Privacy Online

Sabine Trepte • Leonard Reinecke
Editors

Privacy Online

Perspectives on Privacy and
Self-Disclosure in the Social Web

 Springer

Editors
Sabine Trepte
University of Hamburg
Department of Psychology
Von-Melle-Park 5
20146 Hamburg
Germany
sabine.trepte@uni-hamburg.de

Leonard Reinecke
University of Hamburg
Department of Psychology
Von-Melle-Park 5
20146 Hamburg
Germany
leonard.reinecke@uni-hamburg.de

ACM Codes: K.4, K.5, K.6.5, H.4, H.5
ISBN 978-3-642-21520-9   e-ISBN 978-3-642-21521-6
DOI 10.1007/978-3-642-21521-6
Springer Heidelberg Dordrecht London New York

Library of Congress Control Number: 2011932726

Cover design: deblik

Printed on acid-free paper

Springer is part of Springer Science+Business Media (www.springer.com)

Preface

Privacy is a basic human need, and losing privacy is perceived as an extremely threatening experience. Privacy embraces solitude, personal space, or intimacy with family and friends and as such, it is a ubiquitous and trans-cultural phenomenon. Privacy leverages well-being; without privacy we are at risk of becoming physically or mentally ill.

Our fundamental need for privacy is contrasted by a second powerful mechanism of social interaction: self-disclosure to others is similarly important for social functioning and psychological well-being. We need to self-disclose to bond with others, form meaningful relationships, and receive social support. A lack of ability to self-disclose causes clinical symptoms such as loneliness and depression.

Striking the right balance between creating private spaces and self-disclosure is a complex task, if not the most challenging one in interacting with others. Today, in times of online communication and the Social Web, this task is further complicated by two confusing facts:

Firstly, our online communication is usually accessible to a vast number of people. On social network sites, it is very common for several hundred online friends to have access to the personal information, status updates, and private pictures of a profile owner. In addition to these online friends as a "known audience," there are other "unknown audiences," such as advertisers who purchase the users' aggregated profile information from social media companies to address their target audiences.

Secondly, many users appear not to feel threatened in terms of their need for and experiences of privacy when communicating online. On social network sites, micro-blogs, or in forums, they publish a vast amount of information that is considered private or even intimate in other contexts. Although they are aware of their data's publicity on an abstract level, many feel free to speak and to open up to others.

Consequently, we are facing a new situation that demands answers to a variety of pressing questions: Does online self-disclosure change our need for and experiences of privacy? What are the benefits of self-disclosure online? How does the loss of informational privacy influence our online communication?

These and many more questions will be addressed in the following chapters. We are extremely grateful to the authors who contributed to this volume. All of the chapters offer new theoretical approaches to online privacy. The work presented here goes far beyond a summary of existing research: it offers new theoretical models on the psychological functioning of online privacy, novel ideas on the hows and whys of online privacy, and intriguing solutions for some of the most pressing issues and problems in the field of online privacy.

We would like to thank the German Research Foundation (Deutsche Forschungsgemeinschaft, DFG) for supporting the work and the meetings of the "Young Scholar's Network on Privacy and Web 2.0" – a group of scientists from five different countries dealing with online privacy – that have generated fruitful discussions and helped develop many of the ideas expressed in this volume. We hope that these ideas will stimulate future research and contribute to our understanding of the complex challenges to privacy in an online world.

The volume *Privacy Online* is dedicated to those that inspire us and allow for creativity, change, and new perspectives: our families, solitude, and personal space.

Hamburg, August 2011   *Sabine Trepte*
                                                                                     Leonard Reinecke

Contents

Contributors

Bernhard Debatin Ohio University, Athens, OH, USA
debatin@ohio.edu

Nicole B. Ellison Michigan State University, East Lansing, MI, USA
nellison@msu.edu

Paige L. Gibson University of Illinois at Chicago, Chicago, IL, USA
plg2uic@gmail.com

Rebecca Gray Michigan State University, East Lansing, MI, USA
grayreb2@msu.edu

Nina Haferkamp Technical University of Dresden, Dresden, Germany
nina.haferkamp@tu-dresden.de

Maren Hartmann Berlin University of Arts, Berlin, Germany
hartmann@udk-berlin.de

David J. Houghton University of Bath, Bath, UK
d.j.houghton@bath.ac.uk

Cornelia Jers University of Hohenheim, Stuttgart, Germany
cornelia.jers@uni-hohenheim.de

Adam Joinson University of Bath, Bath, UK
A.Joinson@bath.ac.uk

Nicole C. Krämer University of Duisburg-Essen, Duisburg, Germany
nicole.kraemer@uni-due.de

Cliff Lampe Michigan State University, East Lansing, MI, USA
lampecli@msu.edu

Kevin Lewis Harvard University, Cambridge, MA, USA
kmlewis@fas.harvard.edu

Wiebke Loosen Hans-Bredow-Institute for Media Research at the University of
Hamburg, Hamburg, Germany
w.loosen@hans-bredow-institut.de

Wiebke Maaß Hamburg Media School, Hamburg, Germany
w.maass@hamburgmediaschool.com

Ben L. Marder University of Bath, Bath, UK
b.l.marder@bath.ac.uk

Stephen Margulis Grand Valley State University, Grand Rapids, MI, USA
margulis@gvsu.edu

Zizi Papacharissi University of Illinois at Chicago, Chicago, IL, USA
zizi@uic.edu

Jochen Peter University of Amsterdam, Amsterdam, The Netherlands
j.peter@uva.nl

Oliver Quiring University of Mainz, Mainz, Germany
quiring@uni-mainz.de

Leonard Reinecke University of Hamburg, Hamburg, Germany
leonard.reinecke@uni-hamburg.de

Jan-Hinrik Schmidt Hans-Bredow-Institute for Media Research, Hamburg,
Germany
j.schmidt@hans-bredow-institut.de

Charles Steinfield Michigan State University, East Lansing, MI, USA
steinfie@msu.edu

Monika Taddicken University of Hamburg, Hamburg, Germany
monika.taddicken@uni-hamburg.de

Mike Thelwall School of Technology, University of Wolverhampton,
Wolverhampton, UK
M.Thelwall@wlv.ac.uk

Sabine Trepte University of Hamburg, Hamburg, Germany
sabine.trepte@uni-hamburg.de

Patti Valkenburg University of Amsterdam, Amsterdam, The Netherlands
p.m.valkenburg@uva.nl

Asimina Vasalou University of Bath, Bath, UK
minav@luminainteractive.com

Jessica Vitak Michigan State University, East Lansing, MI, USA
vitakjes@msu.edu

Joseph B. Walther Michigan State University, East Lansing, MI, USA
jwalther@msu.edu

Mike Z. Yao City University of Hong Kong, Hong Kong, PR China
mike.yao@cityu.edu.hk

Marc Ziegele University of Mainz, Mainz, Germany
ziegele@uni-mainz.de

Part I
Approaches

Chapter 1
Introduction to Privacy Online

Joseph B. Walther

Even before the various networks supporting online communication converged as the Internet, tensions existed between users' desires to communicate online in very personal ways and their assumptions that their disclosures would or should be treated as privileged and private. These tensions have not abated with the advent of social media. Just as it was with the most bare-bones, text-based online communities of the past, it is with contemporary media: The more users disclose of themselves, the more they may enjoy the benefits these systems have to offer. At the same time, the more they disclose, the more they risk what they themselves consider breaches of their privacy. In light of this ongoing issue, this volume is not only timely in the manner in which it addresses these tensions as they are manifest in contemporary social media platforms, it also contributes to a tradition of research on the dualism of privacy, privilege, and social interaction that online communication has incurred as far back as (or farther than) the advent of the Internet itself.

Three complicating factors that have and continue to confront users of online systems include (1) a misplaced presumption that online behavior is private, (2) that the nature of the Internet at a mechanical level is quite incommensurate with privacy, and (3) that one's expectation of privacy does not constitute privileged communication by definition.

Perhaps it is due to the analogous offline activities which online communication resembles or replaces, that many Internet users notoriously post information online which they do not anticipate will be seen by others than the specific group they imagined when posting. A personal face-to-face conversation is fleeting. A phone call is most likely to be confined to the dyad that conducts it. A social party on held private property is presumably self-contained. These settings allow participants to maintain their sense of privacy consistent with the definitions reflected in Stephen Margulis's Chap. 2, that focus on individuals determining for themselves when,

J.B. Walther (✉)
Michigan State University, East Lansing, MI, USA
e-mail: jwalther@msu.edu

S. Trepte and L. Reinecke (eds.), *Privacy Online*,
DOI 10.1007/978-3-642-21521-6_1, © Springer-Verlag Berlin Heidelberg 2011

how, and to what extent their communications are transmitted to others (except of course by hearsay rather than by duplication and transmission). The presumptions accompanying these precedent settings may be hard to dispel, and it may be difficult for Internet users (at least those who are not digital natives) to recognize that online exchanges are neither fleeting nor confined. This divergence has led to many surprises and disappointments. These include the notorious anecdotal reports of students or employees being terminated or punished as a result of posting depictions of or statements reflecting illegal, insulting, or foolish behavior on their social network profiles.

These disparities between traditional communication settings and new media may be due in large part to the mechanical infrastructure of the Internet. The *psychological* privacy afforded by communication channels may lull users into a false assumption of *informational* privacy, a central distinction that informs the thesis of Sabine Trepte and Leonard Reinecke's Chap. 6. This may be true of the phone call and the conventional letter (which can also be intercepted), as well as the Internet. But the Internet is, at its root, a store-and-forward technology. That is, in order for the Internet to work as it does it must be able to capture, retain, and transmit the information which users enter into it (see Walther 2002). This differs from face-to-face, telephonic, and written exchanges. Yet many Internet users fail to realize that something once put online more or less stays online and may be retrieved by others and replicated, despite the subsequent inclination or efforts of the original poster to protect or remove it. Moreover, the nature of systems' architectures facilitate, if not determine, the propagation of social information, an argument articulated in contemporary terms in Zizi Papacharissi and Paige Gibson's work in Chap. 7 that includes "sharability" among the characteristics defining social media's very makeup.

Users also frequently believe that the expectation of privacy that they had when conversing or posting online constitutes some legal protection against that information being shared. Although the expectation of privacy does indeed privilege certain forms of communication under US law, the domains to which these legal restrictions apply are far more narrow than many Internet privacy advocates suggest. That is, the law privileges only conversations between patients and their doctors or therapists, and attorney-client conversations. Yet the myth prevails that any conversation is privileged that took place with an expectation of privacy, however misplaced that expectation may have been, contributing to what Bernhard Debatin refers to in Chap. 5 as "ignorance and a false sense of security (that) play an important role" in users' approach to the privacy of their online postings.

This position has been propagated by numerous researchers who have argued that if Internet users believe that they communicate privately online, then it is unethical and may be illegal to analyze their messages for research purposes and that human subjects review boards should almost never allow it (Frankel and Sang 1999; see also Hudson and Bruckman 2004; McArthur 2001). Counterarguments have been raised along the lines that, again according to US legal doctrines, messages that have been captured and stored in a publically-accessible space have no privilege whatsoever (Walther 2002) aside from copyright protection (Jacobson 1999), and that the analysis of such messages requires no more human subjects protections than analyzing newspaper content. It is clear that journalists who wish to quote from publically-available online communities and other social media do so quite regularly and without seeking permission, as discussed by Wiebke Loosen in Chap. 15, and as Jan-Hinrik Schmidt discusses in Chap. 12, Twitter users "retweet" others' messages without reservation to audiences unintended by the original source. By definition and in practice, it appears, if anyone in the Internet-using public can see one's messages, the messages are in the public domain.

In light of this, educating users about their online footprints seems to be a more promising objective than to change laws or admonish researchers and other viewers to behave differently with respect to online information. As Mike Yao points out in Chap. 9, despite norms and customs affecting "privacy issues offline, to which a set of well-established cultural, social, and legal norms may be applied, the burden of online privacy protection is primarily shouldered by an individual's own conscious effort." More effective efforts should be devoted to helping users to understand the nature of the Internet in order to develop, according again to Debatin (Chap. 5), "an enlightened understanding of technology and its unintended consequences" in terms of a "*privacy literacy* that enables them to...make educated choices." Yao (Chap. 9) depicts what may be required in terms of shaping those choices in terms of attitudes and subjective norms, while Kevin Lewis's Chap. 8 shows how the normative behavior of one's Facebook friend network influences the behavior of privacy setting adoptions over time.

Just as history shows that controversies over online privacy are not new, it also shows that technological efforts for the protection of privacy have a long line of succession, especially in realms in which the Internet provides unique benefits to its users. In Chap. 16, Jochen Peter and Patti Valkenburg describe the unique affordances that Instant Messaging and social media offer adolescents for communication that is vital to their development. Online communication, especially that which may be done anonymously, pseudonymously, or confidentially, allows for the exploration of identity generally and for the examination of sexual identity as well.

Whereas Peter and Valkenburg limit their focus to adolescents, the use of the Internet for identity exploration and sexual exploration by adults has also been a focus of research and speculation for some time. In an adult context, similar behaviors are described in exploratory or therapeutic rather than developmental terms (Cooper et al. 1999; Turkle 1995, resp.). Such exchanges were frequently noted on Multi-User Discussions (MUDs), where the pseudonymity provided by these systems has been described as a critical enabling feature of such virtual spaces for identity exploration (Stone 1995). Yet controversy arose even within these text-only pseudonymous venues, when users who had developed strong relationships with others through their pseudonymous selves felt betrayed at the outside publication of doubly-pseudonymized quotations (see Bruckman 2002), foreshadowing quite precisely what boyd (2007, p. 2) has since characterized as the privacy-threatening aspects of social network sites ("persistence, searchability, exact copyability, and invisible audiences"). Moreover, just as MUD users developed intimacy with one another by divulging their secrets as well as their real-life names and email addresses (Jacobson 1996; Parks and Roberts 1998). Like the text-based virtual reality use of the past, "social Web use offers advantages and gratifications that increase in direct proportion to the degree of self-disclosure," according to Monika Taddicken and Cornelia Jers in Chap. 11 of this volume. Yet then as now such intimacy comes at jeopardy of privacy, just as Debatin (Chap. 5) points out that for contemporary users of social media, "their level of privacy protection is relative to the number of friends, their criteria for accepting friends, and the amount and quality of personal data provided" online. These risks can be mitigated somewhat, according to Nicole Ellison and colleagues in Chap. 3, by limitations in friending behaviors, privacy settings, and disclosures.

Another form of Internet-enabled therapeutic exchange came as users asked for and received advice on deeply personal issues on discussion systems such as Usenet News. It appears that such personally-revealing and advice-oriented exchanges remain valued activities among older Internet users today, according to Wiebke Maaß in Chap. 17. When Usenet was at its peak, individuals who posted to some of its discussions shielded their identities through the use of *anonymous remailers*. They often did so when addressing stigmatizing issues such as certain illnesses, sexual dysfunctions, or psychological problems. Anonymous remailers posted messages to Usenet without the user's identifying address (see Bacard 2010). By appending a pseudonym to the message instead, users could track which replies subsequently developed that addressed their own original posting. They could post follow-up messages using the same pseudonym via such systems. *Traceable remailers* kept a record of the original sender's address, so that other users could respond by email to the pseudonymous address, whereupon the remailer sent replies back to the original sender. Indeed, anonymity was one of the major attractions for the use of online versus offline social support (Walther and boyd 2002), where, unlike offline social support, both men and women communicated similarly (cf. Mike Thelwall in Chap. 18). Despite growing technological sophistication of anonymous remailers, their use for slander, copyright violations, or potentially subversive political whistle-blowing (much as WikiLeaks provides today) made them susceptible to international subpoenas calling on their operators to reveal the identity of users and thereby abridge the privacy such systems offered. This led the most famous of these systems, anon.penet.fi, to be shut down by its operator rather than be opened to police (see http://w2.eff.org/Privacy/Anonymity/960830_penet_closure. announce). The rise of alternative and easier-to-use web applications has displaced both MUDs and Usenet discussions to a great extent, yet as Peter and Valkenburg make clear, newer systems still benefit users' psychosocial development by providing apparently private communication opportunities.

Yet even in contemporary social media, with full view of one's name and a plethora of identifying features, users actively manage their online self-presentations, as Nicole Krämer and Nina Haferkamp detail in Chap. 10. Indeed, social network sites enable individuals the "*mass management* of real world ties," as Marc Ziegele and Oliver Quiring suggest in Chap. 13. These tendencies sit rather uncomfortably alongside Joinson and colleagues' assertion in Chap. 4 that social network sites provide to at least those whom individuals have granted certain privileges a "radical transparency" about a profile owner's self and behaviors, that may even include, as Maren Hartmann's Chap. 14 points out, the disclosure of individuals' geographic locations by their location-aware mobile phones. It is somewhat paradoxical that, on the one hand, "social network sites. . .are thriving on users' willingness to disclose and consume personal information," as Joinson et al. reflect, plus the fact most of one's Facebook "friends" are known to a profile owner offline to at least some extent (Ellison et al. 2007), but that, on the other hand, impression management activity remains fertile within these sites.

The paradox may be resolved to some extent by noting that impression management has limited and unintended effects. Facebook users can readily identify elements on their own profiles (including their online photos) and in those of their friends that are distorted and not quite true offline (DeAndrea and Walther in press). Although they excuse themselves and their close friends for such exaggerations, they attribute greater hypocrisy and blame for such distortions to those of their friends who they know less well. It is unclear whom individuals are trying to mislead with these inaccurate self-presentations, given the radical transparency of which Joinson and colleagues write. Perhaps it is themselves, as another part of the psychosocial development that Peter and Valkenburg describe of adolescents.

In sum, the chapters in this book offer readers much more than a thorough and contemporary treatment of online privacy and the social web. They offer a sophisticated collection of installments on topics that are quite traditional in their concern and quite under development as Internet communication technologies continue to evolve. They offer a glimpse of the future as well, not only by exploring emergent issues that are arising with new technological applications. They do so by suggesting theory-based research agendas that can guide inquiry beyon the current incarnation of social technologies, just as the privacy issues that arose with the development of earlier Internet communication technologies have morphed but remain with us today.

References

Bacard A (2010) Anonymous remailer F.A.Q. http://www.andrebacard.com/remail.html. Accessed Mar 2011

boyd d (2007) Why youth (heart) social network sites: the role of networked publics in teenage social life. http://www.danah.org/papers/WhyYouthHeart.pdf. Accessed Dec 2010

Bruckman A (2002) Studying the amateur artist: a perspective on disguising data collected in human subjects research on the Internet. Ethics Info Technol 4:217–231

Cooper A, Scherer CR, Boies SC, Gordon BL (1999) Sexuality on the Internet: from sexual exploration to pathological expression. Prof Psychol Res Pract 30:154–164

DeAndrea DC, Walther JB (in press) Attributions for inconsistencies between online and offline self-presentations. Commun Res

Ellison N, Steinfield C, Lampe C (2007) The benefits of Facebook "friends": social capital and college students' use of online social network sites. J Comput Mediat Commun 12:1143–1168; Article 1. http://jcmc.indiana.edu/vol12/issue4/ellison.html

Frankel MS, Sang S (1999) Ethical and legal aspects of human subjects research on the Internet: a report of a workshop June 10–11, 1999. http://www.aaas.org/spp/dspp/sfrl/projects/intres/report.pdf. Accessed 15 May 2002

Hudson JM, Bruckman A (2004) "Go away": participant objections to being studied and the ethics of chatroom research. Info Soc 20:127–139

Jacobson D (1996) Contexts and cues in cyberspace: the pragmatics of naming in text-based virtual realities. J Anthropol Res 52:461–479

Jacobson D (1999) Doing research in cyberspace. Field Methods 11:127–145

McArthur RL (2001) Reasonable expectations of privacy. Ethics Info Technol 3:123–128

Parks MR, Roberts LD (1998) "Making MOOsic": the development of personal relationships on line and a comparison to their off-line counterparts. J Soc Pers Relat 15:517–537

Stone AR (1995) The war of desire and technology at the close of the mechanical age. MIT Press, Cambridge

Turkle S (1995) Life on the screen: identity in the age of the Internet. Simon & Schuster, New York

Walther JB (2002) Research ethics in Internet-enabled research: human subjects issues and methodological myopia. Ethics Info Technol 4:205–216; Rpt. http://www.nyu.edu/projects/nissenbaum/ethics_wal_full.html

Walther JB, boyd s (2002) Attraction to computer-mediated social support. In: Lin CA, Atkin D (eds) Communication technology and society: audience adoption and uses. Hampton Press, Cresskill NJ, pp 153–188

Chapter 2
Three Theories of Privacy: An Overview

Stephen T. Margulis

2.1 Introduction

This chapter reviews the current most important theories of privacy.[1] The review is addressed to those unfamiliar with theories of privacy. It is my goal to provide those readers with a foundation on which to build. To this end, the chapter summarizes the two best articulated and best supported theories of privacy (Altman 1975; Westin 1967) as well as Petronio's (2002) communication privacy management (CPM) theory, an important extension of Altman's theory that is particularly suited for the study of social networking. Additionally, this chapter considers two larger issues about what privacy is: issues in defining privacy and lessons to be learned from Altman's and Westin's theories. I begin with the three theories of privacy.

Irwin Altman's and Alan Westin's theories were selected because they have stood the test of time. Both figure prominently in major reviews of privacy in the 1970s (Margulis 1977), 1980s (Sundstrom 1986, Chap. 13), and 1990s (Newell 1995). Moreover, they have paved the way for others, particularly Petronio's CPM theory.

---

[1]This chapter draws heavily on two articles by the author in the *Journal of Social Issues* (Margulis 2003a, b). The author wishes to thank Wiley-Blackwell for allowing the use of this material. I wish to thank Sandra Petronio for her very helpful review of her theory and for providing published and unpublished material.

S.T. Margulis (✉)
Grand Valley State University, Grand Rapids, MI
e-mail: margulis@gvsu.edu

S. Trepte and L. Reinecke (eds.), *Privacy Online*,
DOI 10.1007/978-3-642-21521-6_2, © Springer-Verlag Berlin Heidelberg 2011

2.2   Westin's Theory

Westin's (1967) theory of privacy addresses how people protect themselves by temporarily limiting access of others to themselves. For Westin (1967, p. 7)

> Privacy is the claim of individuals, groups, or institutions to determine for themselves when, how, and to what extent information about them is communicated to others. [Moreover] ... privacy is the voluntary and temporary withdrawal of a person from the general society through physical or psychological means. ...

Westin (1967) proposes that people need privacy. Privacy, in concert with other needs, helps us to adjust emotionally to day-to-day interpersonal interactions. For Westin, privacy is both a dynamic process (i.e., over time, we regulate privacy so it is sufficient for serving momentary needs and role requirements) and a non-monotonic function (i.e., people can have too little, sufficient, or too much privacy). Westin specifically limits his theory to Western democracies because privacy is consistent with the sociopolitical values of these democracies. For Westin, privacy is neither self-sufficient nor an end in itself, but a means for achieving the overall end of self-realization.

Westin postulates four states of privacy. *Solitude* is being free from observation by others. *Intimacy* refers to small group seclusion for members to achieve a close, relaxed, frank relationship. *Anonymity* refers to freedom from identification and from surveillance in public places and for public acts. *Reserve* is based on a desire to limit disclosures to others; it requires others to recognize and respect that desire. The states are the means by which the functions (purposes or ends) of privacy are achieved. The states are, in effect, the "hows" of privacy.

Westin also posits four functions (purposes) of privacy. They are, in effect, the "whys" of privacy. *Personal autonomy* refers to the desire to avoid being manipulated, dominated, or exposed by others. *Emotional release* refers to release from the tensions of social life such as role demands, emotional states, minor deviances, and the management of losses and of bodily functions. Privacy, whether alone or with supportive others, provides the "time out" from social demands, hence opportunities for emotional release. *Self-evaluation* refers to integrating experience into meaningful patterns and exerting individuality on events. It includes processing information, supporting the planning process (e.g., the timing of disclosures), integrating experiences, and allowing moral and religious contemplation. The final function, *Limited and protected communication*, has two facets: limited communication sets interpersonal boundaries; protected communication provides for sharing personal information with trusted others (Westin 1967).

For Westin (1967), privacy operates at the individual, group, and organizational/institutional levels. This is an early statement of the multiple levels often associated with privacy (cf. Petronio 2002). Although Westin's definition of privacy is often cited, it is his privacy states and functions that have occasioned research. The research supports (to varying degrees) and extends the states and functions; it examines the relationships between the states and functions; it applies the states and functions to specific contexts (see Margulis 2003b, pp. 413–415, for a summary of this research).

Nevertheless, possibly because Westin is a political scientist and lawyer, and not a behavioral scientist, questions remain. Do Westin's four functions flow into one another? Do they co-occur or overlap in time or do they occur independently? Do specific dimensions of privacy underlie Westin's states? Are privacy factors organized hierarchically? Can the functions be understood as traits? Finally, Westin's endorsement of organizational-level privacy is problematic because he models the organization on an individual who acts alone rather than as a collective. (See Margulis 2003b, p. 418, for supporting information and citations.)

2.3 Altman's Theory

Altman, like Westin, has influenced how we understand privacy. Altman's analysis of privacy focuses on individual and group privacy and behavior (i.e., privacy-regulating mechanisms) operating as a coherent system. He takes a dynamic and a dialectical perspective on privacy regulation (i.e., it is a process that paces and regulates interaction with others; we change how open or closed we are in response to changes in our internal states and external conditions) (Altman 1990; Margulis 1977). Because Altman is a social and an environmental psychologist, social interaction is at the heart of his theory and Altman uses the environment to provide mechanisms for regulating privacy.

Privacy, for Altman, is "the selective control of access to the self" (1975, p. 24). Privacy has five properties. Firstly, privacy involves a dynamic process of interpersonal boundary control. Secondly, Altman differentiates desired and actual levels of privacy. Thirdly, privacy is a non-monotonic function, with an optimal level of privacy (desired = actual level) and possibilities of too much privacy (actual > desired level) (e.g., crowding) and too little (desired > actual level) (e.g., social isolation). Fourthly, privacy is bi-directional, involving inputs from others (e.g., noise) and outputs to others (e.g., oral communication). Fifthly, privacy operates at the individual and group level (Altman 1975; Margulis 1977).

For Altman, there are multiple behavioral mechanisms for regulating privacy (e.g., territorial behavior, cultural norms) that operate as a coherent system. Consequently, one mechanism can substitute for another (e.g., a nod of approval for the word "yes"), can amplify another (e.g., shout "no" and slam a door shut), or can modulate another (e.g., offer an apology for locking one's door). Moreover, Altman posits a hierarchy of privacy functions, the most central of which is creating self-identity.

In Altman's approach, three features of privacy are particularly important. Firstly, privacy is inherently a social process. Secondly, a proper understanding of psychological aspects of privacy must include the interplay of people, their social world, the physical environment, and the temporal nature of social phenomena (Altman 1990). Thirdly, privacy has a cultural context; specifically, privacy is a cultural universal but psychological manifestations are culturally-specific (Altman 1975, 1977).

Altman's theory has received impressive empirical support (see Margulis 2003b, p. 419, for a summary). It also has stimulated theory development by others (see Margulis 2003b, pp. 419, 421, 422). Lastly, Altman's theory of privacy is sufficiently comprehensive to be a general theory about the regulation of social interaction (Margulis 1977).

The central issue with Altman's theory is whether his boundary concept is a metaphor or a theoretical construct. In this regard, Petronio (2002), whose theory builds on Altman's ideas, regards it as a metaphor.

2.4   Petronio's CPM (Communication Privacy Management) Theory

The most valuable privacy theory for understanding interpersonal computer-mediated communication, such as blogging and social networking, was stimulated by Altman's dialectical conception of privacy as a tension between opening and closing a personal boundary to others (see Child et al. 2009). That theory is Petronio's (2002) CPM (communication privacy management) theory.

In CPM theory, privacy boundaries can range from complete openness to complete closedness or secrecy. An open boundary reflects willingness to grant access to private information through disclosure or giving permission to view that information, thus representing a process of revealing. On the other hand, a closed boundary represents information that is private and not necessarily accessible, thus characterizing a process of concealing and protecting. The relationship between the boundaries is dialectical, consistent with Altman's thesis, because we continuously adapt our level of privacy and disclosure to internal and external states because we simultaneously need to be open and social as well as private and preserve our autonomy. Moreover, we achieve desired levels of privacy and disclosure through the use of privacy rules. That is, when we make a decision to disclose private information, we use a rule-based privacy management system that regulates the degree of boundary permeability (how much is told) and that manages linkages (who we want to know the information) and the level of shared ownership with others. Using this rule-based management system allows CPM theory to consider *how* decisions are made about revealing and concealing private information (Petronio 2002).

Five propositions underpin CPM theory (Petronio and Durham 2008). The first proposition is that private information is defined in terms of ownership in that when people believe the information belongs to them, they count it as private. The second is that because they define private information as something they own, they therefore believe they have the right to control the distribution of that information (Petronio and Reierson 2009). The third is that people develop and use privacy rules, based on personally important criteria, to control the flow of private information. These rules impact the management of individual and collective (i.e., dyadic and group) privacy boundaries. Individual privacy rules are based on cultural values, gendered orientations, motivational needs, contextual impact, and risk-benefit ratio criteria. The fourth is that once private information becomes shared, a collective privacy boundary is formed and others receiving private information become co-owners of that information. From the perspective of the original owner, co-owners have fiduciary responsibilities to manage and therefore jointly control this private information in a way that is consistent with the original owner's rule. Privacy rule coordination between the original owner and co-owner is negotiated and revolves around decisions about permeability, co-ownership responsibilities, and linkage rules. *Linkage rules* determine who else can know (become a co-owner of) the information. *Permeability rules* determine how much others can know about the information. *Ownership rules* determine how much control co-owners have over co-owned information. (For an instrument to measure these three factors, see Child et al. 2009.) These rules might be implicit (e.g., based on a person's assumption that the other person has learned the requisite rules/norms) or explicit because of a need to clarify or modify an existing rule or to introduce/negotiate a new rule (Child et al 2009; Petronio 2002). These privacy rules are dynamic: they change, grow, or remain stable for periods (Petronio 2002).

Privacy rules also have several attributes (Petronio 2002). Firstly, privacy rules may become so routine that they form the basis for privacy orientations. Routinization can be aided by the use of sanctions to control the use of privacy rules. Nevertheless, these rules are often subject to change. Secondly, we must manage our individual and collective boundaries. Collective boundaries require interpersonal coordination (see Petronio 2002, p. 32f, for a discussion of collective coordination patterns). Thirdly, effective boundary management might fail. For example, there can be boundary turbulence because a co-owner feels no obligation to protect the discloser's private information. Whatever the reason, ineffective boundary management means that co-owners need to take corrective action to ensure effective boundary management (Petronio 2002).

The fifth proposition of Petronio's CPM theory, as noted, is that when privacy rules are not coordinated between the original owner and co-owner, there is a possibility of *boundary turbulence* because people do not consistently, effectively, or actively negotiate collective privacy rules. Boundary turbulence occurs when co-owners fail to effectively control (manage) the flow of private information to third parties.

In sum, CPM theory extends Altman's original proposal of privacy regulation, as Altman has noted, by articulating "[a] most complicated set of dynamics" and by articulating the operation of communication privacy management at the individual, dyadic, and group levels (Petronio 2002, p. xvi). And like Westin, Petronio also focuses on the management of private information.

For applications of CPM theory to interpersonal computer-mediated communication and blogging, see Child and Petronio (2011), Child et al. (2009), Child and Agyeman-Badu (2010).

2.5   What Privacy Is: Issues in Defining Privacy

Privacy is an elusive concept because it is an elastic concept (Allen 1988). The psychological concept subsumes a wide variety of philosophical, legal, behavioral, and everyday definitions. Moreover, the relationships between privacy and cognate concepts (e.g., deception, secrecy, anonymity) are debatable because of disagreements about the boundaries of privacy as a concept (see, e.g., Margulis 2003a, 2009). Also, in the moral domain, there is disagreement about whether privacy is best understood as protecting "behavior which is either morally neutral or valued by society" (Warren and Laslett 1977, p. 44), a common perspective, or whether privacy also can support illegitimate activities, such as misuse of a public office (Westin 1967), vandalism (Altman 1975), and morally dubious behavior like lying (Derlega and Chaikin 1977). Lastly, there is no agreement on the proper philosophical frame within which to define privacy. In this regard, the theories of Altman, Petronio, and Westin are consistent with the limited-access perspective (Allen 1988) but there are other perspectives. (See Tavani 2007, for four perspectives, including limited access.)

I examined the variability in definitions of privacy, primarily in psychological analyses of privacy but also in studies of how people defined privacy (cf. Newell 1998). Based on my examination, I inductively derived "an abstract skeleton" of the means and ends of privacy: "Privacy, as a whole or in part, represents control over transactions between person(s) and other(s), the ultimate aim of which is to enhance autonomy and/or to minimize vulnerability" (Margulis 1977, p. 10). This "skeletal" definition, so to speak, failed to note that, in the privacy literature, control over transactions usually entailed limits on or regulation of access to self (Allen 1988), sometimes to groups (e.g., Altman 1975), and presumably to larger collectives such as organizations (e.g., Westin 1967). Because I inductively derived the definition from a wide range of examples, it follows that the variation in specific definitions reflects how the terms and the relationships among terms, in the abstract skeleton, were interpreted within those definitions. In individual cases, it also reflected the additional concepts and/or relationships that were included in a definition. For example, the concept of control, in the abstract skeleton, has been interpreted as social power (Kelvin 1973) and as personal control (Johnson 1974). Johnson's (1974) distinction between primary (direct) and secondary (indirect) personal control over the attainment of privacy-related outcomes illustrates the use of an additional concept.

Although I concluded that the psychological concept emphasizes privacy as control over or regulation of or, more narrowly, limitations on or exemption from scrutiny, surveillance, or unwanted access (Margulis 1977), there have been (e.g., Pennock and Chapman 1971) and continue to be legal and philosophical analyses of the meaning of privacy, some of which, as noted (e.g., Tavani 2007), would have us go beyond the limited-access perspective (Allen 1988) or raise questions about the boundaries of privacy (e.g., Davis 2009). In the final analysis, privacy remains an elastic concept. Therefore, if you intend to use a behavioral theory of privacy, you should determine whether its definition of privacy meets your requirements.

2.6   What Privacy Is: Lessons from Two Theories of Privacy

One way to examine the core of privacy is to compare the commonalities and differences in the two best supported theories of privacy: the theories of Altman (1975) and Westin (1967).

Both theories discuss how individuals and groups control or regulate access to themselves (i.e., both illustrate the limited-access approach). Both theories describe our need for privacy as a continuing dynamic of changing internal and external conditions, to which we respond by regulating privacy in order to achieve a desired level of privacy. In turn, achieved privacy can affect internal states and external conditions. Both agree that attempts to regulate privacy may be unsuccessful: we may achieve more or less privacy than we desired. Both agree that privacy can take many forms. Both agree that privacy has universal characteristics and that the nature of the forms that privacy can take is probably culturally-specific. Both agree that privacy can support illegitimate goals. Both differentiate the forms (or the hows) from the functions (or the whys) of privacy. Both agree that the functions of privacy include opportunities for self-evaluation and that privacy contributes to self-identity and individuality. The principal difference is that Altman's theory is relatively inclusive of privacy phenomena because it emphasizes social interaction but Westin's is less so, often focusing on information privacy, a subset of social interaction. (In this regard, CPM theory also focuses on information privacy.) That two independent, well-supported theories share so much in common suggests that they provide a reasonable foundation for understanding the fundamentals of privacy as a psychological concept.

Westin (2003) also has described three distinct empirically-derived (not theoretically-derived) positions on privacy that the public holds. The High-Privacy position assigns a high(er) value to privacy claims and seeks comprehensive governmental interventions to protect privacy. (See Bennett 1995, for an overview, and Lyon and Zuriek 1996, for examples of the High-Privacy position.) The Balanced-Privacy position values privacy claims but advocates tailored (e.g., sectoral) governmental interventions to address demonstrated abuses as well as voluntary organizational initiatives to promote individual privacy. (See Etzioni 1999, and Westin 1967, for different approaches to Balanced Privacy.) The Limited-Privacy position usually assigns a lower value to privacy claims than to business efficiency and societal-protection interests and it opposes governmental intervention as unnecessary and costly. (For an example, see Singleton 1998.) I would add a variant on the Limited-Privacy position, based on the claim that openness ought to trump privacy. This position has its roots in humanistic psychology (e.g., Jourard 1971). Interestingly, a contemporary advocate of this position is Mark Zuckerberg, the founder and CEO of Facebook, currently the largest social networking site (Vargas

2010), although his motives have been questioned (e.g., Lyons 2010). As useful as these three positions on privacy could be in research on privacy attitudes of social media users, there are questions about the generalizability of these three positions on privacy (Margulis et al. 2010).

References

Allen AL (1988) Uneasy access: privacy for women in a free society. Rowman & Littlefield, Totowa

Altman I (1975) The environment and social behavior: privacy, personal space, territory, crowding. Brooks/Cole, Monterey

Altman I (1977) Privacy regulation: culturally universal or culturally specific? J Soc Issues 33(3):66–84

Altman I (1990) Toward a transactional perspective: a personal journey. In: Altman I, Christensen K (eds) Environment and behavior studies: emergence of intellectual traditions. Plenum, New York, pp 335–355

Bennett CJ (1995) The political economy of privacy: a review of the literature. Paper prepared for the center for social and legal research, DOE genome project (Final draft), University of Victoria, Department of Political Science, Victoria

Child JT, Agyeman-Badu E (2010) Blogging privacy management rule development: the impact of self-monitoring skills, concern for appropriateness, and blogging frequency. Comput Hum Behav 26:957–963

Child JT, Pearson JC, Petronio S (2009) Blogging, communication, and privacy management: development of the blogging privacy management measure. J Am Soc Inf Sci Technol 60(1):2079–2094

Child JT, Petronio S (2011) Unpacking the paradoxes of privacy in CMC relationships: the challenges of blogging and relational communication on the internet. In: Wright K, Webb L (eds) Computer mediated communication in personal relationships. Hampton Press, Cresskill, pp 21–40

Davis S (2009) Privacy, rights, and moral value. In: Matheson D (ed) Contours of privacy. Cambridge Scholars Publishing, Newcastle upon Tyne, pp 153–179

Derlega V, Chaikin AL (1977) Privacy and self-disclosure in social relationships. J Soc Issues 33(3):102–115

Etzioni A (1999) The limits of privacy. Basic Books, New York

Johnson CA (1974) Privacy as personal control. In: Carson DH (ed) Man-environment interactions: evaluations and applications (Part II, Vol. 6: Privacy, S.T. Margulis, vol. ed). Environmental Design Research Association, Washington, DC, pp 83–100

Jourard SM (1971) The transparent self. (rev edn). Van Nostrand Reinhold, New York

Kelvin P (1973) A social-psychological examination of privacy. Br J Soc Clin Psychol 12:248–261

Lyon D, Zuriek E (1996) Surveillance, privacy, and the new technology. In: Lyon D, Zureik E (eds) Computers, surveillance, and privacy. University of Minnesota Press, Minneapolis, pp 1–18

Lyons D (June 7, 2010) Facebook's false contrition. Newsweek, p 20

Margulis ST (1977) Conceptions of privacy: current status and next steps. J Soc Issues 33(3):5–21

Margulis ST (2003a) Privacy as a social issue and a behavioral concept. J Soc Issues 59(2):243–262

Margulis ST (2003b) On the status and contribution of Westin's and Altman's theories of privacy. J Soc Issues 59(2):411–429

Margulis ST (2009) Privacy and psychology. In: Matheson D (ed) Contours of privacy. Cambridge Scholars Publishing, Newcastle upon Tyne, pp 143–151

Margulis ST, Pope JA, Lowen A (2010) The Harris-Westin index of general concern about privacy: an exploratory conceptual replication. In: Zuriek E, Stalker LH, Smith E, Lyon D, Chan YE (eds) Surveillance, privacy, and the globalization of personal information: international comparisons. McGill-Queen's University Press, Montreal & Kingston, pp 91–109

Newell PB (1995) Perspectives on privacy. J Environ Psychol 14:65–78

Newell PB (1998) A cross-cultural comparison of privacy definitions and functions: a systems approach. J Environ Psychol 18:357–371

Pennock JR, Chapman JW (eds) (1971) Privacy: Nomos XIII. Atherton Press, New York

Petronio S (2002) Boundaries of privacy: dialectics of disclosure. State University of New York Press, Albany

Petronio S, Durham W (2008) Understanding and applying communication privacy management theory. In: Baxter LA, Braithwaite DO (eds) Engaging theories in interpersonal communication. Sage, Thousand Oaks, pp 309–322

Petronio S, Reierson J (2009) Regulating the privacy of confidentiality: grasping the complexities through CPM theory. In: Afifi T, Afifi W (eds) Uncertainty and information regulation in interpersonal contexts: theories and applications. Routledge, New York, pp 365–383

Singleton S (1998) Privacy as censorship: a skeptical view of proposals to regulate privacy in the private sector. (Policy Analysis No. 295) The Cato Institute, Washington, DC

Sundstrom E (1986) Workplaces: the psychology of the physical environment in offices and factories. Cambridge University Press, New York

Tavani H (2007) Philosophical theories of privacy: implications for an adequate online privacy policy. Metaphilosophy 38(1):1–22

Vargas JA (Sept 20, 2010) Letter from Palo Alto: the face of facebook. The New Yorker, pp 54–64

Warren C, Laslett B (1977) Privacy and secrecy: a conceptual comparison. J Soc Issues 33(3):43–51

Westin AF (1967) Privacy and freedom. Atheneum, New York

Westin AF (2003) Social and political dimensions of privacy. J Soc Issues 59(2):431–453

Chapter 3
Negotiating Privacy Concerns and Social Capital Needs in a Social Media Environment

Nicole B. Ellison, Jessica Vitak, Charles Steinfield, Rebecca Gray, and Cliff Lampe

3.1 Introduction

Social network sites (SNSs) are becoming an increasingly popular resource for both students and adults, who use them to connect with and maintain relationships with a variety of ties. For many, the primary function of these sites is to consume and distribute personal content about the self. Privacy concerns around sharing information in a public or semi-public space are amplified by SNSs' structural characteristics, which may obfuscate the true audience of these disclosures due to their technical properties (e.g., persistence, searchability) and dynamics of use (e.g., invisible audiences, context collapse) (boyd 2008b). Early work on the topic focused on the privacy pitfalls of Facebook and other SNSs (e.g., Acquisti and Gross 2006; Barnes 2006; Gross and Acquisti 2005) and argued that individuals were (perhaps inadvertently) disclosing information that might be inappropriate for some audiences, such as future employers, or that might enable identity theft or other negative outcomes.

The focus of this early work on negative outcomes of use, in the absence of research that considered motivations for use, presented a confusing portrait of the Facebook user. Our initial research exploring the "benefits of Facebook Friends" (Ellison et al. 2007) was inspired by the discrepancy between high usage patterns and a focus on negative outcomes. Our research has employed the social capital framework as a way of exploring the positive outcomes of SNS use. A stream of research by the authors has explored social capital outcomes of Facebook use (Ellison et al. 2007, 2010, 2011; Steinfield et al. 2009). The social capital approach has been replicated in other contexts, such as Valenzuela et al.'s (2009) study of Facebook use and civic engagement.

N.B. Ellison (✉) • J. Vitak • C. Steinfield • R. Gray • C. Lampe
Michigan State University, East Lansing, MI, USA
e-mail: nellison@msu.edu

S. Trepte and L. Reinecke (eds.), *Privacy Online*,
DOI 10.1007/978-3-642-21521-6_3, © Springer-Verlag Berlin Heidelberg 2011

One question not yet addressed by scholarship in this area is the relationship between privacy and social capital outcomes. Our conception of privacy speaks to the ability of individuals to control when, to what extent, and how information about the self is communicated to others (see Westin 1967; see also Chap. 2 of this volume for a further elaboration on theories of privacy by Margulis). In many cases, disclosing information about the self is necessary in order to reap the benefits from these technological tools. After all, members of one's social network cannot suggest a new job possibility if they do not know s/he is looking, nor can they offer social support if they do not know it is needed. By lowering the barriers to communicating with a wider network of weak ties (Donath and boyd 2004; Ellison et al. 2007), SNSs enable individuals to broadcast requests for support or information. Self-disclosure is also a means by which individuals learn about and develop relationships with one another (Berger and Calabrese 1975); however, this process entails revealing information about the self that one might not want to share with a wider audience.

This chapter will consider how SNS users balance the desire to share personal information (and thus potentially accrue the social capital benefits associated with disclosure) and the need to control these disclosures (by minimizing the risks associated with sharing private information). We describe three strategies by which users can control the audience for their disclosures on SNSs: Friending behaviors, managing audiences via privacy settings, and disclosures on the site. Below we briefly discuss social capital, privacy, and information disclosure on SNSs before presenting some preliminary findings about SNS privacy behaviors and social capital.

3.2   Literature Review: Overview of Social Capital

The concept of social capital has received considerable attention across numerous disciplines over the past three decades (Adler and Kwon 2002). Social capital broadly refers to the accumulated resources derived from the relationships among people within a specific social context or network (Bourdieu 2001; Coleman 1988; Lin 2001; Portes 1998; Putnam 2000). Some have expressed concern that the concept lacks theoretical and operational rigor – for example, Portes (1998) notes that conceptualizations of social capital can alternatively refer to the mechanisms that generate it (the relationships between people) or its outcomes (the resources one may obtain from these relationships). We emphasize social capital as an outcome that stems from relationships among people. Hence, being embedded in a network of relationships is a necessary precursor of social capital, but in and of itself is not synonymous with social capital.

Putnam (2000) distinguishes between two forms of social capital: one emanating from weak ties that he calls bridging social capital, and a second that is derived from strong or intimate ties like family relations, called bonding social capital. Bridging social capital is best understood in relation to groundbreaking work by

Granovetter (1973), who observed that weak ties tend to be outside of one's dense local network and, by virtue of these ties having links to new people, help promote the diffusion of non-redundant information. One's strong ties, however, are likely to be connected to each other, suggesting that much of the information flowing through a close-knit network of relationships is redundant. Such strong ties are a source of bonding social capital and are associated with trust, reciprocity, emotional support, and tangible resource provision (Putnam 2000).

More recently, researchers have examined how Internet use influences people's abilities to form and maintain social capital, given that it provides many new ways to interact with a wide variety of others ranging from close contacts to relative strangers (Resnick 2001; Wellman and Gulia 1999; Williams 2006). Ellison et al. (2010) summarize this body of literature by grouping the findings into three basic categories: (1) those that find that Internet use enables people to generate new social capital (e.g., Hampton and Wellman 2003; Rheingold 1993), (2) those that find that Internet use diminishes people's stock of social capital (e.g., Kraut et al. 1998; Nie 2001), and (3) those that find that Internet use reinforces people's offline relationships and supplements social capital development (e.g., Quan Haase and Wellman 2004; Uslaner 2000).

We view social capital as a particularly relevant outcome to consider when examining use of SNSs, given that many of the core features of such sites are explicitly designed to facilitate the formation and maintenance of connections among people – connections that are sustained through communication about the self. Our own and others' research in the past half decade provides strong empirical support for the hypothesis that greater use of SNSs is associated with different types of social capital benefits (Burke et al. 2010; Ellison et al. 2007, 2011; Steinfield et al. 2008, 2009). Ellison et al. (2007) found that, even after controlling for a range of demographic attributes, general Internet use, and psychological well-being, the more intensely students used Facebook, the greater their reported bridging, bonding, and maintained social capital. Steinfield et al. (2008) investigated bridging social capital and Facebook use longitudinally, finding evidence for a causal effect of SNS use on levels of bridging social capital. Research in organizational settings also suggests a positive association between SNS use and both bridging and bonding social capital (Steinfield et al. 2009). Ellison et al. (2011) extended this work, finding that not all usage of Facebook resulted in social capital growth. Rather, students who reported greater use of Facebook in a social information-seeking capacity – specifically to learn more about people with whom they had some form of offline connection – had higher levels of social capital. Finally, using a sample of adult US Facebook users, Burke et al. (2010) found that more active users of Facebook (i.e., those who engaged in directed communication) reported higher levels of bridging and bonding social capital.

While the general relationship between SNS use and social capital has been established in a number of studies, to date no academic work has considered how privacy relates to social capital in the SNS context. We take this question up in the next section.

3.3 Privacy and SNSs: An Overview

In defining SNSs, boyd and Ellison (2008) assert that SNSs contain three components that distinguish them from other online sites: (1) a user-constructed public or semi-public profile, (2) a set of connections to other users within the system, and (3) the ability to view one's own list of connections, as well the connections made by others in the system. Indeed, these public displays of connections are a defining feature of SNSs, differentiating them from most other forms of social media (Donath and boyd 2004). Decisions about whom to connect with on SNSs are a key component of users' ability to control their personal information. Similarly, users can control access to personal information through their disclosure behaviors – the kinds of information they include on their profile or share via status updates. A third critical area, and the subject of much of the literature, revolves around privacy settings.

Previous research examining privacy on SNSs is in disagreement over how privacy settings, Friending behaviors, and disclosures interact. For example, while Acquisti and Gross (2006) found little relationship between privacy concerns and certain types of disclosures, more recent studies have found that a high level of privacy concerns leads to fewer disclosures on SNSs (Krasnova et al. 2010; Stutzman et al. 2011). The relationship between these variables is further complicated by the presence of multiple audiences (e.g., high school friends, family, coworkers) within a single space (boyd 2008b), and users may employ a variety of strategies to mitigate risks associated with disclosures made to unintended audiences, such as using pseudonyms or employing advanced privacy controls.

In an online realm where individuals may benefit from sharing personal information, control over the audience for this information is critical. Privacy on SNSs is a multi-faceted issue, requiring attention on the user's part, both to protect information from third-party data collection and to manage personal impressions across a variety of contexts and relationships. The relationship between privacy concerns and privacy behaviors is complex. Facebook users generally believe that others in their network are more at risk than they are in regards to negative privacy-related outcomes (Debatin et al. 2009). Past research on privacy and SNSs has explored the relationship between privacy concerns and actual behavior on SNSs, privacy "violations" that have left SNS users feeling vulnerable, and the distinction between social privacy and institutional privacy. For example, Acquisti and Gross (2006) found that one's privacy concerns were a weak predictor of SNS use, and that among those who had joined an SNS, there were no differences in the likelihood to make disclosures such as one's birthday, mobile number, or address between those who reported a high level of privacy concerns and those who reported low-level concern. Tufekci (2008) found similar results regarding the relationship between privacy concerns and disclosures through an SNS, but also found that students employed audience management strategies such as using a nickname or adjusting profile visibility.

Perhaps the greatest focus of SNS privacy literature has been user awareness of settings and visibility to others using the site. It was not uncommon for early SNS researchers to find Facebook users relatively unaware of the activity, accessibility, and extent of their social networks despite reporting privacy concerns (Acquisti and Gross 2006; Strater and Richter 2007). In their study of Facebook users' attention to and use of privacy controls, Strater and Richter (2007) found that participants often experienced difficulty navigating the privacy settings of the Facebook interface during interviews, while Barnes (2006) observed that teenage SNS users appeared unaware or ignorant of the public nature of the content they shared through the sites. In more recent work, however, Stutzman and Kramer-Duffield (2010) found that 83% of respondents indicated using any Facebook privacy settings, while 58% of respondents indicated they had made their Facebook profile Friends-only.

Structural changes to Facebook have elicited public discussions about privacy issues and SNS use. In September 2006, Facebook introduced the News Feed, which aggregated the activities of a user's Friends and presented them in a reverse chronological order stream on the user's homepage. This meant that behaviors that were previously visible only by visiting one's profile, such as adding a Friend or joining a group, were highlighted in the News Feeds of one's Facebook Friends. The new visibility of Facebook activities inevitably left some Facebook users feeling as though they needed to monitor actions they formerly performed without hesitation; as boyd (2008a) wrote, "With Facebook, participants have to consider how others might interpret their actions, knowing that any action will be broadcast to everyone with whom they consented to digital Friendship" (p. 16).

3.4 Identity and Information Disclosure in SNSs

While both research and popular narratives point to numerous privacy concerns associated with using SNSs (Acquisti and Gross 2006; Lenhart and Madden 2007), information disclosures on SNSs – through one's profile information, interactions with other users, and the public display of one's connections – seem to be a necessary component of accruing benefits from one's network. As noted by Ellison et al. (2010), the information provided in SNS profiles (e.g., contact information, background data, personal characteristics) can lower the barriers to initial interaction and facilitate formation of common ground. Studies indicate that trust and willingness to share information were higher on Facebook, which requires users to provide their real name, than on MySpace, which does not have such a requirement (Dwyer et al. 2007). Furthermore, research by Mazer et al. (2009) found that perceptions of credibility on an SNS increased with greater information disclosure.

In reviewing the extant literature on self-presentation through SNS profiles, Ellison et al. (2010) conclude that access to personal identity information supports the relationship-formation process. Moving beyond purely "social" SNSs such as Facebook, DiMicco et al. (2009) provide support for this argument through a study of workplace SNS use, finding that employees use profile information to engage in "people sensemaking," which the authors describe as "the process a person goes through to get a general understanding or gist of who someone is" (p. 1). In other words, information gathered from a user's profile may aid in establishing common ground, which, in turn, may facilitate communication and coordination processes (Clark and Brennan 1991; Olson and Olson 2000). Research suggests that profile information in Facebook may help users find common ground with one another (DiMicco and Millen 2007; Dwyer et al. 2007; Lampe et al. 2007) and support relationships. For example, Lampe et al. (2007) grouped profile elements into three distinct categories – referent, interest, and contact information – and found that the more information users completed in each of these profile categories, the greater the size of their network, thus suggesting that disclosures within the profile aid in relationship formation. Another category of information included in a user's profile – the display of friend networks – may also serve to establish common ground and encourage more honest self-disclosures (see e.g., Donath and boyd 2004).

In addition to the role that the public display of connections may play in vetting a user's identity, users may consider their audience prior to making disclosures through an SNS. Recent work by Marwick and boyd (2011) and Hogan (2010) has begun to consider how individuals navigate audiences through social media, focusing on the concept of context collapse, or the idea that sites such as Facebook flatten audiences and make it challenging to employ different self-presentational strategies for different groups and individuals on the site. Privacy settings may help segregate audiences, but as Hogan suggests, users may simply take a lowest common denominator approach and only make disclosures that are appropriate for all members of their network. As with other privacy-based concerns, SNS users must balance concerns about their content being viewable by a variety of audiences with their desire to receive benefits from interactions on the site.

Recent research takes a more granular approach to exploring how user activity influences overall outcomes on SNSs. This work suggests that in order to reap benefits from use, dynamic disclosure beyond entering information into profile fields is needed. Burke et al. (2010) obtained both server-level and survey data from a large (N = 1,193) sample of Facebook users and found that users who were actively engaged with Facebook had higher levels of social capital and other measures of well-being. They identified a "consumption" pattern of use (similar to lurkers in other contexts) comprised of users who clicked on Friends' profiles but did not contribute content themselves. This type of use was not associated with greater social capital levels and, in fact, was associated with increased loneliness. On the other hand, users who posted often and engaged in directed communication with Friends reported higher bonding social capital. Similarly, Kim and Lee (2011) find that honest self-presentation contributes indirectly to subjective well-being and is mediated by perceived social support. They write, "Facebook friends are more likely to provide support when they know that the user is in need for support; only when such need is properly communicated through self-disclosure facilitated by honest self-presentation are users likely to receive support from Facebook friends (p. 362)." Other work has examined bloggers' self-disclosure behavior, finding a similar relationship between self-reported disclosure and social capital measures (Ko and Kuo 2009).

In summary, research suggests that the provision of identity information and other disclosures on SNSs are key to extracting relational benefits from their use, but the large, diverse networks supported by SNSs can complicate these disclosures through context collapse and other considerations.

3.5   A Preliminary Investigation of Privacy and Social Capital

The relationship between privacy and social capital is complex. At the most basic level, it seems reasonable to assume that in order to accrue social capital benefits from one's social network, an individual must disclose information about the self, which may entail privacy concessions. For example, a Facebook user who only accepts friend requests from close offline friends may lack access to the bridging benefits associated with having a diverse network of weaker acquaintances. Likewise, Facebook users who do not actively engage in direct interaction through the site but instead spend their time reading content by others should be less likely to reap bonding benefits, such as emotional support, through the site.

We conducted two studies in 2010 that explored factors related to privacy and social capital, including users' privacy settings, Friending habits, disclosures on the site, and perceptions of social capital. The first was a survey of undergraduates at Michigan State University, while the second included interviews with a national sample of adult Facebook users. Below we discuss privacy-related findings of both studies.

3.5.1   Quantitative Analysis of Undergraduates

Each year that we collect data from undergraduates on their use of Facebook, we include a few items probing privacy and social capital variables. In our most recent dataset, collected in March and April of 2010 (N = 299), we asked questions about their privacy settings, the types of disclosures they make on the site, and their Friending behaviors (such as the number of Facebook Friends and the number of "actual" friends in their Facebook network), as well as the bonding and bridging social capital measures used in previous research (see Ellison et al. 2007).

When looking specifically at possible privacy-enhancing behaviors, we asked about two basic strategies: changing privacy settings from the default and limiting specific content to individuals or groups within one's network. We believe this second item is of special interest when considering how users are managing audiences within an SNS; by taking a more granular approach to restricting access and distributing content, users may be more willing to make greater disclosures through the site, which in turn, could lead to greater social capital gains. We found that a majority of participants (78%) reported engaging in this strategy of restricting access to content to specific Friends. To probe further into the relationship between this behavior and our other variables of interest, we ran a series of independent sample t-tests, using the advanced privacy settings measure as the grouping variable. Significant differences emerged between those who reported using this feature and those who had not for a number of variables. First, when looking at our social capital measures, we found that participants who employed these privacy settings reported higher perceived bonding and bridging social capital. Furthermore, this group of participants reported having more Facebook Friends as well as more "actual" friends within their Facebook network. See Table 3.1 for means, standard deviations, and t-scores.

Next, we focused on two Friending behaviors: the total number of Facebook Friends a user has connected with through Facebook, as well as their perceptions regarding how many Facebook Friends they consider to be "actual" friends. As these were both continuous variables, we created a dichotomous variable for each, encompassing the lowest and highest quartiles of responses. Independent sample t-tests revealed that, similar to our previous analysis, there were significant differences in participants' reported social capital, such that participants reporting the most Facebook Friends and actual (Facebook) friends reported greater perceived bonding and bridging social capital than those reporting the fewest number of Facebook and actual friends. See Table 3.2 for details.

Table 3.1 Results from independent sample t-tests for employing advanced privacy settings

	Advanced privacy settings			
	Have not used this feature		Have used this feature	
Bridging SC, t(368) = −3.64, p < 0.001	M = 3.60	S.D. = 0.67	M = 3.90	S.D. = 0.69
Bonding SC, t(114) = −2.324, p = 0.022	M = 3.51	S.D. = 1.03	M = 3.79	S.D. = 0.80
Facebook Friends, t(174) = −4.08, p < 0.001	M = 343.17	S.D. = 223.26	M = 462.40	S.D. = 284.93
"Actual" friends, t(174) = −3.12, p = 0.002	M = 161.97	S.D. = 151.57	M = 229.25	S.D. = 217.53

Table 3.2 Results from independent sample t-tests for Friending behaviors

	Friending behaviors			
	Lowest quartile		Highest quartile	
Facebook Friends				
Bridging SC, t(189) = −6.53, p < 0.001	M = 3.47	S.D. = 0.72	M = 4.11	S.D. = 0.64
Bonding SC, t(178) = −5.32, p < 0.001	M = 3.38	S.D. = 0.90	M = 4.00	S.D. = 0.69
"Actual Friends" in Facebook network				
Bridging SC, t(178) = −6.66, p < 0.001	M = 3.54	S.D. = 0.81	M = 4.20	S.D. = 0.56
Bonding SC, t(184) = −5.41, p < 0.001	M = 3.46	S.D. = 0.95	M = 4.10	S.D. = 0.69

For total Facebook Friends, lowest quartile is <240 Friends, highest quartile is 600+ Friends. For actual friends, lowest quartile is <61 friends, highest quartile is 300+ friends

Finally, to address how disclosures fit into this framework, we ran analyses using a weak two-item original scale assessing participants' disclosure habits through the site (registering their agreement with the statements, "When I'm having a bad day, I post about it on Facebook" and "When I receive a good grade in class, I post about it on Facebook" on a five-point Likert-type scale ranging from Strongly Disagree to Strongly Agree). Participants indicated a below-midpoint level of agreement with these statements (scale $M = 2.54$, $S.D. = 1.13$), suggesting that they are not using Facebook as a way to share certain types of personal information about themselves. Furthermore, we found no significant relationship between this variable and privacy settings, social capital, or Friending behaviors but suspect this is due to the weakness of this measure. We expect that a better measure of disclosures, such as that employed in Burke et al. (2010), or one that captures more interaction-based disclosures happening outside the "status update" context, would be more likely to produce insight into social capital and privacy behavior dynamics.

Overall, we believe this initial analysis supports our conceptualization of multiple possible privacy behaviors and their potential relationship to social capital, although more granular measures and multivariate analyses are needed to flesh out these dynamics more fully. For example, the positive relationship between use of advanced privacy settings and the number of Friends (both total and actual) may reflect a strategy by which users with larger Friend counts (which are more likely to include those from different spheres) need to place these friends into groups, or the fact that those who feel comfortable creating lists also feel more comfortable accepting different types of people as Friends. The positive relationship between participants' use of the advanced privacy settings and both bridging and bonding social capital suggests that tools for managing audiences within an SNS may aid users' efforts to maximize rewards derived from interactions with network members, perhaps because users who are able to direct their disclosures to a subset of Friends may actually disclose more deeply and honestly. This interpretation contains face validity, especially in light of the positive relationship between both forms of social capital and participants' reported Facebook and actual friends on the site (potentially reflecting wider, more diverse networks and greater access to close friends).

While our measure of disclosures was extremely limited, it could be that users employ privacy settings as an effective means of managing the audiences for their disclosures. For example, a college student who wants to post pictures from a weekend party could block family members from seeing any content related to the event. An alternative interpretation of the low level of agreement with our disclosure measure is that users are employing the lowest common denominator strategy (see Hogan 2010), in that they choose not to make disclosures that are unsuitable for *any* of their audiences. This merits further research, especially when considering that those who use advanced privacy settings and have more Friends on the site report more bonding and bridging social capital.

3.5.2 Qualitative Study of Adult Facebook Users

During late 2009 and early 2010, we conducted 18 in-depth interviews with adult Facebook users aged 25–55 regarding their use of the site. Among the themes to emerge, comments on privacy reflected a balancing of tensions, whereby several users commented on their attempts to maximize benefits (i.e., gains in social capital) while minimizing risks through strategies related to privacy settings, disclosures, and Friending behaviors.

Our participants exhibited a wide range of attitudes regarding the relationship between privacy and disclosures made through Facebook. On one extreme, some participants said that because they employed privacy settings to restrict access to content, they freely shared content through the site. For example, a male participant said that because he limited his profile to friends only, "there's not much I won't post in there." At the other extreme, one user's privacy concerns were so high that she rarely made disclosures of any kind through the site. When asked if she thought her decision to not actively participate in the site made it less useful for her when compared with other users, she agreed, saying, "I don't get as much out of Facebook as I think a lot of people that I know do."

Participants voiced a number of strategies for making disclosures through Facebook while managing multiple audiences. For example, a female participant said she did not post many status updates because she saw them as "polluting" her Friends' pages with irrelevant information, which might have a negative impact on people with whom she regularly interacted offline. A male graduate student described Friend Lists so he could post updates about his teaching experiences but make them non-viewable to specific groups, such as his former students or current professors, saying, "Whenever I do post, people are kind of separated into the limited profile, like the student group, and that kind of filters out what I would say to those people anyway."

An older female participant's comments most closely reflect users' attempts to maximize rewards while minimizing risks of disclosure. She said she uses Facebook because of its convenience in keeping in touch with her children, extended family, and geographically dispersed friends, but she refrains from going into depth in the content she posts to the site:

> It's very public and I'm a private sort of person. So while some people would say [by] just being on Facebook, I'm sharing more about myself than they would consider reasonable or safe or whatever, I have limits to what I would post and, you know, things I won't, so it just depends. There is a balance that you can be involved in a social networking site and share personal information, but without going overboard... I have my own level of privacy concerns and I don't put a lot of things out there that other people seem to feel the need to share with the world.

A final theme to emerge from our interviews that relates to our variables of interest reflects the notion of "Facebook literacy" among older users, such that users who may not be familiar with the various privacy settings available to control content distribution may experience more negative outcomes of their use or may use the site in ways that do not promote social capital benefits. For instance, a number of the adults we spoke to commented that they were unsure about their privacy settings or did not know how to limit content to specific Friends or groups of Friends. We speculate that users with low Facebook literacy might be reluctant to engage in certain kinds of interaction on the site because they are unsure how to limit their audience, which, in turn, could lower the social capital benefits they gain from those interactions. Alternatively, if this lack of understanding leads to assumptions of privacy in a public or semi-public space, there could be negative consequences for the discloser. For example, a male participant said he had become more careful in posting content to Friends' pages after he got in trouble at work because a Friend of a Friend saw a wall post he wrote that included negative comments about a coworker. Based on these preliminary data from our interviews with adult Facebook users, we suspect that efforts to increase user awareness about our three privacy-related behaviors (especially those surrounding privacy settings) are important for enabling those with low Facebook literacy to reap social capital benefits from these tools.

3.6   Conclusion

In this chapter, we have argued for a conception of privacy that acknowledges that users have many options for controlling access – privacy settings are just one. Users may also choose to limit their actual disclosures by reducing the number of disclosures or limiting the content of their disclosures to mundane topics. Friending criteria also play a role. For instance, very selective Friending is one strategy by which users may control audiences. These three areas – Friending, disclosures, and privacy settings – can be seen as operating in conjunction with one another. We were not able to fully flesh out the relationships among these behaviors given our current data, but hope that future investigations will utilize more granular measures of social, technical, and communication-based activities to describe privacy strategies. Research should also explore the interactions of these behaviors among various populations. For example, two chapters in this book consider how adolescents (see Peter and Valkenburg, this volume, Chap. 16) and seniors (see Maaß, this volume, Chap. 17) navigate privacy and disclosures in an online space. These populations, often neglected in academic studies, are migrating to SNSs at a rapid rate, and their concerns and behaviors should be considered as well when developing models of privacy online.

In addition to focusing on user actions, considering the structural aspects of these technologies themselves in relation to privacy is also important. For example, it can be difficult for users to determine who can see which posting (e.g., to know who is included in the "Friend of a Friend" group), which Friends are being displayed in the News Feed, or what a privacy action (e.g., "blocking" another user on Facebook) will actually do. When on Facebook, for instance, it is fairly easy to gain access to the photo album of a non-Friend after a mutual Friend comments on a photo. While access to this kind of information may be positively related to bridging social capital, which is associated with novel information from weak ties, it may also result in negative personal or professional outcomes associated with the unanticipated disclosure of information about the self to unintended audiences. Helping users to understand how they can control their information by using tools in the system, and aiding in understanding the implications of those tools, allows users to choose how much they share and with whom. This kind of knowledge, and the self-efficacy that accompanies it, will help enable users to maximize the potential social capital benefits from these sites while minimizing the harms that can accompany sharing some kinds of disclosures with some audiences. As noted in our qualitative findings, the role self-efficacy plays in encouraging social capital accrual through disclosures on SNSs must be considered. boyd and Hargittai (2010) found that those with low overall Internet skills are less likely to change their Facebook privacy settings and are less confident in doing so. If these populations experience negative outcomes from their SNS use (due to less optimal use of privacy settings) and fewer positive outcomes (because they are not empowered to share disclosures that may be necessary to read these benefits), they may be less likely to continue using these sites than those with higher levels of Internet skills.

In conclusion, we believe privacy behaviors on SNSs are not limited to privacy settings; Friending behaviors and disclosures are also strategies by which users may control their audience. The degree to which users employ these strategies may be instrumental for gaining social capital and avoiding privacy risks because they give users the opportunity to calibrate their disclosures to various subsets within their overall Facebook network. The intersection of privacy and social capital is an important topic, and we are hopeful that research continues to explore this topic to help enable more equable access to "the benefits of Facebook Friends" (Ellison et al. 2007).

References

Acquisti A, Gross R (2006) Imagined communities: awareness, information sharing, and privacy on the facebook. In: Privacy enhancing technologies: 6th international workshop, PET 2006, Springer, Cambridge, pp 36–58

Adler P, Kwon S (2002) Social capital: prospects for a new concept. Acad Manag Rev 27(1):17–40

Barnes S (2006) A privacy paradox: social networking in United States. First Monday 11(9): n.p

Berger CR, Calabrese RJ (1975) Some explorations in initial interaction and beyond: toward a developmental theory of interpersonal communication. Hum Commun Res 1:99–112

Bourdieu P (2001) The forms of capital. In: Granovetter M, Swedberg R (eds) The sociology of economic life, 2nd edn. Westview Press, Boulder, pp 96–111

boyd d (2008a) Facebook's privacy trainwreck: exposure, invasion, and social convergence. Convergence 14:13–20

boyd d (2008b) Taken out of context: American teen sociality in networked publics. PhD Dissertation, University of California, Berkeley boyd dm, Ellison NB (2008) Social network sites: definition, history, and scholarship. J Comput Mediat Commun 13:210–230

boyd d, Hargittai E (2010) Facebook privacy settings: who cares? First Monday 15(8)

Burke M, Marlow C, Lento T (2010) Social network activity and social well-being. In: Proceedings of ACM CHI 2010: conference on human factors in computing systems, ACM, New York, pp 1909–1912

Clark HH, Brennan SE (eds) (1991) Grounding in communication. APA Press, Washington, DC

Coleman JS (1988) Social capital and the creation of human capital. Am J Sociol 94(Supplement): S95–S120

Debatin B, Lovejoy JP, Horn A, Hughes BN (2009) Facebook and online privacy: attitudes, behaviors, and unintended consequences. J Comput Mediat Commun 15:83–108

DiMicco JM, Millen DR (2007) Identity management: multiple presentations of self in facebook. In: Proceedings of the 2007 ACM conference on supporting group work, ACM Press, Sanibel Island, pp 383–386

DiMicco JM, Geyer W, Dugan C, Brownholtz B, Millen DR (2009) People sensemaking and relationship building on an enterprise social networking site. In: Proceedings of the 42nd Hawaii international conference on system sciences. (CD-ROM), Computer Society Press, Hawaii

Donath JS, boyd d (2004) Public displays of connection. BT Technol J 22(4):71–82

Dwyer C, Hiltz SR, and Passerini K (2007) Trust and privacy concern within social networking sites: a comparison of facebook and MySpace. In: Proceedings of the Americas conference on information systems 2007, AIS, Keystone

Ellison N, Steinfield C, Lampe C (2007) The benefits of Facebook "friends": exploring the relationship between college students' use of online social networks and social capital. J Comput Mediat Commun 12:1143–1168

Ellison N, Lampe C, Steinfield C, Vitak J (2010) With a little help from my friends: how social network sites affect social capital processes. In: Papacharissi Z (ed) The networked self: identity, community, and culture on social network sites. Routledge, New York, pp 124–145

Ellison NB, Steinfield C, Lampe C (2011) Connection strategies: social capital implications of facebook-enabled communication practices. New Media Soc

Granovetter MS (1973) The strength of weak ties. Am J Sociol 78(1360):1480

Gross R, Acquisti A (2005) Information revelation and privacy in online social networks. In: Proceedings of the workshop on privacy in the electronic society, ACM, Alexandria, pp 71–80

Hampton K, Wellman B (2003) Neighboring in Netville: how the Internet supports community and social capital in a wired suburb. City Commun 2(4):277–311

Hogan B (2010) The presentation of self in the age of social media: distinguishing performances and exhibitions online. B Sci Technol Soc 30:377–386

Kim J, Lee JE (2011) The facebook paths to happiness: effects of the number of facebook friends and self-presentation on subjective well-being. CyberPsychol Behav Soc Netw 14:359–364

Ko H, Kuo F (2009) Can blogging enhance subjective well-being through self-disclosure? CyberPsychol Behav 12:75–79

Krasnova H, Spiekermann S, Koroleva K, Hildebrand T (2010) Online social networks: why we disclose. J Inf Technol 25:109–125

Kraut R, Patterson M, Lundmark V, Kiesler S, Mukopadhyay T, Scherlis W (1998) Internet paradox. a social technology that reduces social involvement and psychological well-being? Am Psychol 53:1017–1031

Lampe C, Ellison N, Steinfield C (2007) A familiar face(book): Profile elements as signals in an online social network. In: Proceedings of the SIGCHI conference on human factors in computing systems, ACM, New York, pp 435–444

Lenhart A, Madden M (2007) Social networking websites and teens: an overview. Pew Internet & American Life Project, Washington, DC

Lin N (2001) Building a network theory of social capital. In: Lin N, Cook K, Burt R (eds) Social capital theory and research. Transaction Publishers, New Brunswick, pp 3–30

Marwick AE, boyd d (2011) I tweet honestly, I tweet passionately: twitter users, context collapse, and the imagined audience. New Media Soc 13:113–114

Mazer JP, Murphy RE, Simonds CJ (2009) The effects of teacher self-disclosure via facebook on teacher credibility. Learn Media Technol 34:175–183

Nie NH (2001) Sociability, interpersonal relations, and the internet. Am Behav Sci 45:420–435

Olson GM, Olson JS (2000) Distance matters. Hum Comput Interact 15:139–178

Putam R (2000) Bowling Alone: The collapse and revival of American community. New York: Simon & Schoster

Portes A (1998) Social capital: its origins and applications in modern sociology. Annu Rev Sociol 22:1–24

Quan-Haase A, Wellman B (2004) How does the internet affect social capital? In: Huysman M, Wulf V (eds) Social capital and information technology. MIT Press, Cambridge, MA, pp 113–135

Resnick P (2001) Beyond bowling together: socio-technical capital. In: Carroll J (ed) HCI in the new millennium. Addison-Wesley, New York, pp 647–672

Rheingold H (1993) The virtual community: homesteading on the electronic frontier. MIT Press, Cambridge, MA

Steinfield C, Ellison NB, Lampe C (2008) Social capital, self-esteem, and use of online social network sites: a longitudinal analysis. J Appl Dev Psychol 29:434–445

Steinfield C, DiMicco JM, Ellison NB, Lampe C (2009) Bowling online: social networking and social capital within the organization. In: Proceedings of the fourth international conference on communities and technologies, ACM, New York, pp 245–254

Strater K, Richter H (2007) Examining privacy and disclosure in a social networking community. In: Proceedings of the 3rd symposium on usable privacy and security 2007, ACM, New York, pp 157–158

Stutzman F, Kramer-Duffield J (2010) Friends only: examining a privacy-enhancing behavior in facebook. In: Proceedings of the 28th international conference on human factors in computing systems, ACM, New York, pp 1553–1562

Stutzman F, Capra R, Thompson J (2011) Factors mediating disclosure in social network sites. Comput Hum Behav 27:590–598

Tufekci Z (2008) Can you see me now? Audience and disclosure regulation in online social network sites. Bull Sci Technol Stud 11:544–564

Uslaner EM (2000) Social capital and the Net. Commun ACM 43(12):60–64

Valenzuela S, Park N, Kee K (2009) Is there social capital in a social network site?: facebook use and college students' life satisfaction, trust, and participation. J Comput Mediat Commun 14:875–901

Wellman B, Gulia M (1999) Net surfers don't ride alone: virtual communities as communities. In: Kollock P, Smith M (eds) Communities and cyberspace. Routledge, New York, pp 167–194

Westin AF (1967) Privacy and freedom. Atheneum, New York

Williams D (2006) On and off the Net: Scales for social capital in an online era. J Comput Mediat Commun 11:593–628

Chapter 4
Digital Crowding: Privacy, Self-Disclosure, and Technology

Adam N. Joinson, David J. Houghton, Asimina Vasalou, and Ben L. Marder

4.1 Introduction

In this chapter, we introduce and develop the concept of "digital crowding." Traditionally, crowding has been conceptualized as excessive social contact or insufficient personal space (Altman 1975). Under these circumstances, not only do people show signs of stress, but they also engage in a number of techniques to escape excessive social contact (Baum and Valins 1977). For instance, studies of students in shared, crowded spaces find that they spend more time in their bedrooms than in social spaces, are more likely to seek friendships outside of the crowded area, and even sit further away from strangers in waiting rooms (Baum and Valins 1977). We argue that while much of the discussion of privacy and technology has focused on information flow and leakage, it has ignored the interactive, interpersonal impact of new technology. In this chapter, we begin by examining the key issues raised by technology for privacy. We then discuss earlier, non-technology focused theories that cover interpersonal aspects of privacy. Finally, we examine some ways in which technology might impact on interpersonal privacy, with a specific focus on social network sites.

4.2 Privacy, Technology, and Digital Crowding

Concerns about the privacy impact of new technologies are nothing new. Back in 1996, Schatz Byford argued that, "at no time have privacy issues taken on greater significance than in recent years, as technological developments have led to the

A.N. Joinson (✉) · D.J. Houghton · A. Vasalou · B.L. Marder
University of Bath, Bath, UK
e-mail: A.Joinson@bath.ac.uk

S. Trepte and L. Reinecke (eds.), *Privacy Online*,
DOI 10.1007/978-3-642-21521-6_4, © Springer-Verlag Berlin Heidelberg 2011

emergence of an 'information society' capable of gathering, storing and disseminating increasing amounts of data about individuals" (Schatz Byford 1996, p. 1). In the UK, 11 million children's details have become accessible to the scrutiny of 390,000 trained professions (BBC News 2009a); workplace surveillance is an established practice (BBC News 2003; Joinson and Whitty 2008); and social network sites (SNSs) are thriving on users' willingness to disclose and consume personal information (Joinson 2008) while at the same time they provide users with mixed mechanisms for privacy protection (Bonneau and Preibusch 2009). Recent developments to increase the personalization of website experiences also pose a problem, with customers who value informational transparency being the least likely to accept personalization and profiling (Awad and Krishnan 2006).

We are increasingly building Internet services that elicit ever more detailed disclosure from individuals. One driver of this is the move towards more socialized use of technology. For instance, most SNSs cease to function as intended if people do not disclose information about themselves in the form of profiles, photographs, status updates, or tweets and, increasingly, their location (e.g., Burke et al. 2009). The most popular SNS, Facebook, has a strict "real name" policy, meaning that this disclosure is usually connected to a non-anonymous individual who relies only on the privacy settings of the site (and the trustworthiness of the organization behind the site) to protect their privacy. This move towards increased sharing – termed "radical transparency" – led Facebook founder Mark Zuckerberg to claim in 2010 that privacy is no longer a "social norm" (BCS 2010). This ideological position is based on two key assumptions – firstly, that openness and transparency is a positive force in society, and secondly, that openness is generally beneficial in interpersonal relations. Facebook has ten "principles" that outline this ideology – the first being *"people should have the freedom to share whatever information they want, in any medium and any format"* (Facebook 2011). Other principles expound the importance of *"the freedom to access all of the information made available to them by others,"* and, *"the freedom to build trust and reputation through their identity and connections."* However, this identity must be "real" – the terms and conditions of Facebook (Oct 2010 version) stipulate that users *"will not provide any false personal information on Facebook"* (Facebook 2010). Indeed, Facebook already prevents users from creating usernames with "Fake" in the name, and employs algorithms to attempt to distinguish "real" from "fake" users (Breyer and Zuckerberg 2005). This creeping transparency is not limited within Facebook – the use of Facebook Connect as an identity management system that allows users to log onto other sites using their Facebook credentials further increases the spread of personal, identifiable information across the Internet.

The privacy issues raised by SNS use are well documented (e.g., Bonneau and Preibusch 2009; Christofides et al. 2009). Users post personal, identifiable information on their own and other's profiles (Christofides et al. 2009; Young and Quan-Haase 2009). They post, share, and tag photographs of themselves and others (Binder et al. 2009; Gross and Acquisti 2005; Nov and Wattal 2009), update their status with inappropriate information (BBC News 2009b), boast about illegal activity (BBC News 2010), and openly discuss their personal relationships on "walls" (a semi-public forum) (Houghton and Joinson 2010). Such information revelation can be detrimental to the user or can implicate others (Acquisti and Gross 2006, 2009; Christofides et al. 2009), and is often based on optional self-disclosure and encouraged by site settings (Acquisti and Gross 2006; Bonneau and Preibusch 2009; Burke et al. 2009; Nov and Wattal 2009).

It is not just self-disclosed information that puts users under threat but the visible communications linked to them by "friends." This co-creation of users' profiles is carried out through actions such as wall posts, comments, and the tagging of photos or location. Arguably, these activities may be thought to pose a greater risk than disclosure by users themselves, for the reason that concerns over privacy and possible harms may not be fully internalized by other users within the decision to disseminate information (e.g., Houghton and Joinson 2010). Protection from this can be offered through site privacy settings, which allow users control over who and what can contribute to their online image, although these are often too simple or too complex (Bonneau and Preibusch 2009).

However, threats originate not only from users' and their friends' posting of information but from outside access. While a user can be careful and deliberate in what information they post, outside access can also result in privacy violations and personal harm. The use of unsecured login connections by SNSs may allow third parties easy access to account information (Gross and Acquisti 2005). The default settings of SNSs allow profile pictures, demographic data, and network groupings to be visible to anybody with an Internet connection. The seemingly benign informational aspects that users share about their lives, such as contact information (including mobile phone numbers and e-mail addresses), hometown, sexual and political preferences, date of birth, and partner's name, can be mined, stored, and abused (Acquisti and Gross 2006, 2009; Acquisti and Grossklags 2004; Christofides et al. 2009; Govani and Pashley 2005; Gross and Acquisti 2005; Nov and Wattal 2009; Tufekci 2008; Young and Quan-Haase 2009). This can result in phishing, information leakage, social security fraud, identity fraud, and both online and offline stalking (Acquisti and Gross 2009; Gross and Acquisti 2005; Hasib 2009; Westlake 2008).

Not all privacy threats on SNSs come from loss of *information privacy* or *control* over personal information – they may also come from excessive social contact, or *digital crowding*. We argue that the evolution of SNSs has led to a situation akin to offline crowding where inability to control interaction, in particular the boundaries between self, small intimate groups, and the public audience, leads to deleterious consequences both for the individual concerned and for the quality of social relations between people. Our argument is based on an analysis of the nature and role of self-disclosure and privacy maintenance in social interaction, and the ways in which SNSs disrupt established practices. Specifically, we argue that SNSs may create digital crowding in three main ways:

1. By disrupting the dynamic nature of boundary regulation as social interaction progresses, through the use of discrete privacy settings and preferences.
2. By providing multiple audiences, with limited or overly complicated methods to control sharing within set boundaries.

3. By encouraging unfettered sharing of personal information that intrudes upon other users.

In the following section, we discuss the nature of self-disclosure, its role in relationships, and its links to privacy theory.

4.3 Self-Disclosure, Relationships, and Privacy Theory

Self-disclosure has been defined as *"the process of making the self known to other persons"* (Jourard and Lasakow 1958, p. 91). This results in the sharing of knowledge between pairs of individuals, individuals within groups, or between an individual and an organization (Joinson and Paine 2007; Petronio 2002). The notion of simply "disclosing more" must appreciate the duality of self-disclosure that can be measured along two dimensions, breadth and depth (Spiekermann et al. 2001). Breadth is related to the quantity of information, and depth to the quality (Spiekermann et al. 2001). Depth can range from biographic information to deeper aspects such as revelations of trust violations or one's sexual fantasies (Joinson and Paine 2007). Altman and Taylor (1973) suggest a penetrative, "layered" model of disclosure, akin to an onion. The core layer contains fewer, but deeper, aspects of personality. Towards the peripheral layers of the model are an increasing number of personality aspects, although somewhat shallower. For example, being empathetic would be a core personality construct, whereas types of clothing and basic interaction with others are towards the peripheral layers (Altman and Taylor 1973). Breadth varies along two planes, frequency and category. Category refers to the number of elements within each layer and frequency refers to their occurrence (Altman and Taylor 1973).

Self-disclosure is critical to the development and maintenance of relationships. Uncertainty reduction theory (URT) (Berger 1979; Berger and Calabrese 1975) posits that greater knowledge of others is associated with greater liking, and uncertainty has been linked to relationship problems (Knobloch 2007). In a meta-analysis of liking and self-disclosure, Collins and Miller (1994) report three distinct self-disclosure effects: (1) people who disclose are liked more, (2) people disclose more to those they like, and (3) people like those to whom they have previously disclosed. Open disclosure has consistently been related to marital satisfaction and feelings of love (e.g., Hendrick 1981; Rubin et al. 1980), and levels of disclosure from one partner to another in dating couples predicts liking (Sprecher 1987).

Variations in the breadth and depth of self-disclosure are a form of regulation (Derlega and Chaikin 1977) that serves on the one hand to maintain privacy and on the other hand to determine the type of relationship kept with others; by controlling disclosure, individuals manage the degree of intimacy in a relationship. To give an example, in a public space we cannot help but reveal some peripheral information, such as our clothes, gender, and approximate age. We keep other members of the public in a non-intimate relationship with ourselves by concealing deeper aspects of our lives. During the process of regulation, people (or individuals) allow themselves to be open and accessible to varying degrees. In order to manage this openness, they engage in a process of *boundary* regulation. Altman (1975) likens boundaries of interpersonal relationships to a selectively permeable cell membrane where the flow of inputs and outputs can be adjusted to reach a desired level of privacy. An important aspect of this theory is that privacy is non-monotonic and is determined as a dialectic process involving a desire for and against various interaction types. The dialectic process suggests that the achievement of privacy requires a balance of opposing forces. For example, the desire to reveal information opposes the desire to conceal information. Depending on the circumstances at a particular moment, one may choose a position on such a continuum that aids the achievement of the desired level of privacy (Altman 1975). In the context of relationships, desired levels of privacy are partly driven by an individual's need to maintain certainty about another individual or group. Certainty allows them to develop informed judgments about others' personality orientation in order to predict their attitudes or behaviors in a variety of situations (Berger and Bradac 1982; Berger and Calabrese 1975). To achieve certainty requires reciprocal information disclosure between those involved while managing the boundaries of communication (Berger 1993; Berger and Bradac 1982).

The dialectic management of disclosure and privacy is subject to norms as individuals interact in line with the social situation they are in (Berger and Bradac 1982). At a cocktail party, it is the social norm to interact with unknown others and begin the conversation with reciprocal peripheral information sharing, slowly moving conversation towards more central constructs (Altman and Taylor 1973; Berger and Bradac 1982). However, an individual that shares too much information in such an environment would be labeled a social deviant (Altman and Taylor 1973) and suspicions would be raised as to their objectives (Berger and Bradac 1982). For example, taking off one's clothes in a public environment is not only a social *faux pas*, but also illegal. However, change the environment to a doctor's surgery and this is in line with expected social norms (Berger and Bradac 1982). It is not just the environment that dictates social norms and expectancies of self-disclosure, but also the nature of the relationship between the interaction partners. In the above example of the doctor's surgery, the doctor-patient relationship alongside the environment of the doctor's surgery dictates that we can take off our clothes, and it is acceptable. If one were to get naked in the doctor's surgery but in front of the receptionist, it would again become a social taboo (Berger and Bradac 1982).

From a relational perspective, the decision to disclose information to others is subject to a series of explicit and implicit rule negotiations. Groups or individuals with whom people share become co-owners and may feel entitled to disclose the shared information further (Petronio 2002). When discussing the state of a romantic relationship with a close friend, it can be explicitly stated, "don't tell anyone," or it can be expected that the friend knows this implicitly (Petronio 2002). Therefore, alongside privacy norms that are shaped by individual characteristics (e.g., gender, culture), norms are communicated when individuals enter pre-existing boundaries (e.g., the family) or are negotiated when new boundaries are formed (Petronio 2002).

4.4   Boundaries, SNSs, and "Digital Crowding"

We contend that a privacy threat of SNSs that has been underrepresented in the extant academic literature comes from excessive self-disclosure, socialization, and social contact – what we term "digital crowding." As discussed above, the regulation of boundaries and management of disclosure are central to maintaining interpersonal distance between people, and thus establishing different types of relationships. Just as excessive physical contact can lead to a sense of crowding, we hypothesize that excessive digital social contact via SNSs may lead to *digital crowding*.

We focus on two ways in which digital crowding – through excessive contact or sharing – can be detrimental to privacy and the quality of relationships. The first is the dangers inherent in radical transparency or unregulated openness. The second is through overlapping social spheres and users' inability to maintain dynamic boundaries.

4.4.1   Digital Crowding and Radical Transparency

As discussed above, much social media involves disclosure in some form – whether location, identity, pictures, contact information, or more intimate aspects of one's life. Indeed, many of the services currently popular simply do not work without disclosure – or the design of the site is such to encourage sharing and openness.

While there is ample evidence that self-disclosure is generally positive in relationships, this is not universally true. Non-disclosure, secrecy, and deceit are also key components of successful relationships (Afifi et al. 2007; Burgoon and Hale 1988; Petronio 1991), and over-disclosure can be as detrimental to relationship development as unwillingness to disclose (Altman and Taylor 1973; Berger and Bradac 1982). While studies of the mere exposure effect (Zajonc 1968) consistently show that familiarity and repeated exposure to objects is associated with increased liking, there is also evidence that over-exposure leads to reduced liking (Erdelyi 1940; Smith and Dorfman 1975). Norton et al. (2007) found that although people expected that increased knowledge of possible romantic partners would be associated with increased liking, this was rarely the case, and more often than not it was associated with reduced liking. In a similar vein, Stafford and Reske (1990) found that students in geographically distant relationships reported being more in love than those who lived in the same town. Before the radical transparency that SNSs imposed, Walther (1996) argued that it is the ability while online to manage the flow of information, and to self-present selectively, that leads to "hyperpersonal interaction." Similarly, Petronio (1991) notes that, *"There are good reasons to balance openness with secrecy in a relationship,*" and Afifi et al. (2007) argue that, "*withholding information is sometimes benign or even useful*" (Afifi et al. 2007, p. 78).

However, in the era of radical transparency there is little scope for secrecy. With its emphasis on sharing, lack of sharing not only leads to a reduced user experience on many web 2.0 sites, but could also be seen as anti-normative (or at least, contrary to the principles and terms and conditions of Facebook). As noted by other privacy researchers (e.g., Acquisti and Gross 2009; DeCew 1997), sharing does not need to be intimate to impinge on privacy – indeed, with the opportunity to collect information about others across time and locations, and to aggregate and process that data, the multitude of banalities usually seen on social media services may be more telling than the single intimate outpouring. With the advent of social media and particularly SNSs, alongside "radical transparency," it is inevitable that we will end up knowing more about people, and also more likely that we end up disliking them because of it.

4.4.2 Digital Crowding and Overlapping Social Spheres

Self-disclosure is used in different ways in different types of relationships (e.g., between same-sex friends, romantic partners, colleagues). Typically when the most popular SNSs were launched their content was targeted at specific markets. Myspace was aimed at teenagers and music lovers, LinkedIN at professionals in high tech industries, and Facebook at university students. However, the growth in the popularity of these sites, alongside a loosening of entry rules, has brought a widening of user demographics. To give an example, Facebook began by confining entry to people with a Harvard e-mail address, followed by a slow roll out across US campuses using the same ".edu" criteria. When opened up globally, it again began with a focus on university campuses, to be followed in 2006 by being open to all potential users. In recent years Facebook has become popular not only with older generations, but also with social groups very different to those associated with the site in the early days (Gonzalez 2010). Furthermore, it should be noted that not just users, but also uses themselves may change over time as usage of any complex software is expected, to some extent, to be socially shaped (Dutton et al. 2004; MacKenzie and Wacjman 1985; Selwyn et al. 2005). Widening demographics, especially age, has a crucial role within the nature of shared information across boundaries, as users start to befriend parents, grandparents, employers, religious elders, and teachers. As a consequence, a user's profile may be scrutinized by a number of critical members from different social spheres simultaneously.

Skeels and Grudin (2009) define this group co-presence as "a situation in which many groups important to an individual are simultaneously present in one context and their presence is salient for the individual." People generally make decisions on what information they share based on which distinct persons or groups are the intended audience (Davis et al. 2005; Jones and O'Neill 2010; Lederer et al. 2004).

Privacy issues occur when content meant for one social sphere becomes visible to another. This simultaneity of surveillance can present a challenge for users who endeavor to control information flows (Hewitt and Forte 2006). The chance that harm may arise out of negative broadcasts increases, particularly when we consider that information online is "persistent" and subject to record permanence (Binder et al. 2009; Sparck Jones 2003).

While Facebook provides mechanisms for controlling access to information from different spheres, in the form of "friends lists," lack of use or over complexity make it likely that they are not effective in separating groups. Binder et al. (2009) refer to this as the "*problem of conflicting social spheres*," which they argue leads to an increase in "tension" either between the maintainer of the network and one of their connections, or directly between connections (boyd and Ellison 2008).

Binder et al. (2009) argue that this increased diversity leads to tension, particularly when the ties involve kinship. They propose that such tension could arise out of disparities between the norms of different social spheres (Binder et al. 2009). Similarly, DiMicco and Millen (2007), in a study of IBM employees, found that managing profiles with regards to visibility to work-related friends could cause problems. What is fundamental to both these pieces of research is that different social spheres hold different norms, values, and expectations. The issues of conflicting social spheres require rule negotiation and boundary maintenance, otherwise the boundaries become turbulent (Petronio 2002). Failure to manage boundaries successfully may encourage individuals to become enclosed in their own "self" boundary, severely restricting information throughput (Altman 1975), and thus the content disclosed to SNSs.

From the perspective of privacy and communication, these overlapping social spheres cause a number of problems. Firstly, we argue that it becomes difficult for a person to manage their boundaries – either through negotiation or acceptance of norms of behavior. Because we may be sharing with multiple audiences, each with its own understanding of what is and is not appropriate, the time and effort to negotiate sharing becomes prohibitive. Secondly, we argue that the role of trust is subverted since while we may have trusted "friends" with whom we have implicit or explicit rules about disclosure, we may also have "friends" who are considerably less close, and with whom there are either no set expectations and rules, or the rules are loosely defined and based on social norms of behavior. The offline equivalent is Altman's (1975) notion of crowding, where a failure of two privacy mechanisms – control over territory and personal space – leads to *too much* social contact. In instances of overbearing social contact, the individual (or group) will try to close the boundary around the self to prevent information disclosure, or others gaining access to them, to regain control. Consequently, this individual becomes isolated, creating dissonance between their desired level of privacy and their experienced level of privacy.

Overcrowding offline has been studied in terms of personal space, considered to be less than 50 cm between two or more individuals. This distance, like privacy, is non-monotonic. It can differ depending on environment, gender, age group, role, activity, social class, region, desire to be intimate or personal with another, and culture (Aiello and Jones 1971; Beaulieu 2004; Evans and Howard 1973; Freedman 1975). For many SNS users, the online equivalent to personal space is equidistant across audiences and environments. As well as loss of control and the aforementioned issues of information flow on SNSs, individual differences of appropriate disclosure and intimacy demonstrate an array of possible reasons that personal space can be violated, resulting in "digital crowding."

In online instances we suggest that any unwanted information disclosure or "cross-talk" between multiple audiences that results in the release of information from core layers of the self-construct, is akin to others physically encroaching on one's intimate or personal space. Both core constructs and personal space relate to intimacy, and a deep level of information, requiring trust for its disclosure or contact. A variation of individual and cultural preferences affects both concepts, and both result in the individual using behavior as a mechanism to regain control. In physical crowding of personal space one might step back from the intruder. In the release of core information, one might close the self-boundary and become isolated. Therefore, difficulties can emerge online when social spheres overlap, when information is leaked to those considered "peripheral" when it is intended for close friends. There may be an emotional reaction, a feeling of privacy violation, and a behavioral mechanism to overcome it.

Digital crowding can also occur from the bombardment of peripheral information disclosure by another: the increased intensity of revelation of the shallower aspects of daily life by other users. An offline example would be a friend that telephones you several times a day with mundane or trivial personal concerns that could be solved easily without consultation, or a child consistently pestering its parents for sweets on a shopping trip. To give an online example, this translates to the continual posting of mundane, useless information via status updates that can result in frustration and annoyance of its readers, ultimately ending in the de-friending of individuals.

We hypothesize that the failure of online privacy mechanisms and site designs that allow crowding to occur, such as those on SNSs, will effectively result in the same outcome – *stress and eventual withdrawal*. Paradoxically for SNSs, the success of a site makes it more likely that crowding will occur, meaning that the seeds of failure are sown only in success.

For users, there are a number of possible ways that digital crowding can be reduced. One option is to rely on existing privacy mechanisms to reduce crowding – that is, to engage with the myriad of privacy settings in order to differentiate social spheres, and to re-establish manageable boundaries. This approach will require perseverance to change the settings in parallel with changes to the dynamic social communication boundaries. An alternative approach is one increasingly seen on sites like Twitter – establishing multiple accounts (e.g., one for work, one for family and friends). Multiple sites could also fulfill this option – for instance, LinkedIn for work, Facebook for social interaction. Users might also establish their desired state of privacy behaviorally – for instance, by limiting the depth of the information about the self that is communicated to others. This solution suggests that the information communicated by users will become increasingly banal as they gain more contacts in different social spheres, assuming that they do not manage their privacy via the site settings.

Failure to adopt multiple accounts, multiple sites, or the privacy settings offered on social media may result in a withdrawal or inhibited posting of content. SNSs encourage continual content provision by their users – otherwise the site lacks any real motivation for visiting (Burke et al. 2009). The danger for sites is that digital crowding encourages withdrawal – and hence less engagement with the site. An alternative method of controlling digital crowding is to severely limit who is added to the "friends" list on a user's account. For example, users conscious of these data control issues may only have a small social network of strong ties, but even in these cases, the privacy settings of these strong ties may render the network penetrable.

4.5   Conclusion

People are able to maintain their interpersonal boundaries by managing the amount and depth of information they disclose to others. New technology, in particular social media, makes this more difficult – the sites often rely on disclosure for functionality, personal information can be aggregated across time, and the complexity of privacy settings often makes it difficult for users to differentiate multiple audiences. Together, these effects might equate to a form of *digital crowding*, where excessive social contact prompts users to search for coping mechanisms or to withdraw. The danger, otherwise, is a reduction in liking between contacts and increased tension between an individual and members of different social spheres. The writing of this chapter was supported by funding by the EPSRC ("Privacy Value Networks", Grant reference: EP/G002606/1).

References

Acquisti A, Gross R (2006) Imagined communities: awareness, information sharing, and privacy on Facebook. Paper presented at the Privacy Enhancing Technology workshop, Cambridge

Acquisti A, Gross R (2009) Social insecurity: the unintended consequences of identity fraud prevention policies. Paper presented at the workshop on the economics of information security, University College London

Acquisti A, Grossklags J (2004) Privacy attitudes and privacy behavior: losses, gains, and hyperbolic discounting. In: Camp J, Lewis R (eds) The economics of information security, vol 12. Kluwer Academic Publishers, NY, pp 165–178

Afifi TD, Caughlin J, Afifi WA (2007) Exploring the dark side (and light side) of avoidance and secrets. In: Spitzberg B, Cupach B (eds) The dark side of interpersonal relationships, 2nd edn. Erlbaum, Mahwah, pp 61–92

Aiello JR, Jones SE (1971) Field study of the proxemic behavior of young children in three subcultural groups. J Pers Soc Psychol 19(3):351–356

Altman I (1975) The environment and social behavior. Wadsworth, Belmont

Altman I, Taylor DA (1973) Social penetration: the development of interpersonal relationships. Holt, Rinehart and Winston, New York

Awad NF, Krishnan MS (2006) The personalization privacy paradox: an empirical evaluation of information transparency and the willingness to be profiled online for personalization. MIS Q 30(1):13–28

Baum A, Valins S (1977) Architecture and social behavior: psychological studies of social density. Erlbaum, Hillsdale/New York

BBC News (2003) Bugged by the boss. BBC news. http://www.bbc.co.uk/wales/weekinweekout/stories/buggedbytheboss.shtml. Accessed 14 Feb 2011

BBC News (2009a) MP's fears at child risk register. BBC news. http://news.bbc.co.uk/1/hi/england/somerset/8127265.stm. Accessed 14 Feb 2011

BBC News (2009b) Facebook remark teenager is fired. BBC news. http://news.bbc.co.uk/1/hi/england/essex/7914415.stm. Accessed 14 Feb 2011

BBC News (2010) A burglar who taunted police on Facebook is jailed. BBC news. http://news.bbc.co.uk/1/hi/england/manchester/8492500.stm. Accessed 14 Feb 2011

BCS (2010) Zuckerberg: privacy no longer a social-norm. British Computer Society. http://www.bcs.org/content/conWebDoc/34018. Accessed 14 Feb 2011

Beaulieu CMJ (2004) Intercultural study of personal space: a case study. J Appl Soc Psychol 34(4):794–805

Berger CR (1979) Beyond initial interaction: uncertainty, understanding, and the development of interpersonal relationships. In: Giles H, St. Clair R (eds) Language and social psychology. Blackwell, Oxford, pp 122–144

Berger CR (1993) Uncertainty and social interaction. In: Deetz SA (ed) Communication yearbook 16. SAGE, London, pp 491–502

Berger CR, Bradac JJ (1982) Language and social knowledge. Uncertainty in interpersonal relations. Edward Arnold, London

Berger CR, Calabrese RJ (1975) Some explorations in initial interaction and beyond: toward a developmental theory of interpersonal communication. Human Commun Res 1:99–112

Binder J, Howes A, Sutcliffe A (2009) The problem of conflicting social spheres: effects of network structure on experienced tension in social network sites. Paper presented at the CHI 2009, Boston

Bonneau J, Preibusch S (2009) The privacy jungle: on the market for data protection in social networks. Paper presented at the workshop on the economics of information security, University College London

boyd dm, Ellison NB (2008) Social network sites: definition, history, and scholarship. J Comput Mediat Commun 13(1):210–230

Breyer J, Zuckerberg M (2005) Mark Zuckerberg discusses Facebook. (Video recording, 26 Oct), http://ecorner.stanford.edu/authorMaterialInfo.html?mid=1567. Accessed 2 Jan 2010

Burgoon JK, Hale JL (1988) Nonverbal expectancy violations: model elaboration and application to immediacy behaviors. Commun Monogr 55(1):58–79

Burke M, Marlow C, Lento T (2009) Feed me: motivating newcomer contribution in social network sites. Paper presented at the CHI 2009 conference, Boston

Christofides E, Muise A, Desmarais S (2009) Information disclosure and control on Facebook: are they two sides of the same coin or two different processes? Cyberpsychol Behav 12:341–345

Collins NL, Miller LC (1994) Self-disclosure and liking: a meta-analytic review. Psychol Bull 116(3):457–475

Davis M, Canny J, House N, Good N, King S, Nair R, Reid N (2005) MMM2: mobile media metadata for media sharing. Paper presented at the 13th annual ACM international conference on Multimedia, Hilton, Singapore, 6–11 Nov 2005

DeCew JW (1997) In pursuit of privacy: law, ethics, and the rise of technology. Cornell University Press, Ithaca

Derlega VJ, Chaikin AL (1977) Privacy and self-disclosure in social relationships. J Soc Issues 33(3):102–115

DiMicco JM, Millen DR (2007) Identity management: multiple presentations of self in Facebook. Proceedings of the 2007 international association for computing machinery conference on Supporting group work, ACM Press, Sanibel Island, pp 383–386, 4–7 Nov 2007

Dutton WH, Cheong PH, Park N (2004) The social shaping of a virtual learning environment: the case of a university-wide course management system. Electron J e-Learn 2(1):69–80

Erdelyi M (1940) The relation between "radio plugs" and sheet sales of popular music. J Appl Psychol 24(6):696–702

Evans GW, Howard RB (1973) Personal space. Psychol Bull 80(4):334–344

Facebook (2010) Statement of rights and responsibilities. Facebook. http://www.facebook.com/terms.php?ref=pf. Accessed Oct 2010

Facebook (2011) Facebook principles. Facebook. http://www.facebook.com/principles.php. Accessed 17 Feb 2011

Freedman JL (1975) Crowding and behavior. W.H. Freeman, San Francisco

Gonzalez N (2010) About CheckFacebook.com. http://www.checkfacebook.com/. Accessed 15 Feb 2010

Govani T, Pashley H (2005) Student awareness of the privacy implications when using Facebook. http://lorrie.cranor.org/courses/fa05/tubzhlp.pdf. Accessed 6 Oct 2009

Gross R, Acquisti A (2005) Information revelation and privacy in online social networks. Paper presented at the 2005 ACM workshop on privacy in the electronic society, Alexandria

Hasib AA (2009) Threats of online social networks. Int J Comput Sci Netw Secur 9(11):288–293

Hendrick SS (1981) Self-disclosure and marital satisfaction. J Pers Soc Psychol 40(6):1150–1159

Hewitt A, Forte A (2006) Crossing boundaries: 'Identity management and student/faculty relationships on the Facebook'. Paper presented at the Computer Supported Cooperative Work 2006, Banff, Alberta, Canada

Houghton DJ, Joinson AN (2010) Privacy, social network sites, and social relations. J Technol Human Serv 28(1):74–94

Joinson AN (2008) 'Looking at', 'looking up' or 'keeping up with' people? Motives and uses of Facebook. Paper presented at the CHI 2008 – Online Social Networks, Florence

Joinson AN, Paine CB (2007) Self-disclosure, privacy and the Internet. In: Joinson AN, McKenna KYA, Postmes T, Reips U (eds) The Oxford handbook of Internet psychology. Oxford University Press, Oxford, pp 237–252

Joinson AN, Whitty M (2008) Watched in the workplace. Infosecurity 5(1):38–40

Jones S, O'Neill E (2010) Feasibility of structural network clustering for group-based privacy control in social networks. Paper presented at the proceedings of the sixth symposium on usable privacy and security (SOUPS) 10, Microsoft, Redmond WA, USA

Jourard SM, Lasakow P (1958) Some factors in self-disclosure. J Abnorm Psychol 56(1):91–98

Knobloch LK (2007) Perceptions of turmoil within courtship: associations with intimacy, relational uncertainty, and interference from partners. J Soc Pers Relat 24(3):363–384

Lederer S, Hong J, Dey A, Landay J (2004) Personal privacy through understanding and action: five pitfalls for designers. Pers Ubiquit Comput 8(6):440–454

MacKenzie D, Wacjman J (1985) The social shaping of technology. Open University Press, Buckingham

Norton MI, Frost JH, Ariely D (2007) Less is more: the lure of ambiguity, or why familiarity breeds contempt. J Pers Soc Psychol 92(1):97–105

Nov O, Wattal S (2009) Social computing privacy concerns: antecedents and effects. Paper presented at the CHI 2009, Boston

Petronio S (1991) Communication boundary management: a theoretical model of managing disclosure of private information between marital couples. Commun Theory 1(4):311–335

Petronio S (2002) Boundaries of privacy. State University of New York, Albany

Rubin Z, Hill CT, Peplau LA, Dunkel-Schetter C (1980) Self-disclosure in dating couples: sex roles and the ethic of openness. J Marriage Fam 42(2):305–317

Schatz Byford K (1996) Privacy in cyberspace: constructing a model of privacy for the electronic communications environment. Rutgers Comput Technol Law J 24:1–74

Selwyn N, Gorard S, Furlong J (2005) Adult learning in the digital age. Routledge, London
Skeels MM, Grudin J (2009) When social networks cross boundaries: a case study of workplace use of facebook and linkedin. Paper presented at the proceedings of the ACM 2009 international conference on supporting group work, Sanibel Island, FL, USA
Smith GF, Dorfman DD (1975) The effect of stimulus uncertainty on the relationship between frequency of exposure and liking. J Pers Soc Psychol 31(1):150–155
Sparck Jones K (2003) Privacy: what's different now? Interdiscip Sci Rev 28(4):287–292
Spiekermann S, Grossklags J, Berendt B (2001) E-privacy in 2nd generation E-Commerce: privacy preferences versus actual behavior. Paper presented at the ACM conference on Electronic Commerce, Tampa, 14–17 Oct 2001
Sprecher S (1987) The effects of self-disclosure given and received on affection for an intimate partner and stability of the relationship. J Soc Pers Relat 4(2):115–127
Stafford L, Reske JR (1990) Idealization and communication in long-distance premarital relationships. Fam Relat 39(3):274–279
Tufekci Z (2008) Can you see me now? Audience and disclosure regulation in online social network sites. Bull Sci Technol Soc 28(1):20–36
Walther JB (1996) Computer-mediated communication: impersonal, interpersonal, and hyperpersonal interaction. Commun Res 23(1):3–43
Westlake EJ (2008) Friend me if you Facebook: generation Y and performative surveillance. Drama Rev 52(4):21
Young AL, Quan-Haase A (2009) Information revelation and Internet privacy concerns on social network sites: a case study of Facebook. Paper presented at the C&T '09, Pennsylvania
Zajonc RB (1968) Attitudinal effects of mere exposure. J Pers Soc Psychol 9(2):1–27

Chapter 5
Ethics, Privacy, and Self-Restraint in Social Networking

Bernhard Debatin

5.1 Approaches to Privacy

Privacy is a basic human need. It is anthropologically and psychologically rooted in the sense of shame and the need for bodily integrity, personal space, and intimacy in interpersonal relationships. Especially in modern Western cultures, it is understood as a necessary condition for individual autonomy, identity, and integrity (Altman 1975; Westin 1967; see also Margulis, this volume, Chap. 2). The desire for privacy is historically variable and has increased noticeably throughout the process of modernization. As Jürgen Habermas (1962) has shown in his seminal study *The Transformation of the Public Sphere*, this process led to the emergence of the private sphere as a corollary to the public sphere: the private sphere offers the protection and freedom necessary for the undisturbed growth and self-fulfillment of the modern subject, who then, as a citizen, can participate in exchanging opinions and forming public discourse in the communicative space of the public sphere.

Privacy is to be distinguished from secrecy. While privacy can be understood in a broad way as the "right to be let alone" (Warren and Brandeis 1890) and the right not to reveal information about *oneself*, secrecy refers to blocking or hiding *any* type of information. A person's privacy is characterized by "a series of concentric circles of intimacy in which the degree of intimacy diminishes from the innermost circle outward" (Hodges 2009, p. 277f.). The more intimate something feels to a person, the more it is considered a private issue that will only be shared with someone who is close to them. While specific personal information, such as embarrassing facts, will sometimes be kept secret by an individual, secrecy has usually more to do with keeping certain places, persons, or information hidden from *any* unauthorized eye (e.g., arcane places, secret agents, state or business secrets).

B. Debatin (⊠)
Ohio University, Athens, OH, USA
e-mail: debatin@ohio.edu

S. Trepte and L. Reinecke (eds.), *Privacy Online*,
DOI 10.1007/978-3-642-21521-6_5, © Springer-Verlag Berlin Heidelberg 2011

There is no single definition of privacy because it is a complex and ambiguous notion, serving as an umbrella term for a variety of loosely related issues and problems (Solove 2008). However, it can be conceptualized in both positive and negative terms. Privacy is *positively* conceptualized as an individual's control over his or her circles of intimacy in four dimensions: personal space in the physical dimension, personal integrity in the psychological dimension, interaction with others in the social dimension, and personal data in the informational dimension (Leino-Kilpia et al. 2001). It can be defined *negatively* as the absence of invasion of privacy by the government, businesses, or other actors. The focus here is on different types of privacy violations and their disruptive or destructive effects on the integrity of certain human activities; consequently, much attention is given to attempts to protect privacy from intrusions. In his taxonomy of privacy, Solove (2008, pp. 101–170) identifies four types of *privacy problems*, most of which are related to informational privacy: firstly, information collection, encompassing surveillance and interrogation; secondly, information processing, with the sub-types of aggregation, identification, insecurity, secondary use, and exclusion; thirdly, information dissemination, including breach of confidentiality, disclosure, exposure, increased accessibility, blackmail, appropriation, and distortion; fourthly, invasion of one's private sphere, in the forms of intrusion or interference with personal decisions. Similarly, Nissenbaum (2010, pp. 21–64) identifies three types of technology-based privacy problems: tracking and monitoring, aggregation and analysis, and dissemination and publication. However, in order to avoid "conceptual sprawl," her notion of privacy focuses on "public/private" as a guiding normative distinction in the three dimensions of actors, realm/space, and information. Here, the right to privacy is not understood as mere access control but as the "right to appropriate flow of personal information" while maintaining the "contextual integrity" of the information (Nissenbaum 2010, p. 127).

5.2 Privacy Protection

Because of the rapid advances of information technology and its enormous processing and storing capacity, privacy protection has become particularly important in the informational dimension. Moreover, the ubiquity of information and communication technology also increasingly permeates the other three dimensions of privacy (For a systematic and detailed discussion of information technology-based invasions of privacy, see Nissenbaum 2010, pp. 21–64). For instance, personal space and territorial privacy are subject to invasive technologies, such as the increasing use of surveillance cameras at workplaces and in public or semi-public places (e.g., in shopping malls and airports) or the use of RFID tracking devices (Van den Hoven Aspen and Vermaas 2007). Personal communication can easily be intercepted and retained with wiretapping technology and the surveillance of e-mail and other Internet-based communication media, as warranted under the USA PATRIOT Act (Solove et al. 2006, pp. 107ff). Bodily privacy is infringed upon by large-scale biometric checks at stadiums and other gathering places and also by the much debated body scanners in airports (Lombard 2010).

Privacy can be protected through three main mechanisms: *legal* regulation, *ethical* self-regulation, and privacy-enhancing *technology.* These three mechanisms will be discussed briefly in the following.

In modern societies, privacy enjoys specific *legal* protection, although the extent and range of the protection varies considerably. While most countries explicitly recognize basic privacy rights in their constitutions and have adopted comprehensive and general data protection laws, the United States Constitution does not mention a right to privacy. Yet, the protection of personal beliefs in the first Amendment, the search and seizure limits of the third and fourth Amendments, and the self-incrimination limit of the 5th Amendment protect at least certain aspects of personal privacy. In addition, a good dozen Supreme Court decisions have used the liberty clause of the 14th Amendment to establish a somewhat broader right of privacy. However, case law decisions and sectoral legislation, such as the Health Information Privacy Protection Act (HIPPA), the Family Educational Rights and Privacy Act (FERPA), and the Children's Online Privacy Protection Act (COPPA), only lead to "patchwork coverage" and fail to guarantee privacy as a basic right (Bennett and Raab 2006, p. 132).

Privacy as a basic human right is guaranteed in the UN Declaration of Human Rights (United Nations 1948, Art. 12), the European Convention on Human Rights (ECHR 1950, Art. 8), and many other international agreements and national statutory laws. Initially, legal regulations focused on preventing intrusion into personal privacy, home, family, and correspondence, but the rapid development of information technologies soon necessitated specific data protection laws. For instance, the OECD "Guidelines governing the protection of privacy and transborder flows of personal data" define basic fair information practices and principles (FIPP) regarding individual rights and accountability in the collection, use, purpose, and security of data (OECD 1980, Part 2). The Data Protection Directive of the European Union (European Parliament 1995) even defines *information privacy* explicitly as a basic human right. This stands in stark contrast to the situation in the US, where "the government is constitutionally prohibited under the First Amendment from interfering with the flow of information, except in the most compelling circumstances" (Cate 1999, pp. 179f.). Differences in national and international law, the lack of comprehensive privacy laws in some countries, and the rapid evolution of technology make legal regulation a cumbersome, inconsistent, and often outdated instrument of privacy regulation.

A different approach is voluntary *ethical self-regulation* of privacy. Although ethical regulation lacks the power of external sanctions (such as a legal penal system), it can be quite effective, particularly if based on the binding power of socially entrenched norms. Informal privacy norms are akin to rules of etiquette and personal morality. They govern reasonable expectations of privacy in interpersonal relationships, groups, and subcultures. More formal norms of privacy are embedded in professional norms, ethics codes, and express policies of organizations and institutions that typically deal with any kind of personal information. Such formal policies often mix different types of privacy regulation, such as privacy commitments, privacy codes, privacy standards, and privacy seals (Bennett and Raab 2006, pp. 151–175). Professional discretion and confidentiality thus belong to the privacy standards that clients may reasonably expect in their interactions with agencies such as health care providers or educational institutions.

As Nissenbaum (2010, pp. 129ff.) has shown, all of these norms are entrenched in specific contexts, within which they regulate the flow of personal information, which is why they are referred to as informational norms. From this perspective, the right to privacy can be understood as a right to *context-appropriate flow* of personal information. In other words, privacy does not mean the indiscriminate control of personal information, but a highly differentiated practice of sharing and withholding information depending on its meaning and sensitivity in different contexts. Consequently, violations of privacy are seen as violations of contextual integrity or "breaches of context-relative informational norms" (Nissenbaum 2010, p. 140). This contextual approach to privacy not only allows a detailed descriptive analysis of privacy, it also provides a strong normative basis for an ethical critique of privacy invasion as an unjustified transgression of contextual integrity. The transgression would be deemed unjustified whenever (a) expectations of the established context-appropriate flow of information are breached, and (b) the novel flow is not morally superior to the existing contextual norms and practices (Nissenbaum 2010, p. 164). The task of the ethical evaluation is, then, "to compare entrenched and novel flows in terms of values, ends, and purposes of respective contexts" (Nissenbaum 2010, p. 227). The concept of contextual integrity thus provides both a rational explanation of the moral outrage individuals feel when their privacy is invaded and an ethical framework for assessing the legitimacy of their claims.

The technicization of privacy invasion, particularly in the realm of information technology, has led to an increased demand for the third approach to privacy protection, i.e., *privacy-enhancing technology*. This approach is broader than just protecting privacy with the help of specific information technology. For centuries, simple mechanical solutions have been used to protect people's privacy: screens, curtains, doors, fences, and sound insulation protect against the unwanted gaze and eavesdropping; sensitive paper documents are locked in filing cabinets and often shredded after their intended purpose expires. In digital information environments, technological privacy protection can be achieved through access control and privacy-sensitive data management. *Access* can be controlled with a variety of hard- and software tools, such as authentication tools, firewalls, spyware detectors, filters, secure connections, and privacy settings. In addition to this, privacy-sensitive digital *data management* employs techniques such as data encryption, anonymization tools, blocking of data aggregation, automatic data expiration, and secure data deletion tools (Bennett and Raab 2006, pp. 177–202).

Unfortunately, much as fences can be climbed and locks picked, digital access control and data management tools can be circumvented or hacked into. The reliability and trustworthiness of privacy technologies are thus rather questionable. They are a necessary but not sufficient condition for informational privacy. Sole reliance on such technologies often creates a false sense of security and may actually lead to careless and imprudent behavior. As will be shown in Sect. 5.4, citizens must not only insist on their privacy rights but also acquire *privacy literacy,* which encompasses an informed concern for their privacy and effective strategies to protect it. First, though, ethical arguments that analyze the normative status of privacy and develop moral principles to justify its protection must be considered.

5.3   Ethical Justification of Privacy Protection

Similar to the conceptualization of privacy, the ethical justification of privacy and its protection can be founded on positive and negative arguments. The *positive* argument claims that the social-psychological need for privacy and the legal right to privacy imply that privacy possesses a specific moral value for individuals, relationships, and society, and therefore deserves special protection. Privacy is regarded both as an inherent value and as interrelated with a number of other essential human values, among them moral autonomy and freedom, equality and justice, dignity and self-fulfillment, and trust and variety in relationships. Privacy also draws moral value and legitimacy from its crucial role for the functioning of key social institutions and the well-being and freedom of citizens (Nissenbaum 2010, pp. 67–83; Solove 2008, pp. 77–100). The demand for privacy protection thus rests upon value-based moral claims and can be ethically justified by the moral value of privacy and its links to related basic values.

A central value and guiding principle of the positive ethical justification of privacy and its protection is the individual's right to *self-determination*, i.e., the right to freely determine what is necessary and desirable for a fulfilling and meaningful life and to freely pursue one's social, cultural, political, and economic development. Self-determination is thus part of an individual's autonomy and freedom. Self-determination and autonomy are, as Kant has shown, intrinsically connected: "Autonomy of the will is the property the will has of being a law unto itself" (Kant 1785/1964, p. 108). In short, self-determination of the free will is the basis for moral action and at the same time an inalienable natural right. Applied to privacy, self-determination is the underlying moral principle and right that enables individuals to control access to their private sphere and to regulate the flow and context of their information. Self-determination can thus be regarded as a basic positive moral and legal principle of privacy protection (Baker 2008, p. 10).

Given the ubiquity and influence of information technology in our society, *informational self-determination* has become a central positive concept in the privacy debate and also in privacy policy. As Hornung and Schnabel (2009, p. 85) have pointed out, privacy and informational self-determination guard the borders among different societal contexts, "as they prevent sensitive information from one context (e.g., the working world, medical treatment, family life, etc.) from proliferating into other ones." They also stress the fundamental role of informational self-determination for the development of autonomous individuals and for their unhampered participation in the political process. It is noteworthy that, in a groundbreaking decision, the German Federal Constitutional Court in 1993 established the right to informational self-determination and data protection, linking them explicitly to "the fundamental values those rights are assumed to protect and which were identified by the German Constitutional Court as human dignity and self-development" (Rouvroy and Poullet 2009, p. 46). The right to informational self-determination is also expressed in the 1995 data protection directive of the European Union (European Parliament 1995). Even though some countries do not recognize the right to informational self-determination, the significance of this concept cannot be overemphasized.

The *negative* ethical argument for protecting privacy is based on the harm principle (Mill 1851/1991), which postulates the duty to avoid harming others for one's own benefit. As an ethical principle, harm avoidance is not just built upon a selfish interpretation of the Golden Rule, which simply advises us not to harm others so that we will not be harmed. Rather, it is based on a universal appreciation of a shared capacity for suffering, human connectedness, and compassion (Linklater 2006). It also does not exclude the causation of *any* harm (otherwise, for example, many medical procedures would be impossible). Instead, it specifically refers to harm that both violates a person's right and at the same time can actually be avoided without creating greater harm elsewhere. This necessitates applying a cost-benefit analysis that weighs the interest in invading a person's privacy against the individual's right to and need for privacy.

In media ethics, for instance, the cost-benefit analysis is typically based on two interdependent criteria: firstly, a privacy invasion is only acceptable if no other means are available for obtaining the needed information; secondly, any invasion of privacy requires the existence of an overriding public interest (Hodges 2009, p. 281). This approach, however, has been criticized insofar as it leaves open what exactly constitutes an overriding public interest, so that definitional power is inevitably vested in the privacy invaders, as they can always claim a higher interest in the name of the public. In the media, intrinsic journalistic news values and the frequently invoked audience's "right to know" quickly cancel out the individual's privacy claims (Christians 2010, p. 209). However, protection of privacy is a matter of general ethics and must not be subordinated to the imperatives of professional ethics or, worse, pragmatic purposes (Christians 2010).

There are two approaches to remedy this problem: *Firstly*, a balance test, as proposed by Whitehouse (2010), demands that the benefit to the public must be considerably higher than the potential damage to the journalistic profession and the victim of privacy invasion. Here, too, the cost-benefit ratio remains somewhat speculative and arbitrary because it lacks clear and fair criteria for determining what constitutes "considerably higher" benefits. *Secondly*, the "informed consent" criterion is based on the maxim of informational self-determination and thus requires the unforced and well-informed consent of the individual whose privacy is at risk (Van den Hoven Aspen and Vermaas 2007, p. 285). For private citizens (as opposed to public figures), an overriding public interest could only be claimed if public safety is at stake and if no alternative, less invasive courses of action are available to reach the same goal.

While it makes sense that the public interest might override the individual's right to privacy in certain instances, the issue becomes much more complicated when special interests, such as businesses, are the driving force of privacy invasion. Nissenbaum (2010, p. 111) argues that such particular interests are often disguised as legitimate superior values, with the result that costs and benefits are unevenly distributed at the expense of the individual. An ethically justifiable approach, however, would require a fair distribution of costs and benefits. This could be achieved with the above described framework of contextual integrity, which would weigh the context-relative norms of the individual's flow of information against the new flow intended by the special interest actor. The invasion of privacy would only be justified if the new flow was demonstrably at least as beneficial to the individual as to the special interest.

However, the contextual integrity framework has two minor conceptual flaws: one is its preference for existing norms in present contexts, which may lead, as the author concedes, to conservatism and the "tyranny of the normal"– just because a social practice is well established does not mean it is a morally good practice. The suggested remedy, the principle of moral superiority, is somewhat weak because it relies on the optimistic assumption of a commonly accepted morality and is based on a circular assessment of "how effective each (competing practice) is in supporting, achieving, or promoting relevant contextual values" (Nissenbaum 2010, p. 166). Here, a *normative ethical* concept that provides a standard of moral quality would be needed, such as the question of whether a new technology or a new flow of information fosters autonomy, self-determination, and self-fulfillment for both individuals and society as a whole; in other words, a standard that foregrounds an emancipatory potential.

The second flaw is that the contextual integrity framework provides little room for the individual as an autonomous decision maker. The comparison of the context-relative norms of the existing flow of information to those of the new flow seems to operate like a court with the assumption of a generally accepted morality as the judge. However, based on the principle of individual self-determination and autonomy, one could argue that the *informed consent* criterion should govern the comparison, and not some external moral force. This would also imply that the default setting for privacy decisions must be positive consent: the *proactive opt-in* choice, rather than the retroactive opt-out (Bowie and Jamal 2006, p. 330).

Though preferred by online businesses, opt-out solutions are always problematic from an ethical point of view because they shift the burden to the individual: the opt-in approach disallows any privacy invasion unless the individual explicitly agrees to share his or her information. Contrary to this, the opt-out approach implicitly allows the invasion of privacy unless the user actually opts out. In addition, individuals often do not know about the opt-out possibility, and opt-out solutions often entail confusing piecemeal procedures or are hidden at the end of lengthy and complicated user agreements (Bowie and Jamal 2006, p. 330). Indeed, true self-determination and actual consumer choice can only be achieved through opt-in as the default standard (Gandy 1993; Bowie and Jamal 2006). The more consumer-friendly privacy laws in the European Union often include an opt-in requirement while US law, favoring business interests, does not even require general opt-out procedures (Bowie and Jamal 2006, p. 331).

In conclusion, the above discussion on the ethical justification of privacy protection has shown that privacy and its protection are not negligible or secondary values. Rather, they belong to the inner core of basic human rights and needs. The discussion of privacy must be centered on the idea of contextual integrity and the individual's right to self-determination. This, then, provides the basis for an ethical approach to privacy that prioritizes the individual's privacy rights over others' interest in privacy invasion. It leads to three moral principles:

1. The positive right to self-determination and the negative duty to minimize harm require a fair distribution of costs and benefits, determined by the comparison of the existing and the intended flow of information.
2. Individuals must have access to informed and positive consent (opt-in) when their context-appropriate flow of personal information is in danger of being breached.
3. An overriding interest in privacy invasion is justified only under special circumstances, such as a threat to public security or the individual, and only when no other, less invasive procedures would reach the same goal.

5.4   Privacy Protection in Online Social Networks

Privacy protection in online social media seems to be an oxymoron. After all, the main purpose of participating in social networks is the exchange of information, most of it highly personal, and the maintenance and expansion of one's social relationships. The informal character of online social networking and the possibility to communicate casually with few words through wall posts and status updates enables users to manage a large number of rather superficial contacts with relatively little effort – a phenomenon discussed in network sociology as "weak ties in the flow of information" (Gross and Acquisti 2005, pp. 2f.). The pervasiveness and user-friendliness of social networking sites provide additional motivation for users to post frequently. Thus, they voluntarily disclose large amounts of personal information and contribute continually to the creation and maintenance of extensive dynamic user profiles.

However, social networking sites pose many privacy risks for their users, ranging from unauthorized use of their information by government agencies and businesses to attacks by hackers, phishers, and data miners (Lynch 2010; Clark and Roberts 2010; WebSense 2010). Risks can also result from harmful activities by other users, such as cyberstalking, harassment, and reputation damage (boyd and Ellison 2008; Hoy and Milne 2010; Mishna et al. 2009). The potential risks can actually be plotted on two dimensions: a horizontal axis, which is visible to the user, and an invisible vertical one. The horizontal axis represents social interactions among the users, where people present themselves though their profiles and engage in communicative exchanges. The vertical axis is the systematic collection, aggregation, and use of data by the networking company. The horizontal interactions occur in the visible tip of the iceberg, while the data generated by the users trickle down into the submerged part of the iceberg. For the average user, the vertical invasion of privacy and its potential commercial or criminal exploitation by third parties therefore tend to remain invisible (Debatin et al. 2009, p. 88; Nissenbaum 2010, pp. 221 ff.).

The situation is aggravated by insufficient, sloppy, and misleading privacy practices in online social networks, which have been criticized early on (Jones and Soltren 2005; Privacy International 2007). The world's largest online social network Facebook, which had over half a billion users at the end of 2010, is known for its cumbersome and confusing privacy features and its invasive and deceptive practices (EPIC 2010). The default setting for its privacy features is usually at the lowest, most open level and opt-out procedures are burdensome and convoluted, which means that users have to be very proactive if they want to protect their privacy effectively. All in all, social online networks perform poorly with respect to privacy protection and data security. A 2010 study by the German consumer organization "Stiftung Warentest" found data protection in online social networks to be rather weak. In the overall evaluation, only two of the ten networks tested showed "minor flaws," while four displayed "clear flaws" and four "severe flaws"–among the latter were the mega-networks Facebook, LinkedIn, and MySpace (Test 2010).

Studies on online privacy behavior have shown that social network users tend to be rather careless with their personal data. Most users have a general awareness of possible risks but do not act accordingly: they often know little about privacy policies and use privacy settings inconsistently or not at all (Debatin et al. 2009). The most common privacy risk management strategy is *building fences*, i.e., managing spatial boundaries by using the "friends only" setting to restrict the visibility of one's information, while users are "less aware of, concerned about, or willing to act on possible "temporal" boundary intrusions posed by future audiences because of the persistence of data" (Tufekci 2008, p. 33). And even the "friends-only" strategy is only used by a third to a half of the users (Ellison et al. 2007; Debatin et al. 2009). Moreover, the term "friend" is ambiguous in the online world, designating soulmates, acquaintances, and strangers alike. Most Facebook users have hundreds of friends, and statistically, about one third of users will accept complete strangers as friends (Jones and Soltren 2005; Jump 2005).

Even if a user profile is restricted to "friends only," the restriction can easily be bypassed through tagging, so that at least the friends of the friend who tagged something can view this information. Worse yet, the "friends only" restriction obviously affects only the horizontal dimension of interactions among users, but has no impact on the vertical dimension of data harvesting by the networking company and its partners. Therefore, it is highly questionable if one can call the "friends only" strategy a real "privacy-enhancing behavior," as Stutzman and Kramer-Duffield (2010) suggest. Might this particular strategy – like privacy technologies in general–simply create a false sense of security among its users?

This would be consistent with the finding that users tend to be satisfied with the mere idea of privacy control without much real control: while they may use privacy restrictions, "they do not quite understand that their level of privacy protection is relative to the number of friends, their criteria for accepting friends, and the amount and quality of personal data provided in their profiles, which they tend to divulge quite generously" (Debatin et al. 2009, p. 102).

Though ignorance and a false sense of security play an important role, it remains perplexing why social networking users tolerate deep invasions of their privacy. An important explanation lies in the expected benefits of social networking. The most important gratification is arguably the social capital from creating and maintaining contacts and friendships (see Ellison et al., this volume, chap. 3). In addition, social media are now deeply rooted in everyday habits and routines. Routinized social networking allows users to maintain relationships while keeping people at a ritualized distance, thus enabling large scale weak ties management (Debatin et al. 2009, p. 101). However, whether social network users follow a rational choice model in weighing the benefits and risks, such as Petronio's communication privacy management model (Xu et al. 2008), is still questionable. Similarly unconvincing is the hypothesis that they are just willing to take more risks than other people (Fogel and Nehmad 2009; Ibrahim 2008). More likely, disclosure of private information in online social networks happens through a kind of bargaining process in which the perceived concrete benefits of networking outweigh the abstract interest in guarding one's privacy. The potential impact of the disclosure is a hypothetical event in the future, while the benefits of social networking are tangible and immediate. Moreover, in analogy to a third-person effect, possible risks are typically projected into the environment and thus seen as happening to others, not to oneself (Debatin et al. 2009).

It is noteworthy, though, that users react with outrage to concrete and visible violations of their privacy. When Facebook launched the "News Feed" in September 2006, a feature that tracks users' activities and displays them on the pages of their friends, users protested massively against this intrusive feature. They formed anti-News Feed groups on Facebook, including the 700,000 member group "Students Against Facebook News Feed." Facebook reacted to this by introducing specific privacy controls for the News Feed (boyd 2008). Similarly, the Facebook advertising platform Beacon, which broadcasted online shopping activities to the users' friends, met great resistance when it was introduced in November 2007. Facebook responded by first offering various opt-out features and then, after continuing protests, changing to an opt-in policy for Beacon (Nissenbaum 2010, p. 223).

These privacy invasions visibly breached users' reasonable expectations of the context-appropriate flow of their personal information. Applying the three moral principles introduced earlier, the following conclusions can be drawn: Firstly, the comparison of the existing and novel flow shows in both cases that costs and benefits were unfairly distributed, thus violating *principle 1*. Secondly, massive protest led to a repair of the disrupted flow of information (appropriate privacy control tools in one case, and opt-in in the other). This reinstated *principle 1* and followed the requirements of *principle 2*. Thirdly, there was obviously no overriding interest and no lack of alternative options that might have justified the continuation of the invasive practices, as stated in *principle 3*. Finally, these examples also show that moral outrage, public discourse, and political pressure are necessary to effect change in privacy policies and practices. Only then can businesses and governmental agencies be held accountable and compelled to adhere to fair privacy standards.

5.5   Conclusion: Toward an Ethics of Self-Restraint

In order to have a vital public discourse about privacy invasions, they must be brought to light and no longer be carried out under cover of invisibility or obscured by "technological constraints." Unfortunately, the widespread focus on technological solutions to privacy problems not only results in a false sense of security, it also encourages unthinking self-subordination to ostensible technological constraints. This is part of the broader problem that technology creates a universe of immanence with its own putatively inherent necessities and constraints, leading people to believe that there are no alternatives to technological solutions and that they have no agency and responsibility (Jonas 1984a).

The first step toward regaining agency and responsibility is the development of an enlightened understanding of technology and its unintended consequences. In the case of privacy in social media, it means that users develop *privacy literacy* that enables them to see through the technological veil and to make educated choices. In other words, users of social media need to develop an *informed concern* about their privacy, avoiding both moral panic and ignorant or naive indifference toward information technology. This implies that users must inform themselves proactively about the potential negative impact of social media on their privacy and that they must acquire the skills necessary to mitigate or entirely prevent negative consequences.

A privacy-literate user would thus not simply make use of technical privacy settings, because they are merely *spatial* access barriers that can always be bypassed somehow. Additionally, this user would employ *temporal* privacy protection, i.e., limit the availability of free floating private information from the outset so that it cannot be abused in the future. As long as there are no effective mechanisms for user-driven data annulment, any personal information that is put out on the Internet must be considered *as if* it were public, because information in digital networks is persistent and can arbitrarily be copied, distributed, and repurposed without the original owner's knowledge and consent. Reducing the flow of information is therefore a reasonable and effective strategy for maintaining the integrity of personal information. Admittedly, this would require users to readjust their expectations and behavior in social networking environments. It would require a user-centered *ethics of self-restraint* as the guiding principle of operation (Jonas 1984b). In a Kantian test of universalization, users who follow the principle of self-restraint should always ask themselves, when posting information, *if they can at the same time will that this information become known not only to their friends but to the whole world.*

This should not be misread as carte blanche for social network owners and others to harvest user data. Rather, the user's informed concern and the subsequent ethics of self-constraint are corollaries to the three principles set forth above. Thus, the onus is on all parties involved:

- Network owners and third parties are expected to follow principles of fair information practices, i.e., to respect the user's right to self-determination, to foster a fair distribution of costs and benefits, and to employ positive consent (opt-in) as a default. The ethics of self-restraint can be applied to them too, as they should put themselves in the shoes of their users and ask *if they, in the position of the user, could at the same time will that their information become known not only to their friends but to the whole world.*
- Users have a responsibility to be sufficiently educated about their choices and actions in social media. After all, truly informed consent presupposes the user's informed concern for his or her privacy.
- And finally, ethicists, educators, system developers, and service providers are also responsible for creating an environment that fosters *privacy literacy* among the users of social media and in society as a whole.

A turn toward respectful, fair, and open information practices, based on informed consent and the ethics of self-restraint, may sometimes mean short-term losses with regard to the data harvesting business. However, long-term benefits will not only be enjoyed by users who interact in a safer and more trustworthy environment, they will also extend to social network owners and third parties because they can be trusted and will thus gain and sustain a positive reputation among their customers.

References

Altman I (1975) The environment and social behavior: privacy, personal space, territory, crowding. Cole Publishing Company, Monterey, CA

Baker DJ (2008) Constitutionalizing the harm principle. Criminal Justice Ethics 27:3–28, Summer/Fall 2008

Bennett CJ, Raab CD (2006) The Governance of Privacy: Policy Instruments in Global Perspective, Cambridge, MA, London: MIT Press, 2 ed.

Bowie NE, Jamal K (2006) Privacy rights on the internet: self-regulation or government regulation? Bus Ethics Q 16(3):323–342

boyd d (2008) Facebook's privacy trainwreck: exposure, invasion, and social convergence. Convergence: The International Journal of Research into Media Technologies 14(1):13–20

boyd d, Ellison NB (2008) Social network sites: definition, history, and scholarship. JComput-Mediat Commun 13:210–230.http://jcmc.indiana.edu/vol13/issue1/boyd.ellison.html. Accessed 12 Jan 2011

Cate FH (1999) The changing face of privacy protection in the European Union and the United States. Ind L Rev 33:173–233

Christians CG (2010) The ethics of privacy. In: Meyers C (ed) Journalism ethics: a philosophical approach. Oxford University Press, Oxford, pp 203–214

Clark LA, Roberts SJ (2010) Employer's use of social networking sites: a socially irresponsible practice. J Bus Ethics 95:507–525

Debatin B, Lovejoy J, Hughes B, Horn A (2009) Facebook and online privacy: attitudes, behaviors, and unintended consequences. J Comput-Mediat Commun 15(1):83–108. http://onlinelibrary. wiley.com/doi/10.1111/j.1083-6101.2009.01494.x/pdf Accessed 11 Jan 2011

ECHR (1950) European convention on human rights. Registry of the European Court of Human Rights 2010., http://www.echr.coe.int/NR/rdonlyres/D5CC24A7-DC13-4318-B457-5C9014916D7A/0/ ENG_CONV.pdf Accessed 15 Dec 2010

Ellison N, Steinfield C, Lampe C (2007) The benefits of Facebook "friends": exploring the relationship between college students' use of online social networks and social capital. JComput-Mediat Commun 12, 4. http://jcmc.indiana.edu/vol12/issue4/ellison.html Accessed 5 Dec 2010

EPIC (2010). Social Networking Privacy. Epic.Org Electronic Privacy Information Center. http:// epic.org/privacy/socialnet/ Accessed 10 Dec 2010

European Parliament (1995). Directive 95/46/EC of the European Parliament and of the Council of 24 October 1995 on the protection of individuals with regard to the processing of personal data and on the free movement of such data. Official Journal L 281, 23/11/1995 P. 0031 – 0050. http://eur-lex.europa.eu/LexUriServ/LexUriServ.do?uri=CELEX:31995L0046:en:HTML Accessed 15 Dec 2010

Fogel J, Nehmad E (2009) Internet social network communities: risk taking, trust, and privacy concerns. Comput Hum Behav 25:153–160

Gandy OH Jr (1993) The panoptic sort: a political economy of personal information. Westview Press, Boulder, CO

Gross R, Acquisti A (2005) Information revelation and privacy in online social networks. Workshop on Privacy in the Electronic Society (WPES). http://privacy.cs.cmu.edu/ dataprivacy/projects/facebook/facebook1.pdf Accessed 22 Dec 2010

Habermas J (1962) Strukturwandel der Öffentlichkeit. Untersuchungen zu einer Kategorie der bürgerlichen Gesellschaft. Darmstadt: Luchterhand Verlag. English Edition: Habermas J (1989) The Structural Transformation of the Public Sphere: An Inquiry into a category of Bourgeois Society (trans. Burger, T.). Cambridge, MA: MIT Press.

Hodges L (2009) Privacy and the press. In: Wilkins L, Christians CG (eds) The handbook of media ethics. Routledge, New York, pp 276–287

Hornung G, Schnabel C (2009) Data protection in Germany I: the population census decision and the right to informational self-determination. Comput Law Security Review 25:84–88

Hoy MG, Milne G (2010) Gender differences in privacy-related measures for young adult facebook users. J Interactive Advertising 10(2):28–45

Ibrahim Y (2008) The new risk communities: social networking sites and risk. Int J Media Cult Polit 4(2):245–253

Jonas H (1984a) The imperative of responsibility: in search of ethics for the technological age. University of Chicago Press, Chicago

Jonas H (1984b) Warum wir heute eine Ethik der Selbstbeschränkung brauchen. In: Ströker E (ed) Ethik der Wissenschaften? Philosophische Fragen. Wilhelm Fink Verlag, München, Paderborn, Wien, Zürich, pp 75–86

Jones H, Soltren JH (2005) Facebook: threats to privacy (white paper, December 14, 2005). http:// www-swiss.ai.mit.edu/6805/student-papers/fall05-papers/facebook.pdf. Accessed 12 Jan 2011

Jump K (2005) A new kind of fame: MU student garners a record 75,000 Facebook friends. Columbia Missourian, 1.9.2005. http://www.columbiamissourian.com/stories/2005/09/01/a-new-kind-of-fame/. Accessed 5 Jan 2011

Kant I (1964) Groundwork of the metaphysic of morals (trans. H.J. Paton). Harper & Row, New York (Original work published 1785 in German)

Leino-Kilpia H, Välimäki M, Dassen T, Gasull M, Lemonidou C, Scott A, Arndt M (2001) Privacy: a review of the literature. Int J Nurs Stud 38:663–671

Linklater A (2006) The harm principle and global ethics. Global Soc J Interdisciplinary Int Relat 20(3):329–343

Lombard E (2010) Bombing out: using full-body imaging to conduct airport searches in the United States and Europe amidst privacy concerns. Tul J Int Comp Law 19(1):337–367

Lynch J (2010). New FOIA documents reveal DHS social media monitoring during Obama inauguration. Electronic Frontier Foundation, 13.10.2010. http://www.eff.org/deeplinks/2010/10/new-foia-documents-reveal-dhs-social-mediaAccessed 11 Jan 2011

Mill JS (1991) On liberty and other writings. Oxford University Press, Oxford (Original work published 1841)

Mishna F, McLuckie A, Saini M (2009) Real-world dangers in an online reality: a qualitative study examining online relationships and cyber abuse. Soc Work Res 33(2):107–118

Nissenbaum H (2010) Privacy in context. technology, policy, and the integrity of social life. Stanford University Press, Stanford

OECD (1980). Guidelines on the protection of privacy and transborder flows of personal data. Organisation for Economic Co-operation and Development, Washington, DC. http://www.oecd.org/document/18/0,3343,en_2649_34255_1815186_1_1_1_1,00.html. Accessed 15 Dec 2010

Privacy International (2007) A race to the bottom: privacy ranking of internet service companies–A consultation report. Privacy International, June 9, 2007.http://www.privacyinternational.org/article.shtml?cmd[347]=x-347-553961. Accessed 22 Dec 2010

Rouvroy A, Poullet Y (2009) The right to informational self-determination and the value of self-development: reassessing the importance of privacy for democracy. In: Gutwirth S, Poullet Y, De Hert P, de Terwangne D, Nouwt S (eds) Reinventing data protection? Springer, New York, pp 45–76

Solove DJ (2008) Understanding privacy. Harvard University Press, Cambridge, MA

Solove DJ, Rothenberg M, Schwartz PM (2006) Privacy, information, and technology. Aspen, New York

Stutzman F, Kramer-Duffield J (2010). Friends only: examining a privacy-enhancing behavior in facebook. In: CHI '10 Proceedings of the 28th international conference on Human factors in computing systems, ACM Digital Library. http://portal.acm.org/citation.cfm?id=1753559. Accessed 26 Dec 2010

Test (2010) Soziale Netzwerke: Datenschutz oft mangelhaft. Stiftung Warentest – test.de, 25. 03. 2010. http://www.test.de/themen/computer-telefon/test/Soziale-Netzwerke-Datenschutz-oft-mangelhaft-1854798-1855785/. Accessed 3 Dec 2010

Tufekci Z (2008) Can you see me now? Audience and disclosure regulation in online social network sites. B Sci Technol Soc 28(1):20–36

United Nations (1948) The universal declaration of rights. United Nations. http://www.un.org/en/documents/udhr/index.shtml. Accessed 15 Dec 2010

Van den Hoven Aspen J, Vermaas PE (2007) Nano-technology and privacy: on continuous surveillance outside the panopticon. J Med Philos 32:283–297

Warren S, Brandeis L (1890) The right to privacy. Harv Law Rev IV(5):193–220

WebSense (2010) Facebook used for phishing attacks and open redirects. In: WebSense Security Labs Blog, 29. 11. 2010. http://community.websense.com/blogs/securitylabs/archive/2010/11/29/facebook-used-for-phishing-attacks-and-open-redirects.aspx. Accessed 12 Jan 2011

Westin AF (1967) Privacy and freedom. Atheneum, New York

Whitehouse G (2010) Newsgathering and privacy: expanding ethics codes to reflect change in the digital media age. J Mass Media Ethics 25(4):310–327

Xu H, Dinev T, Smith HJ, Hart P (2008) Examining the formation of individual's privacy concerns: toward an integrative view. In: International conference on information systems (ICIS) ICIS 2008 proceedings, Paris. http://faculty.ist.psu.edu/xu/papers/conference/icis08a.pdf. Accessed 22 Dec 2010

Chapter 6
The Social Web as a Shelter for Privacy and Authentic Living

Sabine Trepte and Leonard Reinecke

6.1 Introduction

Social network sites are known for intruding their users' privacy per default. The networks use and sell demographic information for targeted advertising (Acquisti et al. 2007). Data are replicated by users and transferred to unknown third parties; the user's utterances (e.g., on fan pages) are searched, analyzed, and scaled in market research (Nissenbaum 2009). Although users seem to be aware of this situation, the majority of users do not complain or change their self-disclosure online (boyd and Hargittai 2010, p. 320; Christofides et al. 2009). We find a very loose and laissez-faire behavior in terms of how users deal with the threats to and their own concerns about informational privacy online. Scholars have termed this contradiction the "privacy paradox," indicating that people seem to know about privacy threats on the one hand, but do not enact their privacy needs on the other (Barnes 2006).

To this notion of paradoxical privacy behavior, we would like to add a notion that we think has been neglected in previous debates and research. From our perspective, users are concerned in terms of informational privacy, but think they have great control in terms of social privacy and even feel that they benefit in terms of their perceived psychological privacy (Burgoon 1982). Informational privacy addresses whether people are able to control which and how much information about them is shared by others. Social privacy refers to the dialectic process of managing proximity and distance towards others. It is given if people feel in control of the amount and kind of interactions they have with others (Burgoon 1982). Psychological privacy is related to the control over emotional and cognitive inputs and outputs. A high level of psychological privacy exists if free speech and thought is possible, and if people may decide with whom to share their feelings and thoughts. That said, we would like to posit here that the majority of users feel threatened in terms of informational

S. Trepte (✉) • L. Reinecke
University of Hamburg, Hamburg, Germany
e-mail: sabine.trepte@uni-hamburg.de

S. Trepte and L. Reinecke (eds.), *Privacy Online*,
DOI 10.1007/978-3-642-21521-6_6, © Springer-Verlag Berlin Heidelberg 2011

privacy online, but that the main benefits that users find in the Social Web are rooted in perceived social and psychological privacy.

In terms of social privacy, the Social Web offers the possibility (or illusion) of controlling with whom to interact and to share information by means of mechanisms such as friends lists on social network sites. In terms of psychological privacy, the Social Web offers tremendous possibilities for publishing one's thoughts and feelings without being censored. In sum, users feel able to control their privacy via privacy settings and friends lists. Thereby, the subjective experience of privacy may be even richer in the Social Web than offline. People create *online spaces of social and psychological privacy* that may be an illusion; however, these spaces seem to be experienced as private and the technical and social architecture of the Social Web supports this notion. Within these online spaces of privacy, people experience the chance to be authentic. We would also go so far as to claim that these online spaces of psychological privacy predominantly seem to exist *because* they allow authenticity. As privacy and authenticity are basic human needs and important for psychological functioning and well-being (Kernis and Goldman 2006), users might accept trading off their informational privacy. The benefits of finding online spaces of psychological privacy that allow for authentic living seem to outweigh the loss of informational privacy.

In this chapter we will elaborate on this line of thought by firstly arguing that although the Social Web poses a threat to informational privacy, it offers online spaces of social and psychological privacy (see Sect. 6.2). We will then review the psychological groundwork on the concept of authenticity (see Sect. 6.3) and argue that privacy allows for authentic functioning (see Sect. 6.4). In the following, we will argue that the Social Web may be perceived as a shelter for authentic living because it offers online spaces of privacy. This experience is rooted in users' perception of successfully controlling audiences, interaction partners, and the content they are publishing (see Sect. 6.5). In our discussion (Sect. 6.6), we will suggest that users accommodate online spaces to their full advantage by (more or less consciously) trading off their informational privacy. We will discuss how this trade-off might affect future online behavior and online services. Also, we will argue that upcoming research on online privacy should be fine-grained in terms of its assumptions about what kinds and types of privacy users do or do not experience online.

6.2 Informational and Psychological Online Privacy: Trading Off One for the Other?

Contemporary conceptions of privacy and privacy management have been strongly influenced by the work of Alan Westin and Irwin Altman. Both Westin and Altman refer to privacy as a dynamic process of boundary management (Altman 1975; Westin 1967). While Westin (2003) defines privacy as "the claim of an individual to determine what information about himself or herself should be known to others" (p. 431), Altman (1975) defines privacy as "selective control of access to the self or to one's group" (p. 18). With their emphasis on controlling or regulating access to the self, both theories can be categorized as examples for "limited-access" approaches to privacy (Margulis 2003, p. 423). Furthermore, both Altman (1975) and Westin (1967) describe privacy as a non-monotonic function: the optimal level of privacy is not reached by a maximum of solitude or isolation. Rather, privacy needs to fluctuate dynamically according to specific situations and individuals may experience too little, just enough, or too much privacy (Margulis 2003). This idea is expressed well in Altman's (1975) distinction between *desired privacy* and *achieved privacy*. While desired privacy represents an individual's desire for a certain level of interaction in a given situation, achieved privacy represents the actual level of contact resulting from interaction in the respective situation. Thus, Altman (1975) describes privacy as an *optimizing process* that aims at matching the levels of desired and achieved privacy. The importance of successful privacy regulation is emphasized by Westin (1967), who argues that privacy is a crucial psychological resource and fosters important processes, such as personal autonomy, emotional release, self-evaluation, and protected communication.

The high complexity of privacy has led to further theoretical developments. Building on the seminal work of Altman, Westin, and other privacy theorists, Burgoon (1982) has developed a multi-dimensional definition of privacy that encompasses the distinction of four interdependent dimensions of privacy:

1. *Informational privacy* is defined as "the ability to control who gathers and disseminates information about one's self or group and under what circumstances" (Burgoon, et al. 1989, p. 134). Informational privacy is strongly affected by the way modern societies collect, store, and process personal information, such as medical or financial records, application data, customer data, and – since the advent of the Internet – a plethora of personal information available through online databases, search engines, or social network sites.
2. *Social privacy*, later referred to as *interactional privacy* by Burgoon et al. (1989), describes an individual's "ability to withdraw from social intercourse" (Burgoon 1982, p. 216) and "any efforts to control one's degree of social contacts" (p. 217). Social privacy is crucial in establishing closeness among some interactional partners while establishing a distance from others.
3. *Psychological privacy* refers to "one's ability to control affective and cognitive inputs and outputs" (Burgoon 1982, p. 224). It thus includes both the freedom to decide what, when, and to whom to disclose personal feelings and thoughts (output), as well as protection from cognitive or affective interference from others, such as persuasive pressures (input). Psychological privacy is an important resource that fosters the development of self-identity, autonomy, and personal growth (Burgoon 1982).
4. *Physical privacy* refers to "the freedom from surveillance and unwanted intrusions upon one's space by the physical presence, touch, sights, sounds, or odors of others" (Burgoon et al. 1989, p. 132) and puts an emphasis on the control over the degree of the physical accessibility or inaccessibility to others (Burgoon 1982).

In the following paragraphs we will focus on informational, social, and psychological privacy and discuss how users perceive all of these dimensions of privacy while surfing the Social Web. As the dimension of physical privacy has limited relevance for online communication and online self-disclosure, it does not seem as important for our considerations about online privacy and will not be discussed further here.

Previous research has predominantly addressed *informational privacy* and users' concerns related to their personal information. A number of studies have looked at general online privacy concerns, for example, with regard to credit card fraud, identity theft, viruses and spyware, unwanted dissemination of personal data or the abuse of personal information (e.g., for marketing purposes), and at online privacy protection behaviors (Buchanan et al. 2007; Cho et al. 2009; Paine et al. 2007; Yao et al. 2007). With regard to the Social Web, studies have been concerned with the breadth and depth of information provided in blogs or social network sites and with the use of privacy settings to protect personal information from unintended audiences (Acquisti and Gross 2006; Debatin et al. 2009; Lampe et al. 2007; Lewis et al. 2008; Tufekci 2008).

Social privacy in online contexts has not been addressed directly in prior research. However, there are many studies indicating how people enact and perceive their social privacy online (Debatin et al. 2009; Lewis et al. 2008). Users have been shown to be very well-informed about how to deal with their privacy settings or friends lists (boyd and Hargittai 2010). Also, they feel to be able to withdraw from interactions (by turning the computer off or leaving the room) at anytime. In particular, the technical features of the Social Web and social network sites enable users to engage in a number of audience management strategies such as joining groups and inviting or ignoring "friends."

Psychological Privacy online has also not been addressed directly in previous research, but there are a number of empirical findings indicating that users may have a strong sense of control with regard to their cognitive and emotional inputs and outputs in online environments. Firstly, self-disclosure as a correlate of privacy and as a form of emotional and/or cognitive output (and hence directly related to psychological privacy) has been shown to be higher in computer-mediated communication as well as in the Social Web when compared with face-to-face interaction (Joinson 2001; Tidwell and Walther 2002). Secondly, subjective feelings of anonymity or intimacy have often been used to explain why self-disclosure is more likely in computer-mediated communication or online than face-to-face (Walther 1996). In two experiments, Joinson (2001) demonstrated that computer-mediated communication was associated with higher levels of spontaneous self-disclosure than face-to-face interaction, and that this effect could be explained through visual anonymity in computer-mediated communication. Furthermore, Tidwell and Walther (2002) demonstrated that in computer-mediated communication, interaction partners engage in more intimate questions and self-disclosure utterances than individuals in face-to-face interaction. These results support the assumption that the computer-mediated setting seems to create a sense of privacy that is experienced in intimate face-to-face settings.

Similar results can be found for Social Web use. A number of studies demonstrate a high amount of disclosure and thus indicate that Social Web users exhibit communication behavior found in contexts experienced as private. The majority of blog and social network site users disclose detailed personal information such as personal feelings and thoughts; also, they grant insights into spheres considered private, such as details about their life with family and friends (Christofides et al. 2009; Debatin et al. 2009; Hinduja and Patchin 2008; Lampe et al. 2007; Nardi et al. 2004; Tufekci 2008; Viegas 2005).

We believe that the "privacy paradox" (Barnes 2006) may not be so paradox if we take a closer look at the users' behavior and experiences. While users may be concerned about the uncontrolled dissemination and potential abuse of their personal data and may thus experience threats to their *informational* privacy, the Social Web seems to foster feelings of *psychological* and *social* privacy. While the following section will present an introduction to basic theoretical conceptions of authenticity, the interaction between privacy and authenticity and the effects of the Social Web on authentic behavior will be discussed further in Sects. 6.4 and 6.5.

6.3 Authenticity

Authenticity is usually termed as having two suppositions: firstly that people know their thoughts and emotions, and secondly that they act in accordance with both (Harter 2002). In previous research on authenticity, it has been found that people can be most authentic if they feel minimally determined by role expectations (Sheldon et al. 1997). As such, authenticity has also been termed as being equivalent to self-determination and as an expression of the so called "true-self" or "core-self" (Kernis and Goldman 2005, 2006). Kernis and Goldman (2006) define authenticity as "the unobstructed operation of one's true- or core-self in one's daily enterprise" (p. 294).

There are different theoretical approaches and a number of suggestions for operationalizing authenticity (Harter 2002; Sheldon et al. 1997; Wood et al. 2008). Kernis and Goldman's (2006) multicomponent conceptualization of authenticity seems to be particularly helpful in defining and further understanding authenticity and authentic functioning. They suggest breaking down authenticity into four separate, but interrelated components:

1. *Awareness* refers to possessing and being motivated to increase knowledge of and trust in one's emotions and cognitions.
2. *Unbiased processing* implies that people are able to objectively process positive as well as negative self-aspects such as emotions, private knowledge, and internal experiences.
3. *Behavior* as a third component of authenticity refers to behavior that reflects one's values, preferences, and needs as opposed to acting falsely to please others, to obtain or to retain rewards. Inauthentic behavior involves being either unaware of or otherwise oversimplifying self-aspects relevant to a behavioral context.

4. *Relational orientation* involves openness, sincerity, and truthfulness in close relationships.

As the four dimensions are separable, a person might be aware of her or his values but might not be able to express these values in a certain setting. The question arising here is whether somebody being aware of his thoughts but lacking expression thereof may still be considered an authentic personality. It also remains questionable whether we can be fully authentic at all, as we are bound to cultural norms and certain role expectations in many settings such as family, work, or leisure time settings. This question has raised quite a degree of consideration in previous research (Sheldon et al. 1997). The authenticity theories rooted in self-determination theory, such as the multicomponent conceptualization of authenticity (Kernis and Goldman 2006), suggest that people can be authentic as long as they are self-determined. This does not necessarily mean unveiling one's true self in a setting that does not seem appropriate to do so. Different approaches for staying authentic may be considered. Firstly, authentic people may actively self-select environments that have the fewest environmental boundaries and thus allow for authentic living:

> By having greater self-understanding, individuals high in authenticity seemingly are capable of self-selecting appropriate niches in their interpersonal milieu that sustain and promote their interpersonal and psychological adjustment. (Kernis and Goldman 2006, p. 320)

Secondly, the expectations set in a certain situation or environment may not be fulfilled. For authentic persons it might be more satisfying if they do not live up to the standard set in a certain environment rather than sacrifice their authenticity for the sake of social norms and expectations. Furthermore, authentic people might see it as an opportunity for individual growth and challenge to face an environment where they have to fight to express their true self while staying in touch with themselves and others.

A positive relationship between authenticity and healthy psychological and interpersonal functioning has been demonstrated in previous research. Well-being (Hodgins and Knee 2002; Kernis and Goldman 2006; Wood et al. 2008), self-esteem, life satisfaction (Kernis and Goldman 2005), and other measures of psychological health or distress such as anxiety, depression, stress, and symptomatology are significantly related to authenticity (Sheldon et al. 1997). The importance of authenticity for healthy psychological functioning may explain why people actively seek spaces where they can be authentic. In the following section we will show that private spaces are particularly suited to enacting authentic behavior.

6.4 How Privacy Fosters Authenticity

How do privacy and authenticity interact? And why do we need privacy to be authentic? Firstly and most importantly for the development of an authentic personality, privacy represents a psychological resource that fosters self-determined behavior (Westin 1967). This psychological impact of privacy is very well represented in Westin's (1967) notion of privacy functions. According to Westin (1967), privacy encompasses four processes that are crucial to psychological functioning: self-evaluation, autonomy, emotional relief and protected communication.

Privacy facilitates *self-evaluation* by creating protected rooms and situations that allow an individual to reflect upon his feelings and identity without the threat of social punishment. With regard to authenticity, self-evaluation appears to be a crucial predisposition for the authenticity component of *awareness* (Kernis and Goldman 2006). Without private situations that allow for self-reflection and evaluation, a person's ability to gather knowledge about his emotions and cognitions is severely limited.

Autonomy, the second function of privacy identified by Westin (1967), refers to the absence of manipulation or dominance by others and has strong implications for the authenticity dimension of *unbiased processing* (Kernis and Goldman 2006). The absence of external manipulation is a crucial precondition for the objective processing of positive and negative self-aspects necessary for authentic behavior and communication.

Furthermore, privacy facilitates *emotional relief* (Westin 1967) by allowing individuals to "lay their mask aside" (p. 35) and to deviate from social norms. This privacy function is very clearly related to the *behavior* component of authenticity (Kernis and Goldman 2006). By creating a break from social norms and expectations, privacy increases the likelihood of behavior that reflects one's values, preferences, and needs.

Finally, *limited and protected communication*, the last of Westin's (1967) privacy functions, refers to the ability to create intimacy and confidentiality as well as boundaries and distance among partners of social interaction. This privacy function is very likely to foster the authenticity dimension of *relational orientation* (Kernis and Goldman 2006). By creating intimate social interactions and enhancing confidentiality and trust among interaction partners, privacy is very likely to increase the willingness for openness, sincerity, and truthfulness in close relationships.

As demonstrated above, the four privacy functions proposed by Westin (1967) can be mapped to the four authenticity components of Kernis and Goldman (2006). In sum, privacy as a psychological resource gives individuals the freedom necessary for an undistorted reflection on the true self and for authentic behavior and self-presentation. The interrelation of privacy and authenticity helps us to understand authentic functioning in the Social Web.

The preceding analysis of privacy functions and authenticity support our initial notion that the Social Web is a particularly well-suited environment for stimulating authentic behavior (cf. Sect. 6.2). The specific features of the Social Web increase the subjective feelings of psychological and social privacy. Online spaces of psychological as well as social privacy, in turn, empower Social Web users to create protected virtual spaces for authentic behavior. A deeper analysis of the mechanisms that foster authentic behavior on the Social Web will be presented in the next section.

6.5 How Online Spaces of Privacy Allow for Authentic Living

Since very early work on the Internet, it has been described as enhancing self-expression (Turkle 1996). Bargh et al. (2002) hold that "[...] we would expect a person to use it first and foremost to express those aspects of self that he or she has the strongest need to express – namely, the true-self [...]" (p. 34).

In the preceding paragraphs we suggested that private spaces may encourage authentic living, that people seem to find these spaces particularly online, and that authentic living leverages well-being and psychological functioning. We showed that authenticity is rooted in self-determination theory (Deci and Ryan 2000), thus it can also be termed as a basic need that people strive to fulfill in their day-to-day life. However, not all people are able to fulfill this need. Their environments may exert strong role constraints and role pressure and thus prohibit authentic living (Kernis and Goldman 2006). Online environments may be forums that enable individuals to be authentic. We posit here that – although the Social Web has often been accused of violating people's informational privacy – it offers "online spaces of privacy" to its users and consequently endorses self-determination and authenticity.

However, what are the underlying psychological mechanisms that make people think they can be authentic in these psychological spaces of online privacy? We suggest that the subjective experience of privacy control grants the experience of authenticity. Thus we assume that people feel they can be authentic online because they create online spaces of privacy by controlling audiences, interaction partners, and content (Ben-Ze'ev 2003). In the following we will differentiate between controlling audiences and interaction partners on the one hand, and controlling content on the other. Whereas the control of audiences refers to social privacy, the control of content refers to psychological privacy.

6.5.1 Control over Audiences and Interaction Partners

Social networks offer a variety of technical settings and mechanisms for privacy management such as friends lists and privacy settings. These allow users to control the groups that they communicate with. This particular architecture is designed to control access and it is very simple to handle. All audience management strategies only need a couple of mouse clicks to be executed. This is not much compared to offline strategies for privacy management and access control, such as architectural features of built environments (Vinsel et al. 1980), the enforcement of social norms, the use of verbal and non-verbal cues, or other distancing behavior (Altman 1975; Burgoon 1982). Users gain the impression of being able to control their social privacy online easily and successfully.

In Sect. 6.3 we showed that two approaches are suited for making authentic behavior likely: one being that people actively select environments where they feel free to show their true self, and the other that people face environmental constraints and see conflicts as an opportunity for individual growth. The first approach seems to be used particularly on social network sites and in other Social Web services (Ben-Ze'ev 2003). Users control access of audiences and interaction partners and thus create niches in which they feel they can be authentic.

We assume that the controlled selection of interaction partners is the presupposition for a sense of self-determination and authenticity. Social privacy, the ability to control the degree of social interaction and the partners of social interaction (Burgoon 1982), relates to the ability to engage in limited and protected communication (Westin 1967) and to create niches that allow for authentic behavior.

Whereas controlling the boundaries to other persons and groups is one mechanism for creating spaces of privacy, the control over content is another. The latter will be described in the following paragraph.

6.5.2 Control over Content

Controlling what emotions and thoughts we share with others is a "sine qua non" for the experience of psychological privacy. Psychological privacy refers to the ability to control emotional as well as cognitive input and output (cf. Sect. 6.2). This seems to be particularly related to the authenticity component "unbiased processing" (cf. Sect. 6.3), which implies that authentic people are able to objectively process positive as well as negative self-aspects such as emotions, private knowledge, and internal experiences. Both terms "psychological privacy" and "unbiased processing" refer to the content of thoughts and emotions. As psychological privacy refers to the ability to control cognitive and emotional inputs and outputs (Burgoon 1982), it shows a direct connection to the absence of external influences hindering authenticity. In other words, the more psychological privacy a person possesses, the higher the person's autonomy (Westin 1967), enabling the person to elude social norms and expectations and to behave authentically.

Results from Schouten et al. (2007) emphasize the importance of perceived controllability of message construction and responses to other messages in computer-mediated communication compared to face-to-face interaction. Based on data from a survey among 1,340 Dutch adolescents, the authors demonstrated that the subjective relevance of heightened controllability in computer-mediated communication was a positive predictor of self-disclosure in instant messaging.

The perceived ability to control affective and cognitive inputs and outputs is the main assumption of psychological privacy (Burgoon 1982). It seems to be amplified through different features of the Social Web. Here we will address two means of controlling affective inputs and outputs.

One means of controlling cognitive output is to reread and edit utterances before posting them online. We believe that the Social Web and particularly social network sites are experienced as a very instantaneous medium. In their status notes, blog posts, or instant messages, users publish information that is comparable to "small talk" information. However, in contrast to face-to-face small talk, status notes may be reread and edited before being published. This editing process may only last a couple of seconds, but increases the experience of control as opposed to face-to-face interaction.

A second means of controlling emotional output is reached by communicating verbally only. Facial cues are not available during interaction in the Social Web and thus emotional output stays under the user's control. Fear, anger, happiness, and concerns are emotions that can be read in someone's face (Berry 1991; Ekman et al. 2001; Hassin and Trope 2000). However, facial cues as an information source about the interaction partner's emotions are not accessible online. Posting a status note on a social network site gives users' the chance to verbally focus on the thoughts they want to express and to filter out unwanted emotional expression. Social Web users might feel psychologically private online, because there is no risk of conflicting messages resulting from verbal and facial expressions. From the perspective of the user, the heightened control over verbal and non-verbal cues in computer-mediated communication, in combination with the heightened control over interaction partners in the Social Web (cf. Sect. 6.5.1), grants access to limited and protected communication, one of Westin's (1967) privacy functions, which refers to the ability to create intimacy and confidentiality as well as boundaries and distance among partners of social interaction. We suggested in Sect. 6.4 that this privacy function may support relational orientation as one component of authenticity (Kernis and Goldman 2006). By creating intimate social interactions and interpersonal trust among interaction partners, privacy is very likely to increase openness, sincerity, and truthfulness.

In sum, we suggest here that users may experience psychological spaces of privacy while surfing the Social Web, because they can edit and reread their verbal expressions online. Also, users may feel psychologically private, because their interaction partners do not see their facial expressions and other non-verbal cues. Both kinds of content control allow for protected communication, increase subjective feelings of psychological privacy, and thus foster authentic behavior in the Social Web.

6.6 Discussion and Future Perspectives

In this chapter we argued that social network site users may feel threatened or even exploited in terms of informational privacy online, but that they benefit in terms of social and psychological privacy. Social privacy is easily found online by controlling and managing audiences and interaction partners. Psychological privacy is created by managing the quantity and quality of personal information that is shared with others. The Social Web offers several mechanisms for regulating access to the self, such as friends lists, privacy settings, and group creation and participation. This fine-grained *"privacy-tuning"* gives users (the illusion of) private spaces. Within these online spaces of privacy, they experience fewer role constraints and expectations than they face in many offline environments. We thus suggested that these online spaces are perceived as spaces for authentic living. The more control a person has regarding the partners involved in social interaction and the content of interaction, the easier it is to create social rooms and situations that foster authentic living.

We validated single steps in our line of thought with prior research stemming from privacy and authenticity theories and from research on the Social Web. However, we made two very new assumptions that require empirical investigation. Firstly, we suggested that people perceive a loss of informational privacy but perceive a considerable amount of social and psychological privacy in online contexts. Secondly, we suggested that in these online spaces of privacy, authenticity is more likely to be shown. We also went so far as to say that these online spaces of privacy are controlled and created *because* they grant spaces for authentic living. Whereas other claims we made in this chapter have been investigated before, these two assumptions need further investigation and empirical validation.

In terms of theory, the critical question about our line of thought seems to be whether the proclaimed "online spaces of social and psychological privacy" are an illusion or whether they carry a certain truth. In terms of data management, psychological and social privacy online are only possible if the data are handled privately. As long as online data (e.g., on social network sites) are scaled, mined, and sold, these data are not private and all utterances that may be perceived as psychologically or socially private are not private from an informational point of view. However, the users' subjective experiences have to be taken into account as well as the objective facts. Therefore, from a psychological point of view, the truth or existence of online privacy may be assessed by simply asking the users what they experience. Furthermore, by putting users in conditions of more or less psychological and social privacy, it would be possible to investigate how these conditions are experienced and how they may affect authenticity. As long as we find authenticity as an effect of "experienced" privacy, we would posit from a psychological perspective that online privacy is surely not an illusion. Privacy would then "exist" as a user experience. Thus, we – as Social Web or privacy scholars and as a society – will have to face the phenomenon that an experience of social and psychological privacy might be a truth for a majority of users and consequently endorses privacy-related behavior such as authenticity online.

The assumption of people experiencing their online lives as private and thus behaving authentically may lead to different scenarios in the future. One would be that the ongoing scaling, mining, and selling of data that currently generates the revenues of social network sites might continue and might be advanced and extended in the future. In this scenario, the networks will make their users feel increasingly private, with the aim of triggering private self-disclosure, because personal data in particular generates revenues from advertisers and targeting companies. In contrast, a second scenario would be that users might become more aware of the illusiveness of their private niches online and might want to create spaces that not only feel private in a psychological and social sense, but also grant informational privacy. They might also become aware that privacy is the "currency" of the Social Web and that they trade their informational privacy for server space (e.g., webmail, drop-box services), access to online infrastructure (e.g., social network sites), or online content. In this scenario they may start to claim back their informational privacy online. Online services might then generate revenues by offering services that guarantee informational privacy and bill their users monetarily. Such online spaces that provide psychological and social privacy while protecting the users' informational privacy might eventually be the perfect niche for authentic online behavior. And it could be a chance for social network sites: they would not only demand authentic and open communication from their users, but for a change, could be authentic themselves by communicating what they sell and what they bill their customers.

References

Acquisti A, Gross R (2006) Awareness, information sharing, and privacy on the Facebook. Paper presented at the 6th Workshop on Privacy Enhancing Technologies, Cambridge, 28–30 June 2006

Acquisti A, Gritzalis S, Lambrinoudakis C, De Capitani di Vimercati S (eds) (2007) Digital privacy: theory, technologies, and practices. Auerbach, Boca Raton

Altman I (1975) The environment and social behavior: privacy, personal space, territory, crowding. Brooks/Cole, Monterey

Bargh JA, McKenna KYA, Fitzsimons GM (2002) Can you see the real me? Activation and expression of the "true self" on the internet. J Soc Issues 58(1):33–48

Barnes SB (2006) A privacy paradox: Social networking in the Unites States. First Monday 11(9). http://firstmonday.org/htbin/cgiwrap/bin/ojs/index.php/fm/article/view/1394/1312. Accessed 25 May 2009

Ben-Ze'ev A (2003) Privacy, emotional closeness, and openness in cyberspace. Comput Hum Behav 19(4):451–567

Berry DS (1991) Accuracy in social perception: contributions of facial and vocal information. J Pers Soc Psychol 61(2):298–307

boyd d, Hargittai E (2010) Facebook privacy settings: Who cares? First Monday 15(8)

Buchanan T, Paine C, Joinson AN, Reips U-D (2007) Development of measures of online privacy concern and protection for use on the internet. J Am Soc Inform Sci Tech 58(2):157–165

Burgoon JK (1982) Privacy and communication. In: Burgoon M (ed) Communication yearbook 6. Sage, Beverly Hills, pp 206–249

Burgoon JK, Parrott R, Le Poire BA, Kelley DL, Walther JB, Perry D (1989) Maintaining and restoring privacy through communication in different types of relationships. J Soc Pers Relat 6:131–158

Cho H, Rivera-Sanchez M, Lim SS (2009) A multinational study on online privacy: global concerns and local responses. New Media Soc 11(3):395–416

Christofides E, Muise A, Desmarais S (2009) Information disclosure and control on facebook: are they two sides of the same coin or two different processes? Cyberpsychol Behav 12(3):341–345

Debatin B, Lovejoy JP, Horn A-K, Hughes BN (2009) Facebook and online privacy: attitudes, behaviors, and unintended consequences. J Comput Mediat Commun 15:83–108

Deci EL, Ryan RM (2000) The "what" and "why" of goal pursuits: human needs and the self-determination of behavior. Psychol Inq 11(4):227–268

Ekman P, Friesen WV, Ancoli S (2001) Facial signs of emotional experience. In: Parrott W (ed) Emotions in social psychology: essential readings. Psychology Press, New York, pp 255–264

Harter S (2002) Authenticity. In: Snyder CR, Lopez SJ (eds) Handbook of positive psychology. Oxford University Press, Oxford, pp 382–394

Hassin R, Trope Y (2000) Facing faces: studies on the cognitive aspect of physiognomy. J Pers Soc Psychol 78(5):837–852

Hinduja S, Patchin JW (2008) Personal information of adolescents on the internet: a quantitative content analysis of myspace. J Adolesc 31:125–146

Hodgins HS, Knee CR (2002) The integrating self and conscious experience. In: Deci EL, Ryan RM (eds) Handbook of self-determination research. University of Rochester Press, Rochester, pp 87–100

Joinson AN (2001) Self-disclosure in computer-mediated communication: the role of self-awareness and visual anonymity. Eur J Soc Psychol 31:177–192

Kernis MH, Goldman BM (2005) Authenticity, social motivation, and psychological adjustment. In: Forgas JP, Williams KD, Laham SM (eds) Social motivation: conscious and unconscious processes. Cambridge University Press, New York, pp 210–227

Kernis MH, Goldman BM (2006) A multicomponent conceputalization of authenticity: theory and research. In: Zana MP (ed) Advances in experimental social psychology, vol 38. Elsevier Academic Press, San Diego, pp 283–357

Lampe C, Ellison NB, Steinfield C (2007) A familiar Face(book): profile elements as signals in an online social network. In: Proceedings of the SIGCHI conference on human factors in computing systems, Association for Computing Machinery, New York, pp 435–444

Lewis K, Kaufman J, Christakis N (2008) The taste for privacy: an analysis of college student privacy settings in an online social network. J Comput Mediat Commun 14:79–100

Margulis ST (2003) On the status and contribution of Westin's and Altman's theories of privacy. J Soc Issues 59(2):411–429

Nardi BA, Schiano DJ, Gumbrecht M (2004). Blogging as social activity, or, would you let 900 million people read your diary? In: Proceedings of computer supported cooperative work 2004, Chicago. http://home.comcast.net/~diane.schiano/CSCW04.Blog.pdf. Accessed 10 May 2007

Nissenbaum H (2009) Privacy in context: technology, policy, and the integrity of social life. Stanford Law Books, Palo Alto

Paine C, Reips U-D, Stieger S, Joinson AN, Buchanan T (2007) Internet users' perceptions of 'privacy concerns' and 'privacy actions'. Int J Hum Comput St 65:526–536

Schouten AP, Valkenburg PM, Peter J (2007) Precursors and underlying processes of adolescents' online self-disclosure: developing and testing an "internet-attribute-perception" model. J Media Psychol 10:292–315

Sheldon KM, Ryan RM, Rawsthorne LJ, Ilardi B (1997) Trait self and true self: cross-role variation in the big-five personality traits and its relations with psychological authenticity and subjective well-being. J Pers Soc Psychol 73(6):1380–1393

Tidwell LS, Walther JB (2002) Computer-mediated communication effects on disclosure, impressions, and interpersonal evaluations. Getting to know one another a bit at a time. Hum Commun Res 28(3):317–348

Tufekci Z (2008) Can you see me now? Audience and disclosure regulation in online social network sites. B Sci Technol Soc 28(1):20–36

Turkle S (1996) Life on the screen: identity in the age of the internet. Weidenfeld & Nicolson, London

Viegas FB (2005). Bloggers' expectations of privacy and accountability: an initial survey. J Comput-Mediat Commun 10(3), Article 12

Vinsel A, Brown BB, Altman I, Foss C (1980) Privacy regulation, territorial displays, and effectiveness of individual functioning. J Pers Soc Psychol 39(6):1104–1115

Walther JB (1996) Computer-mediated communication: impersonal, interpersonal, and hyperpersonal interaction. Commun Res 23:1–43

Westin AF (1967) Privacy and freedom. Atheneum, New York

Westin AF (2003) Social and political dimensions of privacy. J Soc Issues 59(2):431–453

Wood AM, Linley PA, Maltby J, Baliousis M, Joseph S (2008) The authentic personality: a theoretical and empirical conceptualization and the development of the authenticity scale. J Couns Psychol 55(3):385–399

Yao MZ, Rice RE, Wallis K (2007) Predicting user concerns about online privacy. J Am Soc Inform Sci Tech 58(5):710–722

Chapter 7
Fifteen Minutes of Privacy: Privacy, Sociality, and Publicity on Social Network Sites

Zizi Papacharissi and Paige L. Gibson

7.1 Introduction

In celebration of a burgeoning celebrity pop culture, Andy Warhol famously proclaimed that in the future, everyone would be famous for 15 minutes. Almost half a century later, being public online has become so easy that one wonders how, in the future, one may be truly private for 15 minutes. Both statements reflect the distance that separates the self from privacy, publicity, and that which lies in between: sociality.

In contemporary democracies, privacy is recognized as a basic human right – the "right to be let alone," as defined by the landmark Warren and Brandeis (1890, p. 195) *Harvard Law Review* article. Allegedly, Warren was inspired to write this article following the intrusive news coverage of his wife's society parties and reached a breaking point after the invasive press coverage of his daughter's private wedding party. Given the prevalence of media platforms that could so easily render a *private* event *public,* Warren and Brandeis (1890) saw it necessary to assert the right to privacy, or, in their words, "the right to an inviolate personality" (p. 211). In modern societies, this distance between public and private continues to dwindle, as contemporary media further blur the lines separating private from public. Social media in particular enable individuals to connect with multiple audiences on online social planes that are neither conventionally public nor entirely private. In the publicly private and privately public era of social media, friends or their acquaintances, not the press, would have tagged photographs of Ms. Warren's guests, making them publicly accessible to outside networks and third parties.

The question of privacy in a digital era, and in particular, in the Social Web realm, resurfaces as the structural affordances of networked spaces remediate the texture of publicity, sociality, and privacy. People digitally record and archive their

Z. Papacharissi (✉) • P.L. Gibson
University of Illionis at Chicago, Chicago, IL, USA
e-mail: zizi@uic.edu

S. Trepte and L. Reinecke (eds.), *Privacy Online,*
DOI 10.1007/978-3-642-21521-6_7, © Springer-Verlag Berlin Heidelberg 2011

performances of self, enacted via social media. The self (and others) can further edit, duplicate, and remix these performances, which, accessible via a variety of search protocols, reach a variety of networked audiences and publics. boyd (2010a) theorizes these properties as the four affordances of networked publics: persistence, replicability, scalability, and searchability. The self traverses from privacy to publicity and back by cultivating a variety of social behaviors or performances. These affordances complicate the circumstances under which the self may do so, and are augmented in architectures that emphasize sharing information by default (Papacharissi 2010; Raynes-Goldie 2010). The challenge for individuals is to manage the persistence, replicability, scalability, and searchability of their performances fluently in environments that prompt (and in some instances reward) sharing.

Shareability, then, presents a fifth affordance of networked digital spaces, as it constitutes an architectural feature of networked structures that encourages sharing over withholding information. What renders networks lively is the flow of information between individual network nodes. Without information flowing between individuals, the network becomes a static, asocial environment (Papacharissi 2009). Stutzman (2006) has referred to this attribute as the inherent sociality of social network communities and has explained that it accounts for the high level of disclosure of personal information online. In order to stay social, but also manage private and public information fluently, individuals must make critical decisions about how to share information in networked environments that thrive on sharing. This chapter examines the conditions that complicate private performances of the self in the context of the Social Web. We use the term private performance because it becomes necessary for the self to adopt behaviors that will semantically (meaning) and syntactically (code) communicate and guarantee privacy. We suggest that an advanced form of digital literacy can enable individuals to *redact* performances of the self online so as to navigate public and private boundaries fluently.

7.2 Privacy on Social Network Sites

Social network sites (SNSs) are abundant in number, diverse in aim and culture, and far-reaching in scope, penetrating the depths and traversing the global expanse of the Internet (boyd and Ellison 2007). SNSs not only account for a great portion of our online activities (Albrechtslund 2008), but the technologies that enable them converge online and offline aspects of our identity (Schneider and Zimmer 2006). In an attempt to distinguish social network sites from other forms of computer-mediated communication (CMC), boyd and Ellison (2007) argued that despite the interchangeable use of the terms social networking site and social network sites, the two terms place emphasis on different activities. Networking highlights the forging of *new* relationships, an idea that is neither accurate for most SNSs nor a differentiating characteristic from other CMC (boyd and Ellison 2007). The argument for this distinction has not been without debate. Understanding social networking sites to be a subset of social network sites, some scholars, like Beer (2008), question the usefulness of drawing such a fine line and criticize the terminological movement toward breadth rather than pointed classification.

Still, the distinction is useful for understanding how individuals perceive their own privacy with regard to the networked platforms they inhabit and the publics they wish to network with, and this analysis pertains to *social network sites*. As boyd (2006) notes, the norm for early adopters of Friendster did not comply with the expectation that they would simply link to their offline friends. Not until this practice became challenging for privacy did users handle their information and friend selection more cautiously. Whether maintaining offline relationships or initiating new ones, the wide range of web services that fall under the heading of "social network site" at their core present the opportunity for individuals to (1) construct a public or semi-public profile within a bounded system, (2) articulate a list of other users with whom they share a connection, and (3) view and traverse their list of connections and those made by others within the system. (boyd and Ellison 2007 p. 211). This chapter will observe this definition in discussing privacy and the self in the context of social network sites.

SNSs have integrated aspects of these features into their architecture in a variety of ways since the launch of the first SNS, Six Degrees.com, in 1997. Friendster presented these features in a way that propelled its popularity in 2002, and some of the most successful features of it were expanded and folded into the design of MySpace, followed by the subsequent launch of Facebook. Each reiteration of these SNSs presented a series of different features, but their defining attribute remains the visible profile displaying social connections embedded in a system centered around people rather than interests (boyd and Ellison 2007). From the frame of their architecture to the daily practices, SNSs are centered on sharing with a penchant for more rather than less (Raynes-Goldie 2010). The SNS profiling structure capitalizes on identifying information (e.g., hometown, date of birth), access information (e.g., location), and expressive information (e.g., status updates and comments) (see DeCew 1997).

The volume, range, and method of sharing personal information across a variety of publics and audiences on SNSs pose an issue of growing concern for users. The persistence, replicability, scalability, and searchability of personal data deposited as individuals forge social connections present privacy challenges. Individuals gradually realize that the physical barriers that enable privacy offline are not inherent aspects of online-networked architectures. The impact of maintaining privacy without the aid of physical barriers is further augmented as SNSs cultivate practices that prompt users to be more public with their information by default. While it is possible for users to edit these settings, the code that belies the structure of the network makes it easier to share than to hide information. For Facebook, progressive updates of profiles are accompanied with revised privacy settings that users must monitor, adjust, and master. As a result, Privacy International has placed Facebook in the second lowest category, that of presenting "substantial and comprehensive privacy threats." Only Google, also infamous for its privacy violations, ranks lower (Debatin et al. 2009). With 500 million plus active users on Facebook alone, half of whom log in many times on any given day (Facebook 2011), the impact of SNSs on privacy, sociality, and publicity is irrefutable, spilling over into offline privacy, too. As Schneider and Zimmer (2006) posit, "Online and off, the digitization of identity mediates our sense of self, social interactions, movements through space, and access to goods and services" (p. 1). The sharing of private information online frequently carries consequences for privacy offline, in a manner that negates the online/offline dichotomy.

The lack of a coherent regulatory framework for privacy protection in the US permits digital traces of consumer behavior that remain on partner and third party sites that users visit, like, or share, to be further exploited. The global nature of communication in networked environments would also challenge the application of nationally oriented regulation. Facebook CEO Mark Zuckerberg has argued that these changes make it easier for users to share information across the social web (Sutter 2010). By contrast, activist groups such as the Electronic Privacy Information Center (EPIC) claim that Facebook frequently pulls a "privacy bait and switch," getting users to provide personal information under one set of privacy terms, then modifying their privacy policies (Chittal 2010, p. 6). The pattern that emerges is that following protests mounted by users and activists, Facebook will take steps to amend privacy settings and make them more accessible and manageable for their members, only to spark further uproar with subsequent site updates. Despite compromises on both sides, this cycle progressively weighs against the consumer, creating a protocol that positions sharing as default and privacy as afterthought.

The (d)evolution of privacy guidelines maps a digital path to sociality taken at the expense of privacy. This is not new: sociality has always required some (voluntary) abandonment of privacy. In order to become social, we must give up some of our private time and space so as to share it with others. The balance between privacy and sociality has always existed; and when attained, it permits individuals to pursue rewarding social lives. Many users find the tug-and-pull between privacy and sociality upsetting now that it takes place on a social plane that digitally records, archives, and tracks social behaviors by default.

The privacy question, in its present form, is an urban problem of modernity. Individuals living in rural communities were preoccupied with privacy, but in ways and for reasons different from ours. In a world where communal practices were emphasized, the desire to be private was frequently associated with the need to hide, and gossip was perceived as a means of expressing solidarity (Norris 2001). Modern and urban life charged individuals with the responsibility of managing their sociality, and their privacy, in unknown and urban territory. Urban environments present a certain measure of distance (Simmel 1971), which might suggest autonomy in defining private boundaries, but with autonomy comes responsibility to delineate and protect private boundaries. Yet, individuals maintain social relationships in both urban and agrarian settings, and in doing so, they gradually confide private information to attain personal closeness with valued others. An optimal balance between disclosure and privacy can be beneficial for the individual's personal approach to sociality. Problems arise when an individual's right to make decisions about their own path to privacy, sociality, and publicity is compromised.

Here, we must emphasize that privacy, defined as the right be let alone, must not be confused with a desire to be left alone. Private individuals are not socially reclusive individuals. We define privacy as control over information about oneself (Taraszow et al. 2010). Thus, we follow Westin's (1967) definition that views privacy as control over the circumstances under which information is shared: "Privacy is the claim of individuals, groups, or institutions to determine for themselves when, how, and to what extent information about them is communicated to others" (Westin 1967, p. 7). This definition is aligned with others who have similarly defined privacy as personal information that an individual does not desire to share with a general public (Hodge 2006; Etzioni 1997; Kaplin and Lee 1997; Richards 2007; Timm and Duven 2008). Privacy thus guarantees decision making autonomy for the self, in environments both digital and non-digital. The following passages will focus on three key aspects of this autonomy: privacy and the self, privacy and the formation of social relationships, and privacy and democracy. We view these three aspects as representative of activity on SNSs and reflective of the underlying utility of privacy.

7.3   Privacy and the Self: Autonomy in Performances of Identity

We rarely fight for privacy simply for its own sake; we fight for its underlying values. Autonomy is central to most understandings of privacy (Hildebrandt 2006). Warren and Brandeis' (1890, p. 195) classic call for the "right to be let alone," the catalyst of privacy law in the United States, is built on the notion of autonomy, or our ability to pursue our own path without impediment or external influence. Privacy is often conceptually reduced to control over our information, and thus placed into a narrative that associates technological progress with the loss of control over personal information (Austin 2010). Therefore, the ability to share more information is perceived as evolutionary and contradictory to the practice of controlling personal information. And yet, what is problematic is not the practice of sharing, nor is control over what is shared synonymous with a lack of sharing.

Facebook's "News Feed" controversy in 2006 perfectly illustrates this paradox (as described in boyd and Hargittai 2010; Debatin et al. 2009; Thompson 2008). The feature broadcasts Friends' actions from profile changes to application-specific activities. Although such information had always been present and accessible, the News Feed highlighted even the most trivial updates, making them immediately visible, unfiltered, and like all information placed on SNSs, persistent, searchable, and replicable (Albrechtslund 2008). Such a change is consistent with the difference between issuing someone a visitor's pass and sending out an invitation for viewing one's information. Perceived as a violation of information control, the News Feed produced significant backlash. Ten thousand people joined a protest group by noon of the launch day; the next day that number rose to 284,000, and it would eventually gain as many as 700,000 members (boyd and Hargittai 2010; Thompson 2008). While the predictions for Facebook's future were grim, as Thompson (2008) reports, "Users' worries about privacy seemed to vanish within days, boiled away by their excitement at being so much more connected to their friends" (p. 8). Sociality prevailed at the expense of privacy, and in fact, Facebook subsequently experienced a massive growth spurt.

The norm that develops dictates that Facebook actively stretch our comfort zones until our social norms catch up with technological progress (Thompson 2008). As a result, technological architectures cultivate a newer paradigm for sociality, one that equates disclosure with being social (Zhang et al. 2010). While individuals have always formed social relationships through disclosure, they typically develop hierarchies of social relations on the basis of what is shared, how, and with whom. In fact, learning how to share is a central process of being socialized into society, as it enables relationships and presentations of the self.

Privacy and control are central issues in performances of the self in various online contexts, which can also be understood as a form of portraiture (Donath et al. 2010). Some have argued that SNSs provide a window to our most private and deeply felt aspects of self, often trivializing the information as they "broadly [cast] the private onto scattered planes of the public" (van Manen 2010, p. 1024). While both academic and public discourses commonly conflate secrecy and privacy, the distinction is important because the violation is not that the information is shared but rather with whom. Secrecy (a concern for what is known) refers to the intentional concealment of information. While secrecy often entails something private, privacy does not refer to an unwillingness to share information but rather the need to control who may know the most intimate aspects of self (Ben-Ze'ev 2003; Bok 1989). Furthermore, it concerns who partakes in our construction of identity.

Identity is something unique to the individual, yet constructing an identity does not take place in isolation nor is it a solitary activity. Privacy allows us the freedom to "[develop] our interests and personalities in a way that is not always compatible with social norms" (Ben-Ze'ev 2003, p. 462; Austin 2010; Poullet 2009). Although claimed as exclusively and uniquely ours, identity is fundamentally social, and the sense of self is developed through the collaborative, collective experiences of our social interactions (Mead 1934). The construction and performance of digital identity is similarly intertwined within a web of complex offline and online social connections (Austin 2010; Baym 2010; Buckingham 2008; Mallan and Giardina 2009; Marwick and boyd 2010). Mallan and Giardina (2009) use the term "Wikidentity" to capture the highly collaborative nature of forming these digital identities. Utopian rhetoric frequently presumes SNSs to be digital places "where one can 'type oneself into being'" (boyd and Ellison 2007, p. 211). However, SNSs are connected, intertwined, and embedded in our offline social spaces, and as a result, the digital self is often met with similar constraints to the offline self (Albrechtslund 2008; boyd 2006).

The networked structure of SNSs affords numerous opportunities for social connection and expression, but with this freedom comes the responsibility of producing a performance of the self that makes sense to multiple audiences and publics without compromising our sense of who we truly are (Papacharissi 2010). Whereas conventions of interaction in the offline world permit us to produce and customize performances to specific social situations and groups, the architecture of SNSs does not reproduce these distinctions, resulting in what Marwick and boyd (2010) have termed "context collapse" (p. 9). Individuals develop several strategies in order to retain the autonomy of their identity online. Some take to self-censorship, imagining their audience to be the most sensitive members, and thus editing their performances. Following the logic of network television, individuals find themselves performing for the lowest common denominator so as to produce a performance that will comply with the expectations of the broadest possible audience. Others become well versed in producing polysemic performances, presentations of the self that contain layers of meaning, signifying different impressions to various audiences. Livingstone (2008) has described how teenagers gauge opportunity against risk as they navigate publicly private and privately public boundaries in search of intimacy, privacy, and self-expression. boyd (2010b) has written about social steganography; the process of hiding in plain sight, by creating a message that signifies different meanings for different audiences. Tufekci (2008) has explained that college students employ various strategies of disclosure and withdrawal to engage in virtual identity hide-and-seek online. Lewis et al. (2008) suggested that personal strategies for privacy are characterized by a unique set of cultural preferences, thus presenting a matter of a "taste for privacy" (p. 79).

Online platforms such as Facebook periodically develop technological workarounds that enable Friends to be divided into separate lists (presumably by social circle) and allow individuals to control who views individual status updates. However, other aspects of the architecture remain open to indiscriminate information sharing, forcing individuals to militate toward a forced self-surveillance (Albrechtslund 2008). More importantly, they require the development and learning of strategies for socializing online. This skill, not yet conveyed through our formal and informal channels of socialization, is for the most part self-taught and remains the primary way for attempting to maintain the autonomy of the self on social network sites.

7.4 Privacy and Social Relationships: Autonomy in Defining Sociality

Privacy is fundamentally relational, as it is concerned with the self (formed through autonomy) and its relationship to the social environment of other selves (Hildebrandt 2006). Just as we write our self into being on SNS, we "write [our] community into being" (boyd 2006, p. 69). Privacy enables the existence of relationship and community. If we share all of ourselves with everyone, that sharing loses all meaning and value. Selectivity permits sharing to become singular and meaningful. Privacy enables the development of significant social bonds with others, and the maintenance of ties weak and strong.

A marker of personal relationships is intimacy. The most pronounced difference between digital intimacy and proximal intimacy is that of distance and its mediated form. It seems that digital intimacy can be equated to the apparent oxymoron of distant intimacy, a phenomenon made possible because of technology's ability in turn to shrink that distance and fill it with the intimacy of the written word (van Manen 2010). Ambient awareness also plays a role in establishing digital intimacy. The constant contact SNSs provide works in a similar fashion to physical proximity in that individuals are able to detect moods through the incessant feed of updates. These updates give one a sense of constant presence, and despite the mundane nature of the individual posts, they work toward building an intricate image of the individual (Thompson 2008; van Manen 2010). In 1998, anthropologist Robin Dunbar posited that there is a threshold to the number of social bonds any one human can have (roughly 150); however, technology has amplified that threshold leading Dunbar to nearly double his original estimates. While the circle of intimates experiences little increase (though technology enables them to become richer), SNSs enable a dramatic expansion of one's sociality with weak ties (Thompson 2008). The level of self-disclosure and self-reflection that comes with SNS activities work not only toward digital intimacy with others, but as "a kind of reflexive sphere of intimacy," as we gain a better sense of our self (van Manen 2010, p. 1028; Thompson 2008).

This reflexive sphere is articulated around the nexus of relationships on one's online profile, termed *Friends*. With SNSs, the notion of friendship, both on and offline, and the term *friend* take on new meaning (Beer 2008; boyd 2006; boyd and Ellison 2007; Debatin et al. 2009). Friendship, as a cultural construct, can differ accordingly; however, the general understanding of friendship usually points to the voluntary nature of the relationship, the existence of mutual liking or affection, and the emotional and practical support that this relationship usually entails. Friendship transcends the restrictive boundaries of professional relationships and may not share the intense mutual responsibility of family. The boundaries of Friends and the motivations for Friending vary widely and remain inconsistent. Friendship has always held some performative element but SNSs have amplified its reach as any number of relational types may now rest under this heading (boyd 2006). The same context collapse that complicates our autonomy can also set hurdles as we manage our relationships. For example, the collapse of personal and professional contexts can lead to one's boss accessing and being offended by an inside joke known only among your close friends. Privacy controls become a way of managing one's audience (boyd and Hargittai 2010). However, when those controls are unsatisfactory the task can be complex and difficult to achieve. Despite the clamor for easier and more manageable privacy controls, SNS technology retains loopholes (Raynes-Goldie 2010). For instance, a friend may comment on one's photo album, thereby granting her friends access to the entire album because the comment is considered noteworthy news on her unfiltered newsfeed. One's right to be let alone is thus dependent upon the definition others hold of privacy and the settings they deem acceptable. People of course encounter similar issues with conflicting conceptions of privacy in offline architectures as well; however, the discrepancies are amplified in SNSs given one's performance is then crowdsourced to one's network of friends.

Interestingly enough, digital intimacy achieved on SNSs frequently becomes a question of autonomy surrendered, but also, autonomy feigned, through controls that suggest greater autonomy than we actually possess. Because the architecture fails to define the context of the space for us, the scope of this public and the expected social boundaries are defined by the breadth and depth of one's Friend list (boyd 2006). As Marwick and boyd (2010) argue, "We may understand that the Twitter or Facebook audience is potentially limitless, but we often act as if it were bounded" either through an imagined audience or ideal reader (writing for oneself) that we use to deal with context collapse (p. 3). Public and private boundaries are blurred as are our perceptions of them. Privacy settings, even when monitored and customized, still serve the purpose of negotiated privacy within the terms that the social network site has defined. The individual, in this case, is only able to attain a compromised or prescribed autonomy defined by the site's architecture. Through privacy settings that have been predetermined, the individual is confined to a few options that s/he has played little or no part in shaping.

We must return to the affordance of shareability, an attribute of social network sites that encourages a culture of sharing, to appreciate the individual preparation that privacy requires on social network sites. Younger users of Facebook acknowledge the privacy risk associated with Facebook use but confess to an inability to react either because they do not possess the necessary technology knowhow to manage privacy settings, or because they worry about the social cost of a reduced presence online (Papacharissi and Mendelson 2010). Within an environment that equates sociality with sharing and differential sharing is typically an afterthought, privacy is bound to be a concern.

Modifications that permit differential sharing across groups of friends are typically introduced with the goal of enhancing sharing but not of guaranteeing privacy. Many become disillusioned with the possibility of an SNS-based identity, viewing it as "a false choice, a sociotechnical scenario devoid of agency" rather than a well-reasoned decision (Bigge 2006, p. 42). However, teens who make avid use of SNSs express acute concern over privacy issues and develop strategies for privacy that are congruent with their skill level, gender, age, and mobility narratives (boyd and Hargittai 2010; Li and Chen 2010; Patchin and Hinduja 2010). Nevertheless, discrepancies persist between how users understand privacy, how they think they are protecting themselves, and how they are actually able to establish privacy online (Acquisti and Gross 2006). Especially for younger adults, attaining balance between privacy and sociality presents a central part of identity play and formation. In environments that encourage sharing over privacy by default, dissonance between learned social behaviors for sociality and privacy can develop easily. Individuals will frequently simply transfer behaviors to the SNS context, neglecting to make adjustments that we typically make when moving from one social context (a bar) to another (a classroom). Indeed, it is this translation of sociocultural norms across contexts that results in a subsequent loss or change in meaning (Lasén and Gómez-Cruz 2009; Winseck 2002). SNSs encourage such forgetfulness by inviting users to share upon entering, much like a movie theater invites viewers to be quiet, and a loud bar requires guests to speak more loudly to friends. In this way, networked social environments make it challenging for individuals to be private in spaces that were designed for sharing, not privacy.

7.5 Private Information Commodified, Privacy a Luxury Commodity

The balance between privacy, sociality, and publicity takes on new meaning as Internet-based platforms, like social network sites, afford sociality and publicity at the expense of personal autonomy in determining privacy. All web-accessible platforms offer services, mostly of a social nature, in exchange for personal information. In turn, these services transform personal information of a private nature into currency. However, regarding information as an economic good contains unique properties that complicate its treatment as a commodity. Firstly, unlike other commodities, information remains with its owner, even when traded or sold. Secondly, the value of information is frequently established subjectively; information of value to some may be irrelevant to others. Thirdly, information can never be fully consumed in the manner other goods and services are used up or depleted. These attributes complicate the trading of information in economic markets, causing problems that range from minor hiccups to major problems in the trading system. They also render privacy, viewed as control over information shared about oneself, a complex problem to manage (Huey 2010).

Information traded in bits via online networked platforms possesses these attributes. In addition, it is characterized by the affordances of persistence, replicability, scalability, and searchability, all of which further augment and complicate the unique properties of information as an economic good. Personal information of a private nature adds further complications to the process, because not all personal information is potentially private. Personal information attains a private nature depending on how individuals subjectively define their unique approach to privacy, sociality, and publicity. Online networked platforms that accept personal information in exchange for access to social services engage in an information trade that frequently does not specify how the individual retains the autonomy to determine privacy, sociality and publicity. Thus, it is not just the personal information that is traded, but also the right to privacy in return for a formula of sociality and publicity presented by the social network site.

Byte by byte, our personal information is exchanged as currency to gain digital access to our own friends. In this manner, personal information is commercialized into the public realm, with little input from the individual in the process. We have explained that individuals develop strategies for managing this relationship, and that social network sites frequently adjust privacy/sociality/publicity settings in response to user reactions. Hence this is not a problem that is irresolvable.

What we try to establish, however, is that it emanates from a premise that commodifies personal information. As personal information is traded in, privacy gradually attains the characteristics of a luxury commodity, in that (a) it becomes a good inaccessible to most, (b) it is disproportionately costly to the average individual's ability to acquire and retain it, and (c) it becomes inversely associated with social benefits, in that the social cost of not forsaking parts of one's privacy in exchange for information goods and services (e.g., free e-mail account, online social networking) places one at a social disadvantage. Luxury goods not only possess a price point beyond the average person's reach, they also connote social status and advantage.

But what renders privacy a luxury commodity is that obtaining it implies a level of computer literacy that is inaccessible to most, and typically associated with higher income and education levels, and certain ethnic groups, in ways that mirror dominant socio-demographic inequalities (Hargittai 2008). As a luxury commodity, the right to privacy, afforded to those fortunate enough to be Internet-literate, becomes a social stratifier; it divides users into classes of haves and have-nots, thus creating a *privacy* divide. This privacy divide is further enlarged by the high income elasticity of demand that luxury goods possess: as people become wealthier, they are able to buy more of a luxury good or higher classes of luxury goods and services. Privacy as a luxury commodity possesses similar elasticity; as people become more and more literate, they will be able to afford greater access to privacy. The goal for regulation is to effectively turn privacy into a normal good – a good that everyone may afford, or even better, a public good. A regulatory solution to the privacy divide must address market factors that render privacy a luxury commodity.

The current state of privacy law in the US mirrors that of the general US regulatory mentality, which is biased toward letting the market self-regulate. Unlike most European countries, there are few laws concerning privacy, and they pertain to the government's use of personal information. The most recent and notable of these are the Financial Modernization Act (Gramm-Leach-Bliley Act of 1999), and the Children's Online Privacy Protection Act (1998) (COPPA). The former specifies that financial institutions must inform customers about their privacy practices, but provides limited control to consumers regarding the use and distribution of personal data. Recently, President Obama and several leading economists criticized the act as prompting subsequent deregulation and leading to the 2007 subprime mortgage financial crisis. Under the Act, individuals are granted some privacy protection but must still proactively make certain that their personal information is not made available to third parties. Children understandably receive greater protection under COPPA, which lays out specific regulations for companies targeting individuals under the age of 13 online. Aside from COPPA, regulatory policy in the US is founded upon the assumption that web operators disclose, but do not adjust or restrict information gathering and distribution practices. Privacy statements are descriptive and explanatory of privacy practices but are not inherently protective of privacy. Such privacy practice disclosures tend to be employed more as legal safeguards for companies and less as guarantees of the safety of personal data (Fernback and Papacharissi 2007).

A regulatory framework must define, protect, and educate about "the right to an inviolate personality" online (Warren and Brandeis 1890, p. 211). Doing so can ensure that individuals retain the right to determine for themselves what this balance between publicity, sociality, and privacy should be. Each individual seeks and is satisfied with a different balance. Regulation can help individuals retain decision-making autonomy in online environments. At the same time, a regulatory framework would require global cooperation in defining privacy in the digital era, which would necessitate the reconciliation of different sociocultural norms and political-economic hierarchies to guarantee individual autonomy over personal information (Flint 2009). Some suggest moving from ego-centered to decentralized, link-driven networks as a workaround, but that would only render a partial solution to the problem (Cutillo et al. 2009). Building safety considerations into the design of social network sites is also an important aspect of managing their potential for inviting and rewarding disclosure of personal information (Livingstone and Brake 2010).

Ultimately, because online environments work glocally, educating the public about the "right to be let alone" (Warren and Brandeis 1890, p. 195) online is an important part of crafting a regulatory solution that ensures privacy becomes a public good for global users. Education, in the form of technological literacy, can then help individuals practice this autonomy fluently in digital environments. As individuals use platforms that blur private and public, it is essential that they retain the right to specify boundaries when necessary. Networked environments that thrive on shareability present both opportunities for the self and challenges for performative autonomy online. Individuals are required to become more conscious editors of their own behavior online. Editorial skills, and the ability to redact, previously associated with specific professions only, become the property of individual citizens and part of a survival toolkit online (Hartley 2000). The idea is not entirely new for socially motivated beings. We frequently edit our social behavior and the information we share with others as we interact with a variety of audiences: friends, work colleagues, acquaintances, and strangers. We even have phrases, norms and acronyms that signal to others when too much information has been shared in an inappropriate context.

The process of self-presentation on social network sites involves both the production of performances and simultaneous or subsequent editing of these performances. Redaction enables the bringing together and editing of identity traces to form and frame a coherent performance. Self-editing has always been a part of how we present the self to others, but online platforms frequently prompt self-sharing by default without permitting self-editing. The kind of literacy that supports performative fluency online rests upon one's own acumen for redaction. Structured around the tendency to delete, or otherwise edit aspects of one's identity, *redactional acumen* enables individuals to present a coherent and polysemic performance of the self that makes sense to multiple publics without compromising one's authentic sense of self. It is this sort of editorial acumen that individuals must find a way to apply to online environments. And it is this editorial acumen that will help individuals to not just attain 15 minutes of privacy online, but also perform their identities autonomously in the digital era.

References

Acquisti A, Gross R (2006) Imagined communities: awareness, information sharing, and privacy on the facebook. Presented to privacy enhancing technologies workshop (PET), Cambridge

Albrechtslund A (2008) Online social networking as participatory surveillance. First Monday 13 (3). http://firstmonday.org/htbin/cgiwrap/bin/ojs/index.php/fm/article/viewArticle/2142/1949.

Austin LM (2010) Control yourself, or at least your core self. B Sci Technol Soc 30(1):26–29

Baym NK (2010) Personal connections in the digital age. Polity Press, Cambridge

Beer D (2008) Social network(ing) sites...revisiting the story so far: a response to danah boyd & Nicole Ellison. J Comput Mediat Commun 13:516–529

Ben-Ze'ev A (2003) Privacy, emotional closeness, and openness in cyberspace. Comput Hum Behav 19:451–467

Bigge R (2006) The cost of (anti-)social networks: identity, agency and neo-luddites. First Monday 12(4). http://firstmonday.org/htbin/cgiwrap/bin/ojs/index.php/fm/article/view/1421/1339.

Bok S (1989) Approaches to secrecy. In: Secrets: on the ethics of concealment and revelation, Vintage Books, New York, pp 3–14

boyd d (2006) Friends, friendsters, and top 8: writing community into being on social network sites. First Monday 11(12). http://firstmonday.org/htbin/cgiwrap/bin/ojs/index.php/fm/article/view/1418/1336

boyd d (2010a) Social network sites as networked publics: affordances, dynamics, and implications. In: Papacharissi Z (ed) Networked self: identity, community, and culture on social network sites. Routledge, New York, pp 39–58

boyd d (2010b) Social Steganography: learning to Hide in Plain Sight. Digital Media and Learning blog. http://dmlcentral.net/blog/danah-boyd/social-steganography-learning-hide-plain-sight Accessed Mar 2011

boyd d, Ellison NB (2007) Social network sites: definition, history, and scholarship. J Comput Mediat Commun 13:210–230

boyd d, Hargittai E (2010) Facebook privacy settings: who cares? FirstMonday 15(8). http://firstmonday.org/htbin/cgiwrap/bin/ojs/index.php/fm/article/view/3086/2589

Buckingham D (2008) Introducing identity. In: Buckingham D (ed) Youth, identity, and digital media. The MIT Press, Cambridge, pp 1–24

Chittal N (2010) The case for staying with facebook. American prospect, web-only edition (14 May). http://www.prospect.org/cs/articles?article=the_case_for_staying_with_facebook

Children's Online Privacy Protection Act of 1998 (1998) § 105–277, 15 U.S.C. § 6501–6508

Cutillo LA, Molva R, Strufe T (2009) Safebook: a privacy-preserving online social network leveraging on real-life trust. IEEE Commun Mag 50:94

Debatin B, Lovejoy JP, Horn A, Hughes BN (2009) Facebook and online privacy: attitudes, behaviors, and unintended consequences. J Comput Mediat Commun 15:83–108

DeCew JW (1997) In pursuit of privacy: law, ethics, and the rise of technology. Cornell University Press, Ithaca

Donath J, Dragulescu A, Zinman A, Viégas F, Xiong R (2010) Data portraits. Leonardo 43(4):375–383

Etzioni A (1997) The new golden rule: community and morality in a democratic society. Basic Books, New York

Facebook (2011) Press room: statistics. http://www.facebook.com/press/info.php?statistics. Accessed 14 Jan 2011

Fernback J, Papacharissi Z (2007) Online privacy as legal safeguard: the relationship among consumer, online portal, and privacy policies. New Media Soc 9(5):715–734

Flint D (2009) Law shaping technology: technology shaping the law. Int Review Law Comput Technol 23(1–2):5–11

Fraser N (1992) Rethinking the public sphere: a contribution to the critique of actually existing democracy. In: Calhoun C (ed) Habermas and the public sphere. MIT Press, Cambridge, pp 109–142

Gramm-Leach-Bliley Act of 1999 (1999) § 106–102, 15 U.S.C. § 1338

Habermas J (1968) Knowledge and human interests. (trans: Shapiro JJ) (1972). Beacon Press, Boston

Habermas J (1992) Further reflections on the public sphere. In: Calhoun C (ed) Habermas and the public sphere. MIT Press, Cambridge, pp 421–461

Hargittai E (2008) The digital reproduction of inequality. In: Grusky D (ed) Social stratification. Westview Press, Boulder, pp 936–944

Hartley J (2000) Communicative democracy in a redactional society: the future of journalism studies. Journalism 1:39–48

Hildebrandt M (2006) Privacy and identity. In: Claes E, Duff A, Gutwirth S (eds) Privacy and the criminal law. Intersentia, Oxford, pp 43–57

Hodge MJ (2006) Comment: the fourth amendment and privacy issues on the 'new' internet. Facebook.com and myspace.com. Southern Illinois Univ Law School J 31:95–122

Huey L (2010) A social movement for privacy/against surveillance? Some difficulties in engendering mass resistance in a land of twitter and tweets. Case West R J Int L 42:699–710

Kaplin WA, Lee BA (1997) A legal guide for student affairs professionals. Jossey-Bass, San Francisco

Lasén A, Gómez-Cruz E (2009) Digital photography and picture sharing: redefining the public/private divide. Knowledge Technol Policy 22(3):205–215

Lewis K, Kaufman J, Christakis N (2008) The taste for privacy: an analysis of college student privacy settings in an online social network. J Comput Mediat Commun 14:79–100

Li N, Chen G (2010) Sharing location in online social networks. IEEE Netw 24:20–25

Livingstone S (2008) Taking risky opportunities in youthful content creation: teenagers' use of social networking sites for intimacy, privacy and self-expression. New Media Soc 10(3):393–411

Livingstone S, Brake DR (2010) On the rapid rise of social networking sites: new findings and policy implications. Child Soc 24(1):75–83

Marwick AE, boyd d (2010) I tweet honestly, I tweet passionately: twitter users, context collapse, and the imagined audience. New Media Soc 20(10):1–20

Mallan K, Giardina N (2009) Wikidentities: young people collaborating on virtual identities in social network sites. First Monday 14(6). http://firstmonday.org/htbin/cgiwrap/bin/ojs/index.php/fm/article/view/2445/2213

Mead GH (1934) Mind, self and society. University of Chicago Press, Chicago

Mendelson A, Papacharissi Z (2010) Look at us: collective narcissism in college student facebook photo galleries. In: Papacharissi Z (ed) The networked self: identity, community and culture on social network sites. Routledge, New York, pp 151–173

Norris K (2001) Dakota: a spiritual geography. Houghton Mifflin, Boston

Papacharissi Z (2009) The virtual geographies of social networks: a comparative analysis of facebook, linkedin and asmallworld. New Media Soc 11(1–2):199–220

Papacharissi Z (2010) A private sphere: democracy in a digital age. Polity Press, Cambridge

Patchin JW, Hinduja S (2010) Trends in online social networking: adolescent use of myspace over time. New Media Soc 12(2):197–216

Papacharissi Z, Mendelson A (2011) Toward a new(er) sociability: Uses, gratifications and social capital on facebook. Media Perspectives for the 21st Century, Stelios Papathanassopoulos (Ed.), pp. 212–231. Routledge

Poullet Y (2009) Data protection legislation: what is at stake for our society and democracy. Comput Law Security Review 25:211–226

Schneider T, Zimmer M (2006) Identity and identification in a networked world. First Monday 11 (12). http://firstmonday.org/htbin/cgiwrap/bin/ojs/index.php/fm/article/view/1417/1335

Simmel G (1971) The metropolis and mental life. In: Levine D (ed) On individuality and social forms: selected writings. University of Chicago Press, Chicago, pp 324–340

Sutter J (2010) Facebook makes it easier for users to share interests across web. *CNN.com*. http://www.cnn.com/2010/TECH/04/21/facebook.changes.f8/index.html.

Stutzman F (2006) An evaluation of identity-sharing behavior in social network communities. Int Digit Media Arts J 3(1):1–7

Raynes-Goldie K (2010) Aliases, creeping and wall cleaning: understanding privacy in the age of facebook. First Monday 15(1). http://firstmonday.org/htbin/cgiwrap/bin/ojs/index.php/fm/article/view/2775/2432

Richards DV (2007) Posting personal information on the internet: a case for changing the legal regime created by S 230 of the Communications Decency Act. Texas Law Review 85:1321–1322

Taraszow T, Aristodemou E, Shitta G, Laouris Y, Arsoy A (2010) Disclosure of personal and contact information by young people in social networking sites: an analysis using facebook profiles as an example. Int J Media Cult Polit 6(1):81–102

Thompson C (2008) Brave new world of digital intimacy. The New York Times. http://www.nytimes.com/2008/09/07/magazine/07awareness-t.html

Timm DM, Duven CJ (2008) Privacy and social networking sites. New Direc Student Serv 124:89–102

Tufekci Z (2008) Can you see me now? Audience and disclosure management in online social network sites. B Sci Technol Stud 11(4):544–564

Warren SD, Brandeis LD (1890) The right to privacy. Harvard Law Review 4(5):193–220

Westin A (1967) Privacy and freedom. Atheneum, New York

Winseck D (2002) Illusions of perfect information and fantasies of control in the information society. New Media Soc 4:93–122

Van Manen M (2010) The pedagogy of Momus technologies: facebook, privacy, and online intimacy. Qual Heal Res 20(8):1023–1032

Zhang C, Sun J, Zhu X, Fang Y (2010) Privacy and security for online social networks: challenges and opportunities. IEEE Netw 24:13–18

Chapter 8
The Co-evolution of Social Network Ties and Online Privacy Behavior

Kevin Lewis

8.1 Introduction

What is the nature of personal privacy in an increasingly digital world? To what extent should we foster greater information exchange among the public at large, versus protect the ability to limit disclosure to the people of one's choosing? And to what extent do people say they care about either? Previous research on online privacy has predominantly been concerned with questions such as these. Noticeably absent, however, has been research examining actual online privacy behavior and its causes. In other words, regardless of whether people *say* they care about online privacy – and regardless of whether they *should* care about online privacy – given the option to disclose more information or less, what factors are predictive of the actual privacy decision that people make?

In this chapter, I use a new longitudinal dataset combined with recent developments in network modeling to examine the co-evolution of college students' friendships and privacy behavior on Facebook. In contrast to past research approaching the subject from theoretical, ethical, or attitudinal perspectives, I take a behavioral approach to the study of online privacy – one grounded in insights from social network analysis. Researchers have long been interested in understanding how friendships evolve among college students (e.g., Newcomb 1961), and increasingly this work has been extended to the online sphere (e.g., Kossinets and Watts 2009; Mayer and Puller 2008; Wimmer and Lewis 2010). At the same time, given the unprecedented global popularity of Facebook on one hand, and media attention regarding its privacy measures on the other, the topic of Facebook and privacy has recently attracted the attention of academic research as well (Debatin et al. 2009). To date, however, no one has examined the interconnectedness of these two topics: How does social network evolution among college students depend on their privacy

K. Lewis (✉)
Harvard University, Cambridge, MA, USA
e-mail: kmlewis@fas.harvard.edu

S. Trepte and L. Reinecke (eds.), *Privacy Online*,
DOI 10.1007/978-3-642-21521-6_8, © Springer-Verlag Berlin Heidelberg 2011

behavior; and how does privacy behavior among college students depend on their social networks?

In the following sections, I first briefly review current findings regarding online privacy behavior and its causes. Next, I sketch seven theoretical mechanisms that we can expect to influence changes in students' network ties on one hand, and privacy settings on the other. I then describe the dataset and methodological tool used in this study; present results from statistical models of the co-evolution of network ties and privacy settings; and conclude with an interpretation of findings, a summary of the limitations of these analyses, and suggestions for future research.

8.2 Previous Research

In the voluminous literature on online privacy, there have been remarkably few published studies on the topic of online privacy behavior; and what research has been published is almost exclusively based on self-report rather than natural observation. Debatin et al. (2009), for instance, found a general disconnect between users' understanding of privacy issues and their willingness to upload large amounts of personal information. However, respondents also claimed to be more likely to change their privacy settings if they had personally experienced a privacy invasion. Tufekci (2008) similarly found little to no relationship between college students' online privacy concerns and information disclosure, while Youn and Hall (2008) examined the relationship between gender and privacy protection behaviors – both using survey data. Finally, Livingstone (2008) used interviews to explore teenagers' use of social networking sites for intimacy, privacy, and self-expression.

In a previous analysis of the dataset used in this study, Lewis et al. (2008) examined the predictors of college students having a private versus a public profile on Facebook. They found that women were more likely to have a private profile than men; that having a private profile is associated with a greater degree of online activity; and that students who have a private profile are characterized by distinct cultural tastes. They also found that students were more likely to have a private profile if their Facebook friends and, especially, their roommates also had private profiles – but due to the cross-sectional nature of the analyses, conclusions about causality were tentative.

Researchers have identified the importance of approaching privacy from a behavioral perspective – particularly as it follows (or fails to follow) from users' privacy-related beliefs or prior experiences. However, most studies are based on self-report rather than actually observed behavior. Further, what little work exists has been largely concerned with assessing the relationship between privacy behavior and one additional variable, rather than modeling this behavior as the outcome of several possible processes; and the one paper exploring actual privacy behavior in a multivariate framework has been unable to make strict causal inferences about privacy behavior as cause or consequence. This is the gap in the literature that the current chapter aims to address.

8.3   Mechanisms of Network and Behavioral Change

In recent years – and corresponding with the development of new longitudinal datasets as well as analytical tools for modeling longitudinal network data – tremendous advances have been made in our understanding of how social networks evolve over time. In an important review article, Rivera et al. (2010) document three types of mechanisms, or causal factors, that can account for the development and persistence of a network tie between two people. Less work has been published on the dependence of behavioral change on one's network environment, but this is quickly changing. Below, I organize this research into a framework of seven types of mechanisms that can be used to understand the joint evolution of social network ties on one hand, and online privacy behavior on the other.

8.3.1   Network Dynamics

8.3.1.1   Relational Mechanisms

The first type of mechanism that Rivera et al. (2010) describe has to do with the impact of current relationships on the formation of new ties. These effects have nothing to do with characteristics of the particular individuals involved – but rather their location in a broader landscape of relations. One of the most widely-documented regularities in social networks is the tendency for friends-of-friends to become friends, or for individuals to "close triangles" in networks. This is because I am much more likely to meet the friends-of-friends than I am to meet other strangers (because, for instance, our shared acquaintance may invite us both to a party), and also because I am much more likely to feel positively towards these people for reasons of structural balance (Davis 1963; Kossinets and Watts 2009). Another regularity is the tendency for people with large networks to accumulate friendships at a faster rate than do people with smaller networks – both because a larger baseline network may be reflective of a more sociable personality, and because "popularity" is attractive to other individuals (cf. Snijders et al. 2010). Finally, every social network is characterized by a particular "density," or baseline tendency for a tie to be present versus absent. Networks of acquaintances, for instance, will naturally have many more ties than networks of close confidants – and unless one controls for this tendency, it will be impossible to pinpoint the contribution of other causal factors.

8.3.1.2   Assortative Mechanisms

A second fundamental determinant of network evolution is the principle of "like attracts like" or "birds of a feather flock together" – often called homophily

(McPherson et al. 2001). Homophily has been studied with respect to a wide variety of attributes, though racial background is typically held to be the most divisive feature of American social networks (but see Wimmer and Lewis 2010). Social networks are also often segregated according to socioeconomic status (Marsden 1988) and gender (Marsden 1987).[1]

8.3.1.3 Proximity Mechanisms

The third set of mechanisms involves the focused organization of social interaction, and amounts to the simple fact that people will be more likely to meet and become friends with others who live, work, or otherwise spend time in the same place (Feld 1981). Among college students in particular, propinquity in living arrangements – e.g., sharing the same residence – has been shown to be one of the most powerful determinants of who befriends whom. Sharing an academic major can at times be equally consequential, given that students are more likely to take classes and study with those in their major (Marmaros and Sacerdote 2006; Mayer and Puller 2008; Wimmer and Lewis 2010).

8.3.1.4 Privacy Mechanisms

Finally, independent of the above three mechanisms, network evolution can also depend on students' privacy behavior in two basic ways. On one hand, students with a private profile may have a greater or lesser tendency to form ties overall, leading to a larger or smaller overall network size than the average student. Comparable to what others (Goodreau et al. 2009; Wimmer and Lewis 2010) have called a "sociality" effect, students with private profiles – whose personal information is hence blocked by default to all non-friends – may tend to extend or receive a larger number of friend requests precisely because this is the only way others may view their information. An opposite effect could also occur, whereby the activation of privacy settings precedes a general conservatism about extending and accepting friend requests and hence leads to students with private profiles forming fewer ties overall. In both cases, I refer to this as a "main effect" of privacy behavior on tie formation (cf. Snijders et al. 2010).

On the other hand, much like the assortative mechanisms above, students may self-segregate not on the basis of demographic characteristics but on the basis of privacy behavior itself. In other words, alongside the tendency to befriend students of the same racial or socioeconomic background, students may display an affinity with others who share their perspective on information disclosure – students with

---

[1]It is also possible that individuals self-segregate based on structural position – people with many ties befriending other people with many ties, and people with few ties befriending other people with few ties (Newman 2002). Such "degree-based" assortative mixing is not considered here.

public profiles seeking out others with public profiles, and students with private profiles seeking out others with private profiles. In both cases, I refer to this as a "similarity effect" of privacy behavior on tie formation (cf. Steglich et al. 2010).

8.3.2   Behavior Dynamics

8.3.2.1   Exogenous Mechanisms

Of all possible explanations for a shift in a given student's privacy behavior, perhaps the most plausible has nothing to do with the student at all. In other words, before considering mechanisms that involve the unique situation of particular students, it is important to account for exposure to "external" events or conditions that affect all students equally and may spur a general change in privacy behavior across the population. Such conditions are not hard to imagine: an incident occurs in the college community that increases general awareness about privacy, or perhaps a newspaper article is published to the same effect. Such a change may also be an effect of the website itself – e.g., Facebook alters the ease with which a private profile may be activated – or an "external" effect of time – e.g., students approaching graduation may be more likely to switch to a private profile to avoid the scrutiny of potential employers. In any case, unless one has specific data on such externalities – or particular reason to believe that some students would be more or less susceptible to their effects than others – such effects may be subsumed under a general "baseline tendency" mechanism representing the baseline likelihood of a student adopting a private profile, all else being equal.[2]

8.3.2.2   Associational Mechanisms

Researchers have long documented the effects of "peer influence" with respect to a wide variety of characteristics and behaviors. Much work, both popular and academic, has addressed the diffusion of ideas, innovations, and trends throughout the population or even the globe (Gladwell 2002; Kaufman and Patterson 2005; Rogers 2003). Other research has focused specifically on interpersonal influence with respect to drug use (Kandel 1978), smoking (Mercken et al. 2010), music tastes (Steglich et al. 2006), and a variety of other (often health-related) outcomes (Smith and Christakis 2008). Each of these findings stems from a fundamental insight of social science: that our behavior depends intimately on the behavior of those with whom we associate. The implication for a longitudinal study of privacy behavior is

---

[2]In stochastic actor-based modeling, one typically also controls for potential curvilinearity in this tendency by including a quadratic term. This is unnecessary here because the behavioral variable is dichotomous.

clear. Above and beyond any tendency to adopt a private profile as a result of external factors, students who are friends with other students who have a private profile may become additionally sensitive to privacy concerns themselves; meanwhile, students who are friends with other students who have a public profile may be less likely to be the sole person to deviate from this norm.

8.3.2.3 Structural Mechanisms

Finally, there are reasons to expect that one's structural position in a social network – irrespective of the specific people to whom one is connected – will have an independent effect on the likelihood of adopting a private versus public profile. One measure commonly emphasized in the networks literature is degree centrality. Sometimes called "neighborhood size," degree centrality refers to one's total quantity of direct network connections (Freeman 1978). While peer influence has to do with the specific people one associates with, then, "degree" effects stem only from having a larger versus smaller friend network. In the context of privacy behavior, students with larger social networks may be particularly informed about public concern regarding online safety. Students with a large social network may also feel as though the costs of a private profile in terms of information sharing are relatively low (because relatively more people will still be able to see their information anyway); although students with a small overall network may be closer, in turn, with each of these friends, and therefore more content to share information only with them and no one else.

8.3.3 Summary

What are the determinants of online privacy behavior among college students? In particular, what is the relationship between college students' online privacy behavior and college students' social network ties? Above, I outlined four general categories of factors that may influence students' friendship choices – relational mechanisms, assortative mechanisms, proximity mechanisms, and privacy mechanisms – and three categories of factors that may simultaneously influence students' privacy behavior – exogenous mechanisms, associational mechanisms, and structural mechanisms. In order to pinpoint the contribution of each of these categories of factors to observed network and behavioral change, it is analytically necessary to control for all of them: Firstly, because two very different mechanisms may produce effects that are otherwise indistinguishable; and secondly, because otherwise it is impossible to disentangle the direction of causality. In particular, if students with private profiles are found to have larger or smaller networks, is this a "main effect" of privacy behavior on network activity, or a "degree effect" of network position on privacy behavior? And if students are found to cluster together according to privacy setting, is this because these students seek each other out ("similarity effect") or because privacy behavior "spreads" among peers ("peer influence")? It is therefore only with appropriately sophisticated modeling tools – combined with fine-grained, longitudinal data on students' networks and privacy behavior – that such questions can be answered.

8.4   Data and Methods

8.4.1   The "Tastes, Ties, and Time" Dataset

Data for these analyses are drawn from the "Tastes, ties, and time" social network dataset (Lewis et al. 2008). Together with colleagues – and with permission from both Facebook and the college in question – I downloaded longitudinal profile and friendship data for the class of 2009 at an American private college ($N = 1640$ at wave 1). Students were located on Facebook using an official class roster with all students' names and e-mail addresses, though the data were immediately stripped of all identifiers. Data draws took place once a year for 4 years, in March of 2006, 2007, 2008, and 2009 – such that we could view the evolution of students' social networks and profile data over the 4 years of college. For the purpose of the following analyses, I restrict attention to those 876 students who (1) were members of the study cohort for all 4 years (i.e., they did not transfer in or out) and (2) had publicly available data on Facebook friendships for all 4 years (i.e., they did not set their Facebook friend data to "private").[3] While procedures for dealing with missing data in longitudinal network studies are available (Huisman and Steglich 2008), given that the central question of this study relates to the interrelatedness between network ties and privacy behavior – and further, that stable model estimation generally relies on having no more than about 20% missing data (Snijders et al. 2008), but 27% of students have missing network data in wave 4 alone – I chose instead to only include students with public Facebook friendship data for all 4 years. While practically motivated, this decision has the unfortunate consequence that those students who arguably disclosed the least – i.e., who hid both profile and network data from non-friends – are not considered.[4]

---

[3]Because it is not possible to distinguish between a student who is not on Facebook and a student who is on Facebook but has hidden herself from searches, I first restricted attention to only those students who could be located on Facebook for all 4 years. Of the 1,421 students who remained in the study cohort for all 4 years, 1,272 (89.5%) met this criterion. The remaining 396 students who were dropped from my analyses were active on Facebook for all 4 years, but did not have available network data for at least one year. Comparing these 396 students with the final population of 876, dropped students were significantly more likely to have a private profile in every wave – creating some risk of selection bias – and significantly more likely to be Asian. Otherwise, however, the two samples were statistically indistinguishable with respect to gender, race, and socioeconomic status.

[4]An alternative approach would have been to simply maximize the available data for each transition period separately (see below). However, this would have the undesirable consequence

In the analyses that follow, the central network variable is the presence or absence of a Facebook friendship between two students, and the central behavioral variable is whether each student maintained a public or a private profile at the time of the data draw.[5] Data on housing assignments and academic majors were provided by the college. Gender was coded based on self-report; racial background was coded based on online photos and any listed affiliations with Facebook groups or college organizations signaling race/ethnicity; and socioeconomic status was coded using the median household income of each student's "hometown" ZIP Code Tabulation Area based on the 2000 Census (coded as missing data in the event of a private profile for all 4 years).

8.4.2 Stochastic Actor-Based Modeling

Stochastic actor-based models were designed to overcome prior limitations in the joint analysis of networks and behavior, and in particular disentangling social selection versus peer influence. In short, these models respect the network dependence of actors; account for alternative possible mechanisms of network and behavioral change; and model the co-evolution of social networks and individual behaviors in continuous time (Steglich et al. 2010).

An accessible introduction to stochastic actor-based models is available in Snijders et al. (2010). Here, it is sufficient to note that the heart of these models consists of two "objective functions" – one for changes in dyadic network ties, and one for changes in individual behavior – that represent the short term "objectives" that each actor will probabilistically pursue. The function $f_i^X(\beta, x, z) = \sum_k \beta_k^X s_{ki}^X(x, z)$ represents the network component of this function for actor i given x state of the network, where effects $s_{ki}^X(x,z)$ correspond to the various mechanisms for network dynamics described above and weights β_k^X are effect strengths. Similarly, the function $f_i^Z(\beta, x, z) = \sum_k \beta_k^Z s_{ki}^Z(x, z)$ represents the behavioral component of this function, where effects $s_{ki}^Z(x,z)$ represent the different mechanisms for behavioral dynamics described above and β_k^Z are effect strengths. In short, the

---

that results could no longer be compared over time, because each model would be estimated over a slightly different subset of students.

[5]It is important to note that this dataset was not compiled with the intention of studying privacy behavior, and hence some distortion in the central behavioral dependent variable was introduced insofar as research assistants were recruited from the college of study. Consequently, an unknown minority of students in the study population may have falsely appeared to have "public" profiles if they happened to be Facebook friends with the specific research assistant assigned to download their profiles. However, because research assistant assignments were random, this scenario would only be more likely to have occurred the more Facebook friends the given student had; and therefore the "degree effect" of Facebook friendships on privacy behavior can be expected to capture (and control for) much of this variation.

strength of these models is that they are able to pinpoint the precise contribution of a number of distinct mechanisms to both network and behavioral change, each while controlling for all of the others.

Previous applications of stochastic actor-based models have primarily focused on adolescent substance use (Mercken et al. 2010; Steglich et al. 2010) as well as visible versus non-visible attributes (de Klepper et al. 2010). These models have yet to be applied to the topic of online social network ties and online behavior of any sort.

8.4.3 Model Specification and Interpretation

At the end of their freshman year, each student at the college was randomly assigned to one of 12 upper-class residences where the student would live during her sophomore through senior years. These residences fall naturally into four "neighborhoods," each containing three residences in relatively close proximity – though the size, individual character, and physical arrangement of each neighborhood varies (neighborhood 1, for instance, is slightly smaller and more geographically isolated from the main campus than the other three). In order to consider possible variation of model parameters across these sub-populations, all results are presented separately for each neighborhood. In order to capture variation in the importance of the various mechanisms over time, results are also presented separately for each "transition period" that was observed: wave 1 to wave 2 (period 1), wave 2 to wave 3 (period 2), and wave 3 to wave 4 (period 3).[6]

Each model contains two distinct components: a set of terms related to network dynamics, and a set of terms related to behavior dynamics. Table 8.1 presents a summary of the mechanisms described above as well as the specific model terms that correspond to each mechanism. Also included are two "rate parameters" that refer, respectively, to the average number of opportunities each student receives to change a network tie and change privacy settings in the given transition period. Interpretation of parameters varies depending on the specific term in question; but in general, a positive and significant "network dynamics" coefficient means that the given mechanism plays a significant role in the evolution of network ties while a positive and significant "behavior dynamics" coefficient means that the given mechanism plays a significant role in the evolution of privacy settings. Negative and significant coefficients indicate that the mechanism is consequential but in the opposite direction.

---

[6]The average within-neighborhood density at wave 1 is 0.076, compared to an average across-neighborhood density of 0.059. At wave 2, these numbers are 0.124 and 0.080 respectively; at wave 3, 0.150 and 0.091; and at wave 4, 0.166 and 0.100.

Table 8.1 Summary of mechanisms and corresponding model terms

Network dynamics	
1. Rate parameter	Rate at which students receive the opportunity to change a network tie
Relational mechanisms	
2. Density	Overall tendency for ties to be present
3. Triadic closure	Tendency for A and B to become friends if A and B are both friends with C
4. Degree accumulation	Tendency for popular students to become more popular[a]
Assortative mechanisms	
5. Gender homophily	Tendency for males to befriend males and females to befriend females
6. Racial homophily	Tendency for students from the same racial background to become friends
7. Socioeconomic homophily	Tendency for students with similar SES to become friends
Proximity mechanisms	
8. Shared residence	Tendency for students who live in the same residence to become friends
9. Shared major	Tendency for students who share the same major to become friends
Privacy mechanisms	
10. Privacy main effect	Tendency for students with a private profile to form more friendships overall[a]
11. Privacy similarity effect	Tendency for students with the same privacy setting to become friends
Behavior dynamics	
12. Rate parameter	Rate at which students receive the opportunity to change privacy settings
Exogenous mechanism	
13. Baseline tendency	Baseline tendency to adopt a private profile
Associational mechanism	
14. Peer influence	Tendency to adopt the privacy behavior of one's friends
Structural mechanism	
15. Degree	Tendency for popular students to have a private profile

[a]Because Facebook friendships are undirected, it is impossible to determine whether this is because popular students/students with a private profile initiate more friendship requests or receive more friendship requests

8.5   Results

From March 2006 through March 2009, and in each of the four neighborhoods, we see a pronounced trend towards more students adopting a private profile over time (Fig. 8.1). At wave 1, a mere 53 students (6.1% of the study population) had a private profile. This number increases to 133 students (15.2%) at wave 2, 190 students (21.7%) at wave 3, and 353 students (40.3%) at wave 4. While a minority of students in each transition period shifted their privacy settings from "private" back to "public," the vast majority of change was in the opposite direction (Table 8.2). These trends were roughly consistent in all four neighborhoods, though

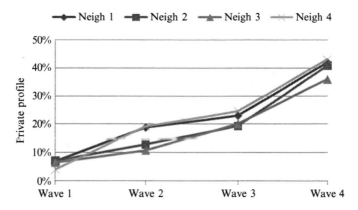

Fig. 8.1 Percentage of students with a private profile in each of four residential neighborhoods

Table 8.2 Descriptive statistics of changes in network structure and privacy behavior

	Wave 1	Period 1	Wave 2	Period 2	Wave 3	Period 3	Wave 4
			Network structure				
Network density							
Neigh 1	0.073		0.132		0.162		0.177
Neigh 2	0.070		0.118		0.142		0.161
Neigh 3	0.075		0.116		0.137		0.151
Neigh 4	0.086		0.130		0.157		0.173
Ties created							
Neigh 1		1088		552		324	
Neigh 2		1280		644		516	
Neigh 3		1159		560		414	
Neigh 4		1155		689		451	
Ties dissolved							
Neigh 1		25		9		44	
Neigh 2		31		37		21	
Neigh 3		36		13		27	
Neigh 4		71		26		62	
			Privacy behavior				
	Wave 1	Period 1	Wave 2	Period 2	Wave 3	Period 3	Wave 4
Proportion private							
Neigh 1	0.068		0.188		0.230		0.419
Neigh 2	0.070		0.127		0.193		0.408
Neigh 3	0.064		0.107		0.201		0.359
Neigh 4	0.040		0.193		0.247		0.430
Public to private							
Neigh 1		25		21		39	
Neigh 2		19		25		51	
Neigh 3		19		28		41	
Neigh 4		36		27		45	
Private to public							
Neigh 1		2		13		3	
Neigh 2		6		10		2	
Neigh 3		9		6		4	
Neigh 4		2		15		4	

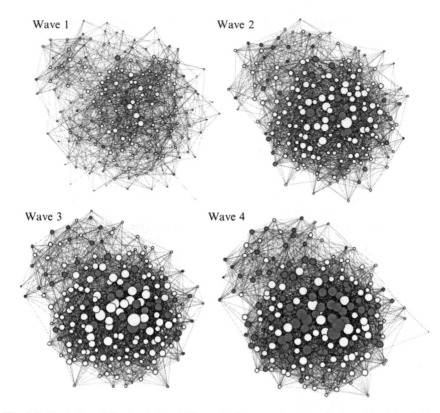

Fig. 8.2 Evolution of Facebook friendships and privacy settings in a single residential neighborhood (Neigh 1, $N = 191$). Nodes represent *students*, and lines represent *Facebook friendships*. Shaded nodes correspond to students with private profiles; node size is proportionate to degree centrality (i.e., larger nodes have more friends). Visualizations were generated using SoNIA (http://sonia.stanford.edu)

students in neighborhoods 1 and 4 (the smallest neighborhoods) displayed a slightly greater overall tendency to adopt a private profile than did students in neighborhoods 2 and 3.

The evolution of privacy behavior can also be visualized a second way, which provides greater insight into the possible interdependence between students' friendship decisions and privacy behavior. Figure 8.2 presents "snapshots" of students' social ties and privacy settings in neighborhood 1 at each of the four waves of observation. In general, we see both a gradual increase in network density (the quantity of ties present) over time, and also a gradual change in privacy behavior as more and more students adopt a private profile. There is also some evidence of clustering according to privacy settings, and a possible tendency – particularly visible at wave 4 – for students with many friends to have a private profile. Statistical models are required to identify the significance of these effects, and also to effectively disentangle the direction of causality between networks and behavior.

8.5.1 Network Dynamics

Results for stochastic actor-based models of Facebook friendships and privacy behavior are presented in Table 8.3. All models were estimated using Siena version 3.18 (Snijders et al. 2008). Given that results are distributed across 12 distinct models (three transition periods for each of four neighborhoods) – each with 15 terms – it is helpful to focus on patterns rather than individual coefficients, and to discuss the network and behavior components of the models separately.[7]

Most consistently, I find robust effects of triadic closure and shared residence for every neighborhood in every transition period. In other words, the two most dominant forces shaping the evolution of students' Facebook friendships is the tendency to become (and remain) friends with one's friends' friends, and to become (and remain) friends with other students who share the same dorm – what could be thought of as social and physical propinquity respectively (cf. Kossinets and Watts 2009).[8] There is also a tendency for Facebook friendships to be relatively sparse overall (i.e., less than half of possible ties are actually present), and for students to befriend others who share the same academic major, given that the "density" (negative) and "shared major" (positive) terms are significant in all but two models. Interestingly, students with relatively many Facebook friendships during period 1 are actually *less* likely to acquire additional friendships (negative, significant "degree accumulation" term for all neighborhoods); and the importance of racial homophily varies according to both neighborhood and period (always significant for neighborhood 3, significant for nearly all neighborhoods in period 3, two neighborhoods in period 1, and only one neighborhood in period 2). Gender homophily does not appear to play a positive role in the evolution of Facebook friendships, although this term is negative and significant for two neighborhoods in period two, suggesting that men and women become friends at a particularly high rate. Finally, socioeconomic homophily is positive and significant only for neighborhood 1 in periods 1 and 2.

With respect to the focal privacy-related mechanisms of this chapter, I find that – even after controlling for all of the effects described above – students' privacy

---

[7]All models were estimated using Siena's unconditional moment estimation and the "initiative/ confirmation" model type for undirected networks (Snijders et al. 2008; see also van de Bunt and Groenewegen 2007). This model type essentially simulates the process whereby Facebook friendships are actually created and dissolved: a tie is created if and only if one student "requests" a friendship and the other student then "accepts," while a friendship can be terminated by either student. All models were run using five phase two subphases and 1,000 phase three iterations. Model convergence was in all cases excellent: the t-ratios for all parameters were less than 0.1 in absolute value.

[8]Technically, positive "network dynamics" coefficients refer to both the tendency for new ties to form *and* the tendency for old ties to be maintained; while negative coefficients refer to both the tendency for new ties *not* to form and the tendency for old ties to be *deleted*. Because friendship deletion is very rare in this network, however (Table 8.2), I focus only on the case of new tie formation for the remainder of my interpretation of results.

Table 8.3 Model results for co-evolution of Facebook friendships and privacy behavior

	Period 1				Period 2				Period 3			
	Neigh 1	Neigh 2	Neigh 3	Neigh 4	Neigh 1	Neigh 2	Neigh 3	Neigh 4	Neigh 1	Neigh 2	Neigh 3	Neigh 4
Network dynamics												
Rate	8.346	8.268	7.825	9.164	3.741	4.545	3.249	4.508	3.019	3.225	2.798	3.686
Density	-0.633*	-0.716*	-0.714*	-0.754	-0.521	-0.720*	-0.790*	-0.396*	-0.857*	-0.791*	-0.948*	-0.920*
Triadic closure	0.354*	0.367*	0.280*	0.244*	0.256*	0.201*	0.225*	0.204*	0.209*	0.194*	0.178*	0.136*
Degree accumulation	-0.006*	-0.005*	-0.002*	-0.004*	-0.003*	-0.001	0.001	-0.007*	-0.012*	-0.001	-0.001	-0.002
Gender homophily	0.017	0.057	0.008	0.042	-0.205*	0.044	0.033	-0.229*	0.087	-0.110	-0.093	-0.002
Racial homophily	0.063	0.201*	0.277*	0.003	0.096	-0.058	0.314*	0.190	0.193*	0.229*	0.344*	-0.068
Socioeconomic homophily	0.911*	0.204	-0.046	0.351	0.971*	-0.119	-0.654*	0.611	0.371	0.102	-0.084	0.418
Shared residence	1.054*	0.909*	0.806*	0.648*	0.964*	0.808*	0.894*	0.817*	0.528*	1.004*	0.787*	0.756*
Shared major	0.575*	0.825*	0.602*	0.448*	0.660*	0.806*	1.019*	0.557*	0.224	0.581*	0.340	0.485*
Privacy main effect	-0.099	0.770*	0.026	0.822*	0.001	-0.766	0.125	-0.146	0.311	-0.652*	-0.128	-0.140
Privacy similarity effect	-0.270	0.683*	0.158	0.163	0.113	-0.029	0.408	-0.038	-0.173	0.211	0.075	0.185
Behavior dynamics												
Rate	0.356	0.689	1.174	0.502	0.727	0.646	0.471	0.726	0.376	0.396	0.348	0.466
Baseline tendency	5.222*	-1.351	-0.021	1.073	-0.038	-0.438	2.150	0.919	-10.740*	0.460	-0.095	1.019
Peer influence	5.245*	2.037	2.875	1.953	2.634	1.617	1.085	4.153*	-7.094	0.281	0.968	4.406*
Degree	-0.078*	0.060*	0.017*	0.003	0.016	0.015	-0.072*	0.012	0.500*[a]	0.043	0.052	0.045

Note: Significant coefficients in bold. $N = 191$ for Neigh 1, $N = 228$ for Neigh 2, $N = 234$ for Neigh 3, and $N = 223$ for Neigh 4. To test that the rate parameters are not zero is meaningless, because if the rate parameters were zero we would observe no network or behavioral change between waves

[a] "Degree" parameter (Neigh 1, Period 3) fixed at this value in order to obtain model convergence

* $p < .05$

behavior plays an independent causal role in the evolution of their social network ties. Firstly, in period 1 and for two out of the four neighborhoods (neighborhoods 2 and 4), students with private profiles are actually more likely to create and maintain friendships than are their peers with public profiles (positive and significant "privacy main effect"). Between their freshman and sophomore years, then, these students either initiate a significantly greater number of new friendships or receive more friendship requests, on average, than do students with public profiles. This pattern actually reverses itself for students in neighborhood 2, however, in the time between their junior and senior years: during this time period, students with private profiles are less likely to initiate (or receive) new ties (negative and significant "privacy main effect"). Finally, to the extent to which students who are friends tend to share the same privacy behavior, there is only scant evidence that this results from a process of social selection whereby students with similar privacy settings seek one another out to become friends: the effect of "privacy similarity" on network dynamics is significant only for neighborhood 2, and only in period 1.

8.5.2   Behavior Dynamics

In the behavioral dynamics section of the model, we see that each of the mechanisms of behavioral change contributes in some way to the evolution of privacy behavior in this population – though effects again vary depending on neighborhood and transition period. In neighborhood 4, the sole significant determinant of privacy dynamics is peer influence: students in this neighborhood are significantly likely to assimilate to the privacy behavior of their peers during the second and third transition periods. In other words, students tend to adopt and maintain the average privacy setting (public or private) held among their Facebook friends – but only following their sophomore year.

Meanwhile, a number of distinct behavioral effects are present for neighborhood 1 (the smallest and most isolated neighborhood, and the neighborhood presented in the visualization above). Between wave 1 and wave 2 (i.e., period 1), model results confirm that students do in fact cluster according to privacy settings – but that this results solely from a process of peer influence rather than similarity-based social selection. Additionally, students in neighborhood 1 in the first transition period have a strong baseline likelihood of adopting a private profile (positive, significant "baseline tendency" effect); but students who have relatively large networks of Facebook friends are less likely to adopt a private profile (negative, significant "degree" effect). No significant behavioral effects are present for this neighborhood in period 2. In period 3, however, the model would not converge after repeated runs. This sometimes happens when a very strong effect is present for a single parameter – i.e., the precise value of the coefficient does not matter, only that the coefficient is very large or very small, and so the model will have trouble converging on a stable estimate. In this case, the problematic parameter was the "degree" effect, which tended towards very high values in estimation attempts. Therefore, I fixed the model parameter at a stable, high value (0.5), and the model had no trouble converging. Conditional on this fixed parameter – indicative of a particularly strong tendency for students with large networks of Facebook friends to adopt a private profile (the visual evidence of which is many large, shaded nodes in wave 4 of Fig. 8.2) – students in that neighborhood actually display a significant baseline tendency *away* from having a private profile, most likely to counterbalance the strength of the degree effect.

Finally, students in neighborhood 2 as well as students in neighborhood 3 (the two largest neighborhoods) display a positive and significant degree effect in the first transition period – an effect which reverses itself in the second transition period for neighborhood 3. In other words, between their freshman and sophomore years, students who have particularly many Facebook friends are particularly likely to adopt a private profile (perhaps to insulate themselves from additional requests); but between their sophomore and junior years, it is students with relatively few Facebook friends who are more likely to adopt a private profile (at least in neighborhood 3).

8.6   Discussion

These findings present the first available insight into the dynamic unfolding of online network and privacy behavior. Despite the very different nature of these ties – friendships documented online – compared to traditional network measures, results for the network dynamics section of the models largely uphold what has been found elsewhere: in particular, the crucial role of both social distance (triadic closure) and spatial distance (co-residence and shared academic major) in determining the shape of social networks. Interestingly, the role of "assortative mechanisms" is less consistent than prior research might lead us to expect: We see no self-segregation among students according to gender; minimal self-segregation by socioeconomic status; and significant racial homophily for only about half of all models. There is also evidence that students with particularly small networks at the end of their freshman year do some "catching up" during the following year only.

Past research on selection and influence has also found that – across a wide variety of attributes that might "spread" through social ties as well as influence their creation – social selection almost always plays a stronger role than does peer influence. In other words, to the extent to which friends in social networks tend to resemble one another, this is largely because they seek one another out rather than become more similar over time (de Klepper et al. 2010). Privacy behavior, there-fore, appears to constitute a rare exception to this trend: I find little evidence that privacy behavior impacts the evolution of students' networks; and to the extent to which it does, this almost always has to do with variation in students' "sociality" according to privacy setting rather than students with similar privacy settings becoming friends. Meanwhile, peer influence indeed plays a significant role in the evolution of students' privacy behavior – but one that also varies considerably across time and context. On one hand, students in neighborhood 1 display a strong tendency to assimilate to the privacy settings of their peers early in college (period 1) but not later. On the other hand, students in neighborhood 4 are influenced by their peers' privacy behavior late in college (periods 2 and 3) but not earlier. Finally, privacy behavior is not only influenced by the specific people with whom one associates, but also by one's structural position: I find multiple significant degree effects on students' privacy behavior, though primarily positive (i.e., students with larger networks are more likely to have a private profile) rather than negative, and primarily early in college (i.e., period 1) rather than later (though students with large networks in neighborhood 1 are particularly likely to adopt a private profile in period 3 – an effect so strong it effectively destabilized the model).

These analyses are limited in a number of ways. Most importantly, they are restricted to students in a particular college setting – a college in which Facebook use was particularly widespread, even in 2006 – which may or may not be generalizable. Without detailed qualitative descriptions of the four neighborhoods, which are here omitted in order to preserve the anonymity of the college, I have only pointed out a few patterns in findings based on the size of the neighborhood(s) in question. Due to practical limitations regarding missing data as well as ambiguities regarding how to interpret students who could not be found on Facebook, I only considered students who could be located on Facebook for all 4 years and who had publicly available friendship data. Finally, while stochastic actor-based modeling represents the most sophisticated available method for modeling the joint evolution of social networks and behavior, there are also nontrivial limitations of applying this method to the study of privacy behavior. Even in the final wave of observation (when private profiles are most widespread), only a minority of students had a private profile; and almost all changes in privacy settings over all three transition periods were due to students moving from "public" to "private" rather than the opposite. Consequently, while all models converged to a satisfactory degree, I was not able to consider additional mechanisms of behavioral change (such as the impact of demographic background on privacy behavior) due to insufficient bidirectional variation in the behavioral variable. Future research should not only replicate these findings in other settings and using other measures of online privacy behavior, but also consider additional mechanisms of network and behavioral change that were not examined here.

This research provides preliminary insight into a topic of clear importance to academics and policymakers alike – yet one that has been strikingly absent from previous work on online privacy. These findings are also noteworthy for future research on network and behavioral evolution more generally. In particular, they demonstrate that mechanisms of change must be sensitive not only to actors' social (i.e., relational) environments, but also to the *time* and *setting* at which this change takes place. Some mechanisms are relevant in certain contexts – here, college residential "neighborhoods" – but not in others; while other mechanisms vary in significance depending on the particular time in the life course (or transition through college) in question. Future research should go beyond simply demonstrating *that* such variation exists, and explore in greater detail how such variation may be systematically related to certain key properties of the local sociohistorical context (cf. Pattison and Robins 2002; van Duijn et al. 2003). While these possibilities are rarely explored, recent advances in available data and methods provide the opportunity for much progress; and as online information disclosure plays an increasingly important role in the conduct of day-to-day life, so we should be increasingly concerned with understanding who is actually disclosing what information, and why.

References

Davis JA (1963) Structural balance, mechanical solidarity, and interpersonal relations. Am J Sociol 68:444–462

de Klepper M, Sleebos E, van de Bunt G, Agneessens F (2010) Similarity in friendship networks: selection or influence? The effect of constraining contexts and non-visible individual attributes. Social Netw 32:82–90

Debatin B, Lovejoy JP, Horn A-K, Hughes BN (2009) Facebook and online privacy: attitudes, behaviors, and unintended consequences. J Comput Mediat Commun 15:83–108

Feld SL (1981) The focused organization of social ties. Am J Sociol 86:1015–1035

Freeman LC (1978) Centrality in social networks: conceptual clarification. Social Netw 1:215–239

Gladwell M (2002) The tipping point: how little things can make a big difference. Little, Brown and Company, New York

Goodreau SM, Kitts JA, Morris M (2009) Birds of a feather, or friend of a friend? Using exponential random graph models to investigate adolescent social networks. Demography 46:103–125

Huisman M, Steglich C (2008) Treatment of non-response in longitudinal network studies. Social Netw 30:297–308

Kandel DB (1978) Homophily, selection, and socialization in adolescent friendships. Am J Sociol 84:427–436

Kaufman J, Patterson O (2005) Cross-national cultural diffusion: the global spread of cricket. Am Sociol Rev 70:82–110

Kossinets G, Watts DJ (2009) Origins of homophily in an evolving social network. Am J Sociol 115:405–450

Lewis K, Kaufman J, Christakis N (2008a) The taste for privacy: an analysis of college student privacy settings in an online social network. J Comput Mediat Commun 14:79–100

Lewis K, Kaufman J, Gonzalez M, Wimmer A, Christakis N (2008b) Tastes, ties, and time: a new social network dataset using Facebook.com. Social Netw 30:330–342

Livingstone S (2008) Taking risky opportunities in youthful content creation: teenagers' use of social networking sites for intimacy, privacy and self-expression. New Media Soc 10:393–411

Marmaros D, Sacerdote B (2006) How do friendships form? Q J Econ 121:79–119

Marsden PV (1987) Core discussion networks of Americans. Am Sociol Rev 52:122–131

Marsden PV (1988) Homogeneity in confiding relations. Social Netw 10:57–76

Mayer A, Puller SL (2008) The old boy (and girl) network: social network formation on university campuses. J Public Econ 92:329–347

McPherson M, Smith-Lovin L, Cook JM (2001) Birds of a feather: homophily in social networks. Annu Rev Sociol 27:415–444

Mercken L, Snijders TAB, Steglich C, Vartiainen E, de Vries H (2010) Dynamics of adolescent friendship networks and smoking behavior. Social Netw 32:72–81

Newcomb TM (1961) The acquaintance process. Holt, Rinehart and Winston, New York

Newman MEJ (2002) Assortative mixing in networks. Phys Rev Lett 89:208701

Pattison P, Robins G (2002) Neighborhood-based models for social networks. Sociol Methodol 32:301–337

Rivera MT, Soderstrom SB, Uzzi B (2010) Dynamics of dyads in social networks: assortative, relational, and proximity mechanisms. Annu Rev Sociol 36:91–115

Rogers EM (2003) Diffusion of innovations, 5th edn. Free Press, New York

Smith KP, Christakis NA (2008) Social networks and health. Annu Rev Sociol 34:405–429

Snijders TAB, Steglich C, Schweinberger M, Huisman M (2008) Manual for SIENA version 3.2. University of Groningen, ICS, Groningen

Snijders TAB, van de Bunt G, Steglich C (2010) Introduction to stochastic actor-based models for network dynamics. Social Netw 32:44–60

Steglich C, Snijders TAB, Pearson M (2010) Dynamic networks and behavior: separating selection from influence. Sociol Methodol 40:329–393

Steglich C, Snijders TAB, West P (2006) Applying SIENA: an illustrative analysis of the coevolution of adolescents' friendship networks, taste in music, and alcohol consumption. Methodology 2:48–56

Tufekci Z (2008) Can you see me now? Audience and disclosure regulation in online social network sites. B Sci Technol Soc 28:20–36

van de Bunt GG, Groenewegen P (2007) An actor-oriented dynamic network approach: the case of interorganizational network evolution. Organ Res meth 10:463–482

van Duijn MAJ, Zeggelink EPH, Huisman M, Stokman FN, Wasseur FW (2003) Evolution of sociology freshmen into a friendship network. J Math Sociol 27:153–191

Wimmer A, Lewis K (2010) Beyond and below racial homophily: ERG models of a friendship network documented on Facebook. Am J Sociol 116:583–642

Youn S, Hall K (2008) Gender and online privacy among teens: risk perception, privacy concerns, and protection behaviors. CyberPsychol Behav 11:763

Chapter 9
Self-Protection of Online Privacy: A Behavioral Approach

Mike Z. Yao

9.1 Introduction

Major shifts in information and communication technologies often reshape the ways in which we produce and share personal information. For example, the development of writing systems allowed personal information to be recorded and stored; the invention of printing technology made it easy to reproduce private information and distribute it to the public; and electronic communications maximized the efficiency and the speed of information sharing. Each of these technological advancements forced human society to redefine the boundaries between the public and private and to re-conceptualize the concept of personal privacy. Not surprisingly, advances in digital communication technologies and the rapid proliferation of social media during the last two decades have once again challenged our views about privacy and privacy protection.

While scholars from various disciplines have all examined the notion of privacy and have each added unique angles to its understanding, there is surprisingly little agreement on its definition and conceptualization. While some saw privacy as the degrees to which people can actively control their own personal information (Bennett 1967; Jourard 1966; Westin 1967), others viewed privacy as a matter of accessibility to one's body and mind (Altman 1975; Leino-Kilpi et al. 2001; Marshall 1974). The concept of privacy has been defined either as a legal prerogative (Warren and Brandeis 1890; Westin 1967), an objective state of being (Jourard 1966; Leino-Kilpi et al. 2001), or a subjective state of mind (Bates 1964). Any discussion of privacy would involve physical, psychological, social, as well as informational aspects (Burgoon 1982; Parrot et al. 1989).

M.Z. Yao (✉)
City University of Hong Kong, Hong Kong, PR China
e-mail: mike.yao@cityu.edu.hk

S. Trepte and L. Reinecke (eds.), *Privacy Online*,
DOI 10.1007/978-3-642-21521-6_9, © Springer-Verlag Berlin Heidelberg 2011

Despite the many different conceptualizations, two general approaches to the study of privacy can be identified in existing literature. On the one hand, the notion of privacy has been treated as a normative and legal concept. From this view, for example, political philosophers and legal scholars have been primarily concerned with questions such as "What is the nature of privacy?" and "How much privacy should a person have?" On the other hand, privacy has been studied as a social and behavioral construct. From this perspective, social scientists have focused on how individuals and/or groups of individuals perceive, protect, and negotiate personal privacy in various social contexts.

In this chapter, I maintain that the protection of online privacy would be best studied from a behavioral perspective. Specifically, I will argue that unlike privacy issues offline, to which a set of well-established cultural, social, and legal norms may be applied, the burden of online privacy protection is primarily shouldered by an individual's own conscious effort. Such efforts, characterized by the adoption of various self-protective strategies to guard personal privacy, might be conceptualized as deliberate and planned behaviors. To support this view, I will first provide an overview of the conceptualizations of privacy from the normative perspective. Then, in the next section, I will discuss the inadequacies of taking such a normative approach to address online privacy issues. In the third section, I will propose a theoretical framework based on the theory of planned behavior (Ajzen 1988) to examine self-protective behaviors. A number of antecedent factors influencing people's attitudes and beliefs with regard to online privacy will also be discussed in this section.

9.2   Normative Perspectives on Privacy

The philosophical foundation of privacy in Western societies can be traced back to ancient times. Konvitz (1966) pointed out that the story of Adam and Eve being expelled from the Garden of Eden could be read as a story about personal privacy. Indeed, nearly all influential thinkers within the Western philosophical tradition have made some sort of distinction between "public" and "private" spaces (Elshtain 1995). The assumption generally has been that there is, or ought to be, a clear boundary separating the private and the public realms in people's lives.

Aristotle saw life itself as divided into public and private spaces. Private homes and households were thought of as the private sphere, or "oikos," and he contrasted these spaces with the public sphere defined by political activities (DeCew 1997). Another Greek philosopher, Epictetus, made a distinction between the private and the public as well (More 1923). He emphasized a distinction between those events or activities that were under our control and those that were not. Epictetus was fascinated with the differences between the inner person – one's own mind and thoughts – and the outer person – one's body and flesh. He argued that it was only our inner self and inner thoughts that were truly under our own control.

John Locke also made a clear distinction between the public and the private. According to Locke (1690), no one person has exclusive rights to nature, which includes land and what is on it. Locke extended the notion of property to every thought, intellectual output, writing, or image a human being could produce. If it belongs to and is acquired by the self through labor and sweat, then it is private property and is considered distinctly separate from what the public owns or what remains in nature.

John Stewart Mill relied on the public/private dichotomy in his thinking as well. He was concerned with the question of when it would be appropriate for society at large (the public) to regulate individual (private) conduct. Mill (1976) argued that there was a realm where people had social responsibilities and where the society could properly restrain people's actions, but that there was also another, more private sphere of action in which the society would have little interest and should not interfere.

Many definitions of privacy have been developed based on these philosophical views on the private and public realms. The concept of privacy has been defined as matters that are personal and secretive (Stephen 1967), a universal human right to be left alone (Cooley 1880; Melvin v. Reid 1931; Warren and Brandeis 1890), the degree of accessibility to an individual ranging from none (i.e., perfect privacy) to complete (i.e., no privacy) (Gavison 1980), or one's ability to control information about oneself (Westin 1967).

While privacy is seen as universally positive in the capitalist Western world, where the right to privacy is a valuable shield for protecting a realm free of the scrutiny and intrusion by others (DeCew 1997), alternative views exist. For example, privacy was viewed as a state of deprivation from the public good and a lack of involvement in the community (see e.g., Arendt 1958). Marx saw privacy as exclusively available to the rich, a protection against the poor (Tucker 1978). Feminist scholars have also argued that too much attention has been given to the private over the public, often to the detriment of women (DeCew 1997). The association between the private sphere and the domestic space that is traditionally occupied by women presents a domain in which women are deprived of power. The domestic life and private space free from public interference has become a haven for men to freely abuse women and oppress their wives and partners while hidden from the watchful eye of public scrutiny (McKinnon 1989).

Despite the lack of a clear and consistent conceptualization of privacy, a review of philosophical and normative views on privacy clearly shows that this concept, as interpreted in the Western philosophies, is not only closely linked to tangible things such as physical spaces, information, and properties, but also to the highly abstract notions of liberty and freedom. Moreover, the conceptual nub of privacy almost always involves a boundary separating the public and the private spheres. This boundary can either be concrete and physical or ephemeral and intellectual.

9.3   Inadequacies of Taking a Normative Approach to Study Online Privacy Protection

It would be relatively easy to find legal and technical solutions for protecting personal privacy when it is defined in terms of physical and observable matters. However, it is far more difficult to reach a consensus on the illusive right to privacy even within a relatively homogeneous cultural system. For example, in the United States, although there is a comprehensive legal system that explicitly identifies a variety of specific situations in which individual's privacy is protected, the US Constitution does not guarantee the right to privacy explicitly (Prosser 1960; Turkington and Allen 1999). The protection of privacy as a generalized human right comes only from the interpretations offered by the Supreme Court Justices (Cate 1997), which may shift from time to time. This reflects the fact that normative beliefs about privacy are highly sensitive to cultural norms and sociopolitical systems. Privacy, as a constant and universally accepted value, would be extremely difficult, if not impossible, to define from a normative perspective.

A normative approach to personal privacy is further challenged by the ever-changing information and communication technologies (ICTs). In the physical world, for example, observable objects and symbols usually mark the boundaries between private and public domains, and the size of personal space can be measured in units of distance. Although different views might exist as to how big or small a person's private space ought to be, the line between where public space ends and where private space starts can nevertheless be easily observed and agreed upon in a given community. However, in the virtual online world, the concept of "space" is merely a metaphor. There is no unit of measurement for virtual space; there are no walls or markers to clearly divide the private and public spheres. To make things more complicated, people from different cultures, often with drastically different privacy beliefs and norms, co-occupy this abstract and metaphorical space. In such a virtual environment, the normative rules and expectations related to personal privacy are irrelevant.

Although there is an ongoing effort for the legislators from governments around the world to expand the right of privacy to the Internet (Turkington and Allen 1999), the difficulties of defining a private space in the virtual world and the explosion of remotely accessible personal information challenge the application of existing legal protections of privacy to the online environment. Furthermore, the ease of data sharing and matching through digital computing also allows new information about a person to be created by merging data from seemingly non-private sources. Such data mining and cross-referencing technologies have also posed great challenges to the normative perspectives on privacy.

It is clear that a normative approach to privacy, relying heavily on social norms and legal traditions, is ineffective when dealing with online privacy threats faced by netizens of the digital world. Internet users would not be able to rely on legal systems to protect their personal privacy, nor could they expect the other users to observe the social and cultural norms of their own. As such, the burden of protecting personal privacy shifts to the individuals themselves.

9.4   Protection of Online Privacy as Planned Behavior

For each individual, the protection of privacy may either be passive or active. Passive protection involves reliance on external entities such as the government or other individuals. This type of protection is generally beyond the direct control of one individual; collective actions and institutional support are required. It is also highly sensitive to cultural and sociopolitical norms. As discussed earlier, the online communicative environment poses a significant challenge to such protection.

Active protection, on the other hand, relies on individuals themselves actively adopting various protective strategies. In the physical world, for example, walls can be reinforced to be soundproof; taller fences can be built to block the views from outside; a door can be closed; a sign can be posted outside a room to indicate the desire for privacy; and a lock can be added to a personal diary. In the virtual world, there are also a number of ways in which people can actively protect their online privacy. For example, Hoffman et al. (1999) found that more than 90% of Internet users had either declined to provide personal information or had fabricated information due to online privacy concerns. Internet users can install firewalls and virus protection software, scrutinize the online information transmission, and use encryption for sensitive data.

From a behavioral perspective, the protection of privacy can be viewed primarily as a process of boundary management through various means of controlling private space (Hall 1966, Sommer 1959) and personal information (Buss 2001; Petronio 2002). Such a protection and management process requires individuals to detect threats to personal privacy from the external environment, weigh such threats against their privacy preferences, evaluate the possible outcomes of either losing or maintaining privacy in a given social situation, and then select and adopt the boundary management strategies accordingly.

9.4.1   A "Theory of Planned Behavior" Model of Online Privacy Protection

In contrast to the offline environment, individuals cannot easily rely on their physical senses to detect threats to privacy online. The often visually anonymous communicative space may also hinder a person's ability to rely on the usual social and cultural cues to evaluate the target of self-disclosure. Additionally, individuals must have a certain amount of knowledge about the Internet and online communication in order to assess privacy risks; many online privacy management strategies also require technical skills beyond that of an average user. Therefore, while privacy management and protection might be performed unconsciously and effortlessly in the offline world, effective self-protection of online privacy must involve deliberate and effortful thoughts and actions.

A dominant approach to understanding deliberative actions people undertake in a variety of domains has been the expectancy-value research tradition. Within this tradition, the theory of planned behavior (TPB) (Ajzen 1988, 1991; Ajzen and Fishbein 2005) is a leading model. The TPB lays out the underlying processes leading to an individual's intention to perform and the actual performance of a target behavior. It maintains that the performance of a particular human action is predominantly determined by the intention to perform it. The TPB postulates three conceptually independent determinants of behavioral intention: The first predictor is the individual's attitude toward the target behavior; it refers to the degree to which a person has a favorable or unfavorable evaluation of the behavior itself and the outcome of performing such a behavior. The second predictor is the subjective norm; it refers to the individual's perceived social pressure to perform or not perform the target behavior. The third predictor of behavioral intention is perceived behavioral control, which refers to the individual's perceived ease or difficulty of performing the target behavior. In combination, attitude, subjective norm, and perceptive behavioral control would lead to the formation of a behavioral intention. As a general rule, the more favorable the attitude and subjective norm, and the greater the perceived control, the stronger the person's intention to perform the behavior in question should be.

Although the usefulness of a TPB-based approach to human actions is most amplified in the research of health-related behaviors such as dieting, quitting smoking, and practicing safe sex (Godin and Kok 1996), this theory is highly generalizable and can be adapted to almost all planned behaviors under volitional control (Ajzen 1988, 1991). With regard to online privacy protection, the TPB should also be a useful theoretical framework because behaviors associated with adopting various boundary management strategies to reduce threats of online privacy are similar to many health-related behaviors. Both types of behavior involve an individual's conscious and deliberate decision to adopt a target behavior in order to prevent a perceived harm.

According to the TPB, the intention to adopt various behaviors and strategies to protect personal privacy on the Internet would be affected by the person's overall evaluations of the necessity and effectiveness of a protective behavior of interest, the perceived social norm regarding privacy protection and behavior, and his/her ability to perform the behavior. For example, one of the privacy protection strategies used most frequently by Internet users is providing false personal infor-mation (Hoffman et al. 1999). When facing a choice of providing either real or altered personal details to a website or another individual (i.e., behavioral inten-tion), Internet users would evaluate the need and effectiveness of lying about personal details (i.e., attitude). While providing a false personal identity might be an effective way to protect privacy, doing so might reduce the chance of forming meaningful social relationships. In this specific social context, people would weigh the risks against the possible benefits and form an overall attitude toward the behavioral choices of either providing real or false personal information (Petronio 2002). Moreover, the intention to lie about personal identity would also be influenced by appropriateness and prevalence of providing false personal information in a given context (i.e., subjective norm). For instance, people are much more likely to stay anonymous or use pseudonyms on a website if other users of the site do so. Finally, the intention and actual action of posting false personal information would be determined by individuals' subjective evaluation of how easy or difficult it would be to not only create but also maintain a fake identity (i.e., behavioral control); it would be much easier for a user to hide behind a fictional identity when posting a one-time comment in a public forum than when using a social networking site regularly.

The application of the TPB in predicting people's online privacy self-protection has received some empirical support. In a study of college students' adoption of four online privacy protection strategies, Yao and Linz (2008) found that the three main constructs in the TPB explained 17% of the variability in behavioral intention and 24% of the variability in the actual adoption of online protective behaviors. This finding is consistent with previous studies that used the TPB to predict other types of planned behaviors.

The primary concern of the TPB is to provide a reliable model that accurately predicts the intention and the actual performance of a wide range of deliberate human actions (Ajzen 1988, 1991). In order to maintain parsimony, antecedents and moderators of these behavior-specific attitudes and beliefs are not included in the TPB's formal model. While this approach provides a robust yet simple theoretical explanation for the underlying process leading to a person's decision to perform a target behavior, the TPB's practical use in promoting a specific social behavior is limited. As such, antecedents of specific attitudes and beliefs must be taken into account when studying a specific type of behavior such as online privacy protection. For instance, the TPB model's capacity for predicting a person's intention to adopt an online privacy protection strategy is determined by this person's attitude toward the strategy, perceived social pressure of using it, and perceived behavioral control over its adoption. From a theoretical standpoint, these variables may be sufficient to explain and predict the target behavior. From a practical standpoint, however, in order to effectively promote online privacy protection, a researcher must also examine the factors that influence privacy-related attitudes and beliefs.

While many situational, contextual, and demographic factors might influence an individual's privacy-related attitudes, beliefs, and behaviors, I will highlight four frequently studied variables in online privacy research within the general framework of the TPB in the remaining part of this chapter: (1) concerns about online privacy, (2) need for privacy, (3) self-efficacy, and (4) Internet use experience. The proposed conceptual framework is illustrated by Fig. 9.1.

9.4.2 Concerns About Online Privacy

By far the most commonly studied online privacy issue is consumer concerns and worries about various online privacy threats. Within a planned behavior framework, such concerns would strongly influence one's attitude toward online privacy

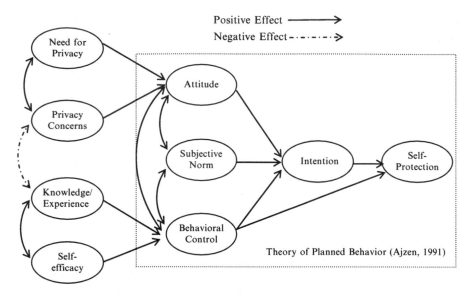

Fig. 9.1 A planned behavior model of online privacy self-protection

protection. The more a person is worried about privacy violation, the more likely he/she would hold a positive attitude regarding the protective strategy.

There is no doubt that Internet users are concerned about online privacy. An analysis of more than 16 opinion polls taken between 1998 and 2002 reveals that nearly two thirds of respondents were either "very" or "somewhat" concerned about privacy when they use the Internet (Metzger and Docter 2003). Hoffman et al. (1999) found that more than 90% of Internet users have either declined to provide personal information or have fabricated information due to online privacy concerns.

Recent development and rapid proliferation of online social media have triggered a new wave of public concerns about online privacy (Barnes 2006; boyd 2008). While social media are great platforms for users to quickly expand and maintain their personal or professional social networks, such a benefit would require users to disclose a large amount of personal information, which would lead to higher risks of privacy violations (boyd and Ellison 2005). Researchers found that sensitive personal information can be constructed from information often found in SNS users' public profiles (Gross and Acquisti 2005). A recent poll of American Internet users has shown that a majority of SNS users were concerned about personal privacy and had reported taking certain steps to minimize potential risks (Lenhard and Madden 2007)

A number of studies examined the factors that may influence consumer online privacy concerns. Phelps et al. (2001) conducted a national mail survey and found that a consumer's attitude toward direct marketing and desire for information control are antecedents to privacy concerns. Specifically, attitude toward direct marketing is negatively associated with online privacy concerns whereas desire for information control is positively related to concerns of online privacy. Demographics such as gender, age, race, and social economic status are also predictors of online privacy concerns (Dommeyer and Gross 2003; Graeff and Harmon 2002; Milne and Rohm 2000; O'Neil 2001; Phelps et al. 2000; Sheehan 1999). For example, Sheehan (1999) surveyed 889 Internet users and found that women are more concerned than men about their personal privacy in information gathering situations (see Thelwall, this volume, Chap. 18 for a more detailed discussion of gender and privacy concerns). Other factors influencing online privacy concerns include perceived creditability of the website (Flanagin and Metzger 2003), perceived security of transaction (Swaminathan et al. 1999), and trust (Jarvenpaa et al. 1999). Yao et al. (2007) found that people's belief in the general right to privacy and technical knowledge were both predictors for concerns about online privacy. Yao and Linz (2008) found that individuals' fear of becoming a victim of online privacy violations had led to a positive attitude toward online privacy protection, but lowered the level of their perceived behavioral control.

9.4.3 A Psychological Need for Privacy

In addition to worries about privacy violation, a dispositional psychological need for privacy would be another important factor that would influence people's attitudes toward online privacy protection. The more an individual desires privacy, the more positive this person's attitude toward online privacy protection is likely to be. Additionally, more need for privacy might also lead to greater concern about online privacy threats and therefore indirectly affect attitude toward online privacy.

The need for privacy has been addressed in several lines of research. The evolutionary perspective, for example, postulates that humans have an innate drive to be gregarious but territorial (Halmos 1953; Klopfer and Rubenstein 1977). Halmos opined that the desire for solitude is natural to both primitive and post-primitive societies; such a desire functions to regenerate social life for its more harmonious living. Klopfer and Rubenstein argued that having some level of privacy is essential to many animals' survival. Most animals exhibit some patterns of social withdrawal. Privacy may also aid survival by reducing competition for food and reproductive resources. Although it is difficult to confirm a hardwired need for privacy, much research has looked at human displays of territoriality as a possible display of such an innate tendency. Territoriality refers to the possessiveness of a physical place, a certain knowledge area, or social status (Altman 1975). Sommer (1966) has distinguished two strategies of territorial defenses – avoidance and offensive display – that are purposed to protect or attain privacy. Marshall (1974) found that people with greater need for privacy tended to have a greater amount of fencing around their homes.

Individual differences in the need for privacy might also be explained from a developmental perspective. For example, family environment may directly influence the development of an individual's independence and autonomy (Ittelson et al. 1974).

Lawton and Bader (1970) found that preference for a private room increases with age from years 10 through 40. Marshall (1974) also found age to be a significant predictor of privacy preference. Wolfe and Laufer (1974) found that with maturation the concept of privacy preference becomes more cognitively complex. Parke and Sawin (1979) found that the use of physical privacy markers and privacy rules at home (e.g., putting signs on the door, knocking before entering the room, etc.) both increased with age among children. Further discussions of a developmental perspective can be found in Chap. 16 of this volume by Peter and Valkenburg in their analyses of adolescents' online privacy preferences, and in Chap. 17 by Maaß, which deals with privacy concerns among elderly Internet users.

A number of recent studies provided empirical evidence that the need for privacy would directly and indirectly influence attitude and beliefs related to online privacy. For example, need for privacy has been found to influence user concerns about online privacy among American college students as well as their counterparts in Asia (Yao et al. 2007; Yao and Zhang 2008). Yao and Linz (2008) also found individuals' need for privacy to be a direct and significant predictor of people's attitude toward online privacy protection strategies.

9.4.4 Self-Efficacy

Perceived self-efficacy is a person's beliefs in his/her capabilities and cognitive resources required to cope with given events (Bandura 1997). Bandura posited that self-efficacy influences how people feel, think, and act. In terms of feeling, a low sense of self-efficacy is associated with depression, anxiety, and helplessness. Individuals with low self-efficacy would also have low self-esteem and harbor pessimistic thoughts about their accomplishments and personal development. In terms of thinking, a strong sense of self-efficacy is thought to facilitate cognitive processes and performance in a variety of settings, including quality of decision-making and academic achievement. In terms of actual behaviors, self-efficacy has a major impact on motivation. People with high self-efficacy choose to perform more challenging tasks (Bandura 1997). These persons set high goals and stick to them. High levels of self-efficacy also allow people to select challenging settings, explore their environments, or create new environments (Schwarzer 1992).

According to the theory of planned behavior (TPB), self-efficacy is a closely related construct to the notion of perceived behavior control. Ajzen (2002) posited that while perceived behavioral control is an evaluation of external factors that may influence the performance of a behavior in relation to one's ability, perceived self-efficacy is an assessment of the actor of a behavior in relation to various external factors. These two concepts are closely related to and predictive of each other (Ajzen 1988, 1991). Thus, one can expect that individuals with higher self-efficacy will be more likely to transfer this sense of confidence to the specific context of online privacy protection through an increased level of perceived behavioral control. A high level of self-efficacy will allow an Internet user to be more confident at using online privacy protection tools. A highly self-efficacious individual will also be more willing to try new protection strategies than will individuals with lower levels of self-efficacy.

9.4.5 Knowledge and Experience of Internet Use

It is intuitively easy to deduce that the more experience people have with various features and functions of the Internet, the more confident or efficacious they will feel about using this medium. Previous research on Internet usage and online privacy has supported this view (LaRose et al. 2001; Yao et al. 2007). As such, individuals with more knowledge and experience of using the Internet might be more likely to adopt various tools and strategies to online privacy through an increase in perceived behavioral control.

However, findings from other studies indicate that an increase in computer knowledge and Internet use experience might also lead to a decrease in concerns about online privacy, and therefore reduce self-protection intention and behavior. For example, in a multiyear longitudinal investigation, the UCLA Center for Communication Policy (2000, 2001, 2003, 2004) found that the level of privacy concern has decreased over time, especially among experienced Internet users. Phelps et al. (2000) found that consumers who had made a catalog purchase via the telephone within the past 6 months were less concerned about disclosing their credit card information than those who had not made a telephone catalog purchase. This finding indicates that as consumers become more familiar with e-commerce, they may be less concerned about privacy issues.

Taken as a whole, these findings are indicative of two contradicting processes at work. On one hand, as discussed earlier, an increase in computer knowledge and Internet use experience may enhance a person's control over the use of online privacy protection tools. Such persons are more likely to use these tools and thus feel less concerned about their privacy. This relationship is consistent with the TPB. On the other hand, however, it can also be argued that an increase in computer knowledge and Internet use experience may lead to a false sense of security, especially if a person does not encounter any negative experience. For example, a computer user may be careless about protecting personal information but, luckily, has never experienced any harmful consequences. As a result, this person is less likely to pay attention to online privacy threats and therefore decide not to utilize online privacy protection tools as a precaution. In other words, there could be a situation where higher levels of Internet use experience may lead to a decrease in perceived threat to online privacy.

9.5   Conclusion

The development of information and communication technologies and the proliferation of social media in recent years have triggered a new wave of public concerns
about personal privacy. However, the social norms and rules pertaining to personal
privacy in the offline world are usually not applicable in this virtual environment.
Protection of privacy in the virtual space thus would require individuals to constantly monitor and evaluate privacy risks, and deliberately adopt various self-
protective strategies. As such, a behavioral approach to the study of online privacy
protection would be more preferable to the normative perspectives.

In this chapter, a general theoretical framework based on the theory of planned
behavior was proposed to predict individuals' self-protection of online privacy.
According to this model, an individual's intention to adopt various protective
strategies is a function of an overall attitude toward the target behaviors, a subjective evaluation of the social norm and pressure related to them, and an overall
perception of behavioral control.

This chapter also discussed several frequently studied variables in online privacy
research within the proposed framework. Specifically, people's online privacy
concerns and their dispositional need for privacy would positively influence their
attitude toward online privacy protection; individuals' perceived behavioral control
might be positively influenced by their sense of self-efficacy and Internet use
experience. However, Internet user experience, in certain conditions, might reduce
concerns about privacy and indirectly reduce the likelihood of online privacy self-
protection.

Compared to previous online privacy research that focused primarily on privacy-
related concerns and preferences, a planned behavior approach does not assume the
link between privacy concerns and self-protection. Indeed, findings from previous
research suggest that, although Internet users report high levels of concern about
online privacy, they have little specific knowledge of practices that may violate
their privacy and little general knowledge of online privacy policies as a whole
(Dommeyer and Gross 2003). Moreover, while many consumers claim to be fairly
well informed about privacy protection strategies, they often do not adopt them
when using the Internet. The use of privacy protection strategies, such as carefully
reading privacy statements, managing cookies, and other precautionary measures,
is low even among those who claim to be very concerned about their privacy
(Berendt et al. 2005; Dommeyer and Gross 2003; Tavani 2000). The proposed
theoretical model may shed light on this seemingly paradoxical pattern by taking
into consideration the psychological process linking one's attitude and actual
behavior.

Overall, this chapter should provide a broad and fundamental understanding for
the rest of the book, focusing on specific issues related to online privacy and
personal boundary management.

References

Ajzen I (1988) Attitudes, personality, and behavior. Open University Press, Milton Keynes

Ajzen I (1991) The theory of planned behavior. Organ Behav Hum Decis Process 50:179–211

Ajzen I, Fishbein M (2005) The influence of attitudes on behavior. In: Albarracin D, Johnson BT, Zanna MP (eds) The handbook of attitudes. Erlbaum, Mahwah, pp 173–221

Altman I (1975) The environment and social behavior. Brooks/Cole, Belmont

Arendt H (1958) The human condition. Chicago, IL: University of Chicago Press

Bandura A (1997) Self-efficacy: the exercise of control. W. H. Freeman, New York

Barnes S (2006) A privacy paradox: social networking in the United States. First Monday, 11. http://www.firstmonday.org/issues/issue11_9/barnes/index.htm

Bates A (1964) Privacy: a useful concept? Soc Forces 42:432–437

Bennett C (1967) What price privacy. Am Psychol 22:371–376

Berendt B, Günther O, Spiekermann S (2005) Privacy in e-commerce: stated preferences vs. actual behavior. Commun ACM 48(4):101–106

boyd d (2008) Facebook's privacy trainwreck: exposure, invasion, and social convergence. Convergence 14:13–20

boyd d, Ellison N (2005) Social network sites: definition, history, and scholarship. J Comput Mediat Commun 13, Article 11. http://jcmc.indiana.edu/vol13/issue1/boyd.ellison.html

Burgoon JK (1982) Privacy and communication. In: Burgoon M (ed) Communication yearbook 6. Sage, Beverly Hills, pp 206–249

Buss A (2001) Psychological dimensions of the self. Sage, Thousand Oaks

Cate FH (1997) Privacy in the information age. Brooking Institute Press, Washington, DC

Cooley T (1880) A treatise on the law of torts or the wrongs which arise independent of contract. Callaghan, Chicago

DeCew JW (1997) In pursuit of privacy: law, ethics, and the rise of technology. Cornell University Press, Ithaca

Dommeyer CJ, Gross BL (2003) What consumers know and what they do: an investigation of consumer knowledge, awareness, and use of privacy protection strategies. J Interact Mark 17:34–51

Elshtain JB (1995) Democracy on trial. Basic Book, New York

Flanagin AJ, Metzger MJ (2003) The perceived credibility of web site information as influenced by the sex of the source. Comput Hum Behav 16:683–701

Gavison R (1980) Privacy and the limits of law. Yale Law J 89:420–435

Godin G, Kok G (1996) The theory of planned behavior: a review of its applications to health-related behaviors. Am J Heal Promot 11:87–98

Graeff TR, Harmon S (2002) Collecting and using personal data: consumers' awareness and concerns. J Consum Mark 19:302–313

Gross R, Acquisti AA (2005) Information revelation and privacy in online social networks. In: Proceedings of WPES'05, ACM, Alexandria, pp 71–80

Hall ET (1966) The hidden dimension. Doubleay, New York

Halmos P (1953) Solitude and privacy: a study of social isolation, its causes and therapy. Philosophical Library, New York

Hoffman DL, Novak TP, Peralta M (1999) Building consumer trust online. Commun ACM 42(4):80–85

Ittelson W, Proshansky H, Rivlin L, Winkel G (1974) An introduction to environmental psychology. Holt, Rinehart and Winston, Oxford

Jarvenpaa SL, Tractinsky N, Vitale M (1999) Consumer trust in an internet store: a cross-cultural validation. J Comput Mediat Commun 5. http://www.ascusc.org/jcmc/vol5/issue2

Jourard S (1966) Some psychological aspects of privacy. Law Contemp Probs 31:307–318

Klopfer P, Rubenstein D (1977) The concept of privacy and its biological basis. J Soc Issues 33:52–65

Konvitz MR (1966) Privacy and law: A philosophical prelude. Law and Contemporary Problems 31:272–288

LaRose R, Mastro D, Eastin M (2001) Understanding internet usage: a social-cognitive approach to uses and gratifications. Soc Sci Comput Rev 19:395–413

Lawton MP, Bader J (1970) Wish for privacy by young and old. J Gerontol 25:48–54

Leino-Kilpi H, Vaelimaeki M, Dassen T, Gasull M, Lemonidou C, Scott A, Arndt M (2001) Privacy: a review of the literature. Int J Nurs Stud 38:663–671

Lenhart A, Madden M (2007) Teens, privacy, & online social networks. Pew internet and American life project report. http://www.pewinternet.org/pdfs/PIP_Teens_Privacy_SNS_Report_Final.pdf

Locke J (1960) The second treatise on government. Bobbs-Merrill, Indianapolis

Marshall NJ (1974) Dimensions of privacy preferences. Multivar Behav Res 9:255–271

McKinnon C (1989) Toward a feminist theory of the state. Harvard University Press, Cambridge, MA

Melvin v. Reid, 112 Cal.App. 92 (1931)

Metzger M, Docter S (2003) Public opinion and policy initiatives for online privacy protection. J Broadcast Electron Med 47:350–374

Mill JS (1976) On Liberty. New York, NY: Penguin

Milne GR, Rohm AJ (2000) Consumer privacy and name removal across direct marketing channels: exploring opt-in and opt-out alternatives. J Public Policy Market 19:238–249

More PE (1923) Hellenistic philosophies. Princeton University Press, Princeton

O'Neil D (2001) Analysis of internet user' level of online privacy concerns. Soc Sci Comput Rev 19:17–31

Parke R, Sawin D (1979) Children's privacy in the home: developmental, ecological and child-rearing determinants. Environ Behav 11:87–104

Parrot R, Burgoon JK, Burgoon M, LePoire BA (1989) Privacy between physicians and patients: more than a matter of confidentiality. Soc Sci Med 29:1381–1385

Petronio S (2002) Boundaries of privacy: dialectics of disclosure. State University of New York Press, New York

Phelps JE, Nowak GJ, Ferrell E (2000) Privacy concerns and consumer willingness to provide personal information. J Public Policy Market 19:27–41

Phelps JE, D'Souza G, Nowak GJ (2001) J Interact Mark 15:2–17

Prosser WJ (1960) Privacy. Calif Law Rev 383:48

Schwarzer R (ed) (1992) Self-efficacy: thought control of action. Hemisphere, Washington, DC

Sheehan KB (1999) An investigation of gender differences in on-line privacy concerns and resultant behaviors. J Interact Mark 13:24–38

Sommer R (1959) Studies in personal space. Sociemetry 22:247–260

Sommer R (1969) Personal space. Prentice-Hall, Englewood Cliffs

Stephen JF (1967) Liberty, equality, fraternity. Liberty Fund, Indianapolis

Swaminathan V, Lepkowska-White E, Rao BP (1999) Browsers or buyers in cyberspace? An investigation of factors influencing electronic exchange. J Comput Mediat Commun 5(2). Retrieved on December 6, 2003, from http://www.ascusc.org/jcmc/vol5/issue2

Tavani H (2000) Privacy-enhancing technologies as a panacea for online privacy concerns. J Inform Ethics fall:26–36

Turkington RC, Allen AL (1999) Privacy law: cases and materials. West Group, St. Paul

UCLA Center for Communication Policy (2000) The UCLA internet report: surveying the digital future: year one. http://www.ccp.ucla.edu. Accessed 7 Oct 2001

UCLA Center for Communication Policy (2001) The UCLA internet report 2001: surveying the digital future: year two. http://www.ccp.ucla.edu. Accessed 21 Jan 2002

UCLA Center for Communication Policy (2003) The UCLA internet report: surveying the digital future: year three. http://www.digitalcenter.org/pdf/InternetReportYearThree.pdf. Accessed 1 Oct 2005

UCLA Center for Communication Policy (2004) The UCLA internet report: surveying the digital future: year four. http://www.digitalcenter.org/downloads/DigitalFutureReport-Year4-2004. pdf. Accessed 1 Oct 2005

Warren S, Brandeis L (1890) The right to privacy. Harvard Law Rev 4:193–220

Westin A (1967) Privacy and freedom. Atheneum, New York (Witte, 1994)

Wolfe M, Laufer R (1974) The concept of privacy in children and adolescence. In: Carson D (ed) Man-environment interactions: evaluations and applications: part 2, vol 6, Privacy. Environmental Design Research Association, Washington, DC, pp 29–54

Yao MZ, Linz D (2008) Predicting internet users' self-protection of online privacy violations. CyberPsychol Behav 11:615–617

Yao MZ, Zhang JG (2008) Predicting user concerns about online privacy in Hong Kong. CyberPsychol Behav 11:779–781

Yao MZ, Rice R, Wallis K (2007) Predicting user concerns about online privacy. J Am Soc Inf Sci Technol 58:710–722

Chapter 10
Online Self-Presentation: Balancing Privacy Concerns and Impression Construction on Social Networking Sites

Nicole C. Krämer and Nina Haferkamp

10.1 Social Networking Sites and Privacy

Reaching the milestone figure of 500 million members in July 2010, the growth of the social networking site Facebook has rapidly accelerated. Currently, its membership figures would make it the third largest country in the world, suggesting that participation in online social networks has become more than a cursory phenomenon. Members of Facebook are required to create an individualized online profile that provides information about themselves, their physical appearance, individual tastes, and preferences (see Liu 2007; Liu et al. 2006), and that highlights certain aspects of their own personality. By means of these features, users inevitably construct and manage impressions of their self. Research has already shown that such a personal webpage even allows a more detailed self-presentation than a casual face-to-face interaction and that people indeed make use of it in order to emphasize certain aspects of their "true" self (Bargh et al. 2002; Haferkamp and Krämer 2010). Additionally, empirical findings indicate that social networking sites (SNSs) are not only a potential means for self-presentation but that people are indeed highly motivated to use this new arena for presenting themselves (Haferkamp and Krämer 2010). In doing this, they even adopt profile elements that have originally been provided for other purposes (e.g., people become a member of a group in order to display their attitudes and interests instead of in order to communicate with others, Haferkamp and Krämer 2009). This tendency might be due to the fundamental motive of every human being to present him/herself in a positive way and, in doing

N.C. Krämer (✉)
University of Duisburg-Essen, Duisburg, Germany
e-mail: nicole.kraemer@uni-due.de

N. Haferkamp
Technical University of Dresden, Dresden, Germany

S. Trepte and L. Reinecke (eds.), *Privacy Online*,
DOI 10.1007/978-3-642-21521-6_10, © Springer-Verlag Berlin Heidelberg 2011

so, gain positive reactions from those forming an impression (Leary 1995; Leary and Kowalski 1990).

However, especially when presenting oneself online, the motive to leave a favorable impression can collide with the motive to maintain privacy. On the one hand, due to their desire to present themselves, users often choose to display individual information such as their physical appearance, individual tastes, likes, hobbies, or even their names or addresses. On the other hand, they are aware of the potential disadvantages when publishing this information in a more or less self-defined community (Lenhart and Madden 2007; Lewis et al. 2008; Livingstone 2008; Reinecke and Trepte 2008; Utz and Krämer 2009). This contradiction regarding the disclosure of private information (especially by teenagers) on an online profile on the one hand and worries about privacy on the other has been called the *privacy paradox* (Barnes 2006).

The main goal of this chapter will be to discuss the conflicting motives and the corresponding strategies. In doing this, we will first comment on the various forms of self-presentation in SNSs and specifically, we will primarily address self-presentation by means of profile elements. Also, we will compare offline and online self-presentation and discuss in what way models from face-to-face self-presentation have to be extended in order to be able to account for online self-presentation. Here, we focus on the two-component model of self-presentation created by Leary and Kowalski (1990) that describes self-presentation as the result of two different processes: impression motivation and impression construction. In addition, we describe different aspects of people's privacy concerns (based on Burgoon 1982) and link them to potential strategies for ensuring privacy when presenting oneself online. In the conclusion, we discuss how users might deal with these conflicting motives and interests and which strategies can be used to balance self-presentation and privacy.

10.2 Defining Self-Presentation from a Social Psychological Perspective and Forms of Presenting Oneself via SNSs

Whenever people want to be perceived in a particular way, certain self-presentation strategies are activated in order to comply with other people's expectations (Leary 1995; Leary and Kowalski 1990). Goffman (1959) describes self-presentation as an attempt to control or guide the impression that others might make of a person by using verbal and nonverbal signals. There have been attempts to distinguish the terms self-presentation and impression management (Schlenker 1980; Schneider 1981), however, no clear-cut distinction has emerged that scholars can agree on. Therefore, common practice is to use the terms interchangeably (Leary and Kowalski 1990). In this chapter, we will use the term self-presentation. More importantly, self-presentation has to be differentiated from self-disclosure: self-disclosure is defined as the act of revealing private information to others and is thus closely related to privacy (Archer 1980). The Internet in particular is a medium that has increased willingness for self-disclosure due to reduced social cues and perceived anonymity (Joinson 2001; Reingold 1993; Tidwell and Walther 2002). Unlike self-presentation and impression management, self-disclosure – as conceptualized, for instance, by Joinson (this volume, Chap. 4) – places a higher priority on the quantity and the kind of personal information provided, while self-presentation focuses on controlling the impressions that other persons form based on the given information. Self-presentation/impression management is therefore more concerned with the quality of information and the (sometimes unconscious yet ubiquitous) intention to influence observers, while self-disclosure solely considers the distribution of information, without necessarily intending to achieve a certain impression effect (although depending on the conceptualization of self-presentation there may be some doubt regarding whether any behavior/display of information is possible without an at least implicit motive to present oneself, Leary 1995).

With regard to online profiles on SNSs, both concepts, self-disclosure and self-presentation, are highly relevant and strongly interrelated. Self-disclosure refers to the act of presenting private information, which is a fundamental precondition for the act of self-presentation online. In contrast, self-presentation refers to the process of (consciously or unconsciously) trying to influence the impression formed by the observer (e.g., through profile pictures or information regarding one's preferences, interests, and hobbies). While the present chapter focuses on *self-presentation* in the Social Web, Joinson (this volume, Chap. 4) describes the role of *self-disclosure* for online privacy.

When discussing differences between online and offline self-presentation as well as strategies to self-present and yet maintain privacy – as we intend to do in the following – it is important to distinguish between different possibilities for self-presentation on social networking sites. The "classic" form of engaging in self-presentation on social networking sites is certainly to display information on sociodemographic aspects, job, hobbies, etc. on the profile. Motives for presenting oneself via this means as well as effects when reading other people's profiles have been analyzed in numerous studies in recent years (boyd and Ellison 2007; Ellison et al. 2006; Haferkamp and Krämer 2010; Mehdizadeh 2010). However, current developments on social networking sites permit various other forms of self-presentation. For example, many SNS providers enable users to provide a short note on their current activities, thoughts, or emotions (e.g., status update on Facebook, Buschfunk on the German equivalent StudiVZ). Here, self-presentation is possible in a similar way as compared to the classic profile elements: people can decide how much and what kind of information they want to present about current aspects of their lives. People use this feature to self-disclose current activities and emotions but inevitably also to engage in self-presentation – since even a statement like "Bored with learning for the next exam" can be seen as a means to influence other people's impressions. Similarly, people can leave postings on walls of their friends and these postings are intended to be seen by the particular addressee as well as his/her friends. This can also be used for self-presentation although the topic of the messages will – according to the function of this particular channel – be more concerned with the addressee instead of the sender. However, even a statement like

"Wow! Summa cum laude! Congrats on your success" certainly also includes self-presentational aspects. Furthermore, it is increasingly popular especially on Facebook to write messages that are sent to a predefined group of friends and that appear as a "News Feed" on their starting page when they open their profile on Facebook. However, this sort of communication is similar to writing e-mails or text messages to a specific group of friends, as the sender can very flexibly decide who should receive this message. This means that – as in every conversation – self-presentation can be present in a more or less implicit or explicit way. Here, the strategies and mechanisms with regard to self-presentation will resemble those known from offline conversation or e-mail. This is due to the fact that (a) self-presentation might be a secondary goal but the primary goal is communication (compared to the [static] self-presentation on the profile where self-presentation is predominant) and (b) communication is directed to a small and well-known group that is selected according to the present communication goal. Given these different possibilities for self-presentation, it is apparent that mechanisms and strategies for self-presentation for each of the features presented above will differ, as do the possibilities for establishing privacy. In order not to risk giving an overly simplistic account of self-presentation and privacy strategies, in the remainder of the chapter we will only focus on self-presentation via profile elements (profile picture, sociodemographic information, jobs, hobbies, groups). This is due to the fact that the profile – as described above – is most closely connected to self-presentation in a pure form. Also, this form of self-presentation differs more clearly from other forms of online and offline self-presentation directed to a clearly defined group of people (e.g., when sending e-mails or talking to a group of people). Related to this, as will be discussed below, the profile is still most interesting with regard to balancing privacy concerns and self-presentation goals. Moreover, the profile (including its usage and functions) has been analyzed in greater detail than the other features, allowing us to base our analysis and conclusions on a rich body of empirical research. However, one question that must be asked is whether design and reception of profile elements are still relevant aspects of SNS usage given that numerous new features, such as status updates, are becoming increasingly popular. Here, against the background of recent results on the importance of, for example, choosing the profile photo (Haferkamp and Krämer 2010), we assume that in spite of the new and widely-used possibilities for using SNSs, the profile still plays a major role and has not lost its importance for self-presentation.

10.3   Impression Construction Online – Extending the Two-Component Model of Self-Presentation

Based on the considerations above, we will now discuss whether self-presentation via profile elements on SNSs and self-presentation offline as it has been described in the two-component model of Leary and Kowalski (1990) differ. In the present section we will first amend the model to make it applicable to the particularities of online self-presentation, and in the next section we will discuss the way in which privacy concerns are influential. Before describing the model by Leary and Kowalski (1990) in greater detail, we must first discuss general differences between offline and online self-presentation via the profile elements of social networking sites. Being able to carefully and consciously choose the presented contents, people have more control over the selected profile elements (e.g., profile picture, group names) on SNSs than they do over verbal and nonverbal cues during spontaneous face-to-face communication. Moreover, in contrast to face-to-face communication, other users' reactions and responses to users' self-presentation online are not directly observable and are difficult to anticipate. Self-presentation online is oriented toward an imagined, "non-present" audience and is inevitably linked to uncertainty.

Thus, online self-presentation differs substantially from offline self-presentation and may challenge our traditional theoretical understanding of self-presentation processes as described, for example, in the model by Leary and Kowalski (1990). The authors describe self-presentation as the result of two different processes: impression *motivation* and impression *construction*. While the former focuses on the desire to create a particular impression in other people's minds, the latter can be regarded as the process of creating this specific impression. Thus, the model considers not only the reasons why people are concerned with others' impressions, but also why people choose one specific self-presentation strategy over another. The *motivation* to conduct self-presentation (impression motivation) is impacted by (a) goal relevance of impressions referring to the desire to reach certain goals by means of one's self-presentation, (b) the adequate value of desired goals, and (c) the discrepancy between the desired and the current image. Secondly, the authors consider the specific *strategy* of creating specific images (impression construction). More precisely, Leary and Kowalski (1990) review five variables that impact a person's impression construction: (a) self-concept, (b) the person's desired identity, (c) role constraints, (d) the current or potential social image, and (e) target values.

By definition, the *self-concept* refers to an individual's perception of "self." Research has demonstrated that offline self-presentation is often consistent with how people see themselves (e.g., Jones and Pittman 1982). The tendency to portray a character different from oneself can generally be seen as an exception. We can thus conclude that the person's self-concept is the primary determinant of the images the person tries to create of him/herself.

Besides the self-concept, the *desirability of a certain identity image* accounts for a specific self-presentation strategy. According to Markus and Nurius (1986), a desirable identity image refers to what a person would like to be and it is thus not surprising that self-presentation is biased in the direction of these desired images.

However, as already discussed in self-completion theory (Gollwitzer 1986), people follow desired identities while sticking to the boundaries of reality. Here, specific *role constraints*, i.e., specific roles within the social system, such as the role of a father/mother or people's occupational status (e.g., lawyer, nurse etc.) constrain people's self-presentation insofar as these roles are related to certain expectancies within the social system. Closely related to this, Leary and Kowalski (1990) focus on a person's *current or potential social image*, i.e., how a person thinks others currently or prospectively regard him/her, as another determining variable of impression construction. Also, information that others have can constrain individual's self-presentation because the person has a low probability of creating an alternative impression (Schlenker 1980). A clear deviation from the current social image involves the risk of misunderstandings and discrepancies between other people's expectations and the current behavior. Finally, the anticipation of other people's values (*target values*) – i.e., the preferences and values of significant others (Jones 1964) – impacts people's self-presentation. That does not necessarily mean that individuals choose to form inaccurate impressions to meet the values of others, rather that they choose to select those impressions that are most likely to meet with desired reactions (Leary and Kowalski 1990).

As the model was developed to predict offline self-presentation, it must be revised with regard to self-presentation online. With regard to *impression motivation*, we argue that the individual motivation is unaffected by the specific "arena" of self-presentation. Rather it should be seen as a necessary prerequisite for engaging in self-presentation in the first place – regardless of whether this takes place on SNSs or in face-to-face communication. Indeed, as alluded to in the introduction, individuals have a strong motive to self-present since a beneficial self-presentation might lead to numerous advantages such as favorable actions and behavior by others (Leary 1995). Therefore, the presentation of one's positive aspects online to a more or less broad audience can be seen as a unique possibility to satisfy this important human need. However, with regard to *impression construction,* various parallels but also differences between online and offline strategies can be observed. Concerning the *self-concept*, a connection to self-presentation has also been confirmed for online contexts: prior research has argued that profiles display a person's true self rather than fake information (Bargh et al. 2002; Haferkamp and Krämer 2010). Gosling, Gaddis, and Vazire (2007) indicate that self-generated images of Facebook users are closely related to how they are seen in everyday life. The authors showed patterns of convergence between impressions formed of the profile owner by strangers, who were merely able to base their impression on Facebook profiles, and the corresponding self-evaluations of the users. We can thus conclude that people want to ensure that others perceive them accurately on SNSs, while their self-concept serves as a guide for creating these impressions (Baumeister and Jones 1978).

Moreover, in line with the assumption on the *desirability of a certain identity image*, Toma and Hancock (2009) examined the role of physical attractiveness in online daters' self-presentation. The authors revealed that less attractive daters enhanced the attractiveness of their profile photograph and lied more about height and age than did attractive daters. This demonstrates that just as in face-to-face settings, people also prefer attractive self-presentations in online contexts.

The third variable, *role constraints,* also impacts self-presentation online, as can be concluded from results showing that women are more concerned with the selection of their profile picture than men are (who in turn are more preoccupied with career issues on profiles; Haferkamp and Krämer 2010).

Also, the influence of the person's *current or potential social image* (how he/she thinks others currently or prospectively regard him/her) will be parallel in offline and online self-presentation. False or inaccurate impressions that are inconsistent with the current social image of a profile user can be identified by observers. For instance, users of the German social networking site StudiVZ stated that their desire to create a realistic impression is based on the apprehension that exaggerated impressions would be detected and disclosed by friends who look at their profile pages (Haferkamp and Krämer 2010). A brief comment on the wall, for instance, could lever out each kind of idealized self-presentation. Therefore, information that others have can constrain individuals' self-presentation because the person has a low probability of creating an alternative impression (Schlenker 1980). Hence, self-presentation online is likely to be guided by the expectations of acquaintances in order to avoid embarrassing discrepancies between the chosen self-presentation and the social image of a person.

While self-presentation online and offline seems to be executed in a similar way as far as the four factors mentioned above are concerned, with regard to the last determinant, *target values*, online and offline self-presentation need to be contrasted: In their model, Leary and Kowalski (1990) postulate that the target values of the audience affect people's selection of images. This does not necessarily mean that they endeavor to choose inaccurate impressions, but rather that they select those impressions that are most likely to meet with desired reactions (i.e., "packaging" [Leary 1995]). From a wealth of attributes that constitute a person, he/she will only choose those aspects that are presumably most appealing to the specific addressee in the specific situation. This type of packaging, however, is not possible with regard to self-presentation online, since there is no feature, for instance, for designing different profiles for different visitors (e.g., friends, parents, colleagues). Although users can decide which particular category is visible to a certain group of people (e.g., via Friend lists, see below), they cannot present adapted information within one profile feature. For instance, users cannot reveal to their closest friends that Lady Gaga is their favorite musician while presenting to another group of people that they like Beethoven. They have to decide whether to disclose or to conceal that Lady Gaga is their favorite singer. Consequently, online self-presentation is constrained by technological boundaries allowing only limited flexibility with regard to online self-presentation. People can compose different forms of online self-presentation based on the *quantity* of information (more or less categories are visible) but they cannot change the *quality* of information within one category. Thus, "packaging" in the sense of selecting the information that might be most appealing to a specific audience (Leary 1995) is rather unlikely. Against the background of people´s goal to leave a favorable impression, several self-presentation strategies are possible that can help in dealing with this problem: (a) They could choose to present all information about themselves (i.e., reveal that they like Lady Gaga AND Beethoven) and trust that each addressee will thereby be provided with all necessary information to build a positive attitude. (b) They could choose to (openly) display only that information that will probably appeal to all sorts of people who have access to their profile. In doing this, people would ensure that their

Table 10.1 Comparison between self-presentation offline and self-presentation online on social networking sites (SNSs) under consideration of the dimension "impression construction"

Impression construction	Self-presentation offline (Leary and Kowalski 1990)	Self-presentation online on SNSs
Self-concept	Primary determinant of the images a person tries to create of him/herself	Users tend to display true self (Bargh et al. 2002), self-concept as a guide for creating online impressions
Desirability of a certain identity image	Self-presentation is biased in the direction of desired images	People tend to present themselves in a positive manner, choosing beautiful profile pictures (Toma and Hancock 2009)
Role constraints	Inconsistent behavior can be identified in communication	Online self-presentation is related to specific offline roles in the social system (e.g., women preoccupied with physical attractiveness, Haferkamp and Krämer 2010)
Current or potential social image	Behavior should meet the expectations of the present interaction partners	Idealized self-presentation online can cause negative comments by friends who know the profile owner from face-to-face communication (Walther et al. 2008)
Target values	Self-presentation can be adapted to each interaction partner ("packaging" [Leary 1995])	"Packaging" is limited, users address a broad audience or a group of people; in order to provide relevant information for all addresses, numerous attributes would have to be presented

self-presentation is suitable for each member who has access. As will be discussed in the following, the first self-presentation strategy certainly conflicts with privacy concerns, while the latter is likely to lead to a superficial and uninformative way of self-presentation and might conflict with the goal of providing a detailed and accurate view of oneself. Table 10.1 provides an overview of the comparison between online and offline self-presentation strategies.

10.4 Informational, Psychological, and Social Privacy and Corresponding Strategies

As has already been mentioned above, self-presentational goals and strategies are likely to conflict with privacy concerns. While optimal online self-presentation might render it necessary to provide a wealth of information about oneself, this strategy is disadvantageous from a privacy point of view. In order to be able to discuss how self-presentational goals and privacy concerns might be balanced, in this section we will present an overview of different aspects of privacy as they have been described by Burgoon (1982). These will then be transferred to online privacy. We will then present different strategies for establishing and maintaining privacy and finally, we will discuss what strategies can be used to achieve a compromise between self-presentation goals and privacy concerns.

10.4.1   Types of Privacy

In an influential paper, Burgoon (1982) distinguished different types of privacy in communication contexts: informational, physical, psychological, and social privacy. While physical privacy is not easily applicable to online communication, the other types relate nicely to specific privacy risks that can be encountered in online settings. For example, by giving factual information such as names and addresses, users' "*informational privacy*," which Burgoon (1982) defined in the context of face-to-face communication as the right to decide to what extent factual data about oneself is released to others, is inevitably threatened. Besides factual information, users also disclose information about their emotional states, thoughts, and preferences when, for instance, they publish status updates or leave comments on the wall of other users' profiles. These private cognitive inputs and outputs only pertain to the individual and are thus part of a person's "*psychological privacy*," defined by Burgoon (1982) as the ability to control affective and cognitive inputs and outputs. However, by expressing them on online profiles, they become public information and can be perceived by other users. Finally, each communication episode between the profile owner and another user displayed on the News Feed is distributed within the Facebook universe. Even friends of users with whom the profile owner is connected can follow this private communication on the News Feed even though they have never met the persons concerned in real life. This public access to the social interactions of social network users is closely connected to "*social privacy*," defined by Burgoon (1982) as the ability to withdraw from social intercourse, for example, to achieve greater intimacy among a selected group of communication partners.

10.4.2   Privacy Strategies

The most obvious privacy strategy for maintaining informational, psychological, and social privacy is certainly to choose to not make the profile and all of its contents publicly available, and to limit the number of people that are granted access by only accepting well-known people as "friends" (for an overview of the strategies, see Table 10.2). However, with regard to self-presentation goals and the related goal of building up social capital (in this case by leaving a favorable impression on strangers in order to facilitate future interactions), this strategy can be seen as disadvantageous. Another, less rigorous way is to employ the so-called Friend list – a technological feature that allows users to organize observers of their online profile into lists. By means of these lists, profile users can decide which kind

Table 10.2 Overview on privacy strategies and corresponding consequences for self-presentation

Privacy strategy	Consequences for self-presentation goal
Invite only a limited number of (well-known) people as friends	Hinders making a favorable impression on potentially interested and interesting strangers
Use Friend list feature to exclude a number of "friends" from privacy-relevant aspects of profile	A number of people do not get any information on specific aspects
Permit access by all friends (and even strangers) to all profile elements but only post superficial, not privacy-relevant information	Information that might be appealing to one group but not to the other is not presented and cannot be employed to make a favorable impression

of profile feature is revealed to a certain audience group and which information stays hidden. Although it is not possible to change the content within one feature, users can decide which piece of information is shown to a specific group of persons. This, for instance, allows users to selectively open more of their profile (e.g., profile pictures, personal information, likes, tastes) to the people closest to them while hiding this private information from rather "official" or loose contacts. By customizing each setting, users can decide which category of information (e.g., profile picture, personal information, status updates) can be perceived by the specific audience. With this feature, a user can differentiate, for example, between acquaintances/strangers (people the user has never met or has met only once in everyday life), friends (i.e., persons the user is also friends with in everyday life), family members (i.e., mother/father/brother/sister), and official contacts (i.e., important occupational contacts such as the user's employer). By employing the Friend list feature, the user might ensure informational, psychological, and social privacy with regard to strangers/acquaintances, psychological, and social privacy with regard to official contacts, as well as psychological privacy with regard to family members. For actual friends probably the least restrictions are necessary. The disadvantage of the Friend list strategy is that a number of people do not get any information about specific aspects of the user. In terms of self-presentation, this could be similarly disadvantageous to the strategy to completely exclude people. A different strategy can be to grant access to information to a large number of people but to provide only superficial and therefore not privacy-relevant information. This complies with one of the self-presentational strategies depicted above in that only information that is compatible with mainstream attributes is displayed. The downside of this, however, is that the user is not able to present any specific information even though it might be appealing to some of the receivers.

10.4.3 Potential Strategies to Solve the Conflict

The previous analyses show that from a self-presentational perspective, it would be best to provide a wealth of information on the SNS profile, which is accessible to a large number of people, while effective privacy strategies all lead to the obstruction of exactly this. In order to solve the conflict, every user has two options: (a) to decide whether self-presentational goals or privacy concerns are more important to him/her personally and to behave accordingly, or (b) to find new strategies that enable him/her to self-present and maintain privacy at the same time. With regard to the first aspect, the individual decision about what to do will be related to the strength of self-presentation motives on the one hand and privacy concerns on the other. Indeed, it has been shown that users with higher privacy concerns conceal more of their profile (Utz and Krämer 2009). However, even when people have high privacy concerns, this does not necessarily mean that they have a low self-presentation motive. In terms of the extended model of self-presentation by Leary and Kowalski (1990), we would state that it is not the impression motivation that is influenced by privacy concerns but the impression construction. This means that even people with high privacy concerns might still want to find a way to convey a specific image even though they are not willing to display private details and actual facts. This conflict – in our view – has already led to the development of at least one new strategy to self-present in a way that is not as detrimental to privacy as the usage of common aspects of the profile: in order to present attitudes, attributes, and preferences, people become members of a group that is then displayed on their profile. Here, instead of communicating on their profile that they have bought a car or even choosing a profile picture with them in front of it, people might simply become a member in the group "I love my car!" In fact, empirical findings have confirmed that group membership is first and foremost used as a means of self-presentation rather than a possibility to communicate with others (Haferkamp and Krämer 2009).

10.5   Conclusions Regarding the Balance Between Privacy and Impression Construction on SNSs

Based on the comparison of online and offline self-presentation, we concluded that a strategy like packaging, in terms of selecting specific information for a specific audience, is not possible when using the profile elements of SNSs. Whereas in real-life situations self-presentation only includes giving information to a selected, perceptible audience, self-presentation online via the profile elements of SNSs is often directed to a broad and sometimes imperceptible audience. Therefore, the two-component model created by Leary and Kowalski (1990) has to be extended for online self-presentation: in contrast to face-to-face contexts, the target values, which are one factor in impression construction, can only be considered when (a) the information given on the person includes a number of different attributes so that it might be appealing to different audiences or (b) by including no specific information at all in order to not contradict any values of any potential recipient.

Given the fact that people have a strong motive to self-present relevant aspects of themselves in order to leave favorable impressions, a reasonable strategy seems to be to provide a wealth of information (except maybe extreme attributes). This strategy, however, conflicts with privacy strategies that are derived from privacy concerns regarding informational, psychological, or social privacy. Thus, the model created by Leary and Kowalski (1990) requires further amendments to be able to account for online contexts: we argue that privacy concerns play a particularly important role in online self-presentation and should be understood as a potential inhibitor that may impact users' impression construction on SNSs and may influence the form of self-presentation that is eventually chosen (see Fig. 10.1).

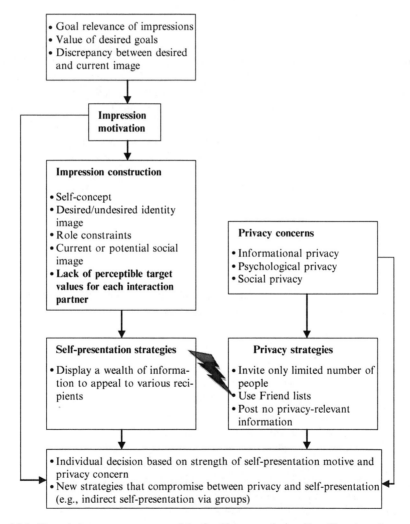

Fig. 10.1 Extended two-component model of self-presentation online (Based on Leary and Kowalski 1990)

The individual decision to disclose more or less information is thus dependent on the relative strength of the impression motivation on the one hand and privacy concerns on the other. Interestingly, another possibility is to engage in self-presentation that is not based on private facts and details but indirectly alludes to important aspects of one's life: here, the display of group memberships has become increasingly popular, allowing an implicit presentation of interests and attributes. This is in line with the creative potential of online users that Walther (1996) described for earlier aspects of computer-mediated communication.

However, our theoretical conceptualization of online self-presentation requires empirical investigations that determine how the factors mentioned combine to affect self-presentational choices. So far, it remains unclear how the factors have to be weighted and whether the eventual decision depends on people's personality and individual motives or whether there are specific situations in which one variable is more salient than the other. Moreover, the question of whether our model can also be applied to Social Web applications other than social networking sites is still unanswered. As mentioned above, the current conceptualization is only valid for applications in which a broad audience is addressed and it is not valid, for example, when presenting oneself in online settings that allow for one-to-one settings as in instant messaging chats (or message services within SNSs). We conceptualized our ideas based on the features of SNSs such as Facebook and more specifically on the profile elements. However, other applications, such as microblogging systems like Twitter (see Schmidt, this issue), demand other data and are characterized by different features and communication opportunities. In conclusion, we believe that our model has provided a first exploratory basis for a theoretical account of self-presentation online under consideration of users' privacy concerns. It should provide a first framework for future research regarding online self-presentation via SNSs.

References

Archer JL (1980) Self-disclosure. In: Wegner D, Vallacher R (eds) The self in social psychology. Oxford University, London, pp 183–204

Bargh JA, McKenna KYA, Fitzsimons GM (2002) Can you see the real me? Activation and expression of the "true self" on the internet. J Soc Issues 58(1):33–48

Barnes SB (2006) A privacy paradox: social networking in the United States. First Monday 11. www.firstmonday.org/issues/-issue11_9/barnes/index.html. Accessed 8 Aug 2008

Baumeister RF, Jones EE (1978) When self-presentation is constrained by the target's prior knowledge: consistency and compensation. J Personal Soc Psychol 36:608–618

boyd dm, Ellison NB (2007) Social network sites: definition, history, and scholarship. J Comput Mediat Commun 13(1):210–230

Burgoon JK (1982) Privacy and communication. In: Burgoon M (ed) Communication yearbook 6. Sage, Beverly Hills, pp 206–249

Ellison N, Heino R, Gibbs J (2006) Managing impressions online: self-presentation processes in the online dating environment. J Comput Mediat Commun 11(2):415–441

Goffman E (1959) The presentation of self in everyday life. Double Day, Garden City

Gollwitzer PM (1986) Striving for specific identities: the social reality of self-symbolizing. In: Baumeister R (ed) Public self and private self. Springer, New York, pp 143–159

Gosling SD, Gaddis S, Vazire S (2007) Personality impressions based on facebook profiles. Paper presented at the international conference on weblogs and social media 2007, Boulder. http:// www.icwsm.-org/papers/3-Gosling-Gaddis-Vazire.pdf. Accessed 2 Mar 2008

Haferkamp N, Krämer NC (2009) When I was your age, Pluto was a planet": Impression Management and Need to belong as motives for joining groups on social networking sites. Paper presented at the annual meeting of ICA 2009 (International Communication Association), Chicago

Haferkamp N, Krämer NC (2010) Creating a digital self: impression management and impression formation on social networking sites. In: Drotner K, Schrøder KC (eds) Digital content creation: creativity, competence, critique. Peter Lang, New York, pp 129–149

Joinson AN (2001) Self-disclosure in computer-mediated communication: the role of self-awareness and visual anonymity. Eur J Soc Psychol 31:177–192

Jones EE (1964) Ingratiation. Appleton, New York

Jones EE, Pittman TS (1982) Toward a general theory of strategic self-presentation. In: Suls J (ed) Psychological perspectives on the self. Erlbaum, Hillsdale, pp 231–262

Leary MR (1995) Self presentation: impression management and interpersonal behavior. Brown & Benchmark, Madison

Leary MR, Kowalski RM (1990) Impression management: a literature review and two-component model. Psychol Bull 107:34–47

Lenhart A, Madden M (2007) Teens, privacy & online social networks. Pew internet & American life project 2007. www.pewinternet.org/pdfs/PIP_Teens_Privacy_SNS_Report_Final.pdf. Accessed 8 Aug 2008

Lewis K, Kaufman J, Christakis N (2008) The taste for privacy: an analysis of college student privacy settings in an online social network. J Comput Mediat Commun 14:79–100

Liu H (2007) Social network profiles as taste performances. J Comput-Mediat Commun 13(1). http://jcmc.indi-ana.edu/vol13/issue1/liu.html. Accessed 10 May 2007

Liu H, Maes PM, Davenport G (2006) Unraveling the taste fabric of social networks. Int J Semantic Web Inf Syst 2(1):42–71

Livingstone S (2008) Taking risky opportunities in youthful content creation: teenagers' use of social networking sites for intimacy, privacy and self-expression. New Media Soc 10:339–411

Markus H, Nurius P (1986) Possible selves. Am Psychol 41:954–969

Mehdizadeh S (2010) Self-presentation 2.0: narcissism and self-esteem on Facebook. Cyberpsychol Behav Soc Netw 13(4):357–364

Reinecke L, Trepte S (2008) Privatsphäre 2.0: Konzepte von Privatheit, Intimsphäre und Werten im Umgang mit "user-generated-content" (Concepts of privacy, intimacy, and values with regard to "user-generated-content"). In: Zerfaß A, Welker M, Schmidt J (eds) Kommunikation, Partizipation und Wirkungen im Social Web. (Communication, participation, and effects in the social web) Band 1: Grundlagen und Methoden: Von der Gesellschaft zum Individuum. Halem Verlag, Köln, pp 205–228

Reingold H (1993) The virtual community. Addison-Wesley, New York

Schlenker BR (1980) Impression management: the self-concept, social identity, and interpersonal relations. Brooks/Cole, Monterey

Schneider DJ (1981) Tactical self-presentations: toward a broader conception. In: Tedeschi JT (ed) Impression management theory and social psychological research. Academic, New York, pp 23–40

Tidwell LS, Walther JB (2002) Computer-mediated communication effects on disclosure, impressions, and interpersonal evaluations. Getting to know one another a bit at a time. Hum Commun Res 28(3):317–348

Toma CL, Hancock J (2009) Self-presentation in online dating profiles: the role of physical attractiveness. Paper presented at the annual meeting of the international communication association, Chicago

Utz S, Krämer NC (2009) The privacy paradox on social network sites revisited: the role of individual characteristics and group norms. J Psychosoc Res Cyberspace. http://www. cyberpsychology.eu/view-.php?cisloclanku=2009111001. Accessed 3 Mar 2010

Walther JB (1996) Computer-mediated communication: impersonal, interpersonal, and hyperpersonal interaction. Commun Res 23:3–43

Walther JB, Van der Heide B, Kim SY, Westerman D, Tong ST (2008) The role of friends' appearance and behavior and evaluations of individuals on Facebook: are we known by the company we keep? Hum Commun Res 34:28–49

Chapter 11
The Uses of Privacy Online: Trading a Loss of Privacy for Social Web Gratifications?

Monika Taddicken and Cornelia Jers

11.1 Introduction

According to Etzioni (1999), the first step in analyzing privacy is to determine whether or not there is a problem. Given the easy availability of private information on the Internet and the seemingly great readiness of Social Web users to disclose personal data, it would appear that the protection of privacy is not a major problem for users. However, empirical evidence demonstrates that Social Web users are in fact quite concerned about their privacy (Barnes 2006; Tufekci 2008; Debatin et al. 2009).

Nevertheless, the individual need for privacy seems to have only little influence on online behavior. This discrepancy between privacy concerns and actual privacy behavior is often referred to as the "privacy paradox" (Barnes 2006; Awad and Krishnan 2006; Norberg et al. 2007). Apparently, extensive concern about the safety of one's private data does not necessarily correspond to privacy-related behaviors such as reducing the accessibility of one's Social Web profile, changing the privacy settings if possible (Acquisti and Gross 2006; Tufekci 2008; boyd and Hargittai 2010), or limiting self-disclosure (Debatin et al. 2009).

The reasons for this are manifold. On the one hand, they include a lack of problem awareness or media competence, such as ignorance of privacy settings and uncertainty about the audience (Debatin et al. 2009; boyd and Hargittai 2010; Acquisti and Gross 2006). On the other hand, it can be assumed that Social Web use offers advantages and gratifications that increase in direct proportion to the degree of self-disclosure (see also the chapter by Peter and Valkenburg in this

M. Taddicken (✉)
University of Hamburg, Hamburg, Germany
e-mail: monika.taddicken@uni-hamburg.de

C. Jers
University of Hohenheim, Stuttgart, Germany

S. Trepte and L. Reinecke (eds.), *Privacy Online*,
DOI 10.1007/978-3-642-21521-6_11, © Springer-Verlag Berlin Heidelberg 2011

volume). Lampe et al. (2007) confirm that the quantity of disclosed information in social networking sites (SNS) is linked to the degree of networking (see also the chapter by Ellison et al. in this volume). Evidently, the disclosure of private information is rewarded with social gratifications.

A suitable approach to study the users' benefits of social media is the uses and gratifications approach. It is widely used in communication science and addresses processes of media use and effects from the users' perspective as well as the question of why people use specific media products and with which gratifications (Rubin 2009). With the help of this approach, it is possible to contrast the costs and benefits of self-disclosure on the Social Web. This allows a detailed focus on the gratifications of Social Web use and the relation between self-disclosure, need for privacy, and these gratifications.

11.2 Social Web Use Versus Privacy: A Users' Dilemma?

The Social Web can be characterized as an endless online pool of easily available private information. Apparently, Social Web users are highly willing to disclose personal data on the Internet and to relinquish control over the amount of contact with others (Pedersen 1997). From a uses and gratifications perspective, this chapter tries to shed light on the aforementioned privacy paradox, and to address the question of why people are concerned about the safety of their personal data but, at the same time, disclose a high amount of these on the Social Web. To do so, it is necessary to theoretically explicate the concepts of self-disclosure and privacy before they can be adapted to the context of the Social Web.

Self-disclosure is an integral component of every social interaction and can be described as "any message about the self that a person communicates to another" (Wheeless and Grotz 1976, p. 338). Self-disclosure, therefore, is a part of the communication process and has to be considered in relation to specific individuals, namely the communication partners (Wheeless 1976). In general, self-disclosure is the basic precondition for every social relationship since it is part of every communication; the passing on of information about oneself, one's thoughts, and one's feelings is necessary to create social proximity (Altman and Taylor 1973; Laurenceau et al. 1998). This means that self-disclosure and the perception of privacy are closely related. The regulation of privacy is not to be understood as a process of retreat, nor is an optimum degree of privacy equal to the highest possible control over one's personal information. Rather, individuals strive for different degrees of self-disclosure in different situations. Thus, both the interactional perspective of privacy and its changeable nature must be highlighted (Newell 1995, p. 100).

Privacy can be defined in many different ways. Basically, it can be seen as "the right to be let alone" (Warren and Brandeis 1890). Despite this general definition, a variety of dimensions and perspectives of privacy have been analyzed by researchers of different scientific perspectives (for an overview see Newell

1995). Although various attempts have been made to create a synthesis of the existing approaches to defining privacy (e.g., Parent 1983; Schoeman 1984; Burgoon et al. 1989; Newell 1995), a unified single account has yet to emerge (Paine et al. 2006). Among the most notable of these existing approaches are the works by Westin (1967) and Altman (1975, 1977). Both researchers focus on control and regulation of access to private information. According to Westin, privacy is "the right to prevent the disclosure of personal information to others" (1967, p. 7). The desire to keep personal information out of the hands of others is central to this concept of privacy. Altman, on the other hand, defines privacy as a "selective control of access to the self or to one's group" (1975, p. 18). According to Altman, the regulation of privacy is a dynamic process of optimization that is influenced by two basic psychological needs: on the one hand, the need to preserve one's privacy and control access to and distribution of personal information, and on the other hand, the need to interact socially and, therefore, to disclose personal information. Accordingly, privacy is perceived as being at its optimum when both needs can be united and the desired and actually achieved levels of privacy correspond (Altman 1975).

Following these arguments, privacy does not mean removing oneself from the presence of others. Rather, different types of privacy have been identified. Different perspectives can be used for a categorization of these types of privacy. For this chapter, it is most important to focus on the individual and interactional perspective. This means that we should highlight the fact that people prefer privacy at some times and not at others. Westin (1967) proposed different types of privacy – solitude, anonymity, reserve, and intimacy – which we will briefly introduce here. We will then connect them to the use of Social Web applications. A summary of the results of our analysis concerning the interrelations of privacy types, the use of the Social Web, and the resulting gratifications and privacy risks are presented in Table 11.1, which may also serve as an advanced organizer for the rest of this chapter. In the following section, we will review and transfer the privacy types proposed by Westin (1967) and discuss their relevance for the Social Web.

Solitude refers to the condition of being alone. This is what lay persons most often define as privacy (for a presentation of literary and historical mentions of privacy, see Hixson 1987). Westin (1967) states that solitude is the most complete state of privacy that individuals can achieve. In this state, the individual is alone and unobserved. That means that solitude refers to a situation where other people cannot see or hear what the individual is doing (Pedersen 1997). Mostly, solitude is regarded as a condition that is either desirable or neutral (Newell 1995).

In the Social Web, solitude is rather uncommon since Social Web applications usually focus on social interactions. However, solitude can be achieved by the individual's use of applications just for themselves. An example of this might be a blog used as a personal diary for (self-) therapeutic reasons and which is inaccessible to an external party. However, in most cases, Internet providers have access to the personal data. Hence, the state of solitude is perceived and not actually given.

Anonymity is defined as a type of privacy that occurs when it is possible to move around in public without being recognized or without being the subject of attention

Table 11.1 Interrelations between privacy types (Westin 1967), Social Web use, self-disclosure, and Social Web gratifications

Type of privacy	Solitude	Anonymity	Reserve	Intimacy
Definition	Condition of being alone and unobserved, other people cannot see or hear what the individual is doing	Condition of moving around in public without being recognized or without being the subject of attention	Controlling of verbal disclosure of personal information to others	Condition of being alone with family or friends to the exclusion of other people to increase interaction
Typical situations and examples in the social web	The use of social web applications purely for personal purposes. Examples: Running a blog as a personal diary; watching videos on YouTube alone	Consuming or participating in the Social Web without providing one's real name. Examples: Taking part in Internet forums using a pseudonym or a nickname, commenting on videos or texts but concealing one's real name	An active and conscious information and impression management is typical for the social web, e.g., within a profile of an SNS. Reciprocal self-disclosure that may happen more or less consciously is typical as well, such as discussions in forums	Intimacy can be found in the social web by using applications that limit access to authorized users. Examples: Running a traveler blog for family and friends; using in-group communication in SNSs for interacting with others
Potential privacy problems	Providers usually have access to the personal data. Hence, the state of solitude is only perceived subjectively and not actually given	Social Web providers might use technical mechanisms to identify their users. The online communication may lead to a higher level of perceived anonymity and to an "online disinhibition effect"	Problem of an unknown and heterogeneous audience that can easily differ from the desired or expected audience. People with different relationships to the audience (e.g., friends, relatives, colleagues): Possibility of "re-contextualization effects" regarding self-disclosed information	Problems occur when the level of intimacy is lower than expected. Users expect to be "intimate" with specific other users and to interact only with them, but in fact other users are often able to read this information as well (e.g., intended audience forwards information to unintended audience)
Gratifications	Affective and cognitive gratifications through consuming and participating use forms without disclosing one's identity Examples: Informing people through writing wiki articles; seeking guidance by reading blogs; having fun by watching YouTube videos	Affective and cognitive gratifications through consuming and participating without disclosing one's identity Personal integrative gratifications through being able to try things out in an anonymous environment with an unknown audience. Examples: Running an anonymous blog about personal experiences and feelings; using nicknames and avatars while using Social Web services	Personal integrative needs can be satisfied by an active impression management. Additionally, cognitive gratifications can be obtained through consciously presenting thoughts and experiences to other users Examples: Identity building by presenting information about oneself on an SNS profile; gaining status through presenting videos on YouTube	Intimacy in the Social Web can facilitate social integrative gratifications. The Social Web may provide even better conditions for intimacy for some people than the offline environment, so that these social integrative needs can be served even better Examples: Keeping in touch with other people through SNSs; sharing one's feelings with others in forums

(Westin 1967). Anonymity can be sought by going unnoticed in a crowd of strangers (Pedersen 1997). Gavison (1984) points out that an individual loses privacy when becoming the object of attention and that this is true whether the attention is conscious and purposeful or inadvertent. Attention is a primary way of gathering information that leads to a loss of anonymity.

In the Social Web, anonymity can be found easily. Lurking (i.e., reading others' contents, such as profiles or discussions) is a good example of this and a wide-spread behavior in the Social Web. In addition, in many Social Web applications, it is possible to become a member of a community without providing one's real name (e.g., by adopting a fake user name). In general, prior research has reported that Internet users perceive a high level of anonymity online (Joinson 2001; Tidwell and Walther 2002). The reasons for this are the limited number of communication channels and, consequently, a reduced perceived presence of other users (Taddicken 2008). The Reduced Social Context Cues Approach (Sproull and Kiesler 1986, 1991) focuses on the limitation of information about communication partners and the actual situation framing the communication. Sproull and Kiesler state: "When social context cues are weak, people's feelings of anonymity tend to produce relatively self-centered and unregulated behavior" (1986, p. 1495). In other words, the communication environment of the Internet has at least two different kinds of impact on its users: Firstly, online communication may influence the state of self-awareness meaning the inward focus on thoughts, feelings, and motives (Duval and Wicklund 1972). Matheson and Zanna (1989) found indeed that online communication increases the state of private self-awareness. Secondly, online communication influences self-disclosure behavior. Suler (2004) found that people "loosen up, feel less restrained, and express themselves more openly" (p. 321) when communicating online and suggested framing this behavior as an "online disinhibition effect".

The possibility of adapting the idea of the Internet as a "limited communication mode" (Taddicken 2008) to the Social Web context has yet to be analyzed. The reduction of social context cues seems to be valid for Social Web applications that provide no detailed user profiles, such as Internet forums, chats, and video platforms. However, a lot of context information about SNS users (profiles, pinboards, photos, etc.) is actually available, even though it is not always directly integrated into the specific communication processes. Also, Social Web providers can use technical mechanisms to identify their users if desired (e.g., IP addresses, log file analyses).

Reserve is a type of privacy that can be achieved in the interaction process. It involves the establishment of psychological barriers against intrusion. Pastalan (1975) defines reserve as the most subtle form of privacy because of its reciprocal nature and the willing discretion of significant others. Pedersen (1997) refers to it as the controlling of the verbal disclosure of personal information to others, especially to strangers.

In the Social Web, it is possible for users to manage information provided consciously with regard to their particular target audience, for example, the details of an SNS profile. There is a wide range of literature on impression management in

SNSs (e.g., Tidwell and Walther 2002; Ellison et al. 2006; Krämer and Winter 2008; see also Haferkamp and Krämer in this volume). In addition to this information, personal details are disclosed during the communication process, such as discussions in Internet forums or dialogs in chats. This reciprocal self-disclosure might occur more or less consciously – as is the case in face to face communication as well.

The process of controlling verbal self-disclosure in the Social Web is affected by the problem of the unknown and heterogeneous audience. Social Web users might often be unaware of who actually reads the information revealed as the audience is temporarily and spatially separated. The desired public of the self-disclosure might differ from the expected audience, which in turn does not have to be identical to the audience reached. But even within the intended public, there are typically people to whom the self-disclosers have different social relations, such as friends, relatives, acquaintances, and colleagues. Regarding the amount, the tone, and the style of the self-disclosed information, this might cause serious consequences for users: information that is suitable to be revealed to close friends, such as party pictures, might be unsuitable for other people, such as parents or (potential) employers. Self-disclosed information can also be redistributed and transferred to other contexts by third parties, for example, by providers that use private information for advertising purposes or even by friends who forward photographs. Consequently, these "re-contextualization effects" may pose a serious threat to the privacy facet of reserve in the Social Web.

Intimacy is another type of privacy that is related to the presence of others. The need for intimacy is described as the need to be alone with family or friends to the exclusion of other people. The intent is to reduce interaction with outsiders while increasing in-group interaction (Pedersen 1997). Westin (1967) defines intimacy as related to an individual's or group's desire to promote close personal relationships. Fried (1984) notes that intimate relationships require the voluntary relinquishment of parts of one's inner self. Pastalan (1975) describes intimacy as a basic need for human contact. According to Gerstein (1984), intimacy includes a certain lack of self-observation. Therefore, Gerstein states that the highest level of invasion is achieved when individuals are observed in an intimate relationship in which they did not intend to be observed at all, even by themselves (Gerstein 1984).

In the Social Web, users may achieve intimacy by limiting access to the information they post online. An example would be a personal blog a traveler runs for his or her family and friends. Furthermore, the Social Web provides the opportunity to have intimate interactions with other users known only online. Separate chat rooms or in-group communication on SNSs are examples of this. However, a problem occurs when the level of intimacy is lower than expected, for example, when people reveal personal information because they are unaware that others have not been excluded. As Gerstein (1984) suggests that intimacy includes a certain lack of self-observation and that the observation of self-disclosure in intimate situations has to be evaluated as the highest level of invasion, this highlights one of the main risks of privacy in the Social Web: users expect to be "alone" with specific other users and to interact only with them, but other users and the providers are often able to read this information as well (e.g., on pinboards).

As demonstrated above, all four privacy types identified by Westin (1967) show significant relations to the use of the Social Web. However, a comprehensive understanding of the privacy-related consequence of Social Web use can only be gained by a careful analysis of the resulting risks and benefits. The wide-ranging discussions on privacy are often dominated by the general idea that privacy is beneficial and that people have a legally protected right to privacy (Newell 1994). At the same time, however, self-disclosure is a behavior that decreases privacy but also promises benefits and gratifications. This seems to be particularly true for Social Web use, where people benefit from presenting information about themselves by gaining social interactions with other users. The uses and gratifications approach (Katz et al. 1974) seems to be a helpful framework for drawing a detailed picture of the benefits of the Social Web. In the following paragraph, we will analyze the gratifications of Social Web use and their relation to self-disclosure and privacy on the basis of this approach.

11.3 Uses and Gratifications in the Social Web

The uses and gratifications approach emphasizes the role of the audience in the process of media use by asking the question "What do people do with the media?" (Katz and Foulkes 1962, p. 378). Consequently, recipients are seen as variably active participants in the process of media use and its effects. Aside from the sociodemographic variables of the audience, psychological and social elements play an important role for understanding this process (Rubin 2009). More specifically, the focus is on motives and needs of the audience, or gratifications as fulfilled needs to explain media choice and behavior. Research grounded in the uses and gratifications approach puts strong emphasis on the role of the individual recipient and the differences between users and their decisions. Thus, the uses and gratifications approach deals with social and psychological origins of needs that generate expectations of the mass media or other sources. These expectations, in turn, lead to differential patterns of media exposure, resulting in need gratifications or other – mostly unintended – consequences (Katz et al. 1974).

The framework of uses and gratifications rests on five assumptions (Rubin 2009; Palmgreen et al. 1985). *Firstly*, it is assumed that when people use media, it is with a clear goal, purpose, and motivation. *Secondly*, people initiate the selection and use of media according to their needs and desires and are variably active communicators in this process. *Thirdly*, social and psychological factors influence, filter, and mediate communication behavior. Users' predispositions, social environment, and interpersonal interactions shape their expectations about the media. *Fourthly*, media compete with other (non-medial) sources of need satisfaction that are considered functional alternatives. *Fifthly*, people are usually more influential in the process of media use than the media itself. Although the uses and gratifications approach quickly became popular and has been applied broadly within communication research, some scholars have criticized the approach and its assumptions. In particular, the lack of clarity of central constructs such as motives and gratifications, the treatment of the audience as being too active, and rational and methodological problems have been criticized (Elliott 1974; Swanson 1977; Lin 1996). Most criticism has been addressed in a variety of studies in the subsequent years. In spite of these advances, parts of the criticism remain.

The uses and gratifications approach was first established in the context of traditional mass media, with studies dealing predominantly with the use of radio and television (e.g., Herzog 1944; Rubin 1979). Nonetheless, the uses and gratifications approach can be seen as especially suitable for studying new media environments because of its general idea of an active audience and its user-centric perspective (Ruggerio 2000; Newhagen and Rafaeli 1996; Rubin 2002).

Several recent studies have dealt with gratifications of Social Web use. Across these studies, four dimensions of needs that can be satisfied by the use of the Social Web became apparent: *cognitive needs*, *affective needs*, *social integrative needs*, and *personal integrative needs* (Leung 2009). It has to be highlighted that these four dimensions are not fully discriminatory but may overlap. The first dimension, *cognitive needs* or *information needs*, is comparable to those needs or gratifications related to the use of traditional mass media. Researchers found that people use blogs to seek guidance (Lee 2006), read wikis in order to learn new things (Rafaeli and Ariel 2008), or watch videos in the Social Web for information seeking (Haridakis and Hanson 2009). In addition to passive consumption, participating or producing forms of use can also fulfill cognitive needs such as influencing public opinion or informing other people through political blogging (Ekdale et al. 2010; Shao 2008). Furthermore, exercising one's knowledge, increasing skills and abilities, and intellectual challenge were identified as chief gratifications of the use of wikis (Nov 2007; Rafaeli and Ariel 2008).

The second dimension can be referred to as *affective needs* or *entertainment needs*. Users experience fun, pleasure, and entertainment when watching or reading the Social Web. Also, sharing videos or other content – i.e., participating – promises the satisfaction of entertainment needs for Social Web users through co-viewing. Furthermore, the production of content in wikis or other applications is used as a means of having fun and passing time (Nov 2007; Rafaeli and Ariel 2008; Haridakis and Hanson 2009).

Social integrative needs are the third important dimension in Social Web gratifications. By using the Social Web in a passive way, social gratifications can be gained through watching friends' entries on SNSs or reading blogs of acquaintances (Ancu and Cozma 2009). Social integrative needs are even more important for participating and producing in the Social Web. This implies sharing one's views, thoughts, and feelings with others, connecting with like-minded people, or communicating with friends and family (Leung 2009; Liu et al. 2007; boyd and Ellison 2008). These needs are particularly well fulfilled by the use of SNSs, but users who write blogs, contribute to wikis, or share videos with others on YouTube also emphasize the importance of social integrative needs. More specifically, the formation of communities, social engagement, and support are named as gratifications by these users (Nardi et al. 2004; Rafaeli and Ariel 2008; Haridakis and Hanson 2009).

The last dimension encompasses *personal integrative needs* or *recognition needs*. In this dimension, aspects such as identity formation and impression management are included – gratifications that are typically linked with Social Web use (boyd 2007; Leung 2009). People try to gain respect and support through active Social Web use, aim to build up their confidence, and like to publicize their experiences (Leung 2009). Producing content in the Social Web is a way of expressing one's feelings and emotions and articulating ideas through writing. In the Social Web, it is possible to experiment in a way that is often more difficult in the offline environment (Nardi et al. 2004; Liu et al. 2007). Additionally, users document their lives in the Social Web and even try to promote their careers and increase their social status (Nov 2007). All of these personal integrative needs are closely related to participating or producing forms of Social Web use. Consuming forms of use, in contrast to this, do not play an important role here.

11.4   Social Web Gratifications and Their Relation to Privacy and Self-Disclosure

As demonstrated above, four relevant need dimensions may be fulfilled by the use of various Social Web applications at different levels of activity. The Social Web partly serves the same functions for the users that traditional media do, such as information and entertainment. On the other hand, the Social Web competes with interpersonal communication with regard to social and personal integrative needs. Regarding privacy issues, it is especially interesting to analyze the extent to which these gratifications are related to self-disclosure.

Consuming forms of Social Web use that do not require any form of self-disclosure are possible with regard to *cognitive needs*. On the one hand, gratifications in this field partly resemble gratifications of using traditional media such as seeking guidance or information. Here, users can take a very passive role that does not reduce any form of privacy. On the other hand, obtaining gratifications such as influencing public opinion or informing people demands some form of self-disclosure. This does not necessarily include the disclosure of one's real name, but, relating to reserve, a certain amount of sharing personal information with others is required. Often, users do not disclose their real names when satisfying information needs through blogging or writing wiki articles, but they do disclose their thoughts and opinions even to strangers to inform these other people and contribute to public discourse.

Only some restrictions to privacy can be expected when looking at *affective needs* of the Social Web. Again, consuming forms of use such as watching videos or reading articles do not necessarily involve any form of self-disclosure. The feeling of anonymity in the Social Web can even improve the opportunity to have fun by consuming content. On the other hand, pleasure or fun can be gratifications that could also be achieved by taking part in the Social Web actively through writing articles or by communicating with other users. Thus, the use of SNSs for entertainment reasons in particular often includes disclosing various amounts of personal information.

Self-disclosure plays an even more important role in fulfilling *social integrative needs*. Exchanging opinions with like-minded people in Internet forums, via blogs, or sharing knowledge with others on wikis affects the privacy type reserve. It is often possible to protect and maintain anonymity despite satisfying these kinds of social integrative needs. On the other hand, gratifications such as communicating with family and friends or keeping in touch with acquaintances inevitably include the self-disclosure of personal information. It is common to use real names on SNSs and many bloggers disclose their identity online. Also, personal feelings, thoughts, and experiences are shared with other users to satisfy social integrative needs. Beside the aspect of reserve, the privacy type intimacy with friends and family is important in this context: although the Social Web allows situations where intimacy with friends or family members can be established through limited access, member registration, etc., the feeling of being alone with other people in the Social Web is often illusive. When somebody writes personal messages to friends on pinboards of SNSs, the friends of both communication partners – often 200 or 300 people – are usually able to follow this interaction. Hence, intimacy with family and friends is in fact decreased with the relocation of a part of the conversation into the Social Web. To summarize, satisfying social integrative needs normally includes a much higher degree of self-disclosure than the aforementioned two gratifications: it is not possible to receive social gratifications without disclosing any form of personal information such as thoughts, feelings, and experiences.

Personal integrative needs are predominantly related to the user's self and identity. Reserve plays an important role in the context of personal integrative needs because it is especially important in controlling the amount and type of information disclosed in the context of forming one's identity. Additionally, anonymity is often a necessary precondition for experiencing and testing one's identity and personality. The impression of being anonymous allows users to feel free to do and try things that finally lead to identity formation, e.g., by blogging about personal feelings and experiences using a pseudonym. In contrast, status and confidence aspects of personal integrative needs require more self-disclosure and sometimes even the disclosure of one's real name if a transfer into the offline world is desired.

We can therefore conclude that Social Web gratifications differ in their relation to privacy issues. Different forms of use correspond to different levels of self-disclosure: while consuming Social Web applications without active participation does usually not demand a disclosure of information, active participation does at least require the disclosure of some experiences and thoughts, sometimes also name and e-mail address. The highest impact on privacy can be expected for producing forms of use.

11.5 Discussion and Outlook

To answer the question of whether or not Social Web gratifications are always accompanied by a loss of privacy and an obligation to self-disclose, we looked at different forms of Social Web activities and different types of privacy. The relations between those phenomena are summarized in Table 11.1. Typical use situations in the Social Web are named for each privacy type affected, together with potential privacy problems that might occur. Additionally, gratifications that are obtained under the specific condition of this privacy type are listed, as well as those that are obtained for relinquishing this privacy form. The table enables a detailed look at the opportunities and risks of the Social Web for its users' privacy. It becomes obvious that there are various situations that enable the linkage or "co-existence" of privacy and Social Web gratifications.

Although a general danger for users' privacy cannot be affirmed after this analysis, some important problems concerning privacy issues and user behavior remain. One crucial question is how aware users are about their self-disclosure in the Social Web. We can assume that many acts of self-disclosure are not the result of an elaborate consideration of its advantages and disadvantages. Rather, users disclose information spontaneously or even unconsciously during communication processes with others. Additionally, users are often not aware of the possible long-term consequences of these acts of self-disclosure. Further studies should examine users' awareness of these problems and their consciousness of their own behavior in the Social Web.

Furthermore, the concepts of privacy, as well as publicity and audience, must be discussed and potentially modified in the light of the diffusion of the Social Web. Does people's understanding of privacy change due to their changing communication behavior? The perception of intimacy may alter with an increasing amount of communicating with closely related people online. For example, the definition of friends seems to change with the growing use of social networking sites: in SNSs, another user is either a friend or not – varying degrees of friendship, such as from best friend to distant acquaintance, simply do not exist.

Taken together, all of these aspects show that further research is needed, as well as a debate on privacy uses and norms.

References

Acquisti A, Gross R (2006) Awareness, information sharing, and privacy on the Facebook. Presentation on the 6th Workshop Privacy Enhancing Technologies, Cambridge, 28–30 June 2006

Altman I (1975) The environment and social behavior. Privacy, personal space, territory, crowding. Brooks/Cole, Monterey

Altman I (1977) Privacy regulation: culturally universal or culturally specific? J Soc Issues 33:67–83

Altman I, Taylor DA (1973) Social penetration: the development of interpersonal relationships. Holt, Rinehart and Winston, New York

Ancu M, Cozma R (2009) MySpace politics: uses and gratifications of befriending candidates. J Broadcast Electron 53:567–583

Awad NF, Krishnan MS (2006) The personalization privacy paradox: an empirical evaluation of information transparency and the willingness to be profiled online for personalization. MIS Quart 30(1):13–28

Barnes S (2006). A privacy paradox: Social networking in the United States. First Monday, 11(9). http://firstmonday.org/issues/issue11_9/barnes/-index.html

boyd dm (2007) Why youth (heart) social network sites: the role of networked publics in teenage social life. In: Buckingham D (ed) Macarthur foundation series on digital learning – youth, identity, and digital. MIT Press, Cambridge, pp 119–142

boyd dm, Ellison NB (2008) Social network sites: definition, history, and scholarship. J Comput Mediat Commun 13:210–230

boyd dm, Hargittai E (2010) Facebook privacy settings: who cares? First Monday 15. http://firstmonday.org/htbin/cgiwrap/bin/ojs/index.php/fm/article/-viewArticle/3086/2589

Burgoon JK, Parrott R, LePoire BA, Kelley DL, Walther JB, Perry D (1989) Maintaining and restoring privacy through communication in different types of relationship. J Soc Pers Relat 6:131–158

Debatin B, Lovejoy JP, Horn A-K, Hughes BN (2009) Facebook and online privacy: attitudes, behaviors, and unintended consequences. J Comput Mediat Commun 15:83–108

Duval S, Wicklund RA (1972) A theory of objective self-awareness. Academic, New York

Ekdale B, Namkoong K, Fung TKF, Perlmutter DD (2010) Why blog? (then and now): exploring the motivations for blogging by popular American political bloggers. New Med Soc 12:217–234

Elliott P (1974) Uses and gratifications research: a critique and a sociological alternative. In: Rosengren KE, Wenner LA, Palmgreen P (eds) Media gratifications research. Current perspectives. Sage, Beverly Hills, pp 249–268

Ellison N, Heino R, Gibbs J (2006) Managing impressions online: self presentation processes in the online dating environment. J Comput Mediat Commun 11(2):415–441 (Article 2)

Etzioni A (1999) The limits of privacy. Basic Books, New York

Fried C (1984) Privacy: a moral analysis. In: Schoeman FD (ed) Philosophical dimensions of privacy: an anthology. Cambridge University Press, Cambridge, pp 371–377 (Reprinted from Yale Law Journal, 1968)

Gavison R (1984) Privacy and the limits of law. In: Schoeman FD (ed) Philosophical dimensions of privacy: an anthology. Cambridge University Press, Cambridge, pp 421–471 (Reprinted from Yale Law Journal, 1980, 89)

Gerstein RS (1984) Intimacy and privacy. In: Schoeman FD (ed) Philosophical dimensions of privacy: an anthology. Cambridge University Press, Cambridge, pp 265–271

Haridakis P, Hanson P (2009) Social interaction and co-viewing with youtube: blending mass communication reception and social connection. J Broadcast Electron 53:317–335

Herzog H (1944) What do we really know about daytime serial listeners? In: Lazarsfeld PF, Stanton FN (eds) Radio research 1942–1943. Duell, Sloan & Pearce, New York, pp 3–33

Hixson WL (1987) Privacy in public society: human rights in conflict. Oxford University Press, New York

Joinson AN (2001) Self-disclosure in computer-mediated communication: the role of self-awareness and visual anonymity. Eur J Soc Psychol 31:177–192

Katz E, Foulkes D (1962) On the use of the mass media as "Escape": clarification of a concept. Public Opin Q 26:377–388

Katz E, Blumler JG, Gurevitch M (1974) Utilization of mass communication by the individual. In: Blumler JG, Kath E (eds) The uses of mass communication, Current perspectives on gratifications research. Sage, Beverly Hills/London, pp 19–32

Krämer NC, Winter S (2008) Impression management 2.0: the relationship of self-esteem, extraversion, self-efficacy, and self-presentation within social networking sites. J Med Psychol 20(3):106–116

Lampe C, Ellison NB, Steinfield C (2007) A familiar face(book): profile elements as signals in an online social network. In: Proceedings of the SIGCHI conference on human factors in computing systems, New York, pp 435–444

Laurenceau J-P, Feldman Barrett L, Pietromonaco PR (1998) Intimacy as an interpersonal process: the importance of self-disclosure, partner disclosure, and perceived partner responsiveness in interpersonal exchanges. J Pers Soc Psychol 74:1238–1251

Lee JK (2006) Who are blog users? Profiling blog users by media use and political involvement. Paper presented at ICA conference in Dresden, Germany. http://www.allacademic.com//meta/p_mla_apa_research_citation-/0/9/2/9/6/pages92964/p92964-1.php

Leung L (2009) User-generated content on the internet: an examination of gratifications, civic engagement and psychological empowerment. New Med Soc 11:1327–1347

Lin CA (1996) Looking back: the contribution of Blumler and Katz's uses of mass communication to communication research. J Broadcast Electronic 40:574–581

Liu S-H, Liao H-L, Zeng Y-T (2007) Why people blog: an expectancy theory analysis. Issues Inform Syst 8:232–237

Matheson K, Zanna MP (1989) Persuasion as a function of self-awareness in computer-mediated communication. Soc Behav 4:99–111

Nardi B, Schiano D, Gumbrecht M (2004) Blogging as social activity or would you let 900 million people read your diary? In: Proceedings of the 2004 ACM conference on computer supported cooperative work, Chicago, pp 222–231. http://portal.acm.org/citation.cfm?id=1031643. Accessed 8 Dec 2010

Newell PB (1994) A systems model of privacy. J Environ Psychol 14:65–78

Newell PB (1995) Perspectives on privacy. J Environ Psychol 15:87–104

Newhagen JE, Rafaeli S (1996) Why communication researchers should study the internet: a dialogue. J Commun 46:4–13

Norberg P, Horne DR, Horne DR (2007) The privacy paradox: personal information disclosure intentions versus behaviors. J Consum Aff 41(1):100–126

Nov O (2007) What motivates Wikipedians, or how to increase user-generated content contribution. Commun ACM 50:60–64

Paine C, Reips U-D, Stieger S, Joinson A, Buchanan T (2006) Internet users' perceptions of 'privacy concerns' and 'privacy actions'. Int J Hum Comput St 65:526–536

Palmgreen P, Wenner LA, Rosengren KE (1985) Uses and gratifications research: the past ten years. In: Rosengren KE, Wenner LA, Palmgreen P (eds) Media gratifications research, Current perspectives. Sage, Beverly Hills, pp 11–37

Parent W (1983) Privacy, morality and the law. Philos Pub Aff 12:269–288

Pastalan LA (1975) Privacy preferences among relocated institutionalised elderly. In: Carson DH (ed) Man-environment interactions, vol 2. Hutchinson & Ross, Stroudsburg, pp 73–82

Pedersen DM (1997) Psychological functions of privacy. J Environ Psychol 17:147–156

Rafaeli S, Ariel Y (2008) Online motivational factors: incentives for participation and contribution in wikipedia. In: Barak A (ed) Psychological aspects of cyberspace: theory, research, applications. Cambridge University Press, Cambridge, pp 243–267

Rubin AM (1979) Television use by children and adolescents. Hum Commun Res 5:109–120

Rubin AM (2002) The uses-and-gratifications perspective of media effects. In: Bryant J, Zillmann D (eds) Media effects. Advances in theory and research. Erlbaum, Mahwah/London, pp 525–548

Rubin AM (2009) Uses-and-gratifications perspective on media effects. In: Bryant J, Oliver MB (eds) Media effects. Advances in theory and research, 3rd edn. Routledge, New York, pp 165–184

Ruggerio TE (2000) Uses and gratifications theory in the 21st century. Mass Commun Soc 3:3–37

Shao G (2008) Understanding the appeal of user-generated media: a uses and gratifications perspective. Internet Res 19:7–25

Schoeman F (1984) Privacy and intimate information. In: Schoeman F (ed) Philosophical dimensions of privacy. Cambridge University Press, Cambridge, pp 403–417

Sproull L, Kiesler S (1986) Reducing social context cues: electronic mail in organizational communication. Manage Sci 32:1492–1512

Sproull L, Kiesler S (1991) Two-level perspective on electronic mail in organizations. J Org Comp Elect Com 1:125–134

Suler JL (2004) The online disinhibition effect. Cyberpsychol Behav 7(3):321–326

Swanson DL (1977) The uses and misuses of uses and gratifications. Hum Commun Res 3:214–221

Taddicken M (2008) Methodeneffekte bei web-befragungen: einschränkungen der datengüte durch ein 'reduziertes kommunikationsmedium'? [Mode effects of Web surveys: Limitation of data quality because of a ,reduced communication mode'?]. Halem, Köln

Tidwell LC, Walther JB (2002) Computer-mediated communication effects on disclosure, impressions, and interpersonal evaluations: getting to know one another a bit at a time. Hum Commun Res 28:317–348

Tufekci Z (2008) Can you see me now? audience and disclosure regulation in online social network sites. B Sci Technol Soc 28:20–36

Warren SD, Brandeis LD (1890) The right to privacy. Harv Law Rev 4:193–220

Westin A (1967) Privacy and freedom. Atheneum, New York

Wheeless LR (1976) Self-disclosure and interpersonal solidarity: measurement, validation, and relationships. Hum Commun Res 3:47–61

Wheeless LR, Grotz J (1976) Conceptualization and measurement of reported self-disclosure. Hum Commun Res 2:338–346

Part II
Applications

Chapter 12
(Micro)blogs: Practices of Privacy Management

Jan-Hinrik Schmidt

12.1 Introduction

Weblogs (or blogs for short) are a prototypical application of the Social Web. They lower the barriers for participating in online conversations and the dissemination of information, blurring the basic dichotomy that is at the heart of traditional mass communication: the separation of roles between sender and receiver, or between producers and users of information (Bruns 2008). Intertwined with this development, blogs (and their younger sibling the microblogs) are also one of those online formats that challenge the classic dichotomy of the private and the public, because they make it feasible to share information of personal relevance with an audience over time and space.

A particularly telling case of the possible tensions between privacy and publicness has been reported by Johnson (2005): a nanny in New York one day told the people she worked for about her private blog. The parents followed the blog for a while and then decided to fire her. The mother, herself a journalist at the "New York Times," explained in a newspaper article (Olen 2005) her outrage that her and her baby's life had been made public on the Internet. Although she did not mention any names, the details provided in her article made it possible to track down the nanny's blog. The nanny, in turn, reacted to her case being made public in the New York Times through blog postings of her own that specifically criticized the sensation-seeking style of the article: "If you have come to this little blog today looking for prurient details of a 'nanny gone wild' and another 'nanny diary' detailing the sordid life of a family she works for, I am very sorry to disappoint you" (N.N 2005). She also announced that she was closing her blog and would blog anonymously to protect her own privacy.

J.-H. Schmidt (✉)
Hans-Bredow-Institute for Media Research, Hamburg, Germany
e-mail: j.schmidt@hans-bredow-institut.de

S. Trepte and L. Reinecke (eds.), *Privacy Online*,
DOI 10.1007/978-3-642-21521-6_12, © Springer-Verlag Berlin Heidelberg 2011

Of course, this story is not representative of bloggers' experiences and neither are these events inherent to or inevitably caused by blogs as such. The individual and social consequences of the appropriation and institutionalization of the format might differ quite substantially. This is especially true for privacy, which should not be conceptualized as a fixed state, but rather as a constant and historically variant process of navigating and managing the boundaries between the private and the public. This includes, as classic theories of privacy have pointed out, maintaining and exercising control over the extent of personal information that is communicated (Westin 1970) or over the access to the self by others (Altman 1975). With regard to (micro)blogs, then, managing privacy refers to the ways people actively use the technology to selectively disclose certain personal information to certain audiences (and also to not disclose certain information to others).

This paper proceeds in three steps: Firstly, it describes the formal characteristics of (micro)blogs and presents empirical findings on their prevalence among onliners as well as on different uses of the technology. It then analyzes (micro)blog-based practices of privacy management by reconstructing their technological evolution as well as some of the shared routines and expectations about self-disclosure and privacy with regard to particular audiences. A summary and outlook to future research conclude the text.

12.2 Formal Characteristics and Prevalence of (Micro)blogs

In a formal way, blogs can be defined as frequently updated websites that display content in a reverse chronological order. Single blog entries ("postings") have unique URLs and can be linked to individually, rather than to the site as a whole. They can also usually be commented on by other users. Microblogs usually impose a limit on the number of characters in a single posting; Twitter, the most prominent if not generic example of a microblogging service, allows for 140 characters within one "tweet." Microblogs also rely on articulated social connections for the structuring of conversations and audiences, because users explicitly establish connections amongst themselves by "following" or "being followed by" other users, and by explicitly referring to other users by replying to or retweeting (i.e., "forwarding") their postings.

Taken together, individual postings or tweets, comments, and articulated connections through hyperlinks, replies, or retweets between (micro)blogs form networks of interconnected texts, usually referred to as the "blogosphere" and the "twittersphere." Not only are these spheres connected (since tweets might refer to blog postings and vice versa) they are also greatly heterogeneous: which information, topics, or events are selected by the (micro)blogger and which are not, how this content is presented in terms of writing style, illustrations, etc., and how these "distributed conversations" (Efimova 2009) within and between blogs are structured, varies greatly. Thus, there is no such thing as "the" blog; rather, blogs and microblogs are prime examples of the contingent and under-determined nature of new media formats (Lievrouw 2002) that allow for or afford various practices, including the ways in which privacy management and self-disclosure are performed.

According to blog monitoring services, the blogosphere has grown from four million blogs in 2004 to approximately 150 million blogs at the beginning of 2011 (Sifry 2004; http://www.blogpulse.com). Twitter, the dominant microblogging service, was estimated to reach 200 million users at the end of 2010 (Murphy 2010). The share of (micro)blog users among the general online population varies between countries and age groups. In the US, around 11% of adult Internet users and 28% of the 12–17-year olds had created a blog in 2009 (Jones and Fox 2009). Within Europe, 11% of the 9–16-year old onliners had written a blog or online diary within the last month (Livingstone et al. 2011, p. 34). 19% of US Internet users were using Twitter (or similar microblogging services) in October 2009 (Fox et al. 2009), while in Germany, it is used by only 1% on a weekly basis (Busemann and Gscheidle 2010, p. 362).

Parallel to this diffusion of (micro)blogs among Internet users, a growing body of research has focused on specific practices and contexts, most notably the relationship and interdependencies with professional journalism (e.g., Lasica 2002; Tremayne 2007; Messner and DiStaso 2008). Other strands of research have examined the role of (micro)blogs within other fields of professional communication, specifically political communication (e.g., Keren 2006; Scott 2007; Park and Thelwall 2008) as well as market communication and organizational communication, including knowledge management (e.g., Böhringer and Richter 2009; Efimova 2009; Puschmann 2010). Somewhat in contrast to this strong research focus on blogging within professional contexts, various studies, by employing different methodologies, agree that the majority of blogs deal with personal issues rather than political, economical, or professional topics as such (e.g., Nardi et al. 2004; Papacharissi 2007; White and Winn 2009).

For example, in a representative survey among US bloggers (n = 233), Lenhart and Fox (2006) found that 37% of bloggers consider "my life and personal experience" as their main topic, with the next most popular topic, "politics and government," reaching only 11%. Accordingly, most bloggers (78%) are inspired to blog by personal experiences, with female and younger bloggers of age 18–29 being even more likely to do so. In a content analysis of n = 457 blogs within a 13 month period between 2003 and 2004, Herring et al. (2007) found that between 65% and 75% belonged to the "Personal Journal" type. A content analysis of n = 207 English tweets found that 41% of all messages were reporting the user's personal experiences (Honeycutt and Herring 2009). And a cluster analysis based on message content of n = 350 randomly selected Twitter users revealed that 80% could be categorized as "meformers," since their tweets predominantly focus on their personal situation, opinions and complaints, or statements and random thoughts (Naaman et al. 2010).

While the composition of a blog's audience, the types of personal information shared, and the particular communicative strategies for disclosing personal information may differ (see below for a more thorough discussion), blogging is nevertheless a fundamentally social activity. It is a hybrid between the modes of "publishing" and "engaging in conversation" – especially in the case of the seemingly paradox online journal, which is both personal and public at the same time. Rather than being an expression of mere "exhibitionistic" self-disclosure, journal-style blogs are used to maintain personal relationships: personal information is disclosed to an audience of readers, which might react to postings by commenting on them or linking to them on their own blogs.

Various studies find that the level of self-disclosure within a personal blog has an impact on the structure and quality of social relations: in a survey of n = 307 female bloggers and a corresponding content analysis of n = 100 blogs (authored by the respondents), Bane et al. (2010) found that bloggers with a high level of self-disclosure on their blogs reported a high number of and higher satisfaction with online friends. Stefanone and Jang (2007), in a survey of n = 154 randomly selected bloggers, found that bloggers with a higher level of extraversion and self-disclosure (as personal traits) not only reported larger strong tie networks, but were also more likely to use blogs to maintain these networks.

Of particular interest for this paper, however, is not the connection between personality traits and blogging behavior, but rather the specific communicative situation in which bloggers engage. It contributes to the emergence of "personal public spheres," which are one of the defining features of the Social Web (Schmidt 2009, pp. 105–128). They are formed when and where users make available information that is personally relevant to them (instead of the information being selected according to journalistic news factors or news values), that is directed to an intended audience of strong and weak ties (instead of the disperse, unconnected, and unknown audience of mass-mediated public spheres), and that is presented mainly to engage in conversation (instead of the one-way mode of publishing).

This new type of public sphere, which is not limited to (micro)blogs but is also visible on social network sites such as Facebook, is blurring the boundaries between the personal and the public. But rather than simply eroding privacy and fostering "digital exhibitionism," as some commentators suspect, personal public spheres reconfigure the context for identity management and relationship management in a more complex way. One the one hand, they contribute to the maintenance of "connected presence" (Licoppe and Smoreda 2005), because they empower users to share information that is relevant to them within an extended network of strong and weak ties. On the other hand they demand certain routines and skills. As Marwick and boyd (2010, p. 11) put it with regard to Twitter: users "must maintain equilibrium between a contextual social norm of personal authenticity that encourages information-sharing and phatic communication (the oft-cited 'what I had for breakfast') with the need to keep information private, or at least concealed from certain audiences." The remainder of the paper explores how exactly this practice of privacy management within (micro)blogs can be described and analyzed

– what do we know about how people use this technology with certain communicative affordances to share personal information with others and to selectively control access to their selves?

12.3 Practices of Privacy Management in (Micro)blogs

There are various approaches that can be used to account for the diversity of blog use (Bruns and Jacobs 2006; Schmidt 2006; Walker Rettberg 2008). Most notably, Herring and colleagues have conducted various studies on blogs as a communicative genre (e.g., Herring et al. 2004, 2005; Herring and Paolillo 2006; see also Puschmann 2010). Here, I will draw upon an analytical model of blogging practices that is based in sociological theory and has been developed in more detail in Schmidt (2007a). In a nutshell, blogging practices consist of and are performed through individual blogging episodes. How individual bloggers select and present content online is framed by the technology or *code* (the underlying software with its specific technological affordances) but also by *rules* (shared routines and expectations) and by *relations* (hypertextual as well as social connections). Along these structural dimensions, we can identify groups or communities of blogging practice, for example, those bloggers who share a specific software such as Wordpress and its features, or those who belong to a specific subculture and use blogs in a certain way to express their subcultural identities and norms (e.g., Hodkinson 2006 for the Goth subculture; Wei 2004 for knitting blogs).

Thus, code, rules, and relations frame the situative use of blogs, for example, by suggesting a certain style of writing, or by providing the technical means to easily link to other content. However, they are also the result of these individually performed episodes: expectations or routines might change over time if bloggers do not follow them, hypertextual and social networks are (re-)produced only by individual acts of linking or commenting, and even the code might be developed further in a reaction to direct or indirect user feedback. Thus, (micro)blogging practices are expressing the recursivity of social action and social structure that has been explained by Giddens' theory of structuration (Giddens 1984).

This analytical model, which accounts both for the social structuredness of blogging and its dynamic nature, can also serve as a framework to look specifically at the development of (micro)blog-based practices of privacy management. In a first step, it allows the reconstruction of the sociotechnical architecture that has evolved from the rather static personal homepages of online diaries to the distributed conversation of the blogosphere, and to the constant and near-live streams and feeds of current (micro)blogging within articulated social networks. In a second step, it can connect these changes in the communicative architecture to prevalent communicative routines and shared expectations, including conceptualizations about the nature and scope of one's audience. Figure 12.1 summarizes the main analytical categories and interdependencies between structure and action, and these are discussed in more detail in the following chapters.

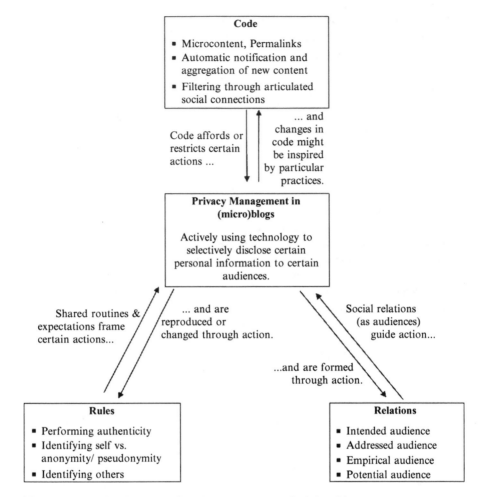

Fig. 12.1 Analytical framework for privacy management in (micro)blogs

12.3.1 Affording Privacy Management: Software Architecture

The term "weblog" was coined by Jørn Barger, who stated in 1997 that a weblog is a "Web page where a Web logger 'logs' all the other Web pages she finds interesting" (cit. by Blood 2004, p. 54). Predecessors of blogs date back to the early 1990s, when individuals such as Tim Berners-Lee and organizations such as the "National Center for Supercomputing Applications" (NCSA) curated regularly updated websites where they provided links to other interesting sites. Around the middle of the 1990s, online journals or online diaries, where people shared and reflected upon personal impressions and experiences (McNeill 2003) provided an additional tradition of online-based communication that blogs drew upon.

Other predecessors include the personal homepage (with its author-centered way of presenting content) and online discussion boards (offering options for commenting on and discussing content).

While the first blogs were edited using regular HTML editors, around the Millennium, various blog hosters such as Pitas, LiveJournal, or Blogger.com launched their services and helped to increase the number of bloggers (Blood 2004). While Pitas provided a field for entering a URL and one for a corresponding text, thus suggesting a form of blogging that consisted mainly of commented links (the "filter blog"), blogger.com offered only one text field. If the user wanted to link to a different site, he/she had to enter the URL manually using HTML tags – this difference in interface design suggested a blogging style that was more similar to the style of diaries: chronicling events, reflecting ideas, or disclosing emotions. Blogs also featured "permalinks" – a unique and stable URL for each single blog posting that can be linked to individually (rather than having to link to the whole blog if one wants to refer to a specific idea or text). The "trackback" function introduced an automatic notification that is added to a blog entry if other blogs link to it.

Microblogging services such as Twitter provide additional options or restrictions for the presentation and connection of content. The most obvious feature is the 140-character limit for each message, which originates from restrictions imposed by using Twitter via mobile phones and text messages. It also encouraged users and developers to invent or co-create communicative routines to overcome these limitations, such as using the "@" symbol to address other users or the abbreviation "RT" for a "retweet" (forwarding another user's message). These social conventions were in turn incorporated into subsequent versions of Twitter, thus stabilizing certain emerging routines technologically. Another interface change made an implicit difference: the textbox for entering a tweet now asks "What's happening?" instead of the former "What are you doing" (Dybwad 2009) – suggesting (but not prescribing) tweets of a somewhat more general relevance than of journaling one's activities.

The specific features such as permalinks, trackbacks, and the comment feature on blog postings, but also the referencing signals of Twitter, make it possible for "distributed conversations" (Efimova 2009) to emerge. Distributed conversations are asynchronous and non-linear conversations where multiple authors refer to and discuss a topic on various sites. While such distributed conversation might be followed or participated in easily within small communities of bloggers, the rapid growth of the blogosphere has made it rather difficult to follow the constant updates. Basically, two technological innovations have proven highly important in assisting readers in keeping up with new content and changing the affordances of information management.

Firstly, the development of the RSS feed format and the corresponding feed readers from 2000 onwards allowed users to subscribe to a variety of blogs. Instead of having to regularly and "manually" visit those sites that are of interest, users aggregate selected sources in their feed reader and this automatically retrieves new and updated content. Secondly, the articulation of social relations became a relevant mechanism for filtering content. The "blogroll," a linklist of favorite blogs on one's own blog, provided an early mechanism for expressing social connection and topical interest. Platforms such as LiveJournal introduced more sophisticated social networking features to the basic blogging functionalities: by adding other users as friends, one could not only selectively give access to certain postings to this group (thus engaging in privacy management; see below), but could also be informed about updates on one's friends' LiveJournal blogs (boyd and Ellison 2007).

On microblogging services such as Twitter, the articulation of social connections has become a basic organizational principle of communication. The act of "following" is akin to subscribing to that account, so that relations on Twitter are not necessarily reciprocal: they do not signify mutual acquaintance (although this can be the case), but more often just interest in those users one follows. By explicitly choosing certain Twitter accounts, a user can customize his/her own repertoire of sources, thus engaging in active information management. The @ feature and the Retweet function, which are both used to relate to other users (by addressing them or forwarding their tweet), also contribute to the organization of conversations on Twitter, thus structuring social relations and networks (Honeycutt and Herring 2009; boyd et al. 2010).

To summarize: (micro)blogs have incorporated several technological innovations that distinguish them from predecessors, such as the easy-to-maintain commented linklist or hosting platforms for online diaries: the shift to regularly updated "microcontent" addressable through permalinks, the automatic notification of new content, the aggregation of these updates in one single "place" (the RSS feed reader or the Twitter interface), and the reliance on articulated social connections to filter information. The resulting technological architecture has not only significantly lowered the barriers for making information accessible to others via the Internet, which includes sharing personal information, but has also contributed to a fundamental shift in the communicative architecture of web-based publics, which is (maybe even more prominently) visible in other Social Web applications as well. Instead of the hypertext networks of separate websites connected by and traversable via hyperlinks that formed the early web, the Social Web is characterized by "streams" and "feeds": afforded by technological features, personal information is constantly made accessible, aggregated, and updated within networked publics that are based on social connections.

12.3.2   Framing Privacy Management: Shared Routines and Expectations

The technological architecture of (micro)blogs only partly explains practices of privacy management. The software use is framed by shared routines and expectations (i.e., social rules) about how to self-disclose and whom to address in a blog. It is not the use of the same tool, but rather the shared knowledge about – often informal and latent – rules that makes a blogger. In this sense, blogging as a practice has to be learned, and the conventions of the blogging genre have to be internalized (Lüders et al. 2010). In doing this, bloggers usually combine existing knowledge about similar genres – such as the paper diary – with reflections about their own experiences and with feedback from people they communicate with through their blog. Additionally, public discourse about the qualities, benefits, or drawbacks of (micro)blogs might influence how bloggers see the genre. Press coverage on Twitter, for example, framed microblogs positively as a tool for maintaining social contact, but also negatively as increasing information overload (Arceneaux and Schmitz Weiss 2010).

The particular rules and expectations about the adequate amount of self-disclosure, about the topics selected for postings, and about the "right style" for blogging differ between sub-genres of blogging. In this respect, corporate blogs or blogs by politicians are different to personal journals, although they use the same software. However, at the core of the rules, expectations, conventions, and norms framing these different blogging practices is the idea of personal authenticity and subjectivity: blogs are considered to be formats where people use their "personal voice" and express their own subjectivity by sharing personal thoughts, observations, or comments about current events. This leitmotif of blogging not only explains the high share of journal-type blogs, but has a direct impact on self-disclosure and privacy.

By following and supporting the norm of authenticity, bloggers predominantly refer to their "real" identity. In their study on blogs run by American teenagers, Huffaker and Calvert (2005) found that a majority of them provided information about their first name (70%), their age (67%), and even additional contact information such as an e-mail address or a phone number (61%). The findings of Herring et al. (2007) point in the same direction: between 66% and 79% of the blogs in their three samples contained first or full names of their authors.

In a survey of 4,220 German-speaking bloggers in 2005, 70% stated that they do not blog anonymously or pseudonymously (Schmidt 2007b). The particular ways through which they disclose personal information varies though: approximately 40% state that they include this information in blog postings; a somewhat smaller share (36%) of bloggers have a separate "about me" page with personal details. Around one in ten bloggers (12%) link to a separate personal homepage from their blog. While anonymity is not the dominating but a prevalent mode of blogging, it is debated in courts whether there is a right to anonymity for bloggers in the legal sense (Barendt 2009). This question is fundamentally tied to issues of free speech, but also touches on the intersection of blogging and journalism, since it raises the question of whether bloggers should enjoy the same protective rights as professional journalists (Hendrickson 2007).

Bloggers also have to build routines on how to deal with the privacy of other people. A non-representative survey on privacy expectations of bloggers (n = 486) conducted by Viegas (2005) found that only 3% always ask for permission before mentioning or citing other people on their blog, while 66% almost never ask; 42% said that they refrain from mentioning names in their blogs, while 21% stated that they almost always reveal them. Common strategies to protect others' identities are to use initials, nicknames, or particular social roles (such as "my daughter" or "my husband") that might identify them to those in-the-know but not to other readers. An exception is usually made for those people who blog themselves – since they have chosen to make certain aspects of their personal life public in their blog, they are considered as having to live with the consequences of being mentioned or linked to by other bloggers as well. Similar findings were reported by Schmidt (2007b) for the German-speaking blogosphere; the survey also found that those people who blog anonymously or pseudonymously were more likely to not disclose information about others or, if they do disclose information, to use only initials etc. instead of full names. These findings indicate that reciprocity norms seem to guide the amount of disclosure about other people.

12.3.3   Performing Privacy Management: Conceptions of Audience

The routines and expectations about self-disclosure or disclosure of others are strongly tied to the conception of the audience. Although (micro)bloggers might reject this term when talking about their own experiences – because they dislike the corresponding notion of acting prominently on a stage or of broadcasting to a diverse group of people (Marwick and boyd 2010, p. 6) – they nevertheless have certain assumptions of their readership. Due to the particular technical affordances of blogging software compared to microblogs, the audience of blogs remains largely invisible – an "unseen audience" (Scheidt 2006) – in the absence of articulated social connections; it is only through comments, through trackbacks and referrer links, or through one's server log files that a blogger can get an impression of the size and composition of his/her audience (Viégas 2005).

Given these limitations and the characteristics of online-based communication in general, where information is persistent, replicable, scalable, and searchable (boyd 2010), four analytical categories of blogs' audiences have to be differentiated: firstly, the *intended audience* comprises a blogger's general idea of the audience he/she wants to reach or address, for example, friends, colleagues, or those interested in a specific topic. Secondly, the *addressed audience* comprises those people that are addressed in a specific blog posting – which might be the same as the intended audience in general, but might also be a specific subset, for example, when a posting or tweet is directed to a particular group of readers for feedback. Empirical studies usually concentrate on the intended audience and find that most bloggers have a vague idea about its composition. Almost half (49%) of the bloggers surveyed by Lenhart and Fox (2006) believed that their audience consisted of people they personally know, about a third (35%) believed that mostly people they have never met personally read their blogs, and 14% believe that it is a mix of personally known and unknown readers. Qian and Scott (2007) report a higher number of bloggers (88%) who identify people they know offline as their main audience.

Both the intended audience and the addressed audience are conceptualizations on the blogger's side, and are an important point of reference for deciding what information to disclose online. However, they do not necessarily correspond with the *empirical audience* that comprises those people who actually take notice of any given posting or tweet. In many cases this will be only a subset of the intended audience, since, for example, not all followers on Twitter will actually read a particular tweet. Problems with regard to privacy arise especially if the empirical audience is larger than the intended audience, for example, when tweets get retweeted or a particular blog posting is found through a search engine. As a result of network effects, the empirical audience might differ significantly from the intended audience: in a large scale analysis of Twitter, Kwak et al. (2010) found that no matter how large the follower base of the original user, a retweeted (forwarded) tweet reaches on average 1,000 users. Qualitative research suggests that especially for teenagers it is the "known, but inappropriate others" (Livingstone 2008, p. 405) who are problematic: parents or teachers reading a blog or discovering a Twitter account that is not intended for them to read.

Finally, the *potential audience* has to be considered. This is mainly determined by the "technological reach" of a blog within the wider context of networked communication. Under the conditions of persistence and searchability in particular, it is hard to assess who might possibly have access to a blog posting or a tweet in the near or in the more distant future. Features of the software code, for example, protecting a Twitter account from non-followers, or blocking search engine robots from a blog, can assist a blogger in restricting his/her potential audience.

12.4   Conclusion

This paper has argued that privacy management in (micro)blogging can be understood and analyzed as a particular practice that is grounded in specific software affordances, in certain shared rules, and in the addressing of particular audiences. More specifically, the technological characteristics of (micro)blog code, which include uniquely addressable microcontent that is regularly updated and aggregated within feeds or streams of text, which in turn are filtered or channeled with the help of articulated social connections, provide a particular communicative architecture for sharing personal information. How exactly these technological features are used to share personal information with others is framed by shared routines and expectations. They evolve, stabilize, and change by combining experiences from (micro)blogging with knowledge about other CMC genres (such as the social network site) as well as with experiences grounded in other spheres of social life (such as the workplace or the home), where selective disclosure has to be performed as well. Important rules of (micro)blogging center around the key norm of authenticity, around the alternative between identifying oneself vs. blogging anonymously or pseudonymously, and around the ethical question of how to disclose information about others, where norms of reciprocity play an important role.

Finally, privacy management in (micro)blogs is inseparably tied to the social relations that are maintained and established through blogging. Not only do articulated social relations, for example, links in blogrolls, subscribed RSS feeds, or one's followers on Twitter assist in filtering information, social relations also become relevant for privacy management in the form of particular audiences: bloggers conceive of an intended audience and might even explicitly write for an addressed audience. In this respect, privacy management is performed for specific audiences. Due to the specific technological affordances, however, the intended or addressed audience might be incongruent with the empirical audience and the potential audience, which in turn can lead to privacy conflicts or failures to control who has access to certain personal information.

Analytically separating and discussing elements of privacy management practices is only a first step in understanding the impact that (micro)blogging has on individual users and social life. Ongoing technological innovation and the convergence with other Social Web applications introduce constant and great dynamics into the way people communicate via (micro)blogs. Not only do we lack more detailed knowledge on the various normative guidelines and shared expectations that frame privacy management under these conditions, especially in a comparative perspective,, but there is also the need to research the congruence or disparities between expectations of privacy and actual behavior. This in turn might lead to a better understanding of appropriate interventions, whether they aim at better and more sophisticated software-based control, or at improved knowledge and skills. Both seem to be necessary to guarantee that users can make the best use of the communication tools while maintaining control over their own personal information and private sphere.

References

Altman I (1975) The environment and social behavior. Brooks/Cole, Monterey

Arceneaux N, Schmitz Weiss A (2010) Seems stupid until you try it: press coverage of twitter, 2006–9. New Media Soc 12(8):1262–1279. doi:10.1177/1461444809360773

Bane CM, Cornish M, Erspamer N, Kampman L (2010) Self-disclosure through weblogs and perceptions of online and "real-life" friendships among female bloggers. Cyberpsychol Behav Social Netw 13(2):131–139

Barendt E (2009) Bad news for bloggers. J Media Law 1(2):141–147

Blood R (2004) How blogging software reshapes the online community. Commun ACM 4(12):53–55

Böhringer M, Richter A (2009) Adopting social software to the intranet: a case study on enterprise microblogging. In: Wandke H (ed) Proceedings of the 9th mensch & computer conference. Oldenbourg, Munich, pp 293–302

boyd d (2010) Social network sites as networked publics: affordances, dynamics, and implications. In: Papacharissi Z (ed) Networked self: identity, community, and culture on social network sites. Routledge, New York, pp 39–58

boyd d, Ellison NB (2007) Social network sites: definition, history, and scholarship. J Comput Mediat Commun 13(1), Article 11. http://jcmc.indiana.edu/vol13/issue1/boyd.ellison.html. Accessed 10 Feb 2011 boyd d, Golder S, Lotan G (2010) Tweet, tweet, retweet: conversational aspects of retweeting on twitter. In: Proceedings of the 43rd Hawaii international conference on social systems, Hawaii, doi: 10.1109/HICSS.2010.412

Bruns A (2008) Blogs, wikipedia, second life and beyond: from production to produsage. Peter Lang, New York

Bruns A, Jacobs J (2006) Uses of blogs. Peter Lang, New York

Busemann K, Gscheidle C (2010) Web 2.0: Nutzung steigt – Interesse an aktiver Teilnahme sinkt. Media Perspektiven 41(7–8):359–368

Dybwad B (2009) Twitter drops "what are you doing?" Now asks "what's happening?" Mashable, 19 Nov 2009. http://mashable.com/2009/11/19/twitter-whats-happening. Accessed 10 Feb 2011

Efimova L (2009) Passion at work: blogging practices of knowledge workers. Novay, Enschede

Fox S, Zickuhr K, Smith A (2009) Twitter and status updating, fall 2009. Pew Research Center, Washington, DC. http://www.pewinternet.org/Reports/2009/17-Twitter-and-Status-Updating-Fall-2009.aspx. Accessed 10 Feb 2011

Giddens A (1984) The constitution of society. Polity Press, Cambridge

Hendrickson L (2007) Press protection in the blogosphere: applying a functional definition of "Press" to news web logs. In: Tremayne M (ed) Blogging, citizenship, and the future of media. Routledge, New York, pp 187–203

Herring SC, Paolillo JC (2006) Gender and genre variation in weblogs. J Socioling 10(4):439–459

Herring SC, Kouper I, Scheidt LA, Wright E (2004) Women and children last: the discursive construction of weblogs. In: Gurak L, Antonijevic S, Johnson L, Ratliff C, Reyman J (eds) Into the blogosphere: rhetoric, community, and culture of weblogs. University of Minnesota. http://blog.lib.umn.edu/blogosphere/women_and_children.html. Accessed 10 Feb 2011

Herring SC, Scheidt LA, Bonus S, Wright E (2005) Weblogs as a bridging genre. Inf Technol People 18(2):142–171

Herring SC, Scheidt LA, Kouper I, Wright E (2007) Longitudinal content analysis of blogs: 2003–2004. In: Tremayne M (ed) Blogging, citizenship, and the future of media. Routledge, New York, pp 3–20

Hodkinson P (2006) Subcultural blogging? Online journals and group involvement among U.K. Goths. In: Bruns A, Jacobs J (eds) Uses of blogs. Peter Lang, New York, pp 187–198

Honeycutt C, Herring S (2009) Beyond microblogging: conversation and collaboration via twitter. In: Proceedings of the 42nd Hawaii international conference on social systems, Hawaii, doi: 10.1109/HICSS.2009.89

Huffaker DA, Calvert SL (2005) Gender, identity, and language use in teenage blogs. J Comput Mediat Commun, 10(2) http://jcmc.indiana.edu/vol10/issue2/huffaker.html. Accessed 10 Feb 2011

Johnson B (2005) The mum, the nanny, her blog and some others. Guardian unlimited technology blog, 20 July 2005. http://www.guardian.co.uk/technology/blog/2005/jul/20/themumthenan? INTCMP=SRCH. Accessed 10 Feb 2011

Jones S, Fox S (2009) Generations online in 2009. Pew internet project memo. 28 Jan 2009. http://www.pewinternet.org/~/media//Files/Reports/2009/PIP_Generations_2009.pdf. Accessed 10 Feb 2011

Keren M (2006) Blogosphere. The new political arena. Lexington, Lanham

Kwak H, Lee CL, Park H, Moon S (2010) What is twitter, a social network or a news media? In: WWW '10: Proceedings of the 19th international conference on world wide web, ACM, New York, pp 591–600

Lasica JD (2002) Blogging as a form of journalism. In: Blood R (ed) We've got blog. How weblogs are changing our culture. Perseus, Cambridge, pp 163–170

Lenhart A, Fox S (2006) Bloggers. A portrait of the internet's new storytellers. Pew Internet & American Life Project, Washington, DC. http://www.pewinternet.org/Reports/2006/Bloggers.aspx. Accessed 10 Feb 2011

Licoppe C, Smoreda Z (2005) Are social networks technologically embedded? Social Netw 27(4):317–335

Lievrouw L (2002) Determination and contingency in new media development: diffusion of innovations and social shaping of technology perspectives. In: Lievrouw L, Livingstone S (eds) Handbook of new media. Sage, London, pp 183–199

Livingstone S (2008) Taking risky opportunities in youthful content creation: teenagers' use of social networking sites for intimacy, privacy and self-expression. New Media Soc 10(3):393–411

Livingstone S, Haddon L, Görzig A, Ólafsson K (2011) Risks and safety on the internet: the perspective of European children. full findings. EU Kids Online, London

Lüders M, Prøitz L, Rasmussen T (2010) Emerging personal media genres. New Media Soc 12(6):947–963. doi:10.1177/1461444809352203

Marwick A, boyd d (2010) I tweet honestly, I tweet passionately: twitter users, context collapse, and the imagined audience. New Media Soc. doi:10.1177/1461444810365313

McNeill L (2003) Teaching an old genre new tricks: the diary on the internet. Biography 26(1):24–47

Messner M, DiStaso MW (2008) The source cycle: how traditional media and weblogs use each other as sources. J Stud 9(3):447–463

Murphy D (2010) Twitter – on-track for 200 million users by year's end. Pcmag.com, 31 Oct 2010. http://www.pcmag.com/article2/0,2817,2371826,00.asp. Accessed 10 Feb 2011

N.N. (2005) Sorry to disappoint you. Instructions to the double, 16 July 2005. http://web.archive.org/web/20050719001851/http://subvic.blogspot.com/2005/07/sorry-to-disappoint-you.html Accessed 10 Feb 2011

Naaman M, Boase J, Lai C-H (2010) Is it really about me? Message content in social awareness streams. In: Quinn KI, Gutwin C, Tang JC (eds) Proceedings of the 2010 ACM conference on computer supported cooperative work, ACM, New York, pp 189–192, doi: 10.1145/1718918.1718953

Nardi BA, Schiano DJ, Gumbrecht M, Swartz L (2004) Why we blog. Commun ACM 47(12):41–46

Olen H (2005) The new nanny diaries are online. New York Times, 17 July 2005. http://www.nytimes.com/2005/07/17/fashion/sundaystyles/17LOVE.html. Accessed 10 Feb 2011

Papacharissi Z (2007) Audiences as media producers: content analysis of 260 blogs. In: Tremayne M (ed) Blogging, citizenship, and the future of media. Routledge, New York, pp 22–38

Park HW, Thelwall M (2008) Developing network indicators for ideological landscapes from the political blogosphere in South Korea. J Comput Mediat Commun 13:856–879. doi:10.1111/j.1083-6101.2008.00422.x

Puschmann C (2010) The corporate blog as an emerging genre of computer-mediated communication: features, constraints, discourse situation. Universitätsverlag, Göttingen

Qian H, Scott CR (2007) Anonymity and self-disclosure on weblogs. J Comput Mediat Commun 12(4), Article 14. http://jcmc.indiana.edu/vol12/issue4/qian.html. Accessed 10 Feb 2011

Scheidt LA (2006) Adolescent diary weblogs and the unseen audience. In: Buckingham D, Willett R (eds) Digital generations: children, young people, and new media. Erlbaum, London, pp 193–210

Schmidt J (2006) Weblogs. Eine kommunikationssoziologische Studie. [Weblogs. A study in sociology of communication]. UVK, Konstanz

Schmidt J (2007a) Blogging practices: an analytical framework. J Comput Mediat Commun 12(4), Article 13. http://jcmc.indiana.edu/vol12/issue4/schmidt.html. Accessed 10 Feb 2011

Schmidt J (2007b) Blogging practices in the German-speaking blogosphere. Empirical findings from the "'Wie ich blogge?!"-survey'. Working paper of the research centre "New Communication Media", No. 07-02. Bamberg. http://nbn-resolving.de/urn:nbn:de:0168-ssoar-9953

Schmidt J (2009) Das neue Netz. Merkmale, Praktiken und Folgen des Web 2.0. [The new net. Characteristics, practices and consequences of Web 2.0.]. UVK, Konstanz

Scott DT (2007) Pundits in muckrakers' clothing: political blogs and the 2004 U.S. presidential election. In: Tremayne M (ed) Blogging, citizenship, and the future of media. Routledge, New York, pp 39–58

Sifry D (2004) State of the blogosphere, October 2004. http://www.sifry.com/alerts/archives/000245.html. Accessed 10 Feb 2011

Stefanone MA, Jang C-Y (2007) Writing for friends and family: the interpersonal nature of blogs. J Comput Mediat Commun 13(1), Article 7. http://jcmc.indiana.edu/vol13/issue1/stefanone.html. Accessed 10 Feb 2011

Tremayne M (ed) (2007) Blogging, citizenship, and the future of media. Routledge, New York

Viégas FB (2005) Bloggers' expectations of privacy and accountability: an initial survey. J Comput Mediat Commun 10(3), Article 12. http://jcmc.indiana.edu/vol10/issue3/viegas.html. Accessed 10 Feb 2011

Walker Rettberg J (2008) Blogging. Polity, Cambridge

Wei C (2004) Formation of norms in a blog community. In: Gurak L, Antonijevic S, Johnson L, Ratliff C, Reyman J (Eds) Into the blogosphere. Rhetoric, community, and culture of weblogs. University of Minnesota. http://blog.lib.umn.edu/blogosphere/formation_of_norms.html. Accessed 10 Feb 2011

Westin A (1970) Privacy and freedom. Atheneum, New York

White D, Winn P (2009) State of the blogosphere 2008. http://technorati.com/blogging/feature/state-of-the-blogosphere-2008. Accessed 10 Feb 2011

Chapter 13
Privacy in Social Network Sites

Marc Ziegele and Oliver Quiring

13.1 Introduction

Are we running out of privacy? Nowadays, for example, we are concerned about whether the maintenance of a private sphere in online environments has become a luxury commodity (Papacharissi 2009). Questions of this kind are justified as online communication plays an increasingly important role in people's everyday life (cf., e.g., Lundby 2009). While it seems exaggerated to stigmatize today's youth as "communication junkies" (Patalong 2010), online conversations are increasingly becoming a functional equivalent to face to face communication (Beer 2008). However, some significant differences between online and "offline" communication remain. Face to face communication may remain largely intimate in some situations. It does not necessarily require the disclosure of personal data nor does it leave behind traces (Dwyer et al. 2007; Tufekci 2008). In contrast, online communication is usually mediated by providers with commercial interests. These providers do not confine themselves to gathering personal data and the content of user communications, rather they try to make conversations as public as possible by default (Gross and Acquisti 2005; Acquisti and Gross 2006). Additionally, the speed of technological progress often exceeds the time Internet users need to cultivate awareness for potential risks resulting from the use of these communication measures (Livingstone 2008). Thus, questions about how users manage their privacy online are topical for a majority of social services of the Social Web.

This is particularly true for social network sites (SNS), which we focus on in this chapter. SNSs are a global and – with respect to their usage – still heavily growing

M. Ziegele (✉) • O. Quiring
University of Mainz, Mainz, Germany
e-mail: ziegele@uni-mainz.de

S. Trepte and L. Reinecke (eds.), *Privacy Online*,
DOI 10.1007/978-3-642-21521-6_13, © Springer-Verlag Berlin Heidelberg 2011

communication phenomenon. Both user numbers across all age groups (Nguyen 2010; Nielsen 2009; see also the chapters by Peter & Valkenburg and by Maaß in this volume) and the time spent on these platforms are currently increasing faster than those of any other Internet service (Nguyen 2010; Nielsen 2009). There is no doubt that SNSs are no longer a niche phenomenon (see boyd and Ellison 2008 for a summary of the historical development of SNSs) and have become a – sometimes essential – part of the daily routine of many Internet users.

Our chapter approaches privacy issues in SNSs from multiple perspectives. In the first section, we discuss SNSs from the perspective of communication services. We provide an explorative taxonomy by systemizing both SNSs' service-determined and their usage-determined features. We then discuss specific privacy theories and conceptualize privacy issues in SNSs as issues of individual autonomy, control of information disclosure, and restriction of personal and spatial access to this information.

The third section expands these considerations of privacy issues in SNSs: we analyze risks and benefits of different degrees of individual information disclosure from a provider- and a user-based view. The relevance of the first perspective results from the fact that – although clearly existing within a majority of Social Web services – "capitalism is [. . .] at risk of looming as a black box in understandings of SNSs" (Beer 2008, p. 524). For an analysis of the latter perspective, we again shift our focus to a more psychological view of privacy. In this context, we gather empirical findings concerning users' privacy behavior in SNSs before closing our chapter with a short discussion.

13.2 Social Network Sites: A Taxonomy

Social network sites can be conceptualized as a specific accumulation of different communication services (Beer 2008) that enable users "to construct a public or semi-public online profile within a bounded system" (boyd and Ellison 2008, p. 2) and to interact with specified network connections – both human and/or institutional ones. SNSs must be distinguished from online social networks because the latter are the results of SNS usage. In other words, SNSs facilitate the organization of online social networks.

In order to analyze potential privacy issues within SNSs, we need knowledge about how people interact on these platforms. However, there is no such thing as a generalizable "SNS usage." Rather, SNSs suggest "genres of behavior through their architectural elements" (Papacharissi 2009, p. 203) but can be accessed in quite individual usage patterns. Thus, while the term "communication service" focuses on the *communicative potential* of SNSs (as the entirety of available communicative tools), the usage of these tools can be conceptualized as *communication modes* (Hasebrink 2004, p. 71). Although communication modes cannot be directly predicted by technological usage potential, it seems important to establish an integrated service- and usage-oriented systematization of SNSs. A taxonomy should include criteria that allow a distinction, for example, between YouTube and Facebook and MySpace *in general,* and in particular for the case of *privacy issues* within these SNSs. Such criteria have loosely been mentioned by different authors (boyd and Ellison 2008; Cachia 2008; Debatin et al. 2009; Beer 2008; Tufekci 2008; Gross and Acquisti 2005). Aggregating them leads to a preliminary classification of SNSs as displayed in Fig. 13.1.

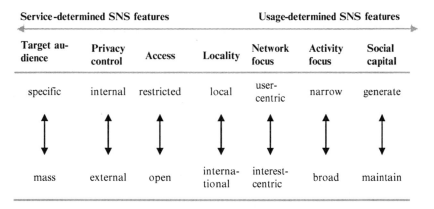

Service-determined SNS features				Usage-determined SNS features		
Target audience	Privacy control	Access	Locality	Network focus	Activity focus	Social capital
specific	internal	restricted	local	user-centric	narrow	generate
mass	external	open	international	interest-centric	broad	maintain

Fig. 13.1 Social network sites taxonomy

   The taxonomy helps to characterize different kinds of SNSs in terms of their major features. For this purpose, it distinguishes service-determined SNS features and usage-determined SNS features. The service-determined SNS features are technological and structural givens that cannot be directly influenced by user activities. For instance, with regard to access, some SNSs are open for every Internet user, while others remain exclusive, "by invitation only" SNSs restricted to a certain audience. In contrast, usage-determined SNS features vary in terms of the users' aims, expected gratifications, and experiences. For instance, with regard to activity focus, some users may just want to use a few of many functions of an SNS to communicate with friends, while others take advantage of a broad spectrum of SNS-provided information, communication, and leisure subservices.

   In the following, we will consider Facebook's current version as well as other SNSs to exemplify service-determined and usage-determined features. One further important aspect when interpreting Fig. 13.1 is that the juxtapositions have to be seen as a continuum rather than dichotomous characteristics of SNSs: for instance, a user's aim when joining a specific SNS might be somewhere between generating and maintaining existing social capital.

   Target audience: Concerning the nature of the targeted audience, Facebook serves as an illustration for both ends of the continuum, specific and mass. Started as a service solely targeting American college students (e.g., Gross and Acquisti 2005), Facebook soon became open to everyone and now explicitly targets a mass audience. Other services within the SNS sector continue targeting more specific audiences (boyd and Ellison 2008): for example, weRead (weread.com) targets book lovers while Buzznet (buzznet.com) aims to bring together people interested in music and pop culture. However, some of these services are starting to integrate Facebook connectivity to increase their reach.

Privacy control: Users' possibilities to internally control disclosed information vary with regard to different spaces within and beyond SNSs (Papacharissi 2009): some services allow their users to specify data visibility (1) beyond the SNS, (2) within the SNS, and (3) within a user's online social network. Other providers make suggestions for "optimized" privacy settings while yet others restrict the user in controlling some of the above mentioned privacy spheres (for example, the German business SNS Xing prevents members without a premium account from browsing other members' profile pages anonymously).

Access: The criteria for membership vary across different SNSs. While Facebook and many other services are open to anyone who can access the Internet, SNSs such as Asmallworld or BeautifulPeople are restricted to a specific – call it exclusive – audience. Similarly, the degree of accessible source code for developers to program mash-ups and third-party applications varies from service to service.

Locality: Facebook is one example of a global SNS. Other services are primarily national (Qzone in China), regional (wer-kennt-wen in Germany), or even hyperlocal (communities of local newspapers).

Network focus: SNSs can be classified by the centrality of user profiles. Services such as MySpace and LinkedIn focus strongly on user profiles and offer a wide range of options for self-expression. Other SNSs build on specific topics such as music, art, and sports. For example, the travelling network TravBuddy (travbuddy.com) centers topics and interest areas on a magazine-style landing page while individual profiles are promoted less prominently. Contrary to boyd and Ellison's (2008, p. 219) view, SNSs forming primarily around interests (not people) obviously do exist. A combination of both perspectives is possible through functional integration: Facebook's public groups are more interest-centric while communicative activities beyond those groups are more user-centric. As a result, the network focus is often primarily usage-determined.

Activity focus: The spectrum of communication (sub-)services offered varies from service to service. Facebook offers a wide range of technological features that might help in obtaining gratifications to satisfy social needs as well as more individualistic information and entertainment needs. In comparison, Twitter, for example, is functionally restricted to the microblogging feature while Flickr concentrates on photo sharing.

Social capital: The perceived extent to which an individual can draw on resources from the network of social ties can be conceptualized as "social capital" (Coleman 1988; Putnam 2000; Ellison et al. 2007; Ellison et al. in this volume). For user activities within SNSs, we suggest differentiating between *generating* social capital – by establishing contact to previously unknown individuals – and *maintaining* social capital by connecting (and interacting) with ties from users' offline social networks (Ellison et al. 2007). In general, most SNSs allow for both activities so that the focus depends heavily on users' communicative behavior.

However, and as already mentioned, many SNSs explicitly suggest genres of behavior. Facebook encourages users to "connect and share with the people *in your life*" (Facebook 2010a, authors' emphasis) to maintain social capital previously created. In contrast, other SNSs focus on building new connections by encouraging users to *publicly* share content or to interact with network members who share *similar interests*. YouTube, digg, and last.fm are just three of many examples where this characteristic form of networking prevails. Although these connections may predominantly remain what Granovetter (1973) calls weak ties, the extension of one's social network by establishing new contacts online might not be as rare as boyd and Ellison (2008, p. 221) assume it to be but rather depends on the specific network under analysis.

As we will show in the following sections, some of these dimensions are particularly important for the analyses of both occurring and potential privacy issues. However, before addressing these issues, we will clarify relevant dimensions that constitute privacy in SNSs.

13.3 Theoretical Approaches to Privacy Online

13.3.1 Informational Privacy

The concept of *privacy as the "right to be let alone"* (Joinson and Paine 2007, p. 242) dates back to the late nineteenth century. The results of an invasion into the private sphere – for instance, by journalists – were described as "mental pain and distress, far greater than could be inflicted by mere bodily injury" (Warren and Brandeis 1890, p. 196). Continuously recurrent legal cases in which celebrities claim their right to be let alone show that this perspective is still topical today. However, this and similar "non-intrusion approaches" do not entirely describe the dimensions of privacy in online environments, where questions of self-regulated access to an individual's personal information and information dissemination play a major role (Joinson and Paine 2007).

In this context, the rapid and global diffusion of Internet access has raised the interest of many scholars from various disciplines who have tried to adapt and extend privacy theories to different forms of online usage (e.g., Cranor 1999; Gadzheva 2008; Metzger 2004; Tavani 2000; Ben-Ze'ev 2003). Here, the concept of *informational privacy* as a distinct category of privacy concerns emerges (Burgoon et al. 1989; Cohen 2000; Tavani 2000). Informational privacy originates in privacy theories by Westin (1967) and Altman (1976). Westin (1967) states that people aim to achieve a situational balance between private and open behavior. Altman (1976) emphasizes that privacy is inherently a social and dynamic process of optimization between disclosure and withdrawal (Tufekci 2008). As a result, an individual might modify or rethink applied privacy mechanisms depending on their success in different social situations (Altman

1976, p. 17). Both theories overlap by focusing on the importance of autonomous control and limited access to an individual's self (Margulis 2003, p. 423). Thus, informational privacy can be understood as "an individual's right to determine how, when, and to what extent information about the self will be released [. . .]" (Joinson and Paine 2007, p. 244; Westin 1967). Within SNSs, it is particularly important to complement this definition with both the addressees of information disclosure – these are single persons, dyads, groups, a disperse public, and/or institutions (see e.g., Schweiger and Quiring 2005) – as well as with the nature of disclosed information. Thus, we expand it to *what information* will be made available *in which way, to whom, when,* and *to what extent."* In other words, informational privacy in SNSs should particularly concern users' *control* of the kind and the content of disclosed information, *autonomy* in (temporal) decision making about information release and withdrawal, and spatial and personal *restriction of access* to private information (see also Sect. 13.4.2).

It becomes clear that extended or public access to personal information alone cannot be considered as a sufficient condition for a loss or a violation of privacy. Many perceived privacy issues may in fact be the result of deliberate privacy abandonment. Individuals who seek to *maintain social capital* may publicly disclose different information to people who use SNSs primarily to generate new social capital (cf. e.g., Ellison et al. in this volume). In contrast, from the user perspective, privacy violations can result from any form of *unwanted or uncontrolled publicness,* regardless of whether specific information is publicly available to one or a thousand persons (see e.g., Joinson and Paine 2007). In other words, privacy issues here occur when users misinterpret the architecture of communication services and/or use communication services in an inappropriate way. This may happen along at least two factors of informational privacy, namely *autonomy* and *control* of information disclosure. Users commenting on their contacts' status updates may *autonomously* decide to disclose the content of their communicative action. However, they might at the same time be unaware of the actual reach of their action – which is likely to exceed the user addressed. The gap between perceived and actual reach can be considered as misinterpretation of the communication service that ultimately results in a *loss of control* over who may access the disclosed information. Other urgent issues occur when SNS providers constrain users in their autonomy so that they may disclose information of different reach *involuntarily.* In terms of our taxonomy, this can occur when providers *limit the amount of internally controllable privacy settings.* For instance, some SNSs provide information on the activity level of their members. Users may be judged by this level although their original intention might have been to use the SNS solely in a passive reception mode. Further involuntary communicative action occurs, for example, when users cannot control whether they may be linked on photos or other multimedia content (see e.g., Debatin et al. 2009).

This perspective of informational privacy largely presupposes the disclosure of *authentic* information about an individual's real self online. In the following section, we assess privacy issues that occur when individuals satisfy inherently social needs with tools of computer-mediated communication (CMC).

13.3.2 Self-Disclosure, Social Network Sites, and Computer-Mediated Communication

It can hardly be denied that within many SNSs, "notions of anonymity and pseudo-nymity [...] have been replaced by performative behavior about the real self" (Cachia 2008, p. 26). Thus, in order to investigate the nature of online privacy issues further, it is important to analyze self-disclosure as the "process of making the self known to others" (Jourard and Lasakow 1958, p. 91; Joinson and Paine 2007). Firstly, and to come back to our taxonomy of SNSs, a high degree of honest self-disclosure is more likely to occur in *user-centric* than in primarily *interest-centric* SNSs (Tufekci 2008; Walther et al. 2010; see also Sect. 13.2). Secondly, within user-centric SNSs, real identity disclosure can be seen as a consequence of the *mediatization of everyday life* (Hartmann 2009; Beer 2008; Thrift 2005, p. 7). From a sociological view, those SNSs increasingly become mundane and "amal-gamate with various non-media activities in social life" (Schulz 2004, p. 98; Beer 2008). As communication services, they provide the architecture for maintaining and managing real world ties and encourage their users to take advantage of these features. In the words of our taxonomy, these SNSs encourage *maintaining social capital* (Haythornthwaite 2007). The *tools* to satisfy (offline) social needs online can instead be found in CMC (see e.g., Etzioni and Etzioni 1999): one key novelty of many user-centric SNSs is that they enable a comfortable *mass management* of real world ties by providing a large spectrum of communication (sub-)services (*activity focus* in our taxonomy). Both one-to-one and one-to-many communication can be executed effortlessly in those SNSs; for example, a user's status update may reach a single recipient or – with no additional effort – a group of specified addressees or a disperse public. This management of real world ties with different communication tools makes many user-centric SNSs hybrid communication phenomena but is also responsible for informational privacy issues becoming prevalent.

In a nutshell: there is a need for a differentiated view on users' privacy behavior in SNSs that addresses (1) different service-determined and usage-determined SNS features (some of them are mentioned in our preliminary taxonomy), (2) the extracted criteria of informational privacy, and (3) SNSs as hybrid communication phenomena where social needs are satisfied with tools of CMC. In the following section, we try to provide further connections between criteria of our taxonomy and the concept of informational privacy by analyzing how SNS providers evaluate different degrees of intimateness and openness.

13.4   Two Perspectives on Privacy in Social Network Sites

13.4.1   A Provider-Based View of Privacy

SNS providers aim to maximize the amount of information users provide and the public visibility of the information disclosed. This is mainly due to *economic* and *network* reasons. The more status updates and personal information users disclose via different communication tools, the more traffic providers can sell to advertising companies. Additionally, information is not only valuable in a quantitative but in a qualitative sense: the content of information can be seen as a commodity that companies convert into opportunities for profit (Thrift 2005; see also Barnes 2006). Every information item participants publish might be used to sell targeted social ads more precisely (Beer 2008; Nielsen 2009). From a provider-based view, a high user consciousness for privacy issues – such as a high awareness of the true visibility of personal information – is seen as a "major obstacle in generating revenue" (Nielsen 2009, p. 5). However, too lax privacy policies result in user discontent and prevent potential users from joining or using the SNS (Economist 2010; boyd 2008; Debatin et al. 2009, p. 84). Therefore, and particularly in *restricted-access SNSs* such as Asmallworld, providers tend to apply strict behavioral rules to determine in which way users can provide what information to whom (Papacharissi 2009). Other providers obviously see one escape from the described dilemma in assuring users that they possess disclosed information while at the same time they reserve some specific exploitation rights (Facebook, 2010b; Nielsen 2009, p. 9). Moreover, one could assume that the more *international* SNSs are, the more complicated it seems to users to control possible third-party access to their information and to demand privacy guidelines that adhere to national specifics in privacy law.

The second reason for providers' endorsement of public information can be derived from the first one: to make SNSs more dynamic and attractive. SNS providers can only build the framework of their product while user activity brings it to life. Providers thus have to rely on "produsers" (Bruns 2006) who actively contribute to shaping the SNS as an attractive product. Regularly updated user profiles, visible activities, and ongoing interpersonal communication suggest to its members that there is always something going on. This potentially increases both users' own activity level and their dwell time, which again can be monetized.

In sum, privacy issues in the relationship between users and providers of SNSs mainly concern the unwanted collection, storage, and dissemination of personal information by providers as well as concerns about potential security leaks from the platforms that might lead to hacking and identity theft (boyd and Ellison 2008). Most of these issues usually remain invisible to the average user (Debatin et al. 2009, p. 88). And despite users seeking to reach a (perceived) optimum between privacy and publicity over time (Lange 2008), new features – such as the Facebook "News Feed" (see e.g., boyd 2008) – tend to circumvent their knowledge about privacy management and eventually make them share more content publicly than they intended to do.

13.4.2   A User-Based View of Privacy

The growing body of empirical research on privacy in SNSs continuously extracts factors that influence the privacy behavior of their users. In Sect. 13.3.1, we suggested three categories of informational privacy: (1) individual autonomy, which may be defined as users' consciousness for how and when privacy settings should be revised; (2) access restriction to private information, which may be assessed in terms of perceived reach and visibility of information disclosure; (3) control of the kind and the content of disclosed information, which may be specified as a deliberation between social benefits versus privacy risks.

13.4.2.1   Autonomy: User Engagement with Privacy Settings

One general reason for privacy issues to occur is users' indifference or lack of knowledge concerning privacy settings in SNSs. Different studies show that while a majority of SNS users seem to be aware of the existence of privacy settings (such as limiting the profile's visibility to specified friends), they seldom make use of this autonomy and change the default settings: for instance, Acquisti and Gross (2006) report significant discrepancies in students' awareness of specific privacy issues and their actual behavior. Similarly, Govani and Pashley (2005) show indifferent user behavior concerning the adjustment of privacy settings on Facebook – even after surveyed users were informed about possible risks of information disclosure. This gap between knowledge about privacy issues and actual behavior has been named the "privacy paradox" (Barnes 2006; Utz and Krämer 2009). While perceiving a high degree of *current* control, the privacy paradox emerges as SNS users often seem too shortsighted concerning *prospective* issues of the current behavior (Dwyer et al. 2007; Tufekci 2008).

In contrast, one factor that leads to an increase in "applied privacy awareness" is the *establishment* of SNSs. This term naturally combines the influence of technological and social developments such as evolving default privacy settings, public attention to SNSs, user experiences, and others. Nevertheless, at this aggregated level, the shift in users' privacy behavior is notable: boyd and Hargittai (2010) use longitudinal data to explain that there were significant increases in the frequency with which users modified Facebook's privacy settings between 2009 and 2010. The same tendency of increased privacy awareness can already be found in Debatin et al.'s 2007 sample (Debatin et al. 2009). Both findings suggest major increases compared to the "vanishing small number of users" (Gross and Acquisti 2005) who had changed their default Facebook privacy settings in 2005. Another reason for users to revise their privacy settings is the personal experience of *invasions into privacy* such as unwanted contacting or profile hacking. Empirical findings by Debatin et al. (2009) substantiate this factor as a strong predictor for an individual to revise their own privacy settings. Furthermore, *demographic factors* are found to influence users' applied privacy behavior, mainly concerning the amount of personal information they disclose (see e.g., Stutzman and Kramer-Duffield 2010; Lewis et al. 2008; Tufekci 2008).

13.4.2.2 Access Restriction: The Influence of Perceived Audience on Privacy Behavior

As already alluded to in the second section of our chapter, the occurrence of privacy issues in SNSs can also be traced back to individual unconsciousness or misperception of the actual visibility of disclosed information: SNS users may not be aware of the audience that is able to access status updates, comments, or profile entries. However, Acquisti and Gross (2006) show that the majority of their surveyed SNS users are aware of the true visibility of their profile – nevertheless, a "significant minority" (p. 53) underestimate its possible reach. Tufekci (2008) substantiates these findings: a comparison between the privacy behavior of Facebook and MySpace users in 2006 and 2007 reveals that 95% of surveyed Facebook users disclose their real names, while this only applies for around 60% of MySpace members. At the time the study was conducted, MySpace profiles were public to every Internet user by default (while the visibility of Facebook profiles could easily be restricted), and thus fewer users were willing to disclose their real name to a possibly unwanted audience. On Facebook, this fear of an unwanted audience was addressed by restricting the profile's visibility – however, and in both cases, most users did not decide to regulate the amount of disclosed information but only to apply the given privacy settings.

While suggesting that SNS users are highly aware of privacy issues, the findings of these and similar studies are often limited: privacy settings in SNSs and communication subservices evolve rapidly and become more sophisticated (Utz and Krämer 2009). However, recent studies concentrate on user profiles as communication subservices and survey college students who might have an increased awareness of privacy issues. For other populations and especially for a wide range of communication modes (e.g., commenting on a photo or a news item in SNSs), it is more likely that privacy awareness has not evolved that much. Here, users might perceive an "imagined audience" that consists either of (a selection of) their network contacts or of a more disperse group of people. As mentioned in our theoretical argumentation, publishing content with this imagined audience in mind might result in a discrepancy between desired and achieved privacy (cf. also Altman 1976; Cachia 2008, p. 27).

13.4.2.3 Control: Pondering the Risks and Benefits of the Presentation of Self

One main motivation behind engaging in SNSs is to start, cultivate, and maintain social relationships (Gangadharbatla 2008; Ellison et al. 2007). When individuals seek sociability, they naturally try to show themselves in a favorable light (Siibak 2009; Zhao et al. 2008). SNSs are an ideal place for strategically creating "highly socially desirable identities" (Utz and Krämer 2009) depending on how individuals would like to be judged by others. Thus, much of what is perceived as privacy issues can instead be seen as *impression management* (Goffman 1959; Krämer and Winter 2008). From this perspective, the nature and the publicity of disclosed personal information has to be co-interpreted as a psychological trade-off between "the need to be seen" (Tufekci 2008, p. 34) and the awareness of possible privacy issues (Livingstone 2008). The specific appearances of impression management vary depending on individual user characteristics and attitudes on the one hand (Krämer and Winter 2008, for a detailed analysis, see Krämer and Haferkamp in this volume) and architectural aspects of communication services on the other hand: while users may want to manage their self-presentation within the business SNS LinkedIn via qualifications and awards (for this might attract future business partners or employers), the prominent exposure of one's network size might serve as a functional equivalent in other SNSs. Concerning the latter, the desire to maximize one's network size can be seen as a reason for SNS users accepting unknown people as Friends (Debatin et al. 2009; Krämer and Winter 2008). In other words, users with a high need for extensive self-presentation online tend to take more risks and consequently also apply less strict privacy settings (Livingstone 2008; Utz and Krämer 2009). At first glance, this seems contradictory to findings by Lewis et al. (2008) who state that private profiles are significantly more common among more active SNS users. For further investigation, future studies should more distinctively analyze the interplay between privacy settings, user activity, and desired social outcomes (e.g., generating or maintaining social capital).

Besides intrinsic factors, (perceived) social norms seem to play an important role in determining personal and spatial access restriction to user profiles as well as the amount and the kind of information individuals provide within SNSs. Lewis et al. (2008) find empirical support for the hypothesis that SNS users are more likely to restrict the visibility of their profile if their network contacts' profiles are private too. Utz and Krämer (2009) extend this finding by revealing significant correlations between users' *perception* of the amount of private profiles in their environment and their actual behavior of restricting the visibility of their own profile.

13.5 Discussion

Despite many SNSs serve as a functional completion to users' offline management of social contacts, individual privacy behavior in both environments is far from being congruent. In this chapter, we have tried to structure the agenda for privacy research in SNSs by (1) systemizing SNSs with both service-determined and usage-determined criteria, (2) denominating privacy issues within SNSs primarily as issues of informational privacy, (3) conceptualizing SNSs as online environments where users satisfy manifold social needs with CMC tools, and (4) advocating the need for integrated analyses of privacy issues in SNSs.

Our suggested taxonomy provides criteria that allow distinctions between SNSs on an inter-service dimension. Furthermore, it can also be applied to analyses of privacy issues within SNSs: while service-determined features constitute the generic privacy framework of an SNS, usage-determined SNS features complement this perspective by allowing analyses of the extent to which privacy issues might occur in different communication modes. As our selective insights into the user perspective on privacy reveal, SNS members currently seem to be quite aware of some *general* risks of disclosing authentic information. As a result, they increasingly try to restore an informational balance by restricting the public visibility of their personal data. However, and in terms of informational privacy, a subversive diminution of autonomy and control still characterizes situations in which people unveil their real identity and at the same time largely cede the surveillance of their private sphere to SNS providers. As our assumptions on the provider-based view of privacy show, this ultimately leads to a discrepancy between users' desired and achieved control. Thus, the privacy paradox currently continues to exist at least below the surface of visible communication processes and *within* users' online social networks, where private information is (imprudently) disclosed to people who are little more than strangers.

As argued in our chapter, an integration of characteristics of CMC with sociological phenomena of the "offline life" might be helpful to analyze this paradox further. In rural areas with close-knit communities, it has long been (and still is) quite usual that information of every kind quickly disseminates across entire villages. Might it be that SNS users act in a similar fashion? The architecture of those online environments facilitates fulfilling social needs such as keeping up with what is going on in one's own narrower and broader environment. And concerning the (inter-)active part of sociability, communication via SNSs increases the probability of receiving immediate and more diverse feedback on own activities (Cachia 2008; Lange 2008).

Apart from these more intrinsic motives for information disclosure, more attention should be paid to the effects of (perceived) external social pressure on the behavior of individual SNS users. As many SNSs are so closely connected to users' offline life (sometimes already a requirement for real world sociability), an online profile without sufficient (authentic) profile information might result in negative results; this leads back to the beginning of our article where we questioned why particularly our youth is so communicative that they are being stigmatized as "junkies." From the described perspective, it is easy to imagine that keeping an orphaned and non-informative online profile might increasingly lead to (offline) victimization.

The increasing interdependence between on- and offline corroborates our approach of conceptualizing SNSs as designed environments where CMC tools are used – and sometimes misused – to satisfy inherently social needs. Individual privacy behavior here remains a multi-faceted phenomenon where voluntary privacy abandonment has to be distinguished from real privacy issues. Our concept to assess these differences was to analyze user privacy behavior with regard to both the concept of informational privacy as well as systematic characteristics of SNSs. Further research should evaluate the empirical capability of our SNS taxonomy and our view on informational privacy to provide a better understanding of whether and why some people really are running out of privacy.

References

Acquisti A, Gross R (2006) Imagined communities: awareness, information sharing, and privacy on the Facebook. In: Golle P, Danezis G (eds) Proceedings of 6th workshop on privacy enhancing technologies, Robinson College, Cambridge, pp 36–58

Altman I (1976) Privacy: a conceptual analysis. Environ Behav 8(7):7–29

Barnes SB (2006) A privacy paradox: social networking in the United States. First Monday 11(4). http://firstmonday.org/htbin/cgiwrap/bin/ojs/index.php/fm/article/view/1394/1312#b1

Beer D (2008) Social network(ing) sites. . . revisiting the story so far: a response to danah boyd & Nicole Ellison. J Comput Mediat Commun 13:516–529

Ben-Ze'ev A (2003) Privacy, emotional closeness, and openness in cyberspace. Comput Hum Behav 19:451–467

boyd dm (2008) Facebook's privacy trainwreck. Convergence 14(1):13–20

boyd dm, Ellison NB (2008) Social network sites: definition, history, and scholarship. J Comput Mediat Commun 13:210–230

boyd d, Hargittai E (2010) Facebook privacy settings: who cares? First Monday 15(8). http://firstmonday.org/htbin/cgiwrap/bin/ojs/index.php/fm/article/view/3086/2589

Bruns A (2006) Towards produsage: futures for user-led content production. http://eprints.qut.edu.au/4863/1/4863_1.pdf

Burgoon JK, Parrott R, LePoire BA, Kelley DL, Walther JB, Perry D (1989) Maintaining and restoring privacy through communication in different types of relationship. J Soc Pers Relat 6:131–158

Cachia R (2008) Social computing: study on the use and impact of online social networking: IPTS exploratory research on the socio-economic impact of social computing. JRC European Commission, Spain. http://ftp.jrc.es/EURdoc/JRC48650.pdf

Cohen JE (2000) Examined lives: informational privacy and the subject as object. Stanford Law Rev 52(5):1373–1438

Coleman JS (1988) Social capital in the creation of human capital. Am J Sociol 94 (Supplement):95–120

Cranor LF (1999) Internet privacy. Commun ACM 42:29

Debatin B, Lovejoy JP, Horn AK, Hughes BN (2009) Facebook and online privacy. Attitudes, behaviors and unintended consequences. J Comput Mediat Commun 15:83–108

Dwyer C, Hiltz SR, Passerini K (2007) Trust and privacy concern within social networking sites: a comparison of Facebook and MySpace. In: Proceedings of the thirteenth Americas conference on information systems, Keystone

Economist (2010) Privacy 2.0, pp 18–19

Ellison NB, Steinfield C, Lampe C (2007) The benefits of Facebook "Friends:" social capital and college students' use of online social network sites. J Comput Mediat Commun 12:1143–1168

Etzioni A, Etzioni O (1999) Face-to-face and computer-mediated communities, a comparative analysis. Inf Soc 15(4):241–248

Facebook (2010) Facebook landing page. http://www.facebook.com

Facebook (2010) Statement of rights and responsibilities. http://www.facebook.com/terms.php? ref=pf

Gadzheva M (2008) Privacy in the age of transparency: the new vulnerability of the individual. Soc Sci Comput Rev 26(1):60–74

Gangadharbatla H (2008) Facebook Me: collective self-esteem, need to belong, and internet self-efficacy as predictors of the iGeneration's attitudes toward social networking sites. J Interact Advert 8(2):5–15

Goffman E (1959) The presentation of self in everyday life. Double Day, Garden City

Govani T, Pashley H (2005) Student awareness of the privacy implications when using Facebook. Paper presented at the privacy poster fair at Carnegie Mellon university school of library and information science, Dec 14, http://lorrie.cranor.org/courses/fa05/tubzhlp.pdf

Granovetter MS (1973) The strength of weak ties. Am J Sociol 78(6):1360–1380

Gross R, Acquisti A (2005) Information revelation and privacy in online social networks. In: Proceedings of the 2005 ACM workshop on privacy in the electronic society, ACM Press, New York, pp 71–80

Hartmann M (2009) Everyday: domestication of mediatization or mediatized domestication. In: Lundby K (ed) Mediatization: concept, changes, consequences. Lang, New York, pp 225–242

Hasebrink U (2004) Konvergenz aus Nutzerperspektive: Das Konzept der Kommunikationsmodi. [Convergence from the user perspective]. In: Hasebrink U (ed) Reihe Rezeptionsforschung, vol 1, Mediennutzung in konvergierenden Medienumgebungen [Vol. 1: media use in converging media environments]. Fischer, München, pp 67–85

Haythornthwaite C (2007) Social networks and online community. In: Joinson AN, McKenna KYA, Postmes T, Reips U-D (eds) The Oxford handbook of internet psychology. Oxford University Press, Oxford, pp 121–153

Joinson AN, Paine CB (2007) Self-disclosure, privacy and the internet. In: Joinson AN, McKenna KYA, Postmes T, Reips U-D (eds) The Oxford handbook of internet psychology. Oxford University Press, Oxford, pp 237–252

Jourard SM, Lasakow P (1958) Some factors in self-disclosure. J Abnorm Soc Psychol 56(1):91–98

Krämer NC, Winter S (2008) Impression management 2.0. The relationship of self-esteem, extraversion, self-efficacy, and self-presentation within social networking sites. J Media Psychol 20(3):106–116

Lange PG (2008) Publicly private and privately public: social networking on YouTube. J Comput Mediat Commun 13(1):361–380

Lewis K, Kaufman J, Christakis N (2008) The taste for privacy: an analysis of college student privacy settings in an online social network. J Comput Mediat Commun 14:79–100

Livingstone S (2008) Taking risky opportunities in youthful content creation: teenagers' use of social networking sites for intimacy, privacy and self-expression. New Media Soc 10(3):393–411

Lundby K (ed) (2009) Mediatization: concept, changes, consequences. Lang, New York

Margulis ST (2003) On the status and contribution of Westin's and Altman's theories of privacy. J Social Issues 59(2):411–429

Metzger MJ (2004) Privacy, trust, and disclosure: exploring barriers to electronic commerce. J Comput Mediat Commun 9(4). http://jcmc.indiana.edu/vol9/issue4/metzger.html

Nguyen J (2010) The state of social networks. http://comscore.com/Press_Events/Presentations_Whitepapers/2010/The_State_of_Social_Networks_in_Asia_Pacific_with_a_Focus_on_Singapore/(language)/eng-US

Nielsen Online (2009) Global faces and networked places: a Nielsen report on social networking's new global footprint. http://blog.nielsen.com/nielsenwire/wp-content/uploads/2009/03/nielsen_globalfaces_mar09.pdf

Papacharissi Z (2009) The virtual geographies of social networks: a comparative analysis of Facebook, LinkedIn and Asmallworld. New Media Soc 11(1–2):199–220

Patalong F (2010) Jugendliche sind Kommunikations-Junkies: Kernergebnisse der JIM-Studie 2010 [Teenagers are communication junkies: core results of the JIM study]. Spiegel Online. http://www.spiegel.de/netzwelt/web/0,1518,731352,00.html

Putnam RD (2000) Bowling alone: the collapse and revival of American community. Simon & Schuster, New York

Schulz W (2004) Reconstructing mediatization as an analytical concept. Eur J Commun 19(1):87–101

Schweiger W, Quiring O (2005) User-generated content on mass media web sites – just a variety of interactivity or something completely different? Paper presented at the 55th annual conference of the international communication association, New York, 26–30 May 2005

Siibak A (2009) Constructing the self through the photo selection-visual impression management on social networking websites. Cyberpsychol J Psychosoc Res Cyberspace 3(1). http://cyberpsychology.eu/view.php?cisloclanku=2009061501&article=1

Stutzman F, Kramer-Duffield J (2010) Friends only: examining a privacy-enhancing behavior in Facebook. CHI Atlanta, 10–15 Apr 2010. http://fredstutzman.com/papers/CHI2010_Stutzman.pdf

Tavani HT (2000) Privacy and the internet. http://www.bc.edu/bc_org/avp/law/st_org/iptf/commentary/content/2000041901.html

Thrift N (2005) Knowing capitalism. Theory, culture and society. Sage, London

Tufekci Z (2008) Can you see me now? Audience and disclosure regulation in online social network sites. B Sci Technol Soc 28(1):20–36

Utz S, Krämer NC (2009) The privacy paradox on social network sites revisited: the role of individual characteristics and group norms. Cyberpsychol J Psychosoc Res Cyberspace 3(2), Article 2

Walther JB, DeAndrea D, Kim J, Anthony JC (2010) The influence of online comments on perceptions of antimarijuana public service announcements on YouTube. Hum Commun Res 36(4):469–492

Warren SD, Brandeis LD (1890) The right to privacy. Harvard Law Rev 4(5):193–220

Westin A (1967) Privacy and freedom. Atheneum, New York

Zhao S, Grasmuck S, Martin J (2008) Identity construction on Facebook: digital empowerment in anchored relationships. Comput Hum Behav 24:1816–1836

Chapter 14
Mobile Privacy: Contexts

Maren Hartmann

14.1 Introduction

> Not sure what Facebook's Wed. announcement will be but I can guarantee two things: It will have to do with mobile & It will violate privacy (MarketingAtom, tweet, 10/31/2010)

On the following Wednesday, Facebook announced several changes to its mobile services, including a new product called "Deals" – a platform for local stores and places to offer deals to nearby Facebook users. The users' location data would be used in the process. The privacy implications were not explicitly addressed in the announcement. This kind of combination of social media and mobility does, however, lead to many questions concerning privacy.

Ever since its first inception as a modern concept, privacy has been a contested terrain – both theoretically and empirically. It is currently facing renewed and increasing challenges. One important set of challenges, as widely discussed in this book and seen in the example, is based in social media applications and services. An additional challenge, less focused on thus far, also relates to new media applications, but at the same time offers a new focus: it is the question of mobility and mobile media, i.e., it is the question of privacy in mobile contexts. The challenges that privacy faces at least double in this context: not only are the existing privacy concerns also relevant here, but the environments in which mobile media are used are also extremely privacy-sensitive. Additionally, the technology provides a privacy challenge through its technical affordances. The basic challenge is the combination of person, location, and activities – both those that are observable from the outside and those that are conducted technologically.

M. Hartmann (✉)
Berlin University of Arts, Berlin, Germany
e-mail: hartmann@udk-berlin.de

S. Trepte and L. Reinecke (eds.), *Privacy Online*,
DOI 10.1007/978-3-642-21521-6_14, © Springer-Verlag Berlin Heidelberg 2011

Three examples may well illustrate privacy issues in mobile contexts: (1) An organization can track an employee who uses a smartphone using a location-based service. However, this employee might not want the employer to know where he/she is at that moment. (2) A car rental company uses the GPS system to track their cars and can thereby charge users in case of contract infringements (cf. Ardagna et al. 2008, p. 308). (3) In the near future, people might use their smartphones to identify a stranger in the street with facial recognition software. All of these examples are based on the combination of privacy and mobility.

The following chapter will focus on the combination of person, location, and activities and the implied challenges therein. In the context of this contribution, the term used to describe this complex set of relations is called "mobile privacy." In many ways, the chapter already offers a conclusion at the very beginning: it begins with the assumption that the combination of privacy and mobility is potentially problematic. Calling it problematic and a challenge hints at a starting point that states that there is still something to protect when we speak of privacy (in contrast to, for example, the view of Google's CEO Schmidt, who does not support anonymity, thus underlining that Google knows where we are and also what we think). The view that mobile privacy is a potentially problematic combination will also not change during the course of the chapter. Instead, the aim is to substantiate the claim and come up with a more differentiated definition of "mobile privacy" at the end.

Two perspectives might be particularly helpful in defining mobile privacy and to explaining its meaning further. The first perspective deals with technological research, the second with a philosophical approach to the contexts of privacy. Whereas the technological studies elaborate on the factual problems of design and privacy settings, the context perspective elaborates on its meaning for the users. Technological research has shown, for example, that users tend to look at the information receiver, the information usage, and the information sensitivity (Beckwith 2003). However, users generally seem to lag behind technological developments. Very often they are not able (or not willing to invest the time) to either find the right information to answer these questions or to accommodate their privacy settings to satisfy their needs. Therefore, some technological studies suggest technological answers to these problems (based on the idea of protecting the user). The perspective of context adds to this point of view that privacy needs are defined alongside with expectations and user interpretations (Nissenbaum 2010). Privacy is dynamic and constantly balanced by its users. To understand mobile privacy, both perspectives should be considered: the technological solutions and the more general explanations.

This chapter will begin with a very brief introduction to both mobility and privacy as theoretical and empirical concepts (Sect. 14.2). We then move on to technological research (Sect. 14.3) and to philosophical research about the contexts of (mobile) privacy (Sect. 14.4). Finally, we will summarize these findings in a definition of mobile privacies (Sect. 14.5).

14.2 Mobility and Privacy

The background to a concept such as mobile privacy includes two obvious references: mobility and privacy. They both appear to be moving in different directions though: mobility is supposedly on the rise and there is talk of a "mobility turn" (see e.g., Urry 2007, p. 6), while privacy is supposedly diminishing (some even say it is heavily threatened (Privacy International 2007)). Both are complex constructs, but they also operate on different levels. Privacy is the more philosophical and therefore debatable, while mobility (depending on the definition) can at least partly be "measured."

14.2.1 Privacy

We will now briefly turn to basic definitions of privacy, since many of these are also helpful in defining current challenges. Privacy is not a topic that needs to be introduced in great detail within the context of this book (see e.g., Margulis' chapter in this volume). Warren and Brandeis famously defined privacy as "the right to be let alone" (Warren and Brandeis 1890). This is relevant for our purpose, since it underlines privacy's *physical nature*, i.e., both place and space are important in this definition. Warren and Brandeis (1890), as legal experts, also managed to extend this idea beyond the material into more abstract realms:

> These considerations lead to the conclusion that the protection afforded to thoughts, sentiments, and emotions, expressed through the medium of writing or of the arts, so far as it consists in preventing publication, is merely an instance of the enforcement of the more general right of the individual to be let alone. ... The principle which protects personal writings and all other personal productions ... but against publication in any form, is in reality not the principle of private property, but that of an inviolate personality. (p. 5)

This combination of physical privacy with more abstract, informational forms can thus already be found in this early approach. It the basis for the combination of privacy and mobility. The informational form becomes even more prominent in another often quoted reference by Professor (Emeritus) of Public Law and Government Alan Westin, who summarized privacy as the ability for people to determine for themselves "when, how, and to what extent, information about them is communicated to others" (1968). To extend Westin a little further, the question of the public should also be considered when thinking about privacy–or rather, the questions of "where" and "in which situation" should be added to his list. Or, as then Privacy Commissioner of Canada, George Radwandski, stated, privacy is "the right to control access to one's person and to personal information about oneself" (2002). Part of that would potentially imply that consent is an important aspect within privacy control (see below).

Partly because of the question of public and private space as well as public and private behaviors, these basic ideas on privacy have also been transferred into the broader context of the question of public life and the necessity thereof for functioning democracies (Weiß and Groebel 2002). The quote by the political theorist Hannah Arendt (1989) is a case in point here:

> The four walls of one's private property offer the only reliable hiding place from the common public world, not only from the common public world, not only from everything that goes on in it but also from its very publicity, from being seen and being heard. A life spent entirely in public, in the presence of others, becomes, as we should say, shallow. (p. 71)

Arendt's (1989) approach points to the fact that possibilities for a retreat are a basis for our participation in public life. At the same time, her statement is not necessarily fitting anymore: today, these retreats are not necessarily the four walls of one's private property. The home remains relevant, but it has become more mobile, and for some people mobile media are even becoming home. Here, too, privacy and mobility are closely related.

These brief privacy references point to two aspects that will be of importance for the definition of mobile privacies (cf. Sect. 14.5). Firstly, privacy is closely related to publicness and they both depend on each other; secondly, privacy is related to both physical and locational questions as well as to informational ones.

14.2.2 Mobility

The other important aspect in "mobile privacy" is obviously the question of *mobility*. The last few years have seen a great rise in interest in the concept of mobility. Its theorizations are blossoming, as are empirical studies with rather diverse foci (tourism, work, etc.). In communication studies, the interest has mainly been fuelled by the increasing emergence of mobile media (see e.g., Green and Haddon 2009). Beginning with mobile phones, which were initially researched as an additional form of mediated interpersonal communication, further applications (such as SMS, then the camera, etc.) soon underlined that the use of these media was not only broadening the media scope, but was also extending the range of environments that was suffused with (mainly individual) media use. Since laptops have become more common (and now smartphones, ipads, etc.), both places as well as environments and hence also forms of use have diversified.

Why is all this relevant in this context? With more mobility, different privacy concerns emerge in different environments. As convergent media, the items referred to above offer such a range of interactions with both people and content that using them in diverse public places and while "on the road" necessarily creates challenges. Mobility is also not a closed and stable entity. Instead, mobility itself is seen to be rather diverse.

The first rough differentiation between types of mobilities is between physical/ material, symbolic/informational, and social mobility. John Urry (2002) differentiates even further and suggests five forms of mobility that he emphasizes as being interdependent:

- Corporeal travel of people for work, leisure, family life, pleasure, migration and escape
- Physical movement of objects delivered to producers, consumers and retailers
- Imaginative travel elsewhere through images of places and peoples upon TV (. . .)
- Virtual travel often in real time on the internet so transcending geographical and social distance; as Microsoft asks: "where do you want to go today?"
- Communicative travel through person-to-person messages via letters, telephone, fax and mobile (p. 1)

For the purposes of defining "mobile privacy," we will follow Urry's (2002) lead. We will use the details of Urry's differentiation and apply them to the mobile privacy definition. The easiest connection between these mobilities and privacy is the right to privacy as a pre-condition for public life, to which the mobile context simply adds an additional emphasis. Somewhat more complex is the right to privacy as something that needs to be created and sustained. Thus, in mobile contexts, different kinds of privacy might be observable and necessary depending on the movement and the related location. Hence, in the following, we will refer to "mobile privacies" with the aim of underlining that there might be different forms of privacies in mobile contexts. Taking Urry's (2002) interdependent forms of mobility into account and assuming that they are all relevant to the mobile privacy question, it becomes clear that privacies are related not only to people, but also increasingly to objects and applications. The combination of privacy as both physical and informational is in many ways the basic description of mobility. The concept of mobilities – especially in Urry's (2002) terms – therefore helps to underline that a set of mobile privacies exists or might need to be created. Below, we will begin to fill this set with some examples.

Let us now turn to two fields of research – technological and philosophical – in terms of mobile privacy.

14.3   A Technology Perspective on Mobile Privacy

A first – and most general – technological answer to mobile privacy can be found in the request for comments (rfc) concerning Mobile IPv6 (Perkins et al. 2010). IPv6 is a protocol that allows nodes to remain reachable while moving around in the IPv6 Internet. The authors suggest that the technical architecture of this protocol should have privacy as the core concern, since users will not usually take care of privacy themselves: "The reason is that most users will not change defaults, and the default be one of privacy, only moving away from it by customer choice" (Perkins et al. 2010). The important technical issue is to keep the default at the highest privacy level rather than the other way round ("opt-in" instead of "opt-out," see also

Debatin's chapter in this volume). This is in stark contrast to existing practices. At the moment, one can observe quite a huge difference in the nature of engagement with the privacy topic when comparing a set of diverse mobile providers. The policies also tend to remain very abstract. Most importantly though, the policies all expect the user to *act*. The default settings will not necessarily offer a satisfying protection for the user. To ask for this to be handled differently generally implies a change in the overall presumption about individuals' responsibilities. Perkins et al. (2010), in line with their user protection strategy, also stress that connecting movement and location data with other data should be avoided: "Architectural changes MUST avoid requiring exposing a mapping between any of a node's identifiers and IP addresses/locators to unknown observers."

The user is also at the heart of Richard Beckwith's research (conducted at Intel Research), which looked at privacy as a design issue (Beckwith 2003). He underlines that some seemingly obvious design choices in the context of privacy are not always the best choices. Unobtrusiveness, for example, is not always a good choice if user awareness is required. This builds on the idea of the relevance of context but also poses the question of consent. How should users provide informed consent when they are not aware of something happening or when they do not understand the full nature of the consequences of their consent? This is one of the core problems of privacy in the mobile media context. Users are expected to be experts concerning their own privacy issues (as with the settings) – and to also adjust these depending on the situation.

According to Beckwith (2003), users tend to look at three aspects in particular: (a) the information receiver, (b) the information usage, and (c) the information sensitivity. Overall, this means that the user needs to know (a) who is involved, (b) what the information will be used for and how this affects the user, and (c) how sensitive the data is (Beckwith 2003). With this information at hand, users can better judge their privacy needs in a given situation. The user problem of needing to actively engage would remain prevalent here though.

However, some of the research presented here emphasizes that the users are not alone in their need to differentiate and act, but rather that the technology can at least partly take over this differentiation (as in Perkins et al. (2010)). This can be demonstrated with the work of Ardagna et al. (2008). They understand *location privacy* as "the right of the users to decide how, when, and for which purposes their location information could be released to other counterparts" (p. 313). Ardagna et al. (2008) differentiate between three different types of location privacy: (a) *identity privacy* ("the main goal is to protect users' identities associated with or inferable from location information"); (b) *position privacy* ("the main goal is to perturb users locations as a way to protect their actual positions"); and (c) *path privacy* ("the main goal is to protect the privacy of those users that are continuously monitored during a certain period of time"). Ardagna et al. then show different technological solutions for all three types of location privacy. These are of particular interest for us, since they offer solutions most concretely in the mobile context. Furthermore, the technological answers are indirectly philosophical as well: they state that users are key to the privacy problem, but mostly in the sense that they need the technology to support them (rather than threaten their privacy).

These technological answers include anonymity but also partial identification. Overall, the idea of a decrease in the accuracy of personal information bound to identities is widely seen as useful (e.g., in something such as "less-than-optimal location tracking"). Depending on which kind of location privacy is meant, different versions of this apply. To a non-technical mind, "less-than-optimal" sounds potentially problematic, but it appears to be a good technological solution. As these references also indicate though, most solutions thus far are technical approximations and still require the other players (users, providers, the legal framework, etc.) to "play along."

One more provocative idea in this context is mentioned by Varun Singh (who also offers other possibilities for differentiations that are not treated here – see Singh 2008). Singh mentions the need for *plausible deniability*, which "allows users to customize their context data, in situations when the users wish to hide or fake their identity" (Singh 2008, p. 6). Singh thereby adds the possibility for a more active take on the overall range of possibilities, re-adjusting our focus back to the active user, but also to the generally accepted rules. It is not a solution for user inactivity, but instead offers a more social (and playful) version of the "less-than-optimal" (as an "other-than-accurate" version). As a "technological" solution, this seems unusual but useful.

Overall, in our technological takes on privacy and mobility, we find an emphasis on the provision of opt-in rather than opt-out mechanisms (now extended to "other-than-accurate" and "plausible deniability"); we find the who/what/how-questions as a possible differentiation as well as different location privacies (identity, position, path). This will be picked up again below. For the moment we ask what they have in common. First of all, they show the range of differentiations necessary to assess the privacy needs and privacy solutions in a given situation. This already implies the question of context, which will be discussed in the next section. They also begin and end with the user and implicitly (and explicitly) emphasize that the user needs to be protected (rather than protection for the freedom to aggregate data, for example). We also see that technological solutions to privacy problems are possible – plus these solutions also tend to imply philosophical answers. In the question of context, we can find both technological and philosophical answers.

14.4 (Mobile) Privacies in Context

One issue that can be found in more than one research field in relation to privacy is the question of context (for an example from the technological field, see Singh 2008). Singh (2008), following Dey (2001), defines context as "[...] a set of suitable environmental states and settings concerning a user, which are relevant for a situation sensitive application in the process of adapting the services and information offered to the user" (p. 1). As shown above, this underlines the need for specific solutions in different contexts (place, time, personal needs, etc. all play a role in this) rather than "one-for-all."

A somewhat broader and therefore very helpful recent book was not without reason entitled "Privacy in Context" (Nissenbaum 2010). In this book, Helen Nissenbaum (a philosopher with an interest in technologies) develops the useful concept of "contextual integrity." She defines the right to privacy as

> a right to live in a world in which our expectations about the flow of personal information are, for the most part, met. [...] achieved through the harmonious balance of social rules, or norms, with both local and general values, ends and purposes. (Nissenbaum 2010, p. 231)

What her concept captures well is not only the dynamic nature of privacy, but also a reliance on expectations. The user, as I have called the person desiring privacy of some sort or another, is key here. This user sometimes balances the risks and benefits and then decides what to do. Such a rational, thoughtful approach is, however, not always possible or not always the case. The user tends to show a gap between perception and action (see also Debatin's chapter in this volume). Not surprisingly then, many of the technological solutions are concerned with easing users' possibilities to determine their level of privacy in given contexts and adding responsibilities to the list of the technology developers and providers (expectations need to be met). Most of the approaches mentioned so far also emphasize the context-related nature of these issues. At the same time, they underline the problem that users should ideally make many informed decisions about their privacy settings in diverse contexts all the time.

What does Nissenbaum (2010) contribute to this problematic? She defines contexts – with an obvious parallel to her privacy definition – as "structured social settings characterized by canonical activities, roles, relationships, power structures, norms (or rules), and internal values (goals, ends, purposes)" (2010, p. 132). She refers to a range of existing social theories (e.g., Bourdieu 1984) and current phenomena (e.g., Google Maps' Street View). This emphasis is clearly useful: (a) as a reminder that this kind of approach does not necessarily have to start from scratch, and (b) because it stresses that contexts are only specific in the given situation. All the aspects mentioned by Nissenbaum (2010), such as roles, relationships, and norms, may play a role in how users define privacy in given contexts. When we take Nissenbaum's (2010) definition and compare it to some of those discussed as part of the technological approaches (Beckwith 2003), however, a problem emerges. While the context of privacy is surely as complex and contingent as Nissenbaum (2010) hints, mobile privacies need to be defined more rigidly – rigid in the sense of "translatable into technological solutions." What Nissenbaum provides is a broad philosophical debate. What the technological debates underline is that the other approach – defining a problematic context and then discussing what is at stake and how it can be solved – is sometimes more productive.

Nissenbaum (2010) does not particularly address the specificities of the mobile context either. Only in (briefly) referring to work of one of her former PhD students, Michael Zimmer, does mobility shine through. Zimmer (2007, in Nissenbaum 2010, pp. 198–199) created the concept of "spheres of mobility." While airports might be one such sphere, a web search might be another (ibid.), i.e., his spheres cover different versions of Urry's (2002) mobilities. A possible combination of airport and websphere (i.e., of corporeal and virtual mobilities), however, is not addressed. The dominance of individual autonomy that Zimmer (in Nissenbaum 2010) proclaims for these spheres of mobility is also rather debatable in the context of mobile privacies and privacy in general.

Another version of context can be found in danah boyd's (2010) work, which claims that "privacy and publicity" is not "a black-or-white attribute for content, when really it's defined by context and the implications of what we've chosen to share" (boyd 2010). She additionally raises the question of (private) material in public places, which might have consciously been put there, but is not necessarily meant to be aggregated. Data aggregation is potentially one of the most contested areas at the moment. If the industry's aim were indeed "to unite information on the customer's age, gender, web-browsing habits, home address and buying patterns with a record of their daily movements, and subject that to behavioral analysis techniques" (Warren 2009), then one important aspect of mobile privacies would be exactly to prevent the different data sets merging. boyd (2010) also emphasizes that public availability is still different to widespread publication. Here, context is more virtual than we had implied thus far – and more content-related – but this, too, is an important aspect.

Overall, Nissenbaum's (2010) emphasis on context is useful. Her approach, however, shows that such an emphasis can also lead to a loss of the specific nature of privacy definitions necessary for acting on them. boyd's (2010) approach seems too limited for our purpose. Nissenbaum's (2010) statement, for example, that certain privacy intrusions in airport settings tend to be acceptable exactly because they take place in airports (Nissenbaum 2010, p. 198), on the other hand, seems to open the doors to a relativity claim. This kind of relativity and generalization is something that most of the technological approaches mentioned previously (cf. Sect. 14.3) would potentially want to work against. It also underlines that the combination of the individual and the social (which the context often is) does not necessarily simplify matters. Nonetheless we hold on to Nissenbaum's (2010) idea of context and contextual integrity as crucial for privacy and to her hint at what factors tend to play a role in such contexts.

14.5 Mobile Privacy

We began with the idea that mobility and privacy are interlinked but provide at least a double challenge: not only do we have to deal with the problems that digital privacy already faces, but we additionally have locality issues to deal with. How the concept of mobile privacy should be defined was not yet clear. In many ways, this double bind problematic was already present in early privacy definitions (see Warren and Brandeis 1890) – but not necessarily as a clear-cut combination or in any sense thought through as mobility. Our journey through different sets of literature provided technological as well as philosophical ideas and also repeatedly the hint at differences in user behavior and attitudes. This was the first step into a rather complex set of differentiations on both very basic, but also somewhat specific levels. We will now look at three different possible combinations that could be useful for a more detailed definition of mobile privacy. A further study would have to apply these empirically and further develop and test them.

Let us begin with the most basic observation made in Sect. 14.2: one point that emerged during the research was that in defining privacy, it makes sense to also include the definitions of publicness (this includes both public space and the public sphere). This would be the basis for a spectrum of privacies, offering a range between publicness and privacy. Another axis that could be added would be the immobility-mobility axis. This would begin to turn the spectrum into a very simple matrix (a mobility-privacy matrix). In this model, the core would not be to limit the definition of mobile privacy to a set of only two primary aspects, but to enable both users and researchers to locate different actions, situations, and contexts on this spectrum/matrix and thereby enable awareness of different variations and implications. It does emphasize the importance of context. The limitations of this spectrum/matrix idea lie clearly in the problematic nature of defining the ends of the scale or rather in the limitation of these to one dimension. Plus it assumes that both privacy/publicness and mobility/immobility are already "measurable." But what about someone sitting in a café using a laptop to access certain Social Web applications – is this person immobile or semi-mobile? Is the location on the scale dependent on the physical or informational level? The same applies to questions of privacy and publicness in this context. This spectrum/matrix then is rather an additional illustration tool in the context of more refined definitions as for instance Nissenbaum's (2010) idea of contextual integrity.

The second possibility is structurally similar to the first, but brings different aspects to the forefront. It combines the who/what/how questions with the location privacies (identity/position/path or who/where/when), both of which were addressed in Sect. 14.3. This then leads to another seemingly simple matrix of who/what/how/where/when of mobile privacy (or rather mobile privacies, cf. Sect. 14.2.2). With regard to content, these are the questions that users should be aware of as sensitive data issues, while technologically, the different nodes related to each question should not be connected with each other identifiably (not even between two of the five nodes). Temporarily, connections will always be necessary, but a common technological answer to this problem seems to be (amongst others) the question of scale. Hence the where and when can be located technologically without being too specific (less-than-optimal).

The second matrix matches well with the first spectrum/matrix suggested above. It provides a set of questions that help to locate nodes on the spectrum/matrix. Nonetheless, this second matrix by far also does not match the complexity of a mobile privacies definition.

We therefore tried a third option. This was in fact a pursuit of the obvious (with the caveat of being work-in-progress): what about the simple combination of Urry's (2002) mobilities with different privacies? We already saw a parallel in the differentiation between physical and symbolic/informational mobilities and the same distinction in terms of privacy. We will therefore use Urry's (2002) five mobilities and map the privacy issues discussed in this contribution onto those:

(a) *Corporeal privacy* as the privacy of the body in its movement but also its attributes (traveling where and for what purposes, meeting with whom, etc.). This builds on Ardagna et al.'s (2008) location privacies as well as Nissenbaum's (2010) contextual integrity.

(b) *Physical privacy* as the privacy of objects, but also of consumption habits, etc., i.e., the combination of the corporeal with other objects. Physical privacy builds on the same references as the corporeal privacy, but additionally emphasizes that not only the person in question, but also related objects, are part of the privacy problematic.

(c) *Imaginative privacy* as a protection of thoughts and imaginations, i.e., of playfulness, of media use, of other kinds of "escape." In terms of the imagination, Singh (2008), with his emphasis on plausible deniability, is the obvious reference. Additionally, suggestions from the social media field (see other contributions in this volume) are relevant for not only the imaginative, but also the virtual and communicative privacy.

(d) *Virtual privacy* as a protection again of online data both in terms of content but also connections (with whom, where, when, what). Virtual privacy reflects most of the questions that were asked in the technological field (cf. Sect. 14.3). Answers can again be found in Ardagna's et al. (2008) identity, position, and path privacies as well as Singh's (2008) playful identities.

(e) *Communicative privacy* as protection related to interpersonal communication on every level and with every medium. Here, too, the basis builds on technological questions and answers. The "opt-in" mechanism suggested by Perkins et al. (2010) is particularly important here, as is any technological aid in obscuring the data (any feasible "less-than-optimal" solution) and Beckwith's (2003), Singh's (2008), and Nissenbaum's (2010) context awareness.

This simple adaptation shows how most of the issues discussed above map nicely onto this range of mobile privacies. In terms of the questions that need to be answered and the ranges of privacy/publicness and mobility/immobility, we are finding parallels to the spectrum and matrices developed above. An empirical mapping and layering of this range of mobile privacies would be a logical next step. This would, as we have seen from the technological answers, at the same time provide useful insights into the applicability of the theoretical concepts implied.

One question that has not yet been explicitly addressed by the set of mobile privacies above is the question of context. In my view, however, it is the combination of the different privacies that makes up the different contexts, i.e., it becomes interesting when, for example, corporeal and virtual privacy meet (as in the café example mentioned earlier). Contexts are therefore different combinations of these mobile privacies.

The privacy of the body as well as of objects is thereby covered as much as different forms of information and communication (as well as imagination – quite an important aspect). In all of them, mobility is implied. Rather than differentiating between the two different sets of privacy and mobility such as in the spectrum/ matrix idea above, here the two aspects are combined into one. It is a set of attributes that still needs to be refined further. But it does (hopefully) underline one of the main points raised in all of the above: that mobile privacy is in fact a set of mobile privacies, and that context is the crucial basis for any informed debate on privacy "on the move." Whether the above is enough to speak of a situation-driven contextual integrity (the ideal) is too early to say.

One other final point: it is important to stress – as actually all of the approaches mentioned have done – that users and their individual, situational needs are the core of any privacy definition. Nonetheless, asking users about their definitions of privacy (rather than their actions) and comparing these definitions to our theoretical ideas could provide an additional insight. Moving even further into the normative, one could say that users should be involved in the process of developing these technological solutions. On the policy level, users might need to be trained to be more aware of the potential consequences of their actions. And companies might need to be forced to move from "opt-out" to "opt-in" instead. Plus clear-cut explanations about what happens with location-based data and about who is using the data should be the norm. Furthermore, the combination of location-based with other data should be made difficult (apart from the basic technological needs). First of all though, the model developed above should be refined, and tested in liaison with technology developers.

Having thought more about technology than usual, one is sometimes tempted to retreat to a totally different scenario instead: the establishment of "no data zones," i.e., zones that are protected from any kind of electronic signal – either going in or out. That does not mean, however, that privacy is not an issue there either...

References

Ardagna CA, Cremonini M, Damiani E, De Capitani di Vimercati S, Samarati P (2008) Privacy enhanced location services information. In: Acquisti A et al (eds) Digital privacy: theory, technologies, and practices. Auerbach, New York, pp 307–326

Arendt H (1989/1958) The human condition. The University of Chicago Press, Chicago

Beckwith R (2003) The human experience. Designing for ubiquity: the perception of privacy. Pervasive Comput 2(2):40–46

Bourdieu P (1984) Distinction: a social critique of the judgement of taste. Harvard University Press, Harvard

boyd d (2010) Making sense of privacy and publicity. Talk presented at SXSW, Austin, 13 Mar. http://www.danah.org/papers/talks/2010/SXSW2010.html. Accessed 6 Dec 2010

Dey AK (2001) Understanding and using context. Pers Ubiquit Comput 5(1):4–7

Green N, Haddon L (2009) Mobile communications: an introduction to new media. Berg, Oxford/ New York

Nissenbaum H (2010) Privacy in context: technology, policy, and the integrity of social life. Stanford University Press, Palo Alto

Perkins C, Johnson D, Arkko J (2010) Mobility support in IPv6. http://tools.ietf.org/html/draft-ietf-mext-rfc3775bis-08. Accessed 10 Jan 2011

Privacy International (2007) The 2007 international privacy ranking. http://www.privacyinternational.org/article.shtml?cmd%5B347%5D=x-347-559597. Accessed 6 Dec 2010

Radwanski G (2002) Letter to the honourable Roy Romanow. http://www.priv.gc.ca/media/le_ehr_020627_e.cfm. Accessed 10 Jan 2011

Singh V (2008) Context-awareness: control over disclosure and privacy in a social environment. TKK technical reports in computer science and engineering, Helsinki University of Technology Department of Computer Science and Engineering. http://www.cse.tkk.fi/en/publications/B/1/papers/VSingh_final.pdf. Accessed 10 Jan 2011

Urry J (2002) Mobility and connections. Unpublished paper. Paris, Apr 2002. http://www.ville-en-mouvement.com/telechargement/040602/mobility.pdf. Accessed 10 Jan 2011

Urry J (2007) Mobilities. Polity, Cambridge

Warren P (2009) The end of privacy? The guardian, 2 Apr 2009. http://www.guardian.co.uk/technology/2009/apr/02/google-privacy-mobile-phone-industry. Accessed 29 Jan 2011

Warren SD, Brandeis LD (1890) The right to privacy. Harv Law Rev 4(5)

Weiß R, Groebel J (eds) (2002) Privatheit im öffentlichen Raum. Medienhandeln zwischen Individualisierung und Entgrenzung? Leske & Budrich, Opladen

Westin A (1968) Privacy and freedom. Atheneum, New York

Chapter 15
Online Privacy as a News Factor in Journalism

Wiebke Loosen

15.1 Privacy and Journalism – A Paradox?

The meaning, value, and organization of privacy are associated with the cultural, normative, and social disposition of a society. Therefore, the distinction and relationship between private and public is in constant transformation (see e.g., Westin 2003, p. 434). It is these circumstances that make investigating privacy so complex. The Italian democracy theorist Noberto Bobbio (1989, p. 1) has stressed this, naming the public/private distinction the often cited "great dichotomy" (in political theory). In occidental thinking, it stands for the fundamental differentiation between a public realm (including everything that is significant for a society as a whole) and a private realm (including everything that is significant for individuals or groups, e.g., the family) (Seubert 2010, p. 9), as well as for the interfaces and ambivalences resulting from the oscillatory connections between both "poles."

These diverse aspects and levels of privacy (e.g., Westin 2003 differentiates between privacy at the political level, at the sociocultural and organizational level, as well as at the personal/individual level) show that privacy is, and also needs to be, a concept in a wide range of disciplines and of inquiry. Privacy has, for instance, been described as an *elastic concept*, associated with a *variety of meanings*, of *multidimensional nature*, relevant on *micro-, meso-* up to *macro-theoretical levels*, which altogether lead to widely different and often wholly separate discourses on privacy (for an overview see e.g., Rössler 2005, p. 2; Burgoon 1982). Therefore, it seems to be less productive or even counterproductive to ask for "a unified, single

W. Loosen (✉)
Hans-Bredow-Institute for Media Research at the University of Hamburg, Hamburg, Germany
e-mail: w.loosen@hans-bredow-institut.de

S. Trepte and L. Reinecke (eds.), *Privacy Online*, 205
DOI 10.1007/978-3-642-21521-6_15, © Springer-Verlag Berlin Heidelberg 2011

account of privacy" (Paine et al. 2007, p. 526), as this necessarily needs to be context-sensitive.

In this chapter, on the one hand, a broad and not prematurely restricted characterization of privacy and privacy-related topics is needed to provide compatibility with journalism and journalism research. This requires an investigation of privacy with respect to public and the public sphere. On the other hand, the attempt to discuss *privacy as a news factor* requires a more precise characterization. Therefore, at least a brief (and selective) revision of some of the several attempts to define privacy as well as of the attempts to synthesize existing literature (e.g., Burgoon 1992) is helpful.

Within psychological literature in particular, Westin's (1967, 2003) and Altman's (e.g., 1975) theories of privacy are very prominent (for an overview see Margulis 2003 or Margulis' chapter in this volume). Both take the idea of *control* over (the access to) specific areas of privacy as a starting point. Westin especially (1967, p. 7) focuses on *information privacy* by defining privacy as "the claim of individuals, groups, or institutions to determine themselves when, how, and to what extent information about them is communicated to others." The (active) term "claim" already demonstrates that this demand can vary individually to a large extent.

This definition addresses an individual level of privacy, and therefore is of limited (or of specific) use where journalism (and its function for society) is concerned. Furthermore, for example, due to the characteristics of contents in networked publics (persistence, replicability, scalability, and searchability; for a detailed discussion see the chapter by Peter and Valkenburg in this volume), individuals' control over information is limited per se. Nonetheless, the definitions of Westin and Altman (and the underlying larger theories of privacy) prove the fundamental role of privacy as a "regulatory process by which a person (or group) makes himself more or less accessible and open to others" (Altman 1977, p. 3) and consequently for self-realization and individual development (Margulis 2003b). This fundamental role may serve as one explanation for the general attraction to, and the critical observation of privacy-sensitive contents in media and journalism as well as for its ambiguity between voyeurism and liberation.

In seeking to systematize the meaning of "private" Rössler (2005, p. 6) suggests three basic types (simultaneously including the overlaps between them): (1) Private modes of action and conduct (in public) (e.g., what clothes I wear on the street); (2) Private knowledge (e.g., who I live with); (3) Private spaces (e.g., dwellings, rooms). Furthermore, she distinguishes a spatial, naturalized meaning of "private" (everything that has its place in the sphere of the private household) as well as its description in terms of dimensions of action and responsibility, and dimensions of interest and concern. Against that background, she differentiates the dimensions of privacy on a more abstract level as: (1) *Decisional privacy* (violations can be defined as illicit interference in one's actions, p. 79); (2) *Informational privacy* (violations can be defined as illicit surveillance, p. 111); (3) *Local privacy* (violations can be defined as illicit intrusions in rooms or dwellings, p. 142).

All of these definitions, meanings, and dimensions reveal the complex structure of privacy as a concept. This complexity even increases when we try to relate privacy to (mass) media and journalism. Nonetheless, the public/private relationship in modern societies and the impacts influencing its transformation cannot be described, discussed, and evaluated without the consideration of (mass) media, for it is evident that privacy has changed under the influence of the developments of electronic media in various ways (Papacharissi 2010; Meyrowitz 2002) that have created a "new visibility" (Thompson 2005). One very self-evident phenomenon is the mobile phone: it has established telephone conversations that are considered as private matters in the public space (Rössler 2005, p. 171).

Basically, it seems to be one of the "constants of media evolution" (Schmidt and Zurstiege 2000, p. 206) that the discursive polarities of public and private have to become a concern of a societal discourse (e.g., with regard to regulations, norms, literacy, etc.) with the advent of every new medium and with every new media technology.

At first glance, privacy and (mass) media seem to be mutually exclusive: the media provide public information, which therefore is not private but public by definition. Nonetheless, private and intimate issues are to a large extent distributed via media and are significant topics of public communication. Thus, privacy in the media always has to be characterized as mediated privacy (Pundt 2008, p. 234), which is produced by the media: "the difference between private and public within the medium itself can clearly only ever be an apparent one – the medium knows privacy only as something publicized" (Rössler 2005, p. 175).

This is true for traditional mass media as well as for the Internet and especially for social media, as they virtually depend on self-disclosure and produce an increasing availability of private information leading to an increased awareness of privacy issues. The availability of private information distributed via social media has introduced a recursive process of individual and mass communication. The boundaries between public and private spheres are rearranged and redefined, and this process of change inspires debates on the individual and societal meaning of public and private spheres.

This chapter addresses these aspects with a focus on journalism as a social system and does this in a dual perspective. (1) The first perspective regards privacy primarily as a *heuristic* for the challenges journalism has to face in a social media environment. (2) The second perspective looks at the meaning of privacy and privacy-related issues for journalism. Against that background, the chapter is structured as follows: firstly, it looks at the relevance and meaning of the public/private distinction in journalism (cf. Sect. 15.2). As social media and their reliance on private information affect journalism in various ways, Sect. 15.3 explores the *(news-) worthiness* of social media within journalism. In an initial attempt, privacy is then considered as a news factor. This perspective requires a brief look into the referring logic of news value research. (cf. Sect. 15.4). Finally, the question is raised of the extent to which privacy and social media offer a chance for journalism to keep (and get) in touch with its declining audiences (cf. Sect. 15.5).

15.2   The Distinction Between *Public* and *Private* in Journalism

> Whatever we know about our society, or indeed about the world in which we live, we know
> through the mass media. (Luhmann 2000, p. 1)

This is by far one of the most cited quotes from the German sociologist Niklas
Luhmann as far as mass media are concerned. Corresponding adaptations and
reformulations of Luhmann's specification of systems theory on the mass media
in journalism research are based on the assumption that processes of self-observation
of society are mainly constituted by the profession of journalism. In a sociological
system theoretical perspective, journalism is defined as a social system that

> [. . .] operates on the basis of a generalized symbolic communication medium which can be
> called 'actuality'. This artificial term includes three dimensions: event-related facts (instead
> of fiction), relevant information (concerning all other function systems in society) and
> current issues (to facilitate the synchronization of society). (Görke and Scholl 2006, p. 651)

This definition illustrates that the journalistic observation of society, and therefore the "performance and provision of themes for public communication" (Rühl
2008, p. 32), follows specific mechanisms to identify themes as *newsworthy* or not
Weischenberg (2007). It is self-evident that all of the above mentioned dimensions
(event-related facts, relevant information, current issues) are not "naturally" given,
but part of a journalistic construction of reality, and therefore observer-related and
relative.

What does this abstract definition of journalism as a social system imply for the
distinction between *public* and *private* in journalism? With this constitutional
definition it becomes obvious that journalism provides *public* communication, a
public service for society, and therefore has a strong preference for the "public side"
of the public/private distinction. As a consequence, more frequently *public*, the
public sphere or even the *public opinion* is the relevant object of inquiry. This does
not mean that privacy is irrelevant, but that it is predominantly defined negatively
with respect to public as *not public* (Pundt 2008, p. 231). In such a (public sphere
theoretical) perspective, privacy is more or less "designated 'the private home' or
the 'realm of intimacy' and not further differentiated" (Rössler 2005, p. 2).

Furthermore, theories of the public sphere mostly focus on a critically diagnosed
decline of the public realm (as a discursive space for public discussion) through the
incursion of intimacy and private issues (e.g., Habermas 1992; Sennett 1977). The
opposite (feminist theoretical) perspective emphasizes the positive effects of a
public awareness for privacy-related issues. It is argued that such issues, which
are often simply qualified as trivial, and not worth a medial presentation nor public
discussion (e.g., home stories, intimate details, personal conflicts), *not* naturally
only need to serve (or be treated as) entertainment and voyeurism (Herrmann and
Lünenborg 2001).

The predominant perspective in communication/media/journalism research is to
look (often with a media critical attitude) into the way privacy-sensitive issues are
dealt within the media (e.g., with reference to daily talk shows, reality TV) and by

journalism (e.g., sensationalized journalism, privatization, and emotionalization in political news). This perspective reveals that what we see in the media is always a medial construction of privacy, a media image of privacy, or rather, of issues qualified (by a scientific, journalistic, or other observer) as privacy-related or privacy-sensitive.

It is exactly this medial construction of privacy that often elicits the question of which private matters may be (or should be) revealed by journalists in the public interest. This matter is intertwined with the role of journalism for and within a society. Normatively, journalism has to balance public interest and the individual's interest. Due to the very fact that both of these interests are located on different layers, in different realms they often conflict and raise different privacy concerns: in one case the unit is seen as the individual (or groups, organizations that have an interest in keeping information private or rather unpublished), and in the other case it is seen as the society (that may have an interest in revelation). For both of them the (self-)disclosure of private information has different meanings, relevance, functions, and consequences. Therefore, the qualification of information as privacy-sensitive is likely to differ from an individual and from a journalistic perspective.

Consequently, the appropriate balance between the two interests – individual and public – is an important object of inquiry in different contexts, for instance, law, politics, ethics, media criticism, and journalism itself. As a result, in journalism, and particularly in its critical (self-)evaluation, the public/private distinction is (implicitly) used as a conceptual framework for demarcating the boundaries between *private* or *of public interest*. This distinction is slightly different from the public/private distinction as it implies that private issues can be of public interest and therefore are an appropriate matter of journalistic revelation. Therefore, in a journalistic perspective the first question is: *newsworthy or not?* In contrast, the decision between *private or of public interest* is subordinated and only occasionally relevant when it comes to deciding whether a public interest outweighs the individual's interest or not. Consequently, *public* or *to be published* is always constructed in contradiction to something else. In journalism, this *something else* can be *private*, but this is not necessarily the case for all situations. It is more likely to be simply *not newsworthy*.

Nevertheless, the coverage of private issues always had a strong newsworthiness in journalism and in several cases the media came under sharp criticism for invading privacy. This is especially true when celebrities, a certain kind of mainstream media, and/or "mediated scandals" (Thompson 2000) or criminal cases are concerned (Imhof and Schulz 1998). In fact, the much cited article "the right to privacy" by the U.S. American lawyers Samuel Warren and Louis Brandeis (1890) already had a media-critical attitude and was written with regard to an increasingly diffused yellow press and the development of new technologies in photography (Solove 2004, p. 57):

> The press is overstepping in every direction the obvious bounds of propriety and of decency. Gossip is no longer the resource of the idle and of the vicious, but has become a trade, which is pursued with industry as well as effrontery. To satisfy a prurient taste the details of sexual relations are spread broadcast in the columns of the daily papers. To

occupy the indolent, column upon column is filled with idle gossip, which can only be
procured by intrusion upon the domestic circle. (Warren and Brandeis 1890)

Since then, privacy has become commoditised and part of the deal between the
(boulevard) media and public figures. This is expressed by the phrase "Janus face of
prominence" (Schneider 2004), since on the one hand celebrities often lament their
loss of privacy, but on the other hand stage their private life within the media to
preserve their public status.

15.3   The (News-) Worthiness of Social Media Within Journalism

All of the above-mentioned examples show that from a normative perspective,
journalism has to take care of privacy concerns. Therefore, privacy concerns were
not raised for the first time when the Internet allowed private persons to distribute
photographs and information about themselves (and others), or with the (scientific
and societal) discourse of online privacy. However, private information distributed
via social media does make a difference, because the creators of such information
may regard it as (semi-)private, whereas journalists may regard it as public (Whittle
and Cooper 2009, p. 2). As a consequence, the perception of privacy, as well as the
way it is dealt within the media and in journalism, is undergoing a fundamental
change. Thus, privacy per se is not a new issue for journalism but its growing
salience is as social media and privacy issues change and challenge longstanding
journalistic conventions about what counts as news.

To illustrate this idea, within the next paragraphs, privacy is primarily used as a
heuristic for the challenges journalism has to face in a social media environment.
All of these challenges can be boiled down to the changing nature of the relationship journalism has to its (former) audience.

With its expansion and institutionalization, the Internet has become not only an
alternative for news production and consumption (Mitchelstein and Boczkowski
2009), but has changed the conditions of (public) communication to a large extent.
Journalism as a genuine media phenomenon is strongly affected by this change as
the Internet is threatening the traditional basis, role, and funding of journalism.

One of the most frequently postulated observations with respect to the new forms
of public communication in an online media environment is the changing nature of
the sender/receiver relationship and the loss of journalism's gatekeeper monopoly
(Bruns 2005). Traditionally, this monopoly is based on a business model with
"news" as a marketable product. It is endangered by the Internet (and a major
economic crisis), and in particular by behavioral changes of audiences and
advertisers induced by new technologies (Downie and Schudson 2009). Furthermore, in a social media environment, the asymmetry between professional
journalists and audience can no longer be maintained and loses its separation effect.
Additionally, user-generated content (that may also contain privacy-sensitive

issues) has become a relevant source for journalism, and participatory journalism practices strongly affect newsroom routines (see e.g. Singer 2010; Domingo et al. 2008; Thurman 2008).

Therefore, journalism has to deal with both the restriction of journalism's ability to include the audience and the increasing demands for inclusion of the audience. This situation exemplifies the (news-) worthiness social media has for journalism: a chance to keep in touch with declining audiences as this former audience has to some extent turned into (inter-)active users and producers.

Journalists "who once controlled the space containing their work now share that space with website users" (Singer 2010, p. 127). Singer's study (like others e.g., Neuberger et al. 2009) on perceived effects of user-generated content on newsroom norms, values, and routines shows that journalists are in a dilemma between doubting their professional autonomy and embracing the change by the more or less deeper insight that they can no longer assume an attitude of passivity on the part of their audience, which a lot of journalists see as a supplemental source and traffic builder (Williams et al. 2010). Traffic to news and media websites increasingly comes from social media such as "Facebook," which reveals the role of social media as disseminators of news (Purcell et al. 2010).

Thus, within the Internet and social media, two principles interact insofar as *journalistic revelation* and *self-disclosure* converge (or collide when it comes to risks and opportunities of privacy) in a recursive process. Thus, contents originally published for a "personal public" (see Schmidt's chapter in this volume) may become journalistic sources and be noticed by a much larger audience via mass medial publication. Therefore, journalism and mass media can be seen as a trigger to publishing private information on the Internet via traditional mass media by relocating the information from a *privately public* realm to a *publicly private* one.

15.4 Privacy as a News Factor

Looking at the previous sections, it may have become apparent that it is not trivial to bring the concept of privacy together with journalism. The same is true for privacy and news factors. Thus, the following explanations are understood as an initial attempt or a first compilation of what becomes relevant when considering privacy as a news factor and when discussing privacy-related news factors. This requires at least a very brief insight into the logic of news factors in the referring research field.

Within news value research, news factors have been used in the attempt to explain which particular characteristics attributed to an event lead journalists to perceive and select contemporary events as newsworthy (Galtung and Ruge 1965). The theory postulates a systematic and stable connection between the characteristics attributable to an event (news factors) and the news value assigned to the respective news item by journalists (Scheufele 2006). A lot of analyses in this research field led to highly differentiated lists of news factors, which vary to a greater or lesser degree (O'Neill and Harcup 2009), even though in particular *relevance, damage/aggression/conflict, elite persons/prominence, continuity, proximity*, and *elite nation* could be shown to affect journalistic selection (Eilders 1997, p. 58). Staab (1990) argues that news factors in news items are not to be regarded as perceived (or even objective) event characteristics, but can rather be seen as a result of journalistic attribution.

Recent studies have increased the explanatory potential of news factors: Eilders (1997, 2006) conceptualizes news factors as *general relevance indicators* in human perception, serving not only as selection criteria in journalism, but also guiding selection processes by the audience (see also Shoemaker 1996). Eilders also stresses that the audience not only selects news according to collectively shared relevance criteria – as represented in the professional routines of journalism – but also according to individual interests and preferences (Eilders 2006, p. 10). This perspective reveals the significant differentiation between individual relevance/subjective importance and societal/collective relevance (Eilders 1997, p. 92; Fretwurst 2008, p. 114).

Selection processes always reduce complexity, and therefore, (journalistic) "selection always also generates that other side of the products presented, that is, the non-selection or the 'unmarked space' of the rest of the world." (Luhmann 2000, p. 37). This "rest of the world" exclusive from media coverage (which has always been important when it comes to media criticism and to suspicions/evidence of/for manipulation and biased information on the media) has become visible and accessible to a much larger extent on the Internet and within social media, and in turn relevant for journalism. As a result, this recursive process is about to change the journalistic perception of newsworthiness and to redefine (at least to some extent) news factors and values. The definition of news as what "is judged to be newsworthy by journalists [...]" (Harrison 2006, p. 13) seems to be increasingly less true in a social media environment. As a consequence, it becomes even more apparent what alternative and media critical approaches argue

> that journalists should be encouraged to counteract the prevailing news factors by, among other things: including more background and context in their reports; reporting more on long-term issues and less on 'events'; paying more attention to complex and ambiguous issues; giving more coverage to non-elite people and nations. (O'Neill and Harcup 2009, p. 170)

In fact, this kind of critique on newspaper reporting was the primary concern of Galtung and Ruge (1965), who proposed some alternative approaches to reporting conflict. In a wider context, this critique describes the conventional motivating factors behind the production of alternative media (Atton 2002, 2009). The emergence of the Internet in particular gave rise to renewed hopes that issues, actors, and arguments marginalized by the mainstream media get a broader public awareness and the public sphere a shift towards participation (Gerhards and Schäfer 2010).

Professional news media and social media observe each other, refer to each other, and use each other as sources. To a large extent, hyperlinks in the blogosphere and on social news sites refer to journalistic content and traditional media (Reese et al. 2007; Messner and Watson DiStaso 2008; Rölver and Alpar 2008; Xenos 2008). For that reason, a certain kind of newsworthiness and certain news factors also seem to be relevant within social media (Eilders et al. 2010). However, one has to keep in mind that news factors are criteria developed for analyses of news media. Thus, news factors were identified in classical investigations of the structural characteristics of news media. Therefore, classical news factors are of limited use when it comes to analyzing social media content. Therefore, the demand for future research on "blog values" (Xenos 2008, p. 501) is comprehensible.

Nonetheless, privacy-related issues and self-disclosure have similarities with traditionally highly important journalistic news factors such as *personification*, *elite persons/prominence*, *cultural proximity*, *social relevance*, *human touch,* and *sex/erotic*. All of them are privacy-related to a greater or lesser extent. The closeness between privacy(−related issues) and the news factor *personification* seems to be most obvious as *personification* is a very common journalistic practice of illustrating a topic by focusing on individuals − a practice that is often used in journalistic formats, for example, interviews, portraits, features, and documentations. This may be realized in terms of *exemplification* (Zillmann and Brosius 2000), for instance, to illustrate the consequences that a revised law has for a family used as a prototype in such a context (Daschmann 2001). A stronger focus on the individual itself can be given in cases of personal destinies or dramas. The collective effectiveness of *personification,* as well as the other above-mentioned factors, can be interpreted with general concepts of *familiarity, identification,* and *parasocial interaction*, which, among other things, can explain the "surveillance function of news" (Shoemaker 1996; Eilders 2006, p. 14).

For a more detailed look, we now come back to the definitions of privacy (cf. Sect. 15.1). At first glance these definitions are of limited use when it comes to defining privacy as a news factor: on the individual level they strongly refer to privacy as "a dialectic and optimizing process" (see Margulis, this volume, Chap. 2) operationalized often with regard to privacy behavior and concerns of individuals (see e.g., Paine et al. 2007). This perspective may be useful for comparing privacy concerns and related attitudes of journalists and recipients as well as their expectations (and expectation expectations) when privacy is concerned, for example, with regard to the treatment of privacy-sensitive issues within the media. On the societal level, the definitions of privacy discussed above often describe the normativity, the value of privacy, for example, in terms of dimensions of responsibility and interest.

In this regard, it is worth noting that nothing is defined as private or as privacy-sensitive "by nature". Things become even more complicated if we ask to what extent privacy-related issues in media coverage are functional or dysfunctional with respect to the role journalism has to fulfill for society.

Keeping this in mind, one can relate the news factor logic almost directly to at least two of the three dimensions Rössler (2006) differentiates (see Sect. 15.1):

• *Local privacy*: Aspects concerning privacy-related issues in terms of private spaces (e.g., home stories, family relationships, intimate relations, daily life)

- *Decisional privacy*: Aspects concerning privacy-related issues in terms of actions and conduct (e.g., with whom a person meets in a restaurant, to which church one goes)

The situation is different when it comes to *informational privacy*, which represents the central dimension of privacy for a lot of theorists as it refers to the control over (the access to) personal information (see Sect. 15.1). As a consequence, this dimension is located on a different level of abstraction than the other two dimensions. *Informational privacy* is less specific than local and decisional privacy and may include information referring to the other dimensions as well. Therefore, whenever (and if logically) possible, there must be a differentiation between whether the referring issue is done/observed in a public or in a private realm and whether it is covered by journalists or relies on self-disclosure (e.g., in an interview). Overall, journalistic coverage can be differentiated with regard to its varying degrees of exposure of privacy-related issues.

This is of course not a "ready to go definition" for an empirical study as these basic dimensions are neither mutually exclusive nor exhaustively defined so far. Above all, it has now become obvious that there are a lot of privacy-related aspects (e.g., journalistic research methods) that cannot be investigated via content analysis, which is by far the dominant method in news value research.

While this perspective focuses on content, another perspective that might be worth looking at refers to the interconnections and recursive processes between journalism and the social media. In this regard, privacy-related issues (which have their seeds in audience participation/inclusion) may be important for *credibility*, *trust*, *authenticity* (for the similarities and differences of privacy and authenticity cf. Trepte and Reinecke's chapter in this volume), and *follow-up communication*. Potentially, they are able to moderate what is often described as the gap (as well as the overlaps) between individual relevance structures and relevance structures of journalism (see e.g., Deuze 2008).

Thus, when one starts to think about "news factors 2.0," as relevance indicators for journalists who want to keep in touch with an audience in a social media environment (and to stay, or rather, to get in touch with the everyday lives of most people), it may come to

- *Actuality* (including three dimensions: event-related facts, relevant information, current issues, see p. 2), which provides or rather stimulates
- *"Topics of/for conversation"* in the sense of follow-up communication; and enables as well as integrates
- *References* to the living environment in terms of individual relevance.

Altogether this may "lead to a journalism," to cite the journalism researcher Mark Deuze (who is paraphrasing the American communications theorist James W. Carey here), "as an amplifier of the conversation society has with itself" (2008, p. 848). This understanding of journalism is not so far away from the 'traditional' definition provided by system theoretical journalism research (Görke and Scholl 2006, p. 651, in the present paper p. 2) – even though the means to facilitate the conversation society has with itself have changed totally. Against that background, one can assume that audience participation within journalism could lead to an amalgamation of individual and societal relevance structures and therefore to the consideration of multiple perspectives on a news item. One consequence may be a stronger representation of privacy-related issues as well.

15.5   Privacy: A Chance to Keep in Touch with the Audience?

Journalism has lost its gatekeeper monopoly. It used to be based on the asymmetry between professional journalism and an audience, which is almost restricted to selective use. This asymmetry can no longer be sustained. The Social Web offers new forms of public communication – and new modes of social participation for the public with significant remarkable implications from a democratic theoretical perspective. There is no doubt that "the people formerly known as the audience" (Rosen 2006) are increasingly important for journalism – and for journalism research. The ongoing debates show quite high expectations for audience participation. It is regarded as an advancement for democracy and as journalism's chance to reconnect with declining audiences. As a consequence, the interrelations and mutual observations between a public sphere constructed by professional journalism and "personal/private public spheres" (Schmidt 2009) within social media are increasing. On the one hand, this may lead to a more commercialized and professionalized use of social media that will decimate the *niches of privacy* within social media and underpin the importance of privacy literacy (see Debatin, this volume, Chap. 5). On the other hand, this may also lead to a sensible combination of issues of societal relevance and of personal/private relevance. The outcome of those interfaces of public and private may be regarded as ambivalent and reflect "the dual nature of privacy as something that can be conceived as both liberating and alienating, emancipative and repressive, beneficial and deleterious" (Rössler 2005, p. 169).

This dual nature of privacy is emblematic of journalism, as balancing ambivalences is part of its identity between market orientation and social responsibility, between advocacy journalism and one of the major invaders of privacy (to some extent accompanied by journalism's self-critical observation of blurring boundaries between private and public). Hence, journalism – what it traditionally has been and what it can or should be in an online environment – is characterized by several paradoxes and journalists have to balance extremely contradictory purposes and demands (Loosen et al. 2008). For instance: they should be fast and accurate, complete and selective, close to the subject as well as keeping a distance, should act autonomously in a state of dependence, listen to the audience and provide orientation, balance transparency and secrecy as well as privacy and public interest. In an online environment, a kind of journalism that supplies privacy even to those who do not supply it themselves is indispensable – to shelter both them and the public sphere.

References

Altman I (1975) The environment and social behavior: privacy, personal space, territory, crowding. Brooks/Cole, Monterey

Altman I (1977) Privacy regulation: culturally universal or culturally specific. J Soc Issues 33(3):67–83

Atton C (2002) Alternative media. Sage, London

Atton C (2009) Alternative and citizen journalism. In: Wahl-Jorgensen K, Hanitzsch T (eds) The handbook of journalism studies. Routledge, New York, pp 265–278

Bergmann J, Pörksen B (2009) Skandal! Die Macht öffentlicher Empörung. von Halem, Köln

Bobbio N (1989) Democracy and dictatorship. The nature and limits of state power. Polity, Oxford

Bruns A (2005) Gatewatching. Collaborative online news production. Peter Lang, New York

Daschmann G (2001) Der Einfluß von Fallbeispielen auf Leserurteile. UVK, Konstanz

Deuze M (2008) The changing context of news work: liquid journalism and monitorial citizenship. Int J Commun 2:848–865

Domingo D, Quandt T, Heinonen A, Paulussen S, Singer JB, Vujnovic M (2008) Participatory journalism practices in the media and beyond: an international comparative study of initiatives in online newspapers. J Pract 2(3):326–342

Donsbach W (1981) Journalisten zwischen Publikum und Kollegen. Forschungsergebnisse zum Publikumsbild und zum in-group-Verhalten. Rundfunk und Fernsehen 29(2–3):168–184

Downie L, Schudson M (2009) The reconstruction of American journalism. Columbia Journalism Review, October 19. http://www.cjr.org/reconstruction/the_reconstruction_of_american.php. Accessed 30 Nov 2010

Eberwein T, Pöttker H (2009) Journalistische Recherche im Social Web: Neue Potenziale, neue Probleme? Zeitschrift für Kommunikationsökologie und Medienethik 11(1):23–32

Eilders C (1997) Nachrichtenfaktoren und Rezeption: Eine empirische Analyse zur Auswahl und Verarbeitung politischer Information. Westdeutscher, Opladen

Eilders C (2006) News factors and news decisions. Theoretical and methodological advances in Germany. Communications 31(2):5–24

Eilders C et al (2010) Zivilgesellschaftliche Konstruktionen politischer Realität. Eine vergleichende Analyse zu Themen und Nachrichtenfaktoren in politischen Weblogs und professionellem Journalismus. Medien & Kommunikationswissenschaft 58(1):63–81

Fretwurst B (2008) Nachrichten im Interesse der Zuschauer. Eine konzeptionelle und empirische Neubestimmung der Nachrichtenwerttheorie. UVK, Wiesbaden

Galtung J, Ruge MH (1965) The structure of foreign news. The presentation of the Congo, Cuba and Cyprus crises in four Norwegian newspapers. J Peace Res 2(1):64–91

Gerhards J, Schäfer MS (2010) Is the internet a better public sphere? Comparing newspapers and internet in Germany and the US. New Media Soc 12(1):143–160

Görke A, Scholl A (2006) Niklas Luhmann's theory of social systems and journalism research. J Stud 7(4):644–655

Harrison J (2006) News. Routledge, London

Hermida A, Thurman N (2008) A clash of cultures: the integration of user-generated content within professional journalistic frameworks at British newspaper websites. J Pract 2(3):343–356

Herrmann F, Lünenborg M (eds) (2001) Tabubruch als Programm. Privates und Intimes in den Medien. Leske & Budrich, Opladen

Imhof K, Schulz P (eds) (1998) Die Veröffentlichung des Privaten – Die Privatisierung des Öffentlichen. Westdeutscher, Wiesbaden

Loosen W, Pörksen B, Scholl A (2008) Paradoxien des Journalismus. Einführung und Begriffsklärung. In: Pörksen B, Loosen W, Scholl A (eds) Paradoxien des Journalismus. Theorie – Empirie – Praxis. VS, Wiesbaden, pp 17–33

Luhmann N (2000) The reality of the mass media. Stanford University Press, Stanford

Margulis ST (2003a) On the status and contribution of Westin's and Altman's theories of privacy. J Soc Issues 59(2):411–429

Margulis ST (2003b) Privacy as a social issue and behavioral concept. J Soc Issues 59(2):243–261

Messner M, Watson DiStaso M (2008) The source cycle. How traditional media and weblogs use each other as sources. J Stud 9(3):447–463

Meyrowitz J (2002) Post-privacy America. In: Weiß R, Groebel J (eds) Privatheit im öffentlichen Raum. Medienhandeln zwischen Individualisierung und Entgrenzung. Leske und Budrich, Opladen, pp 153–204

Mitchelstein E, Boczkowski PJ (2009) Between tradition and change. A review of recent research on online news production. Journalism 10(5):562–586

Muthukumaraswamy K (2010) When the media meet crowds of wisdom. How journalists are tapping into audience expertise and manpower for the processes of newsgathering. J Pract 4(1):48–65

Neuberger C, Nuernbergk C, Rischke M (eds) (2009) Journalismus im Internet. Profession – Partizipation – Technisierung. VS, Wiesbaden

O'Neill D, Harcup T (2009) News values and selectivity. In: Wahl-Jorgensen K, Hanitzsch T (eds) The handbook of journalism studies. Routledge, New York, pp 161–174

Paine C, Reips U-D, Stieger S, Joinson AN, Buchanan T (2007) Internet users' perceptions of 'privacy concerns' and 'privacy actions'. Int J Hum Comput Stud 65:526–536

Papacharissi Z (2010) A private sphere. Democracy in a digital age. Polity, Cambridge

Paulussen S et al (2008) Citizen participation in online news media. An overview of current developments in four European countries and the United States. In: Quandt T, Schweiger W (eds) Journalismus online – partizipation oder profession? VS, Wiesbaden, pp 263–283

Pew Research Center for the People and the Press (2005) The media: more voices, less credibility. A review of pew research center for the people & the press findings. http://people-press.org/commentary/pdf/105.pdf. Accessed 30 Nov 2010

Pundt C (2008) Medien und Diskurs. Zur Skandalisierung von Privatheit in der Geschichte des Fernsehens. Transcript, Bielefeld

Purcell K et al (2010) Understanding the participatory news consumer. How internet and cell phone users have turned news into a social experience. Pew Research Center's Project for Excellence in Journalism, March. http://www.journalism.org/sites/journalism.org/files/Participatory_News_Consumer.pdf. Accessed 6 Dec 2010

Reese S, Rutigliano L, Hyun K, Jeong J (2007) Mapping the blogosphere. Professional and citizen-based media in the global news arena. Journalism 8(3):235–261

Rölver M, Alpar P (2008) Social News, die neue Form der Nachrichtenverteilung? In: Alpar P, Blaschke S (eds) Web 2.0 – Eine empirische Bestandsaufnahme. Vieweg + Teubner, Wiesbaden, pp 259–330

Rosen J (2006) The people formerly known as the audience. PressThink. http://journalism.nyu.edu/pubzone/weblogs/pressthink/2006/06/27/ppl_frmr.html. Accessed 30 Nov 2010

Rössler B (2005) The value of privacy. Polity, Cambridge

Rühl M (2008) Journalism in a globalizing world society: a societal approach to journalism research. In: Löffelholz M, Weaver D (eds) Global journalism research. Theories, methods, findings, future. Blackwell, Malden, pp 28–38

Scheufele B (2006) Frames, schemata, and news reporting. Communications 31(1):65–84

Schmidt J (2009) Das neue Netz. Merkmale, Praktiken und Folgen des Web 2.0. UVK, Konstanz

Schmidt SJ, Zurstiege G (2000) Orientierung Kommunikationswissenschaft. Was sie kann, was sie will. Rowohlt, Reinbek bei Hamburg

Schneider UF (2004) Der Januskopf der Prominenz, Zum ambivalenten Verhältnis von Privatheit und Öffentlichkeit. VS, Wiesbaden

Seubert S (2010) Privatheit und Öffentlichkeit heute. Ein Problemaufriss. In: Seubert S, Niesen P (eds) Die Grenzen des Privaten. Nomos, Baden-Baden, pp 9–22

Shoemaker PJ (1996) Hardwired for news: using biological and cultural evolution to explain the surveillance function. J Commun 46(3):32–47

Singer JB (2010) Quality control. Perceived effects of user-generated content on newsroom norms, values and routines. J Pract 4(2):127–142

Solove DJ (2004) The digital person: technology and privacy in the information age. University Press, New York

Staab JF (1990) The role of news factors in news selection: a theoretical reconsideration. Eur J Commun 5(4):423–443

Thelwall M, Stuart D (2007) RUOK? Blogging communication technologies during crises. J Comput Mediat Commun 12(2). http://jcmc.indiana.edu/vol12/issue2/thelwall.html. Accessed 7 Dec 2010

Thompson JB (2000) Political scandal. Power and visibility in the media age. Polity Press, Cambridge

Thompson JB (2005) The new visibility. Theory Cult Soc 22(6):31–51

Thurman N (2008) Forums for citizen journalism? Adoption of user generated content initiatives by online news media. New Media Soc 10(1):139–157

Warren SD, Brandeis LD (1890) The right to privacy. Harvard Law Review, Vol IV. http://groups.csail.mit.edu/mac/classes/6.805/articles/privacy/Privacy_brand_warr2.html. Accessed 6 Dec 2010

Weischenberg S (2007) Genial daneben: Warum Journalismus nicht (Gegen-)Teil von Unterhaltung ist. In: Journalismus und Unterhaltung. Thepretische Ansätze und empirische Befunde. VS, Wiesbaden, pp 117–132

Westin AF (1967) Privacy and freedom. Atheneum, New York

Westin AF (2003) Social and political dimensions of privacy. J Soc Issues 59(2):431–453

Whittle S, Cooper G (2009). Privacy, probity and public interest. The Reuters Institute for the Study of Journalism, Oxford. http://reutersinstitute.politics.ox.ac.uk. Accessed 06 Dec 2010

Williams A, Wardle C, Wahl-Jorgensen K (2010) Have they got news for us? Audience revolution or business as usual at the BBC? J Pract 3(2):1–15

Xenos M (2008) New mediated deliberation: blog and press coverage of the Alito nomination. J Comput Mediat Commun 13(2):485–503

Zillmann D, Brosius H-B (2000) Exemplification in communication. Erlbaum, Mahwah

Part III
Audiences

Chapter 16
Adolescents' Online Privacy: Toward a Developmental Perspective

Jochen Peter and Patti M. Valkenburg

16.1 Introduction

For many Western adolescents, the use of the Internet for social purposes has become an integral part of their lives. Adolescents are the defining users of the "Social Web," that is, the part of the World Wide Web that is used for socializing and interacting with others. Teenagers far outnumber adults in the use of Social Web technologies, such as instant messaging and social network sites (see e.g., Lenhart et al. 2007). For example, 53% of US and 91% of Dutch adolescent Internet users communicate online through instant messaging (Rideout et al. 2010; Valkenburg and Peter 2009a), and adolescents increasingly use social network sites (e.g., Facebook), blogs, and photo and video sharing sites (e.g., YouTube). Across 13 European countries, 66% of all Internet users aged 15 or older visited social network sites in 2008 (comScore 2009). Finally, data from 2010 show that 74% of all US adolescents aged 13–18 have created a profile on a social network site (Rideout et al. 2010).

Because the Social Web invites the sharing of privacy-sensitive information, adolescents' massive use of Social Web technologies has spurred some controversy about how adolescents deal with online privacy. On the one hand, scholars have pointed to what they call a privacy paradox, that is, a fundamental contradiction in how adolescents and adults deal with online privacy (e.g., Barnes 2006). While adults are concerned about an invasion of their privacy on the Internet, adolescents seem to present personal and sometimes even intimate information on the Internet, particularly on social network sites. As a result of this careless distribution of personal information, adolescents are seen as easy targets for commercial and identity fraud (Moscardelli and Divine 2007), as well as for emotional and sexual abuse (for summaries of these concerns, see e.g., Donnerstein 2009; Hinduja and

J. Peter (✉) • P.M. Valkenburg
University of Amsterdam, Amsterdam, Netherlands
e-mail: j.peter@uva.nl

S. Trepte and L. Reinecke (eds.), *Privacy Online*,
DOI 10.1007/978-3-642-21521-6_16, © Springer-Verlag Berlin Heidelberg 2011

Patchin 2008). On the other hand, it has been argued that the Internet may provide adolescents with just the privacy they need to explore their identity in a relatively safe space, to experiment with intimate issues beyond the confines of face to face communication, and to find information and social support regarding developmentally sensitive issues (e.g., Ben-Ze'ev 2003; McKenna and Bargh 2000; Subrahmanyam and Greenfield 2008).

Despite the uncertainty about what adolescents' extensive use of privacy-sensitive Social Web applications means for issues surrounding their online privacy, research on the topic is scarce. Although several studies have dealt with the issue from an empirical perspective (e.g., Hinduja and Patchin 2008; Lenhart and Madden 2007; Livingstone 2008; Moscardelli and Divine 2007; Patchin and Hinduja 2010; Youn 2009), hardly any study has tried to approach it from a more theoretical angle. This chapter tries to fill this gap. Our aim is to conceptualize and understand the risks, but also the opportunities that surround adolescents' online privacy from a developmental perspective. In the first section, we outline how the functions of privacy correspond both with crucial developmental tasks in adolescence and with the skills that are necessary to achieve these goals. In the second section, we describe fundamental properties of digital information in the Social Web and explain their consequences for online privacy. In the third section, we combine the insights from the two preceding sections and show how and why adolescents use the Social Web for developmental purposes. In the last section, we evaluate the risks and opportunities of adolescents' online privacy within a developmental perspective.

16.2   Privacy and Psychosocial Development in Adolescence

Privacy has been described as an elastic concept (Allen 1988; Burgoon 1982). As a result, definitions of privacy vary between fields and researchers (for an overview, see e.g., Margulis 2003b; see Margulis, this volume, Chap. 2). For example, Altman (1975) has defined privacy as "the selective control of access to the self" (p. 24). Others have described privacy as the ability to exert control over self, information, objects, spaces, and behavior (Wolfe and Laufer 1974), or as the process of creating interpersonal boundaries with which a person or group regulates interaction with others (Derlega and Chaikin 1977). In this chapter, we rely on Westin (1967), who has defined privacy as "the claim of individuals, groups, or institutions to determine themselves when, how, and to what extent information about them is communicated to others" (p. 7). In line with other authors, Westin emphasizes choice and control as features of privacy. Individuals can choose the point of time, mode, and amount of personal information disclosure. In addition, they can control others' access to that information. We focus on Westin's privacy definition for three reasons. Firstly, Westin's definition is widely used and has stood the test of time (Margulis 2003a). Secondly, it focuses on information privacy, which is central for questions about adolescents' handling of personal information in the Social Web. Thirdly, Westin's definition, and the larger theory of privacy in which it is embedded, addresses the psychological level of privacy. This is crucial for our aim of conceptualizing and understanding issues surrounding adolescents' online privacy from a developmental perspective.

In Westin's (1967) theory, privacy plays an important role in the development of individuality. It creates the space for self-exploration and self-assessment, which are essential components in an individual's development, particularly in adolescence. Privacy can be both solitary and social. When privacy is solitary, it allows individuals to manage, for example, bodily and emotional necessities. When privacy is social, it provides individuals with information for their self-evaluation and the development of social competencies. Taken together, privacy enables normal and healthy bodily and psychosocial development (Margulis 2003b). Thus, Westin's theory of privacy suggests that an individual's self-realization is inconceivable without privacy, at least in Western countries (Margulis 2003a).

In the context of self-realization or, more generally, individual development, Westin points out four specific interrelated functions of privacy: personal autonomy, self-evaluation, limited and protected communication, and emotional release. *Personal autonomy* is defined by Westin (1967) as "the desire to avoid being manipulated or dominated wholly by others" (p. 33). Privacy protects personal autonomy by giving individuals the time, space, and opportunity to experiment with emotions, thoughts, and behaviors before making them public. By *self-evaluation*, Westin means that individuals integrate their experiences into meaningful patterns and exert individuality on events. In this context, privacy helps individuals to process information and to decide when to test their own evaluations against the responses of peers.

Limited and protected communication has two aspects. Firstly, privacy in limited communication creates boundaries that ensure the psychological distance necessary for the functioning of interpersonal relationships, regardless of whether they are formal or intimate. Secondly, privacy for protected communication entails individuals being able to share intimate information with people they trust. In protected communications, individuals self-disclose because they know that the intimate information will not be shared with others. *Emotional release,* finally, can be seen as a temporary escape from social obligations. It refers to the liberation from the pressures of playing social roles, respite from the emotional stimulations of daily life, coping with adverse experiences, and the management of bodily and sexual functions.

16.2.1 Linking Privacy Theory and Developmental Theory

Westin's privacy theory (1967) has rarely been related to the fundamental developmental tasks of adolescence. At the same time, developmental theories have hardly ever considered the importance of privacy for the development of individuality. This is striking because concepts such as self-exploration, self-evaluation, and psychosocial development are central to both traditions. Notably, Westin's four specific functions of privacy can easily be linked with four crucial developmental goals in adolescence.

Developmental theorists agree that there are at least four important interrelated developmental goals in adolescence: autonomy, identity, intimacy, and development of the sexual self (e.g., Bukatko 2008; Steinberg 2008). *Autonomy* as a developmental goal in adolescence refers to young people's ability to feel, think, and act independently. Thus, it entails emotional independence, notably in relationships with others; cognitive independence, especially in the development of beliefs, norms, and values; and behavioral independence, particularly in decision-making (Steinberg 2008). The developmental goal of *identity formation* implies that adolescents need to achieve a secure feeling about who they are and who they become (see e.g., Erikson 1968; Harter 1999). The development of a firm sense of identity is accompanied by increasingly complex and abstract self-conceptions, that is, the traits and attributes that adolescents use to describe themselves. *Intimacy* as a developmental goal in adolescence means that adolescents have to acquire the abilities that are necessary to form and maintain close, meaningful relationships with others (see e.g., Buhrmester and Furman 1987; Buhrmester and Prager 1995; Furman and Wehner 1994). Finally, the *development of the sexual self* refers to a firm understanding of oneself as a sexual person. This implies the awareness and acceptance of one's sexual orientation, the development of sexual self-efficacy, and the acquisition of sociosexual skills (Breakwell and Millward 1997; Buzwell and Rosenthal 1996).

From the definition of the four developmental goals in adolescence, it becomes clear that they correspond closely to Westin's (1967) four specific functions of privacy. The link between the developmental goal of autonomy and Westin's privacy function of personal autonomy is self-evident. The goal of identity formation, with its emphasis on the development of a firm sense of one's characteristics, is related to the privacy function of self-evaluation. After all, adolescents can only develop a firm sense of who they are if they evaluate themselves, notably through the responses they get from their peers. The developmental goal of intimacy and its focus on the development of meaningful close relationships corresponds to Westin's privacy function of limited and protected communication. Protected communication in particular enables adolescents to share intimate information with others to form or maintain close relationships. Finally, the development of adolescents' sexual selves is associated with Westin's privacy function of emotional release. Although the emotional release function encompasses more than just sexual functions, it also provides adolescents with the opportunity to deal with sexual issues.

16.2.2   Developmental Goals and Pertinent Skills

The close correspondence between established developmental goals in adolescence and Westin's (1967) four specific functions of privacy suggests that privacy is important or, more precisely, functional for the achievement of these goals (for personal goal achievement via social media use in an older age see also Maaß, this volume, Chap. 17). However, the correspondence between the developmental goals and the privacy functions does not specify how privacy enables adolescents to achieve the various developmental goals. To understand the link between privacy functions and the achievement of developmental goals, we need to look at the skills that are necessary for achieving these goals and that adolescents learn and practice in privacy. As will become clear later, these skills are also essential for our understanding of what adolescents do in the Social Web.

Each of the four developmental tasks outlined above is accompanied by a specific skill. These skills do not develop automatically but have to be learned and practiced. For the development of autonomy, adolescents need to practice *individuation*. Individuation can be defined as the relinquishing of childish dependencies on parents in favor of more mature relationships (Steinberg 2008) that allow for more independency in feeling, thinking, and acting. As Wolfe and Laufer (1974) have shown, the learning of individuation implies the ability to function in aloneness. Privacy enables adolescents to choose to be alone and to control potential intrusion.

For the development of a firm sense of identity, adolescents have to learn how to present themselves to others. Moreover, they have to learn how to adjust their *self-presentation* according to the responses of others (Harter 2003; Leary 1996). Privacy provides adolescents with the opportunity to withdraw from social interaction in order to pre-test new self-presentations in solitude. At the same time, privacy enables young people to engage in social interaction in order to evaluate these new self-presentations through the responses of their peers (Valkenburg et al. 2006).

To develop a sense of intimacy and, more specifically, close relationships, adolescents have to learn to disclose intimate information to others (Franzoi and Davis 1985). This *self-disclosure* is important to validate the appropriateness of cognitions, emotions, and behaviors. In addition, self-disclosure elicits, through the norm of reciprocity, close relationships (Buhrmester and Prager 1995). Privacy enables adolescents to confide in trusted others. It also creates the boundaries that are necessary to reduce the possibility that intimate information shared in self-disclosure is leaked to non-trusted others.

For the development of the sexual self, adolescents need to learn to explore their sexuality (Buzwell and Rosenthal 1996). Adolescents' *sexual self-exploration* is typically accompanied by uncertainty (Breakwell and Millward 1997) and sometimes by moral repercussions. Privacy liberates adolescents from moral pressures and enables them to explore their bodies, to accept their sexual fantasies, and to establish sexual relations with others (Wolfe and Laufer 1974).

In sum, privacy plays an essential role for the attainment of developmental goals in adolescence because it ensures that adolescents can learn and practice the skills that are necessary to achieve these goals. Firstly, privacy is functional for adolescents' accomplishment of autonomy because it creates, through the choice and control of aloneness, the independence necessary for individuation. Secondly, privacy is important for adolescents' identity formation because it provides them with an opportunity for self-evaluation by experimenting with their self-presentation. Thirdly, privacy is essential for adolescents' achievement of intimacy because it creates, through protected communication, the space for self-disclosure. Fourthly and finally, privacy facilitates adolescents' sexual self-exploration by liberating them from moral pressures. The functionality of privacy for the achievement of important developmental tasks through the facilitation of pertinent skills applies both to adolescents' offline and online behavior. However, before we can specify the risks and opportunities of online privacy for adolescents, we need to understand the characteristics that distinguish communication in the Social Web from communication in the offline world.

16.3   Communication in the Social Web

Privacy, as defined by Westin (1967), is essentially about limiting the access of others to personal communication. The risks and opportunities of privacy, then, are inherently social: they are inextricably linked to how others use, or abuse, this personal information. In the Social Web, others can be seen as "networked publics." boyd (2010) defines networked publics as "publics that are restructured by networked technologies. As such, they are simultaneously (1) the space constructed through networked technologies and (2) the imagined collective that emerges as a result of the intersection of people, technology, and practice" (p. 39). Networked publics share many functions of offline or non-networked publics, for example, gathering for social or cultural ends. In contrast to other publics, however, networked publics depend on networked technologies. These technologies shape how information flows in networked publics and how people interact both with this information and with each other (boyd 2010).

The working of networked technologies and, consequently, the functioning of networked publics are closely linked to the properties of bits. As a result, the properties of bits are also important for our understanding of privacy issues in networked publics. A bit (or binary digit) is the smallest information unit in digital computing. Comparing the differences between the properties of bits with those of atoms, Negroponte (1995) has emphasized that bits are superior to atoms because bits facilitate the compression, alteration, duplication, and an efficient and quick transmission of information, notably in wired networks. Based on these properties of bits or, more generally, of digital information, boyd (2010) has pointed out that the bit-based information in networked publics is easier to store, duplicate, distribute, and search than atom-based information in non-networked publics. Specifically, she has identified four affordances of content in networked publics: persistence, replicability, scalability, and searchability.

The *persistence* of content in networked publics refers to the automatic recording and archiving of online expressions. The fact that content in networked publics is by default persistent presents a radical deviation from the common, and deeply entrenched experience that what we say and do is ephemeral. boyd (2010) emphasizes that the persistence of online content is particularly pervasive once it has been distributed in networked publics. When online content has been disseminated in networked publics, it is impossible to delete it. The persistence of content in networked publics is advantageous in asynchronous Internet communication, such as communication through social network sites or e-mail. At the same time, the persistence of such content fundamentally contradicts the notion of privacy as limiting others' access to the content.

The *replicability* of content in networked publics refers to the fact that online expressions can easily be duplicated. boyd (2010) points out two problems that are related to the replicability of digital information. Firstly, original and duplicate cannot be differentiated. Secondly, because digital information can easily be altered, it is difficult to trace back how the original information looked, certainly when the information has been spread in networked publics. Against the backdrop of Westin's (1967) emphasis on individuals' control over and choice of when, how, and to what extent information about them is communicated to others, the replicability of digital information presents a major threat to privacy.

The *scalability* of content in networked publics refers to the potential visibility of online expressions. This affordance captures the opportunity to distribute content to smaller or larger parts of networked publics. It is important to note that scalability in networked publics merely provides the possibility of visibility but does not guarantee it (boyd 2010). The scalability of digital information seems to overlap with the control over the dissemination of personal information that is essential for privacy. However, as boyd emphasizes, the public rather than the individual typically determines what is scaled. What may be intended only for small parts of networked publics may be distributed widely, and what may be aimed at large parts of networked publics may hardly be distributed. As a consequence, the scalability of digital information is more likely to conflict than to harmonize with individuals' privacy.

The *searchability* of content in networked publics refers to the accessibility of online expressions through search (engines). Together with the persistence of digital information, the searchability of such information poses a considerable threat to individuals' privacy. This privacy threat not only affects the retrieval of information about an individual against that individual's will, but also pertains to the possibility that individuals become the target of unwanted contacts.

In conclusion, the affordances of content in networked publics are at odds with the notion of privacy as individuals' control over who has access to information about them. Due to the bit-based character of information in networked publics, it is impossible for individuals to choose and control when, how, and to what extent information about them is communicated to others, as Westin's (1967) definition of privacy would require. However, it is important to note that the affordances of networked communities do not automatically lead to a violation of individuals' privacy. Whether privacy is violated depends largely on how and to what end other members of networked publics use privacy-sensitive information.

16.4 Privacy, Psychosocial Development, and Networked Publics

The two preceding sections have shown two things: firstly, privacy is essential for the achievement of important developmental goals; secondly, the affordances of content in networked publics contradict fundamental properties of privacy. Against this backdrop, it is surprising that adolescents increasingly use networked publics for the privacy-dependent learning and rehearsing of the skills that are necessary for achieving developmental goals. As research has consistently shown, vast numbers of adolescents engage in individuation, self-presentation, self-disclosure, and sexual self-exploration in the Social Web. For example, adolescents use the Social Web to form, maintain, or intensify friendships with peers (e.g., Subrahmanyam and Greenfield 2008), to display personal information on social network sites and personal homepages (e.g., Livingstone 2008; Schmitt et al. 2008), to discuss intimate issues online (e.g., Schouten et al. 2007), and to explore their sexual orientation and various forms of sexuality on the Internet (e.g., Hillier and Harrison 2007; Peter and Valkenburg 2006a). This raises the important question of why adolescents engage so massively in potentially privacy-threatening behavior on the Internet.

One possible explanation is that the same affordances of networked publics that threaten adolescents' privacy may also make them functional for achieving developmental goals, at least from adolescents' own points of view. More specifically, adolescents may experience the persistence, replicability, scalability, and searchability of bit-based information as creating the conditions to learn and practice the skills that ensure the accomplishment of developmental tasks. Thus, whereas the affordances of networked publics may actually reduce adolescents' privacy, adolescents may perceive them as improving their control over personal information and, ultimately, their privacy. In adolescents' view, this privacy eventually helps them to engage in individuation, self-presentation, self-disclosure, and sexual self-exploration.

As mentioned above, the persistence of bit-based information is the reason why communication in networked publics can be asynchronous. Asynchronous communication, in turn, is perceived by adolescents to augment their control over the information they wish to convey (Peter and Valkenburg 2006b; Schouten et al. 2007). This control, finally, allows adolescents to think about, and edit, information that is relevant to individuation, self-presentation, self-disclosure, and sexual self-exploration before sending or posting it. Accordingly, studies have shown that adolescents' sense of control determines the quantity and quality of their self-disclosure (e.g., Schouten et al. 2007), self-presentation (e.g., Schmitt et al. 2008), and sexual self-exploration (e.g., Hillier and Harrison 2007).

The replicability of bit-based information enables adolescents to choose from different types of information about themselves. Textual information can as easily be replicated and posted in networked publics as (audio)visual content. This gives adolescents enormous opportunities to manage the richness of cues they want to convey to others. Adolescents can choose whether they present themselves only through textual descriptions or whether they add more cues, for example, by including pictures or video clips in their self-presentation.

The replicability of bit-based information also implies that the information can be altered (boyd 2010). Thus, adolescents are not only able to manage the richness of cues but they can also modify the very nature of these cues (e.g., by means of specific software). The alteration of information is most obvious when adolescents modify or update textual information on social network sites, as well as when they photo-shop images of themselves before posting them. Consequently, research has suggested that the sense of mastery that accompanies control over the richness and nature of cues, for example, on social network sites, is an important characteristic of adolescents' individuation (Schmitt et al. 2008). Similarly, scholars have pointed out that cue management increases adolescents' opportunities to decide independently about their self-presentation (Calvert 2002). Finally, adolescents' control over the richness and nature of cues seems to facilitate self-disclosure (Valkenburg and Peter 2009b; Walther 1992, 1996), which in turn enhances the intimacy of friendships (Valkenburg and Peter 2007b).

The scalability of content in networked publics is central to adolescents' perception of control over the public to which they present personal information. Adolescents can easily choose whether they convey information in a one-to-one setting (e.g., in closed dyadic instant messaging) or in a one-to-many setting (e.g., on social network sites). As a result, adolescents are able to distribute information about themselves efficiently and to a variety of people. The controlled contact with others may help adolescents to evaluate their identities against a vastly expanded sounding board compared to face to face contacts. Accordingly, studies have demonstrated that the positive feedback adolescents received on their self-presentation on social network sites augmented their self-esteem (Valkenburg et al. 2006). Similarly, when adolescents chose to engage in online self-disclosure to close friends, as opposed to strangers, their psychosocial well-being improved (Valkenburg and Peter 2007a). Finally, studies have shown that young people may use networked publics to form new relationships, which is an important aspect of individuation (Ellison et al. 2007; Peter et al. 2006).

The searchability of bit-based information renders any digital information about persons and things easily accessible for adolescents. Compared to the pre-Internet era, adolescents thus have a greater control and choice for getting in touch with persons and information previously difficult to access. For example, they can easily look up other teenagers whom they may not have met in person for a long time, or with whom they may not have close relationships. The maintenance of these weak ties in particular seems to affect young people's individuation and identity formation positively (Steinfield et al. 2008; Valkenburg et al. 2006). Moreover, because sexual information has become more easily accessible, adolescents can explore sexual issues more conveniently than before, even if some of the available information may be age-inappropriate (Lo and Wei 2005; Peter and Valkenburg 2006a). Similarly, adolescents are provided with the opportunity to look for people who have comparable sexual problems (Hillier and Harrison 2007; McKenna and Bargh 1998) and engage in self-disclosure with trusted others (Subrahmanyam et al. 2006; Suzuki and Calzo 2004).

Thus, the persistence, replicability, scalability, and searchability of bit-based information, along with adolescents' perceptions of choice and control over personal information, may explain why adolescents use the Internet to learn and practice the skills that warrant a successful attainment of developmental goals. However, an analysis of how adolescents deal with online privacy would be incomplete without considering the possibility to engage in anonymous online communication (Ben-Ze'ev 2003). Anonymity (which we conceptualize as relative anonymity given the problems of remaining completely unidentifiable on the web) is not an affordance of content in networked publics but rather of online communication. Adolescents increasingly use Internet applications, such as social network sites, in which anonymity is uncommon. However, they can choose to remain anonymous, for example, when using social support sites (Subrahmanyam et al. 2006; Suzuki and Calzo 2004) or chat rooms (Valkenburg et al. 2005).

Anonymous online communication may be seen as the extreme form of protecting one's privacy. Through the possibility to reveal one's identity, it entails maximum choice and control over when, how, and to what extent information is communicated to others. Research has shown that anonymous online communication is related to the learning and practicing of all skills that are important for the achievement of developmental goals. For example, teenagers use anonymous online communication to get in contact with new people (Peter et al. 2006; Subrahmanyam and Greenfield 2008). Although this may have adverse consequences (Mitchell et al. 2007; Valkenburg and Peter 2007a), it indicates adolescents' individuation. Anonymous online communication also enables adolescents to engage in identity experiments. This is an important aspect of their identity formation and may have positive effects on the development of their social skills (Valkenburg and Peter 2008; Valkenburg et al. 2005). Furthermore, anonymous online communication facilitates adolescents' self-disclosure in terms of relationship and sexual health issues (Suzuki and Calzo 2004). Finally, adolescents engage in anonymous online communication to discuss moral, emotional, and social issues related to teenage sex (Subrahmanyam et al. 2004). Anonymous online communication as a relatively safe way of sexual self-exploration is especially important for gay and lesbian youth. Because same-sex attraction is still accompanied by repercussions and distress, many gay and lesbian adolescents use the Internet for discussing problems surrounding their sexual orientation (Hillier and Harrison 2007).

16.5 Toward a Developmental Perspective of Adolescents' Online Privacy

From a developmental point of view, privacy is an important condition for the successful achievement of developmental goals in adolescence. Not only do Westin's (1967) functions of privacy overlap with developmental goals in adolescence, privacy also enables adolescents to learn and rehearse the skills upon which the successful attainment of these goals depends. In terms of online privacy, adolescents are faced with a much more fundamental privacy paradox than what Barnes (2006) described as the contradiction between privacy-concerned adults and privacy-oblivious teenagers: on the one hand, the affordances of content in networked publics threaten, and potentially violate, adolescents' privacy because they fundamentally reduce adolescents' choice and control over personal information. Adolescents thus have to face the illusion of control. On the other hand, adolescents seem to experience the affordances of content in networked publics as enhancing their choice and control over personal information and, eventually, their online privacy. Overall, communication in networked publics seems to have more positive than negative consequences for adolescents, as current research indicates (for a review, see e.g., Subrahmanyam and Greenfield 2008). Adolescents thus experience the promise and, partly, also the success of control.

Due to the privacy paradox with which adolescents are confronted, adolescents have to negotiate constantly between the risks and opportunities of communicating in networked publics. Their online privacy is permanently threatened and subject to violation. At the same time, however, adolescents feel and experience that they can learn and practice developmentally important skills, often even with positive consequences for their psychosocial development. Of course, the threats to adolescents' online privacy cannot be overestimated. Communicating in networked publics and an adequate handling of privacy issues are crucial tasks that need to be learned. Specifically, adolescents have to realize that whatever they distribute in networked publics is risky and can have adverse consequences, for example, for future relationships, applications, and employment. Moreover, they need to be taught that the more intimate bit-based information is, the more they should abstain from sharing it with others, even if they trust these others. Finally, adolescents need to learn that even the limitation of others' access to personal information, for example, on social network sites, does not protect their privacy as their personal information is still used, for instance, for commercial purposes (see e.g., Debatin et al. 2009).

However, our developmental perspective has also shown that we need to understand adolescents' privacy-sensitive behavior in networked publics in the context of normal, and usually functional, developmental processes in adolescence. Just because individuation, self-presentation, self-disclosure, and sexual self-exploration depend on privacy, they always run the risk of privacy violation, both online and offline. We also need to realize that adolescents may vary in what they consider a violation of their privacy. What may be an intrusion into their personal world for some adolescents may be an acceptable or even desired social interaction for others. Moreover, we have to take into account that notions of privacy may change over time. Livingstone (2008), for example, has highlighted that, in contrast to older generations, many adolescents no longer consider standard information on social network sites, such as age, relationship status, or sexual orientation, private information. Finally, we have to understand that both technologies and the competencies of their users change. The privacy-oblivious behavior of young people on social network sites described some years ago (Gross and Acquisti 2005) was as much a result of technological limitations as a consequence of users' deficiencies. Recent studies have shown that technologies have become more privacy-friendly and adolescents have become more privacy-sensitive (Hinduja and Patchin 2008; Patchin and Hinduja 2010).

In conclusion, a developmental perspective on adolescents' online privacy suggests that online privacy presents "risky opportunities" (Livingstone 2008) to adolescents. Adolescents run considerable risks of their online privacy being violated. At the same time, they are provided with the opportunity to achieve developmental goals. Existing research tends to emphasize either risks (e.g., Barnes 2006; Moscardelli and Divine 2007) or opportunities (e.g., Ben-Ze'ev 2003; McKenna and Bargh 2000), but devotes little attention to how adolescents learn, and can be taught, to balance the two. We believe that much of the promise of future scholarship on the issue lies in embracing both the risks and the opportunities of adolescents' online privacy–and thus its paradoxical nature–from a developmental perspective.

References

Allen AL (1988) Uneasy access: privacy for women in a free society. Rowman & Littlefield, Totowa

Altman I (1975) The environment and social behavior. Wadsworth, Belmont

Barnes SB (2006) A privacy paradox: social networking in the United States. First Monday 11(9), no page numbers

Ben-Ze'ev A (2003) Privacy, emotional closeness, and openness in cyberspace. Comput Hum Behav 19:451–467

boyd d (2010) Social network sites as networked publics: affordances, dynamics, and implications. In: Papacharissi Z (ed) A networked self: Identity, community, and culture on social network sites. Routledge, New York, pp 39–58

Breakwell GM, Millward LJ (1997) Sexual self-concept and sexual risk-taking. J Adolescence 20:29–41

Buhrmester D, Furman W (1987) The development of companionship and intimacy. Child Dev 58:1101–1113

Buhrmester D, Prager K (1995) Patterns and functions of self-disclosure during childhood and adolescence. In: Rotenberg KJ (ed) Disclosure processes in children and adolescents. Cambridge University Press, Cambridge, pp 10–56

Bukatko D (2008) Child and adolescent development. Houghton Mifflin, Boston

Burgoon JK (1982) Privacy and communication. In: Burgoon M (ed) Communication yearbook, vol 6. Sage, Beverly Hills, pp 206–249

Buzwell S, Rosenthal D (1996) Constructing a sexual self: adolescents' sexual self-perceptions and sexual risk-taking. J Res Adolescence 6:489–513

Calvert SL (2002) Identity construction on the Internet. In: Calvert SL, Jordan AB, Cocking RR (eds) Children in the digital age: influences of electronic media on development. Praeger, Westport, pp 57–70

comScore (2009) Tuenti most popular social networking site in Spain. http://www.comscore.com/press/release.asp?press=2733. Accessed 4 Mar 2009

Debatin B, Lovejoy JP, Horn A-K, Hughes BN (2009) Facebook and online privacy: attitudes, behaviors, and unintended consequences. J Comput Mediat Commun 15:83–108

Derlega VJ, Chaikin AL (1977) Privacy and self-disclosure in social relationships. J Soc Issues 33:102–115

Donnerstein E (2009) The internet. In: Strasburger VC, Wilson BJ, Jordan AB (eds) Children, adolescents, and the media. Sage, Thousand Oaks, pp 471–498

Ellison NB, Steinfield C, Lampe C (2007) The benefits of Facebook "friends": social capital and college students' use of online social network sites. J Comput Mediat Commun 12:1143–1168

Erikson E (1968) Identity: youth and crisis. Norton, New York

Franzoi SL, Davis MH (1985) Adolescent self-disclosure and loneliness: private self-consciousness and parental influences. J Pers Soc Psychol 48:768–780

Furman W, Wehner EA (1994) Romantic views: toward a theory of adolescent romantic relationships. In: Montemayor R, Adams GR, Gullotta TP (eds) Personal relationships during adolescence. Sage, Thousand Oaks, pp 168–195

Gross R, Acquisti A (2005) Information revelation and privacy in online social networks (The Facebook case). Paper presented at the ACM workshop on privacy in the electronic society (WPES), Alexandria

Harter S (1999) The construction of the self: a developmental perspective. Guilford, New York

Harter S (2003) The development of self-representation during childhood and adolescence. In: Leary MR, Tangney JP (eds) Handbook of self and identity. Guilford, New York, pp 611–642

Hillier L, Harrison L (2007) Building realities less limited than their own: young people practising same-sex attraction on the internet. 10:82–100

Hinduja S, Patchin JW (2008) Personal information of adolescents on the Internet: a quantitative content analysis of MySpace. J Adolesc 31:125–146

Leary MR (1996) Self-presentation. Impression management and interpersonal behavior. Westview Press, Boulder

Lenhart A, Madden M (2007) Social networking websites and teens: an overview. http://www.pewinternet.org/pdfs/PIP_SNS_Data_Memo_Jan_2007.pdf. Accessed Retrieved 4 Mar 2009

Lenhart A, Madden M, Smith A, Macgill A (2007) Teens and social media. http://www.pewinternet.org/Reports/2007/Teens-and-Social-Media.aspx. Accessed 14 Jan 2010

Livingstone S (2008) Taking risky opportunities in youthful content creation: teenagers' use of social networking sites for intimacy, privacy and self-expression. New Media Soc 10:393–411

Lo V-h, Wei R (2005) Exposure to internet pornography and Taiwanese adolescents' sexual attitudes and behavior. J Broadcasting Electro Media 49:221–237

Margulis ST (2003a) On the status and contribution of Westin's and Altman's theories of privacy. J Soc Issues 59:411–429

Margulis ST (2003b) Privacy as a social issue and behavioral concept. J Soc Issues 59:243–261

McKenna KYA, Bargh JA (1998) Coming out in the age of the Internet: identity "demarginalization" through virtual group participation. J Pers Soc Psychol 75:681–694

McKenna KYA, Bargh JA (2000) Plan 9 from cyberspace: the implications of the internet for personality and social psychology. Personality Soc Psychol Rev 4:57–75

Mitchell KJ, Wolak J, Finkelhor D (2007) Trends in youth reports of sexual solicitations, harassment and unwanted exposure to pornography on the Internet. J Adolesc Health 40:116–126

Moscardelli D, Divine R (2007) Adolescents' concern for privacy when using the internet: an empirical analysis of predictors and relationships with privacy-protecting behaviors. Family Consumer Sci Res J 35:232–252

Negroponte N (1995) Being digital. Hodder & Stoughton, London

Patchin JW, Hinduja S (2010) Changes in adolescent online social networking behaviors from 2006 to 2009. Comput Hum Behav 26:1818–1821

Peter J, Valkenburg PM (2006a) Adolescents' exposure to sexually explicit material on the internet. Commun Res 33:178–204

Peter J, Valkenburg PM (2006b) Research note: individual differences in perceptions of internet communication. Eur J Commun 21:213–226

Peter J, Valkenburg PM, Schouten AP (2006) Characteristics and motives of adolescents talking with strangers on the internet. Cyberpsychol Behav 9:526–530

Rideout VJ, Foehr UG, Roberts DF (2010) Generation M2: media in the lives of 8- to 18-year-olds. Kaiser Family Foundation, Menlo Park

Schmitt KL, Dayanim S, Matthias S (2008) Personal homepage construction as an expression of social development. Dev Psychol 44:496–506

Schouten AP, Valkenburg PM, Peter J (2007) Precursors and underlying processes of adolescents' online self-disclosure: developing and testing an "internet-attribute-perception" model. Media Psychol 10:292–314

Steinberg L (2008) Adolescence, 8th edn. McGraw Hill, Boston

Steinfield C, Ellison NB, Lampe C (2008) Social capital, self-esteem, and use of online social network sites: a longitudinal analysis. J Appl Developmental Psychol 29:434–445

Subrahmanyam K, Greenfield P (2008) Online communication and adolescent relationships. Future Child 18:119–146

Subrahmanyam K, Greenfield PM, Tynes B (2004) Constructing sexuality and identity in an online teen chat room. J Appl Developmental Psychol 25:651–666

Subrahmanyam K, Smahel D, Greenfield PM (2006) Connecting developmental constructions to the Internet: identity presentation and sexual exploration in online teen chat rooms. Dev Psychol 42:395–406

Suzuki LK, Calzo JP (2004) The search for peer advice in cyberspace: an examination of online teen bulletin boards about health and sexuality. J Appl Developmental Psychol 25:685–698

Valkenburg PM, Peter J (2007a) Internet communication and its relation to well-being: identifying some underlying mechanisms. Media Psychol 9:43–58

Valkenburg PM, Peter J (2007b) Preadolescents' and adolescents' online communication and their closeness to friends. Dev Psychol 43:267–277

Valkenburg PM, Peter J (2008) Adolescents' identity experiments on the internet: consequences for social competence and self-concept unity. Commun Res 35:208–231

Valkenburg PM, Peter J (2009a) The effects of instant messaging on the quality of adolescents' existing friendships: a longitudinal study. J Commun 59:79–97

Valkenburg PM, Peter J (2009b) Social consequences of the internet for adolescents: a decade of research. Curr Dir Psychol Sci 18:1–5

Valkenburg PM, Schouten AP, Peter J (2005) Adolescents' identity experiments on the internet. New Media Soc 7:383–402

Valkenburg PM, Peter J, Schouten AP (2006) Friend networking sites and their relationship to adolescents' well-being and social self-esteem. Cyberpsychol Behav 9:584–590

Walther JB (1992) Interpersonal effects in computer-mediated communication: a relational perspective. Commun Res 19:52–90

Walther JB (1996) Computer-mediated communication. Impersonal, interpersonal, and hyperpersonal interaction. Commun Res 23:3–43

Westin AF (1967) Privacy and freedom. Atheneum, New York

Wolfe M, Laufer R (1974) The concept of privacy in childhood and adolescence. In: Carson DH, Margulis ST (eds) Man-environment interactions: evaluations and applications (Part 2), vol 6. Environmental Design Research Association, Washington, DC, pp 29–54

Youn S (2009) Determinants of online privacy concern and its influence on privacy protection behaviors among young adolescents. J Consum Aff 43:389–418

Chapter 17
The Elderly and the Internet: How Senior Citizens Deal with Online Privacy

Wiebke Maaß

17.1 Introduction

The use of the Internet is no longer limited to younger people. Over the past years, more and more elderly people have started using the Internet and today, older persons represent a large group of users that has steadily grown since the year 2000 (Pierce 2009). Although e-mail and search engines are still the most important Internet functions for older people, their use of social media has increased dramatically and nearly doubled from 2009 to 2010 (Madden 2010). While the Internet in general and the Social Web in particular are becoming more important for senior citizens, the question arises of how the older generation deals with privacy online. This chapter analyzes the role of privacy concerns and self-disclosure in seniors' Internet use. For a better understanding of elderly people's online behavior, a short overview of their Internet use is presented (Sect. 17.2). This is followed by a review of the older generation's attitudes toward using the Internet and an outline of the perceived barriers and benefits of using the Internet. Barriers and benefits that users face while using the Internet may also be described as costs and rewards. In their social exchange theory, Thibaut and Kelley (1959) suggested referring to consequences of social interactions as costs and rewards. In this chapter, this conception of costs and rewards will be transferred to social interactions in the Social Web. The particular costs and rewards of Internet use (Sect. 17.3) and online privacy behavior of elderly people (Sect. 17.4) will be elaborated. These theoretical ideas will be complemented with a short empirical analysis of elderly people's self-disclosing behavior within the Social Web (Sect. 17.5). As research in this area is quite limited for the group of older Internet users, this explorative study presents a first insight into the amount of information that elderly people disclose online. Finally, the results will be discussed and conclusions presented (Sect. 17.6).

W. Maaß (✉)
Hamburg Media School, Hamburg, Germany
e-mail: w.maass@hamburgmediaschool.com

S. Trepte and L. Reinecke (eds.), *Privacy Online*,
DOI 10.1007/978-3-642-21521-6_17, © Springer-Verlag Berlin Heidelberg 2011

17.2   Using the Internet in Later Life

Internet adoption rates are higher among younger generations compared to elderly individuals, and this trend is observable throughout several countries of the world. Results of the World Internet Project (Pierce 2010), which analyzed data from ten countries and regions in America, Asia, and Europe, showed that in general, "internet use increases as age decreases" (p. 2). Today, the Internet adoption rate is around 38% among Americans aged 65 years and above, compared to 93% among people aged 18–29 years (Rainie 2010). Although Internet adoption rates are still higher among younger people, Kohut et al. (2006) showed that "the growth rate for adults over 50 has outpaced that for young adults both in the United States and throughout Western Europe" (p. 3). Furthermore, the group of elderly individuals who use the Internet is large due to the demographic structure of the industrial nations. As there is a trend toward "the aging of our population" (Saunders 2004, p. 573), the total number of older people usually exceeds that of younger ones in the industrial nations. Therefore, a relatively low percentage of older Internet users nevertheless represents a high number of elderly people with regard to the absolute values. Sometimes, the number of Internet-using seniors is almost analogous to the number of younger people using the Internet. For example, according to van Eimeren and Frees (2010), 28.2% of German people aged 60 years and above made use of the Internet in 2010, whereas the usage rate within the age group of 14–19 years was nearly 100%. With regard to absolute values, this means that nearly 5.7 million people over 60 years of age used the Internet compared to approximately 5.5 million individuals within the younger age group (14–19 years).

As there are many Internet-using seniors today, they do not form a homogeneous group but vary in their use of the Internet. Nevertheless, there are some Internet functions that seem to be particularly interesting for the majority of the older generation.

One of the most important Internet applications for older individuals that is pointed out by several authors and in different countries is the writing and receiving of e-mails. For example, according to Fox et al. (2001), 93% of seniors with Internet access used e-mails, and this application was described as the number one activity in senior citizens' Internet use. This view is supported by various authors, such as Hilt and Lipschultz (2004), who analyzed seniors within the age of 55–84 years, or van Eimeren and Frees (2010), who found that 75% of the Internet users aged 50 years and above used e-mails at least once a week, making it the most commonly used Internet application within this age group.

Another very important Internet application for elderly people is the use of search engines. For example, Zickuhr (2010) showed that 87% of Internet-using seniors aged 65–73 years made use of this application. Using search engines is also pointed out by other authors as a very important Internet function (e.g., van Eimeren and Frees 2010; Fox et al. 2001), and elderly people use popular search engines such as "Google" or "Yahoo" to find information of personal interest (Hilt and Lipschultz 2004). With regard to the content of information that elderly people are searching for, there are some topics that seem to be of particular interest. For example, Fox et al. (2001) showed that searching the Internet for health and medical information was very common among the older generation, a notion that is also supported by Gatto and Tak (2008). Further important topics are online news in general (Madden 2010) and reading political news in particular (Fox et al. 2001).

In addition to e-mails and search engines as two of the most relevant Internet applications, there are further important functions such as home banking (van Eimeren and Frees 2010), making travel reservations (Zickuhr 2010), file downloading (Sum et al. 2009), as well as online shopping and auctions (Hilt and Lipschultz 2004). Nevertheless, these Internet applications appear to be less important for elderly people than using the Internet for aspects of communication and information.

Taken together, the Internet applications that are most important for elderly people do not seem to differ from those of other age groups. Indeed, these Internet functions are also important for younger Internet users and most of them can be described as key functions that are "uniformly popular across all age groups" (Zickuhr 2010, p.2). Nevertheless, there are differences between age groups with regard to some other Internet applications. With regard to social media, senior citizens appear to be less interested than younger individuals and this tendency can be found in several countries. According to the results of the Global Attitudes Project of the Pew Research Center (2010), there is an age gap with respect to the use of social networking services in each of the 22 nations that were surveyed all over the world.

However, there are two reasons that suggest taking a closer look at elderly people's social media use. Firstly, although younger people dominate the group of social media users today, social media use among elderly individuals has dramatically increased (Madden 2010) and is expected to gain further importance in the future. Secondly, privacy issues are interesting in terms of social media and social networking sites. As the exchange and disclosure of private information can be described as key aspects of social media use, it is interesting to look at how senior citizens deal with online privacy in terms of using such services. Madden (2010) points out that the adoption of such services almost doubled from 2009 to 2010: whereas 25% of Internet users aged 50–64 years and 13% of users aged 65 years and above used social networking sites in 2009, in 2010 these percentages went up to 47% in the age group of 50–64 years, and 26% in the group of Internet users aged 65 years and above. Additionally, Madden (2010) describes that the "use of Twitter and other services to share status updates has also grown among older adults" (p. 3), although this increase was considerably smaller compared to the use of social networking sites such as "Facebook." Nevertheless, compared to 2009, when only 5% of Internet users within the age of 50–64 years used Twitter or another status update service, 11% used these tools in 2010. Furthermore, Pierce (2008) demonstrated that a "large percentage of Internet users 50 and older who are members of online communities report extensive involvement in their communities and benefits from their participation" (p. 1).

With regard to the main focus of this chapter, some key findings can be summarized according to the data presented above. Firstly, elderly people represent a large and steadily growing group of Internet users. Secondly, seniors make use of a broad spectrum of Internet applications and dealing with private information plays an important role for some of these applications. Thirdly, in terms of communication via e-mails or social networking sites, personal information is usually disclosed to some extent. Taken together, the patterns of using the Internet in later life suggest that online privacy is also a relevant issue within the older generation.

17.3   Elderly People's Attitudes Toward the Internet as a Ratio of Costs and Rewards

For a better understanding of senior citizens' Internet use, their attitude toward the Internet should be considered. There are some key aspects that can be seen as barriers against using the Internet as well as some motivating factors. On a more theoretical level, these may be described as costs and rewards, such as in Thibaut and Kelley's (1959) social exchange theory. Thibaut and Kelley's (1959) model was originally used to describe personal relationships; however, here, it will be suggested to determine how elderly people behave in terms of using the Internet. One of the main assumptions of Thibaut and Kelley's (1959) model of social exchange is that the consequences of (social) interactions can be termed as costs and rewards. Thibaut and Kelley (1959) describe costs as various negative components and "any factors that operate to inhibit or deter the performance of a sequence of behavior" (p. 12). Accordingly, there are high costs if "great physical or mental effort is required, when embarrassment or anxiety accompany the action, or when there are conflicting forces or competing response tendencies of any sort" (Thibaut and Kelley 1959, p. 13). On the other hand, the term rewards describes various positive components of an interaction, for example, "pleasures, satisfactions, and gratifications the person enjoys" (Thibaut and Kelley 1959, p. 12).

The relation of costs and rewards leads to specific outcomes of social interactions and these outcomes are important for the formation of social relationships. People try to minimize their costs and maximize their rewards in order to reach "excellent reward-cost positions" (Thibaut and Kelley 1959, p. 31). This set of behaviors can be referred to as *minimax strategy* (e.g., Hogg and Vaughan 2005).

These main assumptions of social exchange theory are very elementary principles that are easily applicable to other research fields. Therefore, the basic principles of social exchange have been used in several different studies and within a variety of contexts, for example, marital relationships (Nakonezny and Denton 2008), the relation between principals and agents (Bottom et al. 2006), and social conformity (Nord 1969). Furthermore, social exchange theory was used in the field of sports (Guillet et al. 2002), knowledge sharing (Liao 2008), and psychotherapy (Derlega et al. 1992). It has also been described as being "among the most influential conceptual paradigms for understanding workplace behavior" (Cropanzano and Mitchell 2005, p. 847).

Thibaut and Kelley's (1959) model may be used here to describe two sets of behavior in terms of their costs and rewards: Internet use and privacy behavior. There are barriers or costs associated with both behaviors on the one hand and perceived benefits or rewards on the other hand. If there is a good "cost-reward ratio" (Hogg and Vaughan 2005, p. 511) and the perceived benefits exceed the barriers, one can assume that there is a higher likelihood of using the Internet. Furthermore, for elderly people who have already decided to use the Internet, this cost-reward ratio can help to describe patterns of online behavior. Different kinds of benefits or motivating factors can be outlined for elderly people's use of the Internet. Gatto and Tak (2008) analyzed participants with a mean age of 71.1 years who pointed out the satisfaction with access to information, positive learning experiences, and the utility of some Internet activities such as online financial services and shopping. Another very important motivation mentioned by the older participants was a sense of connectedness. Similarly, results of Saunders (2004) suggest that elderly people are interested in the use of e-mails because these are able to enhance contacts with children and grandchildren. As all of these factors include aspects of pleasure, satisfaction, or gratification, they can be described as perceived rewards in terms of using the Internet in later life.

With regard to the costs of using the Internet, Gatto and Tak (2008) showed some perceived barriers that were typical for the group of elderly people analyzed. Some of the older individuals mentioned that they were frustrated that it took so much time to learn computer skills. Furthermore, perceived barriers against using the Internet were physical and mental limitations that prevented the older individuals from using the Internet, frustration with the computer equipment, as well as the opinion that they do not have enough time to use the Internet.

Another aspect of perceived barriers was the trustworthiness of information. Some of the older Internet users were concerned about whether they could trust information that was retrieved via the Internet. Results of an analysis of focus groups held with elderly people by Saunders (2004) are in line with the results of Gatto and Tak (2008). Barriers that were mentioned by elderly people were problems in learning how to use computers and finding persons that could support them in acquiring computer skills, as well as physical problems such as reduced eyesight. Furthermore, Saunders (2004) points out that the costs of computers, fear of appearing incompetent or causing damage to the computers, and concerns about junk mail or inappropriate websites were seen as barriers against using the Internet for older people. Taken together, these results are in line with the assumption of Charness and Boot (2009), who reviewed "evidence indicating that attitudes and abilities are among the most powerful predictors of technology use" (p. 253).

Whereas in this section, the costs and rewards of general Internet use were specified, the following section will address privacy behavior as a specific aspect of Social Web use.

17.4   Costs and Rewards of Online Privacy Behavior

While the Internet in general and the Social Web in particular are becoming more important for elderly people, the question arises of how the older generation deals with privacy issues. In this context it has to be considered that research in online privacy among the older generation is quite limited (Chai et al. 2008). Nevertheless, some studies have addressed online privacy behavior already and can help in understanding the way elderly people behave online. With regard to Thibaut and Kelley's (1959) theoretical model, it can be assumed that elderly people will only use Internet services requiring the disclosure of personal data if there is a good ratio of costs and rewards.

17.4.1   Privacy Concerns as Costs of Using the Internet

A very important barrier to using Internet applications are privacy concerns. For example, Gatto and Tak (2008) described that privacy concerns "caused many of the older adults to avoid activities on the Internet that could put their personal information at risk for identity theft" (p. 808). Furthermore, there is some evidence that elderly people are more concerned about privacy issues than younger users. According to an analysis from Burst Media (2009), there are online privacy concerns among all age groups, but these concerns increase with age. Within the age group of 18–24 years, 67.3% of the participants reported concern about privacy issues whereas among participants aged 55 years and above, 85.7% were concerned. Similarly, Zukowski and Brown (2007) found that with increasing age of Internet users, the level of concern for information privacy grows. Moreover, elderly Internet users had a strong desire to control the amount of information that is collected about them. Results from "The Pew Internet & American Life Project" (Fox et al. 2000) were similar: together with women, minorities, and people with less Internet experience, elderly Internet users were one of the groups that seemed to be most concerned about privacy issues online. Another aspect was pointed out by Bühlmann (2006), who investigated online shopping behavior and found that privacy issues are also relevant in this context. The Internet was found to be the most common source of information on products of interest, followed by specialist shops and magazines. Nevertheless, there are barriers to buying products online, the main concern being privacy issues. Fifty-six percent of the participants reported being concerned about online shopping because of potential data abuse, followed by 55% of participants who were concerned because of payment methods.

As mentioned above, privacy concerns can be seen as the costs of using the Internet. As research suggests, the privacy concerns of elderly people are not inappropriate: for example, Chakraborty et al. (2009) assume that the increase in elderly people who use the Internet "has also brought along the problem of privacy invasions and breaches and the senior citizens are among the most vulnerable groups in this context" (p. 1). This view is also supported by other authors. For example, Chai et al. (2008) described elderly people as being particularly vulnerable to privacy attacks. Shrewsbury (2002) argued that older people are "special targets of scams, and the internet broadens their vulnerability, especially as government makes information about citizens readily available" (p. 206). Chakraborty et al. (2009) stressed that there are two reasons that make elderly people vulnerable in terms of online privacy issues. The first reason is that elderly people grew up in a more honest world and therefore tend to trust other people. The second aspect is that senior citizens normally do not spend as much time on the Internet as younger users do. Because of this difference, which is sometimes called the "grey digital divide" (Millward 2003) or the "digital age divide" (Clarke and Concejero 2010), elderly Internet users "are not as knowledgeable about internet frauds" (Chakraborty et al. 2009, p. 1). As mentioned before, although it seems reasonable to investigate online privacy issues of elderly people, there is less research about this topic, as Chai et al. (2008) sum up: "Given the significance and vulnerability of this demographic group, research on information privacy and security of "wired" seniors is paramount, yet, such research is quite limited. Most research regarding cybersecurity and information privacy is with respect to younger generations" (p. 1).

The privacy issues discussed above are contrasted by a number of positive outcomes of Internet use. As social interactions are usually guided by a desire to reach a good ratio of costs and rewards (Thibaut and Kelley 1959), elderly people should also gain perceived rewards from their online self-disclosure. If this were not the case, they would not be motivated to disclose personal data online. Therefore, it appears necessary to take a closer look at the disclosure of personal data and the perceived rewards of this behavior within the next section.

17.4.2 The Benefits of Self-Disclosure as Rewards of Using the Internet

Some evidence about the way elderly people deal with online privacy comes from Pfeil and Zaphiris (2007). According to the results of their qualitative content analysis within an online community for older people, 71% of the analyzed messages included activities of self-disclosure, making self-disclosure the most frequently observed behavior. Pfeil and Zaphiris (2007) assumed that this "shows how important it is for the members of the online community to tell others about themselves" (p. 922). Similar conclusions can be drawn with regard to a study by Mittilä and Antikainen (2006), who analyzed what aspects enhanced the attraction of online communities among adults aged 55 years or above. They found that asking for advice and giving advice, as well as discussion with other members, were common factors of attraction. Furthermore, building new relationships and meeting people online, as well as seeking a dating partner, were important motivations.

All of these behaviors include interpersonal interactions that demand users provide at least some private information.

In addition, there are some studies that focused more precisely on the role of online self-disclosure for interpersonal interactions: Pfeil et al. (2010) analyzed the behavior of members of an online support community for older people and found self-disclosure to be an important factor for the functioning of such a community. The authors analyzed messages that were posted within 6 years in a discussion group focused on the topic of depression within the online community "SeniorNet." The authors investigated threats of interrelated text messages, so called message sequences. With regard to self-disclosure, Pfeil et al. (2010) were able to demonstrate that messages that contained self-disclosure were generally responded to by messages that also contained self-disclosure (this reciprocity effect is also known from general privacy literature, e.g., Archer 1979). According to the authors, these message sequences were used to build "a sense of commonality and togetherness" (Pfeil et al. 2010, p. 354). The authors come to the conclusion that people "talk about themselves, mutually opening up towards each other, often discovering that they have a lot in common. This is then used as the basis for further conversation to happen" (Pfeil et al. 2010, p. 354). Furthermore, the authors showed that there was a strong relationship between messages high in self-disclosure and messages that were related to deep support. Deep support refers to text segments "in which people post support that is customized towards the unique situation of the target that the message is for. It shows that the poster understands the situation of the other, and often includes advise or sympathy for this person" (Pfeil et al. 2010, p. 347). Self-disclosure was often followed by messages that contained deep support and in a similar way deep support was often followed by messages that contained self-disclosure. This suggests that self-disclosing in online support communities is an activity that is often rewarded by social support.

Another study that emphasizes the importance of self-disclosure in senior citizens' Internet use was conducted by Gradis (2003). She analyzed the communication behaviors that were central for building friendships via e-mail within a group of elderly Internet users. The sample of Gradis' (2003) study comprised 90 elderly individuals who held either intergenerational friendships or friendships with peers. Gradis (2003) argues that the content people communicate about is important for the formation of friendships and most friendships are initiated through behaviors that include self-disclosure. The author showed that there were reciprocal patterns of communication behaviors and self-disclosure was one of these behaviors. This finding is in line with the reciprocity effect reported by Pfeil et al. (2010). Moreover, Gradis (2003) suggests "that self promotion (a self presentation strategy) and self disclosure were the most important communication behavioral differences between both senior peer and intergenerational friendship pairs who agreed to maintain friendships as compared with those who did not agree to stay friends" (p. 14). Therefore, self-disclosure was found to be an important factor for the formation and duration of friendships in the analyzed computer-mediated communication.

With regard to Thibaut and Kelley's (1959) theoretical assumptions, it can be summarized that elderly people do provide personal data within the Internet and that the exchange of private information is one of the attraction factors of using the Internet. Therefore, this behavior can be described as a form of reward in terms of Thibaut and Kelley's (1959) ratio of costs and rewards.

17.4.3   The Minimax Strategy in Terms of Online Privacy

As there are perceived costs of online self-disclosure on the one hand and perceived rewards on the other hand, the relationship of these factors should be considered. Although online self-disclosure seems to be important for elderly Internet users, the conditions of self-disclosure have to be considered. Mittilä and Antikainen (2006) describe that the "possibility to meet different kinds of people and discuss with them behind a nickname was one of the seniors' attraction factors" (p. 274). In this regard, they describe anonymity as an important aspect for seniors' use of online communities. There seems to be a tendency to self-disclose on the one hand and to keep up privacy by using synonyms and nicknames on the other hand. This assumption is consistent with the results of a quantitative content analysis from Nimrod (2009). She analyzed the contents and characteristics of 14 leading online communities for elderly people. The five main topics that were discussed within the online communities were fun, retirement, family and health, as well as work and studies. Results showed that the topics discussed ranged from very private issues, for example, fear of death and problems in relationships, to more public topics such as politics. At the same time, Nimrod (2009) points out that most of the participants "use pseudonyms and do not tend to provide identifying details" (p. 390). She further assumes that this "anonymity may enable expressing thoughts and emotions never expressed before and experiencing new roles and relationships" (Nimrod 2009, p. 390).

With regard to Thibaut and Kelley's (1959) theoretical model, the online privacy behavior of elderly people seems to follow a minimax strategy: on the one hand, elderly Internet users self-disclose online to acquire the social rewards of this behavior, for example, social support within an online community. On the other hand, there are several privacy concerns that can be seen as perceived costs of using the Internet, for example, concerns of identity theft. Elderly Internet users try to maximize the social rewards and minimize the costs or risks of this behavior as they often self-disclose while using a nickname. Therefore, the tendency to self-disclose on the one hand and preserve anonymity on the other hand can be seen as using a minimax strategy.

As there are many Internet-using seniors today, these cannot be seen as a homogeneous group. Thus, the theoretical assumption of a cost-reward ratio may not apply to all seniors using the Internet. Nevertheless, social exchange theory seems capable of explaining the usage patterns of a noteworthy part of Internet-using seniors and may be a further step toward understanding the older generations' online privacy behavior. To further investigate elderly persons' online behavior, an explorative study is presented in the next section.

17.5   Disclosing Private Information in Senior Citizens' Social Networking Sites: An Exploratory Study

It was shown above that older individuals often use nicknames to keep up their anonymity in the Social Web. Self-disclosure on the one hand and activities to retain privacy on the other hand may be described as a minimax strategy. However, previous research is quite limited. To date, only scarce information is available about the older generations' online self-disclosure, use of privacy settings, and privacy-related activities. Thus, this study aims to investigate the amount of information elderly people self-disclose online and their strategies to retain their privacy.

In addition to well-established social networking sites such as "Facebook" or "LinkedIn," which address very different groups of people, a variety of online communities that particularly address older users has developed (e.g., www. seniornet.org, www.senior.com). As the studies on online privacy presented above referred to online communities for senior citizens, for example, "SeniorNet" in the study of Pfeil et al. (2010), such a specialized network was also selected for the present descriptive analysis. The network chosen was the German Internet platform "planetsenior.de," which is targeted at seniors aged 50 years and above.

Within the present study, the type of information about the community members that was publicly accessible via the World Wide Web was analyzed. Community members can usually choose between different privacy settings and decide who will be able to see the data they provide. For example, their information may be either limited to certain community members, accessible to all community members, or to all Internet users, (for a taxonomy of social networking sites see Ziegele and Quiring, this volume, Chap. 13).

Measures. To investigate the type and amount of personal information elderly users publish online, the amount of information that was freely accessible via the World Wide Web was assessed. Four categories of personal information were analyzed: first name, surname, marital status, and home state. Furthermore, the number of users providing information in the category "about me," where users can provide a short statement about themselves, and in the category "searching for," where different choices are available (e.g., conversational partner, travelling, or dating) was calculated. Additionally, it was analyzed if users had uploaded a photo on their profile page. The analysis did not consider the type of photo (e.g., portrait of profile owner vs. other motives) and solely assessed the presence or absence of any kind of photo on the profile.

Table 17.1 Categories analyzed within the online community

Category	Number of people who provided data	Percentage
Home state	128	83.66
Marital status	81	52.94
Searching for	59	38.56
Photo	37	24.18
About me	27	17.65
First name	9	5.88
Surname	1	0.65

Total number of profiles analyzed: $N = 153$

Sample. The 153 most current profiles within the age of 50–95 years of planetsenior.de were taken into the sample. Of the 153 profiles analyzed, 44.44% belonged to female users, 55.56% to male users. Users were unable to restrict access to their biological sex within their profiles, thus this information was available for all profiles analyzed.

Results. Personally identifying information, such as first name and surname, were only provided by a minority of users (Table 17.1). Only 9 (5.88%) members reported their first name and only one (0.65%) person provided the surname. Instead, the majority of social networking site members kept their anonymity by using nicknames. In terms of social exchange theory, this behavior resembles the elderly Internet users' attempt to minimize the costs of their online self-disclosure. Nevertheless, users provided more personal information in other profile categories. For example, 52.94% of the users stated their marital status and 83.66% disclosed the state they were living in. A short statement about themselves within the category "about me" was provided by 17.65% of the users, and information within the category "searching for" was reported by 38.56%. Additionally, some kind of photo was provided by 24.18% of the community members.

In line with the results presented in Sect. 17.4.3, senior citizens used nicknames within their profiles and only rarely provided their first name or surname. Particularly compared to data collected in samples of college students, these percentages are low. In Tufekci's (2008) analysis of "Facebook" profiles, 94.9% of users provided their real name, and 62.7% did so in "MySpace." However, this difference between elderly people and college students is not necessarily a mere age effect. As the results refer to different social networking sites, there can also be differences in dealing with online privacy because of different network cultures.

Furthermore, with regard to the social networking site planetsenior.de, marital status, home state, and information within the category "searching for" were disclosed by more than 38% of the users. Statements about the members and photos were provided less frequently, perhaps because these were seen as more private issues. Taken together, a significant amount of information was provided and it has to be considered that the stated details were accessible not only within the social network site but were publicly available for every Internet user. On the other hand, it has to be considered that one cannot prove how much of the data provided is true and how much information is spurious. In this regard, Fox et al. (2000) showed that elderly people sometimes provided fake personal information in order to protect their privacy, although this was more common among younger people: Among Internet users aged 18–29 years, 35% provided fake information about personal aspects, compared to only 17% of Internet users aged 50–64 years.

As this explorative analysis only considered information that was publicly accessible via the World Wide Web, it can be considered a quite conservative approach. One can assume that in some online communities more personal data and identifying details are disclosed but limited to social networking site members. However, the social network site analyzed, planetsenior.de, is just one among several networks in Germany and therefore does not allow a generalization for all senior citizens' social networking sites. Furthermore, the analysis is only an explorative attempt to describe elderly people's online behavior and considered only the information elderly individuals provided through the World Wide Web. There is no information about the amount of personal data that is visible for community members only. Nevertheless, as research on the older generation is scarce, the analysis allows a first insight into the amount of information that elderly people disclose in a social networking site. It shows that profile information seems to differ in terms of how private it is perceived to be. Users seem to be open-hearted with information that would not allow their identification, such as home state. However, they hold back personally identifying information such as their full name.

17.6   Discussion and Conclusion

With regard to the research reviewed above, some key findings can be identified and discussed. Firstly, the Internet is no longer a medium that is limited to younger users. There are notable numbers of "wired" seniors and using the Internet for communicating with others is one of the most important Internet applications for elderly people. With regard to privacy aspects, two trends can be observed. On the one hand, elderly people are particularly concerned about privacy aspects and report more concerns about privacy issues than younger individuals. On the other hand, older individuals provide a lot of personal data online. With regard to Thibaut and Kelley's (1959) theoretical assumptions discussed in this chapter, these two observable trends do not necessarily conflict with each other. It seems plausible to assume that elderly people use a minimax strategy: they try to maximize the rewards of using the Social Web and simultaneously minimize the costs – in this case the privacy concerns – by using nicknames to retain privacy and anonymity. The results of the exploratory analysis support this theoretical assumption. Although the perceived gratifications were not measured, the results regarding the costs are in line with Thibaut and Kelley's (1959) theoretical assumptions. A large number of the analyzed Internet users of a social networking site for senior citizens do self-disclose to a comparatively high extent but the majority use a nickname so that privacy concerns are minimized.

According to social exchange theory, users should be willing to engage in self-disclosure online if there is a good ratio of rewards and costs and the perceived rewards should be higher than the perceived costs. In fact, there are several positive aspects of using the Social Web and providing personal data that can be described as social rewards. For example, as demonstrated by studies of Pfeil et al. (2010) and Gradis (2003), self-disclosure is an important factor with regard to the formation of friendships within the Internet and is closely linked to the amount of social support received in online support communities.

Despite these positive aspects, the possible risks of providing personal information online and the special vulnerability to privacy attacks of elderly people should not be overlooked. It seems important to further investigate privacy behavior and to educate a safe online behavior that is concordant with individual privacy needs and concerns. It can be concluded, that if social media applications are used the right way, there can be many psychosocial benefits for elderly people without them being particularly vulnerable to privacy menaces.

References

Archer RL (1979) Role of personality and the social situation. In: Chelune GJ (ed) Self-disclosure. Origins, patterns, and implications of openness in interpersonal relationships. Jossey-Bass, San Francisco, pp 28–58

Bottom WP, Holloway J, Miller GJ, Mislin A, Whitford A (2006) Building a pathway to cooperation: negotiation and social exchange between principal and agent. Adm Sci Q 51:29–58

Burst Media (2009) Online privacy worries increase with age. http://www.marketingcharts.com/direct/online-privacy-worries-increase-with-age-8229. Accessed 27 Nov 2010

Bühlmann A (2006) Senioren im internet – Ein neuer Markt. [Senior citizens within the internet – a new market]. http://www.seniorweb.ch/files/old/joomla/images/stories/Themen/Konsum/senioren_im_internet_als_neuer_markt_umfrage_auf_seniorweb.pdf. Accessed 27 Nov 2010

Chai S, Rao HR, Bagchi-Sen S, Upadhyaya SJ (2008). 'Wired' senior citizens and online information privacy. Paper presented at the tenth ETHICOMP international conference on the social and ethical impacts of information and communication technology, Mantua, 24–26 Sept 2008. http://www.ccsr.cse.dmu.ac.uk/conferences/ethicomp/ethicomp2008/abstracts/ethicomp2008_chai.php. Accessed 27 Nov 2010

Chakraborty R, Rao HR, Uphadhyahy SJ (2009) BANDES: an adaptive decision support system for protecting online privacy for senior citizen centers. Paper presented at the fourth Pre-ICIS workshop on information security & privacy (WISP) – the official annual workshop of association of information systems SIG/SEC. http://www.security-conference.org/sigsec/WISP2009papers/4.pdf. Accessed 27 Nov 2010

Charness N, Boot WR (2009) Aging and information technology use potential and barriers. Curr Dir Psychol Sci 18(5):253–258

Clarke A, Concejero P (2010) The digital divide – services for the elderly and disabled in 2010 – the PRISMA project. The PRISMA project. http://citeseerx.ist.psu.edu/viewdoc/download?doi=10.1.1.138.1285&rep=rep1&type=pdf. Accessed 25 Oct 2010

Cropanzano R, Mitchell MS (2005) Social exchange theory: an interdisciplinary review. J Manag 31:874–898. doi:10.1177/0149206305279602

Derlega VJ, Winstead BA, Hendrick SS, Berg JH (1992) Psychotherapy as a personal relationship: a social psychological perspective. Psychotherapy 29(3):331–335

Fox S, Rainie L, Horrigan J, Lenhart A, Spooner T, Carter C (2000) Trust and privacy online: why Americans want to rewrite the rules. Pew Internet & American Life Project. http://www. pewinternet.org/~/media//Files/Reports/2000/PIP_Trust_Privacy_Report.pdf.pdf.   Accessed 27 Nov 2010

Fox S, Rainie L, Larsen E, Horrigan J, Lenhart A, Spooner T, Carter C (2001) Wired seniors. A fervent few, inspired by family ties. Pew Internet & American Life Project. http://www. pewinternet.org/~/media//Files/Reports/2001/PIP_Wired_Seniors_Report.pdf.pdf.   Accessed 25 Oct 2010

Gatto SL, Tak SH (2008) Computer, internet and e-mail use among older adults: benefits and barriers. Educ Gerontol 34(9):800–811. doi:10.1080/03601270802243697

Gradis MT (2003) Seniors and friendship formation online. Paper presented at the annual meeting of the international communication association, San Diego, 23–27 May 2003. http://www. allacademic.com/meta/p112117_index.html. Accessed 27 Nov 2010

Guillet E, Sarrazin P, Carpenter PJ, Trouilloud D, Cury F (2002) Predicting persistence or withdrawal in female handballers with social exchange theory. Int J Psychol 37(2):92–104. doi:10.1080/00207590143000243

Hilt ML, Lipschultz JH (2004) Elderly Americans and the internet: E-mail, TV news, information and entertainment websites. Educ Gerontol 30(1):57–72. doi:10.1080/03601270490249166

Hogg MA, Vaughan GM (2005) Social psychology. Pearson, Harlow

Kohut A, Wike R, Speulda N (2006) Truly a world wide web. Globe going digital. The pew global attitudes project. http://pewglobal.org/files/pdf/251.pdf. Accessed 15 Jan 2010

Liao L (2008) Knowledge-sharing in R&D departments: a social power and social exchange theory perspective. Int J Hum Resour Manag 19(10):1881–1895

Madden M (2010) Older adults and social media. Social networking use among those ages 50 and older nearly doubled over the past year. Pew Internet & American Life Project. http:// pewinternet.org/~/media//Files/Reports/2010/Pew%20Internet%20%20Older%20Adults% 20and%20Social%20Media.pdf. Accessed 25 Oct 2010

Millward P (2003) The 'grey digital divide': perception, exclusion and barrier of access to internet for older people. First Monday 8(7). http://firstmonday.org/issues/issue8_7/millward/index. html. Accessed 13 Nov 2010

Mittilä T, Antikainen M (2006) Perceived attraction of online communities among elderly people. In: Maula M, Hannula M, Seppä M, Tommila J (eds) Frontiers of e-business research 2006. Proceedings of ICEB + eBRF 2006, Tampere, pp 267–276. http://www.ebrc.fi/kuvat/ Mittila_Antikainen_paper.pdf. Accessed 29 Nov 2010

Nakonezny PA, Denton WH (2008) Marital relationships: a social exchange theory perspective. Am J Fam Ther 36(5):402–412. doi:10.1080/01926180701647264

Nimrod G (2009) Seniors' online communities: a quantitative content analysis. Gerontologist 50(3):382–392. doi:10.1093/geront/gnp141

Nord WR (1969) Social exchange theory: an integrative approach to social conformity. Psychol Bull 71(3):174–208

Pew Research Center. Global Attitudes Project (2010) Computer and cell phone usage up around the world. Global publics embrace social networking. http://pewglobal.org/files/2010/12/Pew-Global-Attitudes-Technology-Report-FINAL-December-15-2010.pdf. Accessed 14 Feb 2010

Pfeil U, Zaphiris P (2007) Patterns of empathy in online communication. In: Proceedings of the SIGCHI conference on human factors in computing systems, San Jose, pp 919–928.

Pfeil U, Zaphiris P, Wilson S (2010) The role of message-sequences in the sustainability of an online support community for older people. J Comput Mediat Commun 15(2):336–363. doi:10.1111/j.1083-6101.2010.01523.x

Pierce J (2008) New study released by the center for the digital future and AARP shows internet users 50+ are rapidly closing the digital divide with booming online activity. Center for the digital future. http://www.digitalcenter.org/pages/Archive_content.asp?intGlobalId=46&intTypeId=2. Accessed 15 Feb 2011

Pierce J (2009) Annual internet survey by the center for digital future finds large increases in use of online newspapers. Center for the Digital Future. http://www.digitalcenter.org/pdf/2009_Digital_Future_Project_Release_Highlights.pdf. Accessed 25 Oct 2010

Pierce J (2010) World internet project finds large percentage of non-users, and significant gender disparities in going online. World internet project. http://www.digitalcenter.org/pdf/2010_digital_future_final_release.pdf. Accessed 14 Feb 2010

Rainie L (2010) Internet, broadband, and cell phone statistics. Pew internet & American life project. http://www.pewinternet.org/~/media//Files/Reports/2010/PIP_December09_update.pdf. Accessed 29 Oct 2010

Saunders EJ (2004) Maximizing computer use along the elderly in rural senior centers. Educ Gerontol 30(7):573–585. doi:10.1080/03601270490466967

Shrewsbury CM (2002) Information technology issues in an era of greater state responsibilities: policy concerns for seniors. J Aging Soc Policy 14(3/4):195–209

Sum S, Mathews RM, Hughes I (2009) Participation of older adults in cyberspace: how Australian older adults use the internet. Aust J Ageing 26(4):189–193

Thibaut JW, Kelley HH (1959) The social psychology of groups. Wiley, New York

Tufekci Z (2008) Can you see me now? Audience and disclosure regulation in online social network sites. B Sci Technol Soc 28(1):20–36. doi:10.1177/0270467607311484

van Eimeren B, Frees B (2010) Ergebnisse der ARD/ZDF-Onlinestudie 2010 [Results of the ARD/ZDF-online study 2010]. Media Perspektiven 7–8:334–349

Zickuhr K (2010) Generations 2010. Pew internet & American life project. http://www.pewinternet.org/~/media//Files/Reports/2010/PIP_Generations_and_Tech10.pdf. Accessed 14 Feb 2011

Zukowski T, Brown I (2007) Examining the influence of demographic factors on internet users' information privacy concerns. In: Proceedings of the 2007 annual research conference of the South African institute of computer scientists and information technologists on IT research in developing countries, SAICSIT, pp 197–204, Sunshine Coast, South Africa

Chapter 18
Privacy and Gender in the Social Web

Mike Thelwall

18.1 Introduction

The Social Web (e.g., Facebook, Twitter, YouTube, blogs, discussion forums) is about communication, often interpersonal communication. It embeds itself into the lives of users and plays many roles, providing entertainment, supporting friendships, and hosting debates. It is therefore logical to expect some offline gendered communication styles and issues to recur in Social Web usage patterns and goals. Even just in terms of technology uptake there can be clear gender differences: for example, US girls (ages 14–17) were recently almost twice as likely to use Twitter than were US boys (Lenhart et al. 2010).

Online privacy in the Social Web also has a gendered dimension, stemming from offline concerns. One clear example of this is stalking: women are more likely to be the victims of this offence (WHOA 2009), and therefore protecting sensitive details online may be more important for females. There are also purely online phenomena that disproportionately impact women, such as cyberbullying (Dehue et al. 2008), and these also give rise to heightened privacy worries. Despite this, there is relatively little research that focuses on gender and privacy in the Social Web. This chapter therefore draws together relevant material from a variety of sources. Table 18.1 summarizes the key findings.

There are many different definitions and aspects of privacy. This chapter is concerned with privacy defined as: selective control over who accesses personal information, including contact information and personal communication, and control over the contexts in which the information can be used (Altman 1976; Nissenbaum 2004). This excludes privacy in the sense of seclusion, which is not relevant to social activities. Control over the contexts in which information is used is important because of the ease with which web content can be recycled or forwarded.

M. Thelwall (✉)
School of Technology, University of Wolverhampton, Wolverhampton, UK
e-mail: mthelwall@wlv.ac.uk

S. Trepte and L. Reinecke (eds.), *Privacy Online*,
DOI 10.1007/978-3-642-21521-6_18, © Springer-Verlag Berlin Heidelberg 2011

Table 18.1 Key gender-related Social Web privacy differences

Issue	Gender differences
Privacy fears	Females more concerned about others accessing their personal information (Hoy and Milne 2010; Tufekci 2008a)
Avoidance	Males most likely to avoid social websites due to privacy concerns (Youn and Hall 2008)
Privacy protection strategies	Females most likely to use active strategies: anonymous posts (Madden and Smith 2010), inaccurate information (Oomen and Leenes 2008; Youn and Hall 2008), modest photos (Aguiton et al. 2009)
Blogs	Female bloggers more likely to write personal blogs (Viégas 2005) and self-disclose (Hollenbaugh 2010), irrespective of privacy concerns
Social network sites (SNS)	Females more likely to join SNSs (Tufekci 2008b), be more active users (Rosen et al. 2010), and open their profiles to more Friends (e.g., in MySpace: Thelwall 2009); females more likely to read SNS privacy policies and alter privacy settings (Hoy and Milne 2010) and have private profiles (Thelwall 2008b). Females more likely to untag pictures (Hoy and Milne 2010). Females less likely to reveal their phone number (Tufekci 2008a) and address (Acquisti and Gross 2006). Gender differences in types of information reported vary by SNS (Kisilevich and Mansmann 2010; Nosko et al. 2010)
YouTube	Females more vulnerable to personal abuse (see e.g., Burgess and Green 2009, p. 96-97) but nevertheless create many intimate videos (see e.g., Burgess and Green 2009, p. 80; Longhurst 2009)
LGBT issues	SNS profiles can give SNS status clues (see e.g., Jernigan and Mistree 2009). The Social Web offers controlled privacy to "come out" (Alexander and Losh 2010; Burgess and Green 2009, p. 80), get support (Cooper 2010), and find partners (see e.g., Farr 2010)

This chapter introduces *Social Web Gendered Privacy Model*, a new theory of privacy and gender in the Social Web. It then reviews gender-related privacy concerns and practices in the Social Web, including a section on lesbian, gay, bisexual, and transgender (LGBT) issues. For stylistic convenience, I use gender (i.e., learned behavior) and biological sex interchangeably even though the concepts are different (Money and Ehrhardt 1982) because the overlap between the two seems sufficient in this context. The primary privacy concerns that this chapter addresses are the ability to restrict access to personal information, such as home address or relationship status, and freedom from harassment in the sense of unwanted intrusions by others. The latter is perhaps a less obvious choice but is included because harassment is a gendered privacy issue (Allen 1988, pp. 126–129).

18.2   Social Web Gendered Privacy Model

This section introduces Social Web Gendered Privacy Model, a new theory to explain gender differences in privacy concerns and practices in the Social Web. It argues that there are four key gendered components that impact privacy concerns–*physical security, harassment, social communication skills,* and *social communication needs*–and that the first two explain gender differences in privacy concerns, whereas all four are needed to explain gender differences in privacy-related behaviors. The theory argues that women have more *offline* concerns for their physical security and more risk of harassment, and that these concerns make using the Social Web a privacy risk. This translates into caution about using the Social Web and a need to use privacy-protecting strategies (e.g., identity conceal-ment, limiting access to information, withholding personal details). Nevertheless, women have communication needs that are particularly well met by the Social Web, and the Internet's remote access potentially provides protection from physical threats and harassment. Thus, women have the greatest incentives to use the Social Web. Overall, the theory predicts that women will use the Social Web more than men but be more privacy-conscious when using it. They will also tend to use services that meet their needs if they can use them in a way that does not greatly threaten their privacy.

Physical security: Physical security is a greater concern to women, leading to a greater need for privacy for personal information, such as a home address or telephone number. This is because within intimate personal relationships, one of the ultimate sanctions is violence, and although this is *not* predominantly directed by men at women, it has a greater effect on women (Magdol et al. 1997). Violence by men may also be more severe (e.g., beat up rather than punch: Archer 2002). Women may also be more concerned about hiding information that may provoke former partners to violence, such as the existence of a new lover or even just evidence of socializing in mixed gender settings, such as Facebook photographs of parties, since new partners and jealousy are particular causes of extreme violence (Campbell et al. 2003). More widely, rape and sexual assault are crimes that predominantly target, and threaten, women, giving women ongoing physical secu-rity privacy concerns (Fairchild and Rudman 2008). Moreover, there have been many media scares about the potential of the Internet to be used by pedophiles. These scares often involve older men grooming girls online, perhaps hiding their age, then arranging to meet them offline (see e.g., O'Connell 2003). Such stories may create an atmosphere in which women may worry about the potential for strangers to contact or physically locate them. Possibly in response to media pressure, however, MySpace and Facebook have purged large numbers of convicted sex offenders (BBC 2007; MSNBC 2008). Nevertheless, it seems likely that environments that make contact with strangers possible, such as chat rooms, blogs, bulletin boards, and SNSs, will be somewhat associated with risk, particu-larly for women.

Physical security concerns are not necessarily a disincentive to using the Social Web, however, they can also be an incentive to finding web-based (rather than offline) safe environments for various purposes. For instance, women (and LGBT groups) may use the web to build bounded communities that are hidden or protected from outside intrusion.

Harassment: Historically, much theorizing about privacy and gender concerned women's privacy being invaded through non-physical sexual harassment. For instance, it now seems accepted that even in public, people (and women in particular) have the right to anonymity in the sense that others should not draw attention to them in a thoughtless way, particularly if this is systematic harassment or is intrusive (Allen 1988, pp. 126–129). The main gender-related forms of non-physical harassment probably concern inappropriate sexual comments or drawing attention to personal appearance. Inappropriate sexual comments seem to be a risk on the Internet since individuals can be anonymous and hence can be offensive with little risk of being caught. An example of drawing attention to personal appearance is a website from 1995 that listed homepages of random women and rated them for attractiveness (Shade 1996). This is not a legal invasion of privacy but is an overt form of surveillance by drawing attention to women and using their photographs out of context, thus diminishing privacy in the sense of the right to anonymity. (A modern gender-neutral version, HotOrNot.com, is based on self-submission and so is not intrusive.) More generally, women in society seem to be more frequently evaluated by physical appearance and so even the need to post profile photographs in social network sites may be potentially off-putting to females.

Conversely, Internet-based communication can have the advantage of anonymity or protecting personal appearance from scrutiny. For instance, a social network site profile picture may not represent its owner or might present them at their best whilst allowing them to socialize online without worrying about their appearance at the time. Similarly, relatively ephemeral social websites, like many online discussion groups and chat sites, are easy to quit if harassment occurs, minimizing the damage done.

Communication needs: Women and men tend to use different *offline* communication strategies, probably due to socialization into different gender roles in society (Holmes 1995), and hence have different communication needs. For instance, females seem to share more personal information with close friends, whereas males' friendships tend to focus instead on shared experiences, such as sports, and banter (Aukett et al. 1988; Elkins and Peterson 1993). In times of stress women are more likely to desire communication, such as talking to friends or seeking advice, whereas men are more likely to try to solve problems alone or to avoid them. For instance, US women are more likely to seek psychiatric help for emotional problems (Kessler et al. 1981) or medical help for health issues (see e.g., Galdas 2005). Hence, it seems that women have a greater need to use the Social Web than men and to share private personal information and problems online.

Communication needs may not always be satisfactorily resolved online. Women seem to be disproportionately victims (and perpetrators) of online abuse within friendship or acquaintanceship circles, as with the case of cyberbullying (Chisholm 2006).

Communication skills: Women seem to be better at social communication than men and may therefore get more benefits from it. This skill may provide an incentive for females to use the Social Web more. For instance, sentiment is a key component of effective social communication and women are more skilful at detecting sentiment in *offline* communication, are also more effective at encoding (Hall 1984) and decoding (McClure 2000) non-verbal emotional signals, and use positive sentiment more, such as with smiles (Hall et al. 2000). For online communication, people replace non-verbal channels, such as facial expression, with textual equivalents, such as emoticons (see e.g., Fullwood and Martino 2007; Hancock et al. 2007). Women seem to be more successful at this in open online discussions (e.g., newsgroups), although in mixed groups men seem to imitate female styles but with less use of emoticons for "solidarity, support, assertion of positive feelings, and thanks" (Wolf 2000). Similarly, in an early study of e-mail, women found it to have a stronger sense of social presence than men did (Gefen and Straub 1997). Some Social Web evidence that women are better users is that females are disproportionately chosen as Friends and Top Friends in MySpace (Thelwall 2008b) and give and receive more positive sentiment than males in MySpace (Thelwall et al. 2010).

In summary, whilst there are pressures on females to keep them away from the Social Web to protect their privacy and security, the Social Web can also provide relatively secure online alternatives to equivalent offline activities, and can potentially fill female-specific social communication needs that are impossible or difficult to satisfy offline. Moreover, more skilful use of the Social Web by females may lead to greater incentives to use it. The Social Web Gendered Privacy Model suggests that the extent to which women use any particular social website will be largely determined by the strength of these opposing tendencies.

18.3   Privacy Concerns in the Social Web: The Evidence

This section reviews evidence for gender differences in articulated online privacy concerns related to the Social Web. The next section examines privacy-related differences in strategies for using the Social Web. The Social Web Gendered Privacy Model argues that women will be more concerned than men about online privacy, but this hypothesis is not clearly supported by existing evidence. A survey of 5,139 Dutch students found *no* gender differences in general privacy concerns, although it is not clear whether the responses were specific to Internet-related issues (Oomen and Leenes 2008). The study sample was self-selected, with a low response rate to e-mail invitations and other announcements (2.31%) and a low completion rate for the questionnaire (25%), which may account for the unusual results. Alternatively, students in the The Netherlands may be an unusual case. In contrast, an early study of online marketing contexts (i.e., not the Social Web) in the US found that women were more concerned about privacy than men but men were more likely to take steps to actively protect their privacy (Sheehan 1999). A later study of US children found females were more concerned about online privacy than males: girls provided inaccurate information to protect themselves whereas boys tended not to register for new websites instead (Youn and Hall 2008). The remainder of this section deals with the specific case of SNSs.

Privacy concerns vary between online contexts, with SNSs appearing to have the potential to cause the greatest problems. This is due partly to the proliferation of personal information within them but also due to their powerful facilities for spreading that information, such as the News Feed feature in Facebook that controversially broadcasts updates on Facebook activities to Friends (Hoadley et al. 2010). US female students seem to be more concerned than males about unwanted others viewing their SNS profiles (Tufekci 2008a).

A different type of privacy concern is the fear of intrusive advertising or marketing strategies. This is a breach of contextual integrity (Nissenbaum 2009) because information provided in one context is being reused in another. This is relevant to the web in general (Zimmer 2008) but particularly for SNSs: the combination of detailed personal information controlled by the company owning each site and a mass audience with which to perfect marketing strategies makes behavioral marketing particularly powerful. The consequent risk to privacy seems to be widely recognized, for instance, leading to the closing down of Facebook Beacon in September 2009, although it does not seem to have a natural gender dimension. Nevertheless, a study of US Facebook users found that women were more concerned about behavioral advertising (e.g., objecting more strongly to targeted advertising based upon their personal profile information) (Hoy and Milne 2010) and this aligns with US female students being more concerned than US male students with government or commercial access to their SNS information (Tufekci 2008a).

18.4   Privacy Practices in the Social Web

Women are known to typically disclose more information in face to face communication than men (Dindia 2002), and so this may be expected to extend to online contexts that have a flavor of interpersonal communication. Before social network sites, when personal homepages were a major way to express online identities and privacy concerns may have been lower, women seemed to post more personal information online than men. A study of adolescents found that girls' personal homepages contained information about romantic relationships more often, for example, as well as referencing friends and family more frequently (Stern 2004).

Although women seem to be more concerned about online privacy than men, their response seems to be to adjust security settings, when available, or to take more precautions, but to continue posting more personal information than men. For instance, and as a practical privacy step, in public group discussions women seem to be more likely to make anonymous postings (Madden and Smith 2010). One experiment also suggests that women prefer to post more modest pictures of themselves than do men (Aguiton et al. 2009). Another study found opposite findings for Dutch students, however: men were more likely to use pseudonyms or anonymous email addresses and more likely to give false information in response to personal questions (Oomen and Leenes 2008). These practices were especially associated with younger students. It may also be that women perceive risks but make a decision that the benefits from loss of privacy outweigh the risks.

18.5   Blog Posts

Blogs are a popular genre with privacy issues related to self-disclosure. Although prominent blogs are often essentially online newspapers or news filter sites, most blogs are online personal diaries (Herring et al. 2004), with the typical subject being "My life" and the main purpose being "to document [] personal experiences and share them with others" (McCullagh 2008, p. 9; see also Nardi et al. 2004). The diary-like nature of most blogs means that they tend to contain personal information about the author. Blogs are therefore an odd phenomenon in that they are typically used to publically discuss personal matters that would not be widely broadcast in other ways and might also be considered to be private (McCullagh 2008). More generally, the diary format may allow readers to develop an impression of the identity of the author that is more than just the sum of the individual facts.

Blogs kept by women seem to give more detailed personal information even though they are mainly world-readable (exceptions include LiveJournal via its privacy settings). A study of 525 Taiwanese bloggers found that women posting frequently were more likely to value self-expression, whereas men were more likely to value a personal outcome that might arise as a result of blogging (Lu and Hsiao 2009). Other research has shown that females are more likely to self-disclose in their blogs (Hollenbaugh 2010) and a survey of 486 early bloggers found that the vast majority of females (92.5%) characterized their blogs as "personal ramblings" in contrast to a much smaller majority (77.5%) of males (Viégas 2005). This confirms an earlier study of British bloggers, which found women more likely to use blogging as a creative outlet, with this more personal aspect to female blogs perhaps explaining why female bloggers tend to be less prominent than male bloggers (Pedersen and Macaffee 2007).

To set the above in context, when males write diary-like blogs, these seem to have female-like characteristics (Herring and Paolillo 2006), so the key gender factor may be the choice of type of blog to write (e.g., diary vs. information filter) rather than style within the type of blog selected. Moreover, the differences may be less marked or non-existent for younger users (Huffaker and Calvert 2005).

18.6   SNSs

SNSs have gendered privacy concerns related to their use for identity projection and friendship maintenance. The dominant uses of SNSs seem to be for keeping in contact with others and for discovering trivial information about them (Donath 2007; Tufekci 2008b). When considering the posting of personal information online, there are many potential benefits. For instance, posting a personal photograph in Facebook may be seen as a risk but it is an important part of attracting new Friends. Both men and women are more likely to befriend the opposite sex if they have an attractive photo in Facebook so there is equal pressure from this perspective (Wang et al. 2010).

At the most basic level of publication, (US student) women are more likely to use an SNS than men (Tufekci 2008b). Women seem to publish more personal content in SNSs, as a number of studies show. An investigation of US students found that females spent more time maintaining their social network profile and posted more photographs online (Rosen et al. 2010). For the same demographic, women seem to report music, books, and religion more than men but to reveal their phone number much less (Tufekci 2008a). Another study of US university students found that females were more concerned about general privacy issues than males but that gender did not seem to be a factor in the decision to join Facebook. Female students were less likely to post their address, phone number, or sexual orientation, but there were no gender differences in reports of political affiliation or birthdays (Acquisti and Gross 2006). A study of Facebook users from Canadian community or university networks included an examination of gender differences in disclosure but had contrasting findings. Information revealed was generally not significantly different between females and males, except that males revealed more information about their religion and politics (Nosko et al. 2010). Similarly, a study of five Russian SNSs found that males disclosed more about political views and sexual information (e.g., orientation, preferences) in response to standard fields than females, although females tended to reveal more information about non-sexual aspects, such as religion and marital status (Kisilevich and Mansmann 2010). In the same study females were much less likely to reveal their current address. It seems that women may be more active than men in protecting their SNS profile, perhaps because of heightened concerns and more content posted. For instance, young US female Facebook users seem to be more careful about friending and posting personal pictures than males, and are more likely to take the pro-active measure of untagging a posted picture (Hoy and Milne 2010).

One study has gone further than those reviewed above in the sense of building regression models that differentiate between privacy concerns, behaviors, and gender. It found some evidence that male students shared *more* information on Facebook than female students did when privacy concerns and personalization practices were factored out (Stutzman et al. 2011). In other words, males with the same level of privacy concerns and practices as females shared more information, which seems counterintuitive.

The SNS MySpace has been discussed in the press in the context of risks to young people, for instance via stalking. A study of adolescent MySpace profiles has confirmed that a significant minority contain information of potential concern, such as photographs in bathing suits and evidence of illegal activity, and many included information that could be used by strangers to identify them, such as their school name (28%) and phone number (0.3%) (Hinduja and Patchin 2008). This 2006 study may reflect the situation before security issues became more well-known, however, and unfortunately did not give a gender breakdown of the results. Another study found no gender differences in the amount of information published in MySpace profiles that were public, however (Boyle and Johnson 2010). A possible explanation is that people who joined MySpace for friendship were more likely to post personal information, so this motivation may have served to partly offset female tendencies to privacy – female MySpace pages tended to be the most vivid (Boyle and Johnson 2010), however, which suggests implicit personalization.

In terms of caution with regard to language used, in the US, female MySpace users have less strong swearing on their profiles but there is no difference for UK MySpace users (Thelwall 2008a). The number of registered Friends accepted by an SNS member also has implications for privacy, and it appears that women seem to have more Friends than do men (e.g., in MySpace: Thelwall 2009).

Privacy settings can give some control over the important issue of context (Nissenbaum 2009) in the sense of which Friends will be able to view any particular content. Many researchers have called for increased control over context settings so that users can have full control over who can see what (Leenes 2010). Current privacy settings are relatively simple, however. In terms of gender differences, women disproportionately select more restrictive privacy settings. For instance, in MySpace more females than males maintain private profiles (Thelwall 2008b, 2009). Most (71%) US SNS users aged 18–29 change their privacy settings, so this is a widespread practice, even though older users are less concerned with the issue (Madden and Smith 2010). With regard to young US Facebook users, females are more likely to control their privacy settings to keep personal information away from non-Friends and from Facebook's News Feeds, are more likely to monitor the personal settings in Facebook, and are more likely to read privacy policies before joining an SNS (Hoy and Milne 2010).

18.7 YouTube

There are privacy issues associated with posting personal videos on YouTube as well as with personal information in the profiles of registered members. Although not its main feature, YouTube has SNS functionality with member personal pages and Friend-type connections.

Video is a potentially intrusive technology due to the inclusion of moving pictures and sound and the cheap availability of portable camcorders. Women that post videos of themselves seem to be particularly vulnerable to personal abuse and sexist comments because of an apparent culture of lack of restraint in the content of YouTube comments and a predominantly young male audience (see e.g., Burgess and Green 2009, pp. 96–97).

There are several Internet-specific phenomena that involve personal or intimate video and many of these seem to predominantly involve female subjects. One specifically female genre is the childbirth video: a type that is reasonably widespread in YouTube and particularly intimate, although often censored for nudity (Longhurst 2009). Another genre, originating with webcams but spreading to YouTube, is the bedroom video. For instance, one of the most popular early YouTube hits was a video of two girls in a bedroom having fun and dancing to a pop song (http://www.youtube.com/watch?v=-_CSo1gOd48, over 31 million views by September 2010) (Burgess and Green 2009, p. 26). YouTube also hosts a crossover genre, the video log or vlog. These seem to follow blogs in primarily discussing personal issues. Whilst there seems to be no systematic evidence of gender bias, it seems likely that the majority are made by females (see e.g., Burgess and Green 2009, p. 80).

18.8   LGBT Issues

The Social Web Gendered Privacy Model probably applies to LGBT people as much as to females, but with some differences in the details. For example, LGBT individuals probably have greater personal security concerns than heterosexual men – not due to greater risk from intimate relationships or sexual crimes but as potential targets of hate crime violence from intolerant individuals within society. Moreover, in some nations homosexuality or homosexual acts are criminal and can even carry the death penalty. Similarly, the main harassment risks are probably from the insults or insulting behavior of intolerant individuals, perhaps protected by anonymity. No evidence is known about LGBT social communication skill levels but this group has additional communication needs for social support within society (Goodenow et al. 2008).

There are many gender-related privacy concerns for LGBT Social Web users (Cooper and Dzara 2010). Whilst gender is rarely hidden offline, some prefer to reveal their LGBT status only to trusted friends or others with a similar status. This can be a problem for SNSs because of the centrality of public lists of Friends: a person listing several openly gay Friends may be thought to be gay themselves (see e.g., Jernigan and Mistree 2009). This may discourage some people from using SNSs and make others reluctant to openly connect with LGBT friends. Within MySpace, however, many users clearly declare their sexuality as gay, lesbian, bisexual, or queer (Drushel 2010), but the proportion of SNS users that conceal or decide not to declare their sexuality is unknown.

Many have adopted the Web, and YouTube in particular, as a relatively safe medium through which to "come out" or defend themselves in terms of gender (e.g., for transgender see: Burgess and Green 2009, p. 80). There is a risk of abuse but also the potential for support and encouragement. For example, one video author thanked 15 people for their "sweet and nice comments" (URL withheld). The coming out YouTube video is even a recognized genre (Alexander and Losh 2010).

The Social Web also allows the creation of private LGBT enclaves that seem to be particularly valuable for geographically or socially isolated individuals, such as married women with children realizing that they are lesbians and needing support to make difficult life decisions (Cooper 2010). Such enclaves can also help sexual minorities to meet others for offline liaisons safely (see e.g., Farr 2010).

A controversial issue is the license that the Internet has given for amateur story sharing, including slash (Berger 2010) and Yaoi manga (McHarry 2010), which have been criticized in the belief that women invade the collective privacy of gay men by writing fiction about male-male relationships for personal gratification

(Berger 2010). The fear is that gay relationships may be distorted, creating unwanted stereotypes.

Despite the risks to privacy discussed above, particularly for those who conceal their sexuality, it seems that Web 2.0 is beneficial overall for its ability to connect people relatively safely, particularly when overcoming geographic isolation. Moreover, there is anecdotal evidence that, particularly in the US, people tend to "come out" online first because of greater safety.

18.9 Conclusions

A simple message from Social Web privacy research in many different types of site is that women tend to be more concerned about privacy and to take more precautions to protect their privacy in the Social Web, but they also tend to publish more, including information of a personal nature. In terms of the Social Web Gendered Privacy Model, it seems that, for females in general, the benefits of greater social needs and better social communication skills outweigh the greater physical security and harassment fears and the latter are ameliorated by a wide range of privacy-protection strategies, such as giving incorrect information or invoking privacy options. A corollary is that social websites attracting a predominantly male audience should be seen as unusual and examined for evidence of a lack of protection of personal information threatening physical security or a lack of protection from harassment.

In this chapter, almost all studies reviewed have quite serious sampling limitations, such as the use of convenience samples, samples of students alone, snowball sampling, or a particular national group or website. These limitations are not discussed in detail but the conclusions should be interpreted with caution as a result.

The situation for LGBT Social Web users seems to be similar to that for females: whilst the Social Web creates particular privacy issues, its benefits seem to outweigh these threats, with many examples of innovative and positive uses. Women and LGBT web users are particularly at risk of violations of contextual integrity because of the need to provide personal information to meet online goals and the risk of violence or threats if that information is used by unintended others. Nevertheless, these groups also seem to be the ones that gain the most from the Social Web.

Finally, the issue of gender and privacy in the Social Web has received little targeted research and there is a need for systematic investigations into the perceptions of privacy issues and differences in privacy-related behaviors between males and females in all types of social website, and for different nationalities and cultures. This is also true for LGBT Social Web users, about whom there is almost no quantitative evidence. The results of both of these areas of research should also give more general insights into why people use the Social Web and the importance of privacy for decisions about how to use it. This may lead to future Social Web systems that are more sensitive to privacy issues and to tests of the Social Web Gendered Privacy Model to see whether there are important factors missing from it and whether it fits with wider evidence of gender-related privacy issues.

References

Acquisti A, Gross R (2006) Imagined communities: awareness, information sharing, and privacy on the facebook. Lect Notes Comput Sci 4258:36–58

Aguiton C, Cardon D, Castelain A, Fremaux P, Girard H, Granjon F et al (2009) Does showing off help to make friends?. In: Proceedings of the third international ICWSM conference, AAAI, Menlo Park, pp 10–17

Alexander J, Losh E (2010) A you tube of one's own?: coming out videos as rhetorical action. In: Pullen C, Cooper M (eds) LGBT identity and online new media. Routledge, New York, pp 37–50

Allen AL (1988) Uneasy access: privacy for women in a free society. Rowman & Littlefield, Totowa

Altman I (1976) Privacy: a conceptual analysis. Environ Behav 8(1):7–29

Archer J (2002) Sex differences in physically aggressive acts between heterosexual partners: a meta-analytic review. Aggression Violent Behav 7(4):313–351

Aukett R, Ritchie J, Mill K (1988) Gender differences in friendship patterns. Sex Roles 19(1–2):57–66

BBC (2007) MySpace bars 29,000 sex offenders. http://news.bbc.co.uk/2011/hi/technology/6914870.stm. Accessed 21 Dec 2010

Berger R (2010) Out and about: slash fic, re-imagined texts, and queer commentaries. In: Pullen C, Cooper M (eds) LGBT identity and online new media. Routledge, New York, pp 173–184

Boyle K, Johnson TJ (2010) MySpace is your space? Examining self-presentation of MySpace users. Comput Hum Behav 26(6):1392–1399

Burgess J, Green J (2009) Youtube: online video and participatory culture. Polity, Cambridge

Campbell JC, Webster D, Koziol-McLain J, Block C, Campbell D, Curry MA et al (2003) Risk factors for femicide in abusive relationships: results from a multisite case control study. Am J Public Health 93(7):1089–1097

Chisholm JF (2006) Cyberspace violence against girls and adolescent females. Ann N Y Acad Sci 1087:74–89 (Violence and exploitation against women and girls)

Cooper M (2010) Lesbians who are married to men: identity, collective stories, and the internet online community. In: Pullen C, Cooper M (eds) LGBT identity and online new media. Routledge, New York, pp 75–86

Cooper M, Dzara K (2010) The facebook revolution: LGBT identity and activism. In: Pullen C, Cooper M (eds) LGBT identity and online new media. Routledge, New York, pp 100–112

Dehue F, Bolman C, Vollink T (2008) Cyberbullying: youngsters' experiences and parental perception. Cyberpsychol Behav 11(2):217–223

Dindia K (2002) Self-disclosure research: knowledge through meta-analysis. In: Allen M, Preiss RW, Gayle BM, Burrell N (eds) Interpersonal communication research: advances through meta-analysis. Erlbaum, Mahwah, pp 169–185

Donath J (2007) Signals in social supernets. J Comput Mediated Commun 13(1). http://jcmc.indiana.edu/vol13/issue1/donath.html. Accessed 17 June 2008

Drushel BE (2010) Virtually supportive: self-disclosure of minority sexualities through online social networking sites. In: Pullen C, Cooper M (eds) LGBT identity and online new media. Routledge, New York, pp 62–72

Elkins LE, Peterson C (1993) Gender differences in best friendships. Sex Roles 29(7–8):497–508

Fairchild K, Rudman LA (2008) Everyday stranger harassment and women's objectification. Soc Justice Res 21(3):338–357

Farr D (2010) A very personal world: advertisement and identity of trans-persons on Craigslist. In: Pullen C, Cooper M (eds) LGBT identity and online new media. Routledge, New York, pp 87–99

Fullwood C, Martino OI (2007) Emoticons and impression formation. Vis Popular Cult 19(7):4–14

Galdas PM, Cheater F, Marshall P (2005) Men and health help-seeking behaviour: literature review. J Adv Nurs 49(6):616–623

Gefen D, Straub DW (1997) Gender differences in perception and adoption of e-mail: an extension to the technology acceptance model. MIS Quarterly 21(4):389–400

Goodenow C, Szalacha L, Westheimer K (2008) School support groups, other school factors, and the safety of sexual minority adolescents. Psychol Sch 43(5):573–589

Hall JA (1984) Nonverbal sex differences: communication accuracy and expressive style. Johns Hopkins University Press, Baltimore

Hall JA, Carter JD, Horgan TG (2000) Gender differences in nonverbal communication of emotion. In: Fischer A (ed) Gender and emotion: social and psychological perspectives. Cambridge University Press, Cambridge, pp 97–117

Hancock JT, Landrigan C, and Silver C (2007) Expressing emotion in text-based communication. In: CHI '07: Proceedings of the SIGCHI conference on Human factors in computing systems, ACM, New York, pp 929–932

Herring SC, Paolillo JC (2006) Gender and genre variation in weblogs. J Sociolinguistics 10(4):439–459

Herring SC, Scheidt LA, Bonus S, Wright E (2004) Bridging the gap: a genre analysis of weblogs. In: Proceedings of the thirty-seventh Hawaii international conference on system sciences (HICSS-37), IEEE Press, Los Alamitos

Hinduja S, Patchin JW (2008) Personal information of adolescents on the internet: a quantitative content analysis of MySpace. J Adolesc 31(1):125–146

Hoadley CM, Xu H, Lee JJ, Rosson MB (2010) Privacy as information access and illusory control: the case of the facebook news feed privacy outcry. Electron Commerce Res Appl 9(1):50–60

Hollenbaugh EE (2010) Personal journal bloggers: profiles of disclosiveness. Comput Hum Behav 26(6):1657–1666

Holmes J (1995) Women, men and politeness. Longman, New York

Hoy MG, Milne G (2010) Gender differences in privacy-related measures for young adult facebook users. J Interactive Advertising 10(2):28–45

Huffaker DA, Calvert SL (2005) Gender, identity, and language use in teenage blogs. J Comput-Mediated Commun 10(2). http://jcmc.indiana.edu/vol10/issue2/huffaker.html. Accessed 31 July 2010

Jernigan C, Mistree BFT (2009) Gaydar: facebook friendships expose sexual orientation. First Monday 14(10). http://firstmonday.org/htbin/cgiwrap/bin/ojs/index.php/fm/article/view/2611/2302. Accessed Oct 2009

Kessler R, Brown R, Broman C (1981) Sex differences in psychiatric help-seeking: evidence from four large-scale surveys. J Health Soc Behav 22(1):49–64

Kisilevich S, Mansmann F (2010) Analysis of privacy in online social networks of Runet. SIN10. http://infovis.uni-konstanz.de/papers/2010/sin2011p-kisilevich.pdf. Accessed 31 July 2010

Leenes R (2010) Context is everything sociality and privacy in online social network sites. In: Bezzi M, Duquenoy P, Fischer-Hübner S, Hansen M, Zhang G (eds) Privacy and identity management for life. Springer, Berlin, pp 48–65

Lenhart A, Purcell K, Smith A, Zickuhr K (2010) Social media & mobile internet use among teens and young adults. Pew Internet & American Life Project.http://pewinternet.org/Reports/2010/Social-Media-and-Young-Adults.aspx. Accessed 5 Feb 2010

Longhurst R (2009) You tube: a new space for birth? Feminist Rev 93(1):46–63

Lu H-P, Hsiao K-L (2009) Gender differences in reasons for frequent blog posting. Online Info Rev 33(1):135–156

Madden M, Smith A (2010) Reputation management and social media: how people monitor their identity and search for others online. Pew Internet & American Life Project, 26 May 2010. http://pewinternet.org/Reports/2010/Social-Media-and-Young-Adults.aspx. Accessed 9 Sept 2010

Magdol L, Moffitt T, Caspi A, Newman D, Fagan J (1997) Gender differences in partner violence in a birth cohort of 21-year-olds: bridging the gap between clinical and epidemiological approaches. J Consul Clin Psychiatry 65(1):68–78

McClure EB (2000) A meta-analytic review of sex differences in facial expression processing and their development in infants, children, and adolescents. Psychol Bull 126(3):424–453

McCullagh K (2008) Blogging: self presentation and privacy. Inf Commun Tech Law 17(1):3–23

McHarry M (2010) Identity unmoored: Yaoi in the West. In: Pullen C, Cooper M (eds) LGBT identity and online new media. Routledge, New York, pp 185–198

Money J, Ehrhardt A (1982) Man and woman: boy and girl. John Hopkins University Press, Baltimore

MSNBC (2008). Facebook gives sex offenders the boot. http://www.msnbc.msn.com/id/29289048/ns/technology_and_science-security/. Accessed 21 Dec 2010

Nardi BA, Schiano DJ, Gumbrecht M, Swartz L (2004) Why we blog. Commun ACM 47(12):41–46

Nissenbaum H (2004) Privacy as contextual integrity. Washington Law Rev 17(1):101–139

Nissenbaum H (2009) Privacy in context: technology, policy and the integrity of social life. Stanford University Press, Stanford

Nosko A, Wooda E, Molemaa S (2010) All about me: disclosure in online social networking profiles: the case of FACEBOOK. Comput Hum Behav 26(3):406–418

O'Connell R (2003) A typology of cybersexploitation and on-line grooming practices. JISC. http://www.jisc.ac.uk/uploaded_documents/lis_PaperJPrice.pdf. Accessed 8 Sept 2010

Oomen I, Leenes R (2008) Privacy risk perception and privacy protection strategies. In: de Leeuw E, Fischer Hubner S, Tseng J, Borking J (eds) Policies and research in identity. Springer, Boston, pp 121–138

Pedersen S, Macaffee C (2007) Gender differences in British blogging. J Comput Mediat Commun 12(4):1472–1492

Rosen D, Stefanone MA, Lackaff D (2010) Online and offline social networks: investigating culturally-specific behavior and satisfaction. In: Proceedings of the 43 rd Hawaii international conference on system sciences, Institute of Electrical and Electronics Engineers, New Brunswick. http://www.communication.buffalo.edu/contrib/people/faculty/documents/Stefanone_HICSS2010.pdf. Accessed 31 July 2010

Shade LR (1996) Women, the world wide web, and issues of privacy. Feminist Collections 17(2):33–35

Sheehan KB (1999) An investigation of gender differences in on-line privacy concerns and resultant behaviors. J Interact Mark 13(4):24–38

Stern SR (2004) Expressions of identity online: prominent features and gender differences in adolescents' World Wide Web home pages. J Broadcasting Electron Media 48(2):218–243

Stutzman F, Capra R, Thompson J (2011) Factors mediating disclosure in social network sites. *Comput Hum Behav* 27(1):590–598

Thelwall M (2008a) Fk yea I swear: cursing and gender in a corpus of MySpace pages. Corpora 3(1):83–107

Thelwall M (2008b) Social networks, gender and friending: an analysis of MySpace member profiles. J Am Soc Info Sci Technol 59(8):1321–1330

Thelwall M (2009) Social network sites: users and uses. In: Zelkowitz M (ed) Advances in computers. Elsevier, Amsterdam, pp 19–73

Thelwall M, Wilkinson D, Uppal S (2010) Data mining emotion in social network communication: gender differences in MySpace. J Am Soc Info Sci Technol 21(1):190–199

Tufekci Z (2008a) Can you see me now? Audience and disclosure regulation in online social network sites. Bull Sci Technol Soc 28(1):20–36

Tufekci Z (2008b) Grooming, gossip, facebook and MySpace: what can we learn about these sites from those who won't assimilate? Inf Commun Soc 11(4):544–564

Viégas FB (2005) Bloggers' expectations of privacy and accountability: an initial survey. J Comput Mediated Commun 10(3). http://jcmc.indiana.edu/vol10/issue3/viegas.html. Accessed 5 Feb 2010

Wang SS, Moona S-I, Kwona KH, Evansa CA, Stefanone MA (2010) Face off: implications of visual cues on initiating friendship on facebook. Comput Hum Behav 26(2):226–234

WHOA (2009) 2009 Cyberstalking statistics. Haltabuse.org. http://www.haltabuse.org/resources/stats/2009Statistics.pdf. Accessed 8 Sept 2010

Wolf A (2000) Emotional expression online: gender differences in emoticon use. Cyberpsychol Behav 3(5):827–833

Youn S, Hall K (2008) Gender and online privacy among teens: risk perception, privacy concerns, and protection behaviors. Cyberpsychol Behav 11(6):763–765

Zimmer M (2008) The gaze of the perfect search engine: google as an infrastructure of dataveillance. In: Spink A, Zimmer M (eds) Web search: multidisciplinary perspectives. Springer, Berlin, pp 77–99

Index

S. Trepte and L. Reinecke (eds.), *Privacy Online*,
DOI 10.1007/978-3-642-21521-6, © Springer-Verlag Berlin Heidelberg 2011